THE QUEST FOR WORLD ORDER

PERSPECTIVES OF A PRAGMATIC IDEALIST

TOMMY KOH

Edited with an introduction by Amitav Acharya

THE INSTITUTE OF POLICY STUDIES

TIMES ACADEMIC PRESS

© **1998 The Institute of Policy Studies, Singapore**

First published 1998
Times Academic Press
An imprint of Federal Publications (S) Pte Ltd
(A member of the Times Publishing Group)
Times Centre
1 New Industrial Road
Singapore 536196
for
The Institute of Policy Studies
Hon Sui Sen Memorial Library Building
National University of Singapore
Kent Ridge Drive
Singapore 119260

All rights reserved. No part of this publication may be reproduced, stored in a retrieval system, or transmitted, in any form or by any means, electronic, mechanical, photocopying, recording or otherwise, without the prior permission of the publishers.

ISBN 981 210 108 X

Cover design by Duet Design

Printed by Kin Keong Printing Co Pte Ltd, Singapore

All orders for this book should be addressed to:

Federal Publications (S) Pte Ltd
1 New Industrial Road
Singapore 536196

Facts and opinions expressed in this book are strictly those of the author, and do not necessarily reflect the views of The Institute of Policy Studies.

*I dedicate this book to my parents,
Koh Han Kok and See Tsai Ying,
to my beloved wife Poh Siew Aing,
and to our sons, Wei and Aun.*

TABLE OF CONTENTS

List of Abbreviations ix

Foreword xiii

Editor's Acknowledgements xiv

Introduction
- The Essence of a Pragmatic Idealist: Reconciling
  National Interest with Common Good xv

A Vision of World Order
- Can Any Country Afford a Moral Foreign Policy? 1

The United Nations: Reform and Renewal
- The United Nations and the Quest for World Order 10
- The United Nations and Small States:
  The Singapore Experience 19
- Can the United Nations Be Reformed? 27
- The United Nations: Is There Life after Forty? 32
- A New Era in Peacekeeping 46
- An Iconoclastic View of the United Nations'
  Disarmament Activities 52
- The United Nations at Fifty: Time for Renewal 55

North-South Relations: Conflict and Co-operation
- Beyond the North-South Divide 58
- How the Non-Aligned Countries Can Strengthen
  the United Nations 64
- The Western Mass Media and the Third World 70

Negotiations, Bargaining and the Conduct of Diplomacy
- Negotiating with America 81
- The Paris Conference on Cambodia:
  An Example of a Multilateral Negotiation 87

v

- The Earth Summit's Negotiating Process: Some
  Reflections on the Art and Science of Negotiation   97
- Working the Hill: Getting Your Country's Interests
  across to Congress   106
- The Practice of Negotiations: Lessons from the UN   110
- What Can We Learn from the Law of the Sea Conference?   116
- The WTO's First Ministerial Conference:
  The Negotiating Process   120

Setting the Global Agenda: The Law of the Sea and the Environment

- The Achievements and Implications of the
  Third UN Conference on the Law of the Sea   127
- Negotiating a New World Order for the Sea   131
- The UN Convention on the Law of the Sea:
  Implications for Singapore and the Region   144
- The Environment in Southeast Asia: Prospects for
  Co-operation and Conflict   151
- The Earth Summit: Success or Failure?   158
- The Challenge of Sustainable Development   166
- Five Years after Rio and Fifteen Years after Montego Bay:
  Some Personal Reflections   169

Singapore's Role in the Region and the World

- Lee Kuan Yew's Foreign Policy Legacy   175
- A Lilliputian in the Land of the Giants:
  The Work of the Singapore Embassy in Washington   180
- Hong Kong and Singapore are Hard Acts to Follow   197
- Singapore's Regionalization Vision   200
- Explaining the Singapore Miracle   204
- The Relevance of Singapore's Foreign Policy Experience
  for Africa   210
- Indonesia and Singapore: A Strong Partnership   217
- Singapore's External Relations:
  Laying the Foundation for the Post-Cold War Era   222
- Singapore's External Relations: Six Years Later   231

ASEAN and Regional Order: Past and Future

- The Neutralization of Southeast Asia   239
- ASEAN: The Force of Intra-Regional Relations   248
- The Cambodian Conflict: The Question of Peace, Stability and Co-operation in Southeast Asia   255
- ASEAN Diplomacy and the Cambodian Crisis   258
- ASEAN after Cambodia: Towards Greater Dynamism   261
- ASEAN Charts a New Regional Order   265

The Pacific Era: Co-operating for Peace and Prosperity

- The Idea of a Pacific Basin Community   269
- The Dynamic Pacific Rim in the 1990s   274
- A Pacific Century?   280
- APEC: A New Economic Architecture for the Asia Pacific   285
- APEC and Open Regionalism   288
- ASEAN and the Asia-Europe Meeting (ASEM)   291

Asia and the United States: Perceptions and Prescriptions

- De Tocqueville Revisited: American Politics Viewed from a Foreign Perspective   297
- The United States and the Newly Industrializing Countries: The Search for a New Policy   305
- ASEAN's Standing in the United States   311
- The US-Japan Relationship and Its Implications for ASEAN   315
- The Future of US-Japan Relations   321
- The United States and Southeast Asia: A Rationale for Partnership in the Post-Cold War Era   327
- Reflections of a Departing Ambassador: American Values and Economic Problems   335
- An Asian Agenda for President Clinton   341
- Without a Chaperon, Asia Will Dance in the Dark   345

Avoiding a Clash of Cultures: Asia's Role in the New World Order

- Does East Asia Stand for Any Positive Values?   349
- The East and the West: Towards a Convergence of Values   352

- What Holds Societies Together 354
- Revisiting the "Asian Values" Debate 356
- Tolerance, Asian Style 359
- This Way or That, Get on with Good Government 364
- Asians Too, Want Good Environment 367
- Asia and Europe: From Prejudice to Partnership? 369

Personal Experiences
- My First Year at the UN 372
- My Favourite UN Stories 377
- Reflections on a Diplomatic Career 381

Photographs from an Ambassador's Life 385

A Biographical Note 401

Index 403

LIST OF ABBREVIATIONS

ABAC	APEC Business Advisory Council
ACABQ	Advisory Committee on Administrative and Budgetary Questions (UN)
AFTA	ASEAN Free Trade Area
ALF	Africa Leadership Forum
AMM	ASEAN Ministerial Meeting
ANZCERTA	Australia-New Zealand Closer Economic Relations Trade Agreement
ANZUS	Tripartite Security Treaty between the Governments of Australia, New Zealand and the United States
APCEL	Asia Pacific Centre for Environmental Law
APEC	Asia Pacific Economic Cooperation
ARF	ASEAN Regional Forum
ASC	ASEAN Standing Committee
ASCEND 2000	ASEAN Common Plan for Environmentally Sound and Sustainable Development to Year 2000
ASEAN	Association of Southeast Asian Nations
ASEAN-PMC	ASEAN Post-Ministerial Conference
ASEM	Asia-Europe Meeting
ASEP	ASEAN Environment Programme
ASOEN	ASEAN Senior Officials on the Environment
ASSET	ASEAN Subregional Environmental Trust
AWC	ASEAN Working Committee
BERI	Business Environment Risk Intelligence
CANZ	Canada, Australia and New Zealand
CEPT	Common Effective Preferential Tariff
CGDK	Coalition Government of Democratic Kampuchea
COBSEA	Co-ordinating Body on the Seas of East Asia
CSCE	Conference on Security and Cooperation in Europe
CSD	Commission on Sustainable Development

EAEC	East Asian Economic Caucus
EDB	Economic Development Board (Singapore)
EC	European Community
ECC	Economic Coordinating Committee
ECOSOC	Economic and Social Council (UN)
EEC	European Economic Community
EEZ	Exclusive Economic Zone
EU	European Union
FAO	Food and Agriculture Organization
FPDA	Five Power Defence Arrangements
FRG	Federal Republic of Germany
FUNCINPEC	Front Uni National pour un Cambodge Indépendant, Neutre, Pacifique et Coopératif (National United Front for an Independent, Neutral, Peaceful and Cooperative Cambodia)
G15	Group of 15 (Coalition of Developed Countries)
G77	Group of 77 (Coalition of Developing Countries)
GATT	General Agreement on Tariffs and Trade
GDP	Gross Domestic Product
GEF	Global Environment Facility
GNP	Gross National Product
GSP	Generalized System of Preferences (US)
HDI	Human Development Index
HOD	Head of Delegations
IBRD	International Bank for Reconstruction and Development (World Bank)
ICAP	International Civil Aviation Policy
ICC	International Conference on Cambodia
ICJ	International Court of Justice
ICRC	International Committee of the Red Cross
IDA	International Development Agency
IMO	International Maritime Organization
INF	Intermediate-Range Nuclear Forces (Treaty)
IOC	International Oceangraphic Commission

IROR	Internal Rate of Return
ISJCE	Indonesia-Singapore Joint Committee on the Environment
ITA	Information Technology Agreement
IUCN	World Conservation Union
JD	Joint Declaration
JEMS	Junior Executive Managers (ASEAN-EU programme)
JIM	Jakarta Informal Meeting
JMC	Joint Ministerial Committee
KPNLF	Khmer People's National Liberation Front
LOS	Law of the Sea
MCP	Malayan Communist Party
MFN	Most-Favoured-Nation Status
MITI	Ministry of International Trade and Industry (Japan)
MSJCE	Malaysia-Singapore Joint Committee on the Environment
NAFTA	North America Free Trade Area
NAM	Non-Aligned Movement
NATO	North Atlantic Treaty Organization
NSC	National Security Council (US)
NUS	National University of Singapore
OAU	Organization of African Unity
ODA	Official Development Assistance
OECD	Organization for Economic Cooperation and Development
OECS	Organization of Eastern Caribbean States
OIC	Organization of Islamic Conference
OMB	Office of Management and Budget (US)
OSCE	Organization for Security and Cooperation in Europe
PBEC	Pacific Basin Economic Council
PBF	Pacific Business Forum
PECC	Pacific Economic Cooperation Council
PRC	People's Republic of China
PRK	People's Republic of Kampuchea
PUB	Public Utilities Board (Singapore)

SDI	Strategic Defence Initiative
SEANWFZ	Southeast Asia Nuclear Weapon Free Zone
SEM	Single European Market
SIF	Singapore International Foundation
SIPRI	Stockholm International Peace Research Institute
START	Strategic Arms Reduction Talks
UN	United Nations
UNCED	UN Conference on Environment and Development
UNCLOS	UN Conference on the Law of the Sea
UNCTAD	UN Conference on Trade and Development
UNDOF	UN Disengagement Observer Force
UNDP	UN Development Programme
UNDTCD	UN Department of Technical Cooperation for Development
UNEP	UN Environment Programme
UNFICYP	UN Peacekeeping Force in Cyprus
UNFPA	UN Fund for Population Activities
UNGOMAP	UN Good Offices Missions in Afghanistan and Pakistan
UNHCR	UN High Commissioner for Refugees
UNICEF	UN Children's Fund
UNIDO	UN Industrial Development Organization
UNIFIL	UN Interim Force in Lebanon
UNIIMOG	UN Iran-Iraq Military Observer Group
UNMOGIP	UN Military Observer Group in India and Pakistan
UNTAC	UN Transitional Authority in Cambodia
UNTSO	UN TRUCE Supervision Organization
USTR	US Trade Representative
WTO	World Trade Organization
WTO-MC	WTO Ministerial Conference
WWF	World Wide Fund for Nature (formerly known as the World Wildlife Fund)
ZOPFAN	Zone of Peace, Freedom and Neutrality

FOREWORD

Tommy Koh, lawyer, professor and diplomat, has been a dynamic presence on the international scene for the past three decades. This wide-ranging anthology of speeches, papers and articles illuminates that experience, which brought him into close contact with many of the major events and trends of our times: the superpower rivalry; efforts to protect the global environment; conflict resolution and multinational peacekeeping; and the rapid rise of Asia, including his native Singapore, as an economic and political power. He shows us not only the complexity of these issues, but also the intricacy of the negotiating processes through which the nations of the world attempt to harmonize their interests.

Amid an era of historic transformation, Ambassador Koh has remained a steadfast advocate of dialogue and co-operation to resolve problems through mutual accommodation, for the greater common good. He has also been a constant supporter of the United Nations as a unique instrument of global service. The presentation of his views in this publication marks an important contribution to our ongoing work of building a peaceful, just and lawful international society.

Kofi A. Annan
Secretary-General
United Nations

EDITOR'S ACKNOWLEDGEMENTS

Editing a book, which covers Professor Tommy Koh's writings over three decades of professional life, was in itself a remarkable exercise in co-ordination and collaboration. It would have been impossible without the extraordinary enthusiasm and contribution of a number of persons. Professor Koh himself was unfailingly generous with his advice and help and found time from his extremely busy schedule to sit patiently through several long editorial sessions. Arun Mahizhnan of The Institute of Policy Studies was a major inspiration and guiding hand behind the editorial process, providing ideas and suggestions that were invaluable in organizing the book. Shirley Lim of The Institute of Policy Studies, Jenny Tan of the Asia-Europe Foundation and Lily Ng of Singapore's Ministry of Foreign Affairs provided excellent administrative support. Keri Fuller, formerly an editor at the Times Academic Press, played an instrumental role in the initial stages of planning the book. Her successor, Evelyn Ng, worked with considerable energy and dedication to see the project through. I should also mention that Mark Hong of Singapore's Ministry of Foreign Affairs was the first to compile some of Professor Koh's speeches and essays which made my task a lot easier and he too offered valuable comments on my introductory essay. I am deeply indebted to all of them. I also want to thank The Institute of Policy Studies, and Professor Koh in particular, for giving me the opportunity to edit this book on their behalf.

Amitav Acharya
Toronto, Canada

The Essence of a Pragmatic Idealist: Reconciling National Interest with Common Good

Amitav Acharya

People in diplomatic and legal circles around the world recognize Tommy Koh as one of the most accomplished members of these professions. During a long and illustrious career that began in 1962, he has held a number of high-level positions as Singapore's representative abroad, especially in the UN system. Among other things, he has been Singapore's Ambassador to the UN, its Ambassador to the United States (US), its Ambassador-at-Large, the Chairman of the Third United Nations Conference on the Law of the Sea (UNCLOS), the Chairman of the Preparatory Committee for, and the Main Committee of, the United Nations Conference on Environment and Development (UNCED), and the UN Secretary-General's Special Envoy to Russia and the Baltic states. His has been a major presence in countless multilateral negotiations and international events ranging from the International Conference on Kampuchea in 1981 to the inaugural ministerial meeting of the World Trade Organization in 1996.

Despite having held positions with widely different agendas and goals, Koh has been guided throughout his career by a certain vision of foreign policy and world order. Diplomats are more often regarded as tacticians and managers, rather than as thinkers and conceptualizers. Koh clearly belongs to the select group whose practical handling of international affairs underlies a distinct philosophy of world order. It is the basic aim of this book to outline this vision. This book brings together his most important public speeches and writings and captures the essence of his multifaceted role in world affairs: as a negotiator and conciliator, as an agenda-setter and norm-builder, and as an analyst and philosopher. They cover a wide range of themes which preoccupied him in the realm of international relations: from global warming to good governance, from the neutralization of Southeast Asia to the new world order.

Operating on the international stage, Tommy Koh has had to cope with two large challenges. First, he is a self-conscious idealist working within the essentially realpolitik foreign policy framework of Singapore. Second, he is a representative of a small state acting in a world dominated by big powers. How he was able to overcome these challenges and even to use them to his advantage is a story which should be of immense interest and inspiration to leaders, scholars and aspiring diplomats around the world. This is the principal message that emerges from this collection of his writings.

An Idealist in a Realist Milieu

In his professional career, as in personal life, Koh considers himself to be a "pragmatic idealist". The term was coined by U Thant, the third Secretary-General of the United Nations, to describe himself. Koh, an ardent admirer of U Thant, holds a similar perspective on, and approach to, international relations. In essence, pragmatic idealism captures his effort to reconcile his belief in certain principles, especially justice, equality, and co-operation, with the realpolitik approach so commonplace in the world of diplomacy. It represents his faith in certain qualities, such as optimism, honesty, transparency, and reciprocity, as potent weapons against the self-seeking and amoral behaviour of states.

In this context, three aspects of Koh's approach to diplomacy and international affairs are especially noteworthy. First, he believes that a diplomat must strike a careful balance between the promotion of the narrow self-interest of his or her own country and the requirements of a just and peaceful world order. While a Realist may see the two goals as contradictory, and often mutually exclusive, Koh views them to be complementary and sees them as goals which can often be reconciled. For him, it is imperative and possible to align the national interest of one's own country with the common good of humankind.

Second, while Koh takes a fundamentally optimistic view of human nature and world events, his optimism is not naive and ill-considered but informed and cautious. Stressing the positive side of things, whether in analysing a crisis or conducting mediation efforts, is not a matter of projecting one's own outlook. It is a deliberate and effective diplomatic tool to increase the comfort level among the interlocutors. It raises the morale of the entire negotiating process and makes it easier to achieve compromise and consensus.

Third, Koh adheres to a cardinal tenet in international negotiations that success depends on the ability of all sides to recognize and establish the common ground, instead of sticking to uncompromising bargaining positions, however consistent they may be with the national interest of one's own country. He avoids extreme positions and excels in the art of conciliation. Moderation and consensus-building are the hallmarks of his style of diplomacy.

Indeed, to appreciate Koh's perspective and approach, one has to contrast his innate idealism with the hard-nosed realpolitik world view of Singapore's founding leaders. The latter saw international relations as a state of perpetual conflict, in which the foreign policy of sovereign states must be based, as Singapore's long-serving Foreign Minister, S. Rajaratnam put it, on the notion of "Each nation for itself".[1] Another former Foreign Minister, S. Dhanabalan, argued that:

> *The international system comprises sovereign states each admitting to no authority except its own. International relations therefore resembles a Hobbesian state of nature, where each is pitted against all. In such a potentially anarchic situation, order is the prime value. In international politics, as in national politics, order is prior to justice, to morality, to economic prosperity, to any other value that you can think of simply because, in the absence of order, no other value can be realized. In the absence of order the life of states would be as in the life of men in the state of nature – "Nasty, Brutish and Short".[2]*

The Realist tradition in international relations, so vividly reflected in the quote, takes competition and war as a fundamental given of international life, and is sceptical of the importance of international law and organizations in shaping co-operation among states.

International relations is a zero-sum game, an endless contest for power and influence in which the strong usually prevails at the expense of the weak. It is not surprising that such stark pessimism marked the foreign policy philosophy of Singapore's first generation leadership. If anything, it reflected the dire circumstances of the birth of the island republic as a sovereign state. Having been expelled from the Malaysian federation, Singapore enjoyed a fragile relationship with its Malay neighbours. It had serious self-doubts regarding its survival as a small state with a limited population base and an almost total lack of physical resources. Indeed, a related assumption of Realism, shared by many Singaporean policy-makers, is that size and geographic location set limits to a country's foreign policy options, no matter how principled and skilful its diplomacy may be.

Koh is not a subscriber to such views, however. He makes his position very clear in his most famous essay, "Can Any Country Afford a Moral Foreign Policy?":

> ... the logical implication of the stand by the realists is that we live in a world of anomie, that is to say, in a condition of lawlessness, in the absence of any governing structure, in a situation in which there are no laws, principles, rules to govern the conduct between nations. Is this an accurate description of the world in which we live?... In my view it is not.

Koh is perhaps more comfortable with the Liberal-Idealist tradition of international relations although his admiration for Idealists such as Woodrow Wilson and Cyrus Vance is not unqualified. Moreover, he has a healthy respect for the thinking of Realists such as Hans Morgenthau and for the intellectual brilliance of Henry Kissinger. But the main features of the Liberal-Idealist tradition in international relations, including its optimistic view of human nature and its belief in the possibility of co-operation, are important foundations of Koh's own thinking and approach to diplomacy and world order. But Koh is Groatian in his belief in the role of international and lawful regimes in limiting competition and in building co-operation.[3] He subscribes to the view popularized by John Stuart Mill and Norman Angel that expansion of commerce and economic interdependence constrains the use of force in international relations. He appreciates the role of regional and global institutions in promoting co-operation and peace. Most importantly, Koh holds the distinctly un-Machiavellian view that foreign policy should not be amoral.

The term pragmatic idealism easily invites scepticism. "Is it not an oxymoron?" a critic may ask. But Koh firmly believes that idealism accompanied by common-sense pragmatism is desirable, not just from a moral point of view, but also as a practical and efficient way of conducting international relations. He rejects the view that national interest is the only basis for state action, or that the pursuit of national interest justifies the representative of a state to be hypocritical and deceptive. In his view, a diplomat with a reputation for veracity and integrity is more likely to succeed in promoting his/her country's interests than one with a reputation for duplicity. The classic Machiavellian approach is not necessarily the best way to defend one's national interest. Being truthful and principled is the most efficient way to achieve your goals. Being moral is in the interest of your state.

An example of his unorthodox approach can be found in Singapore's position on the US invasion of the small Caribbean country of Grenada in 1983. From a typical realpolitik perspective, it would not have been wise for Singapore's UN representative to lend his voice to the chorus of condemnation of a close friend on which his country depended heavily for its security, and which it considered as a major contributor to the stability and prosperity of the Asia Pacific region. But Koh saw the problem differently. If Singapore did not condemn the US invasion, it would undermine the principle of non-interference which was a basic norm of international relations, and a vital principle for small states like Singapore. Koh thought that failure to protest the US invasion of Grenada would undermine his "moral credibility" in opposing the Soviet intervention in Afghanistan and the Vietnamese invasion of Cambodia. It is worth noting that Koh invoked the same principle in effectively organizing international opposition to the Vietnamese invasion of Cambodia at the UN and in helping develop a common ASEAN position to bring about a diplomatic settlement of the conflict. (See "The Cambodian Conflict: The Question of Peace, Stability and Co-operation in Southeast Asia" and "ASEAN Diplomacy and the Cambodian Crisis".)

As noted earlier, a pragmatic idealist is one who sees no conflict between being moral and being able to defend the national interest. When the UN General Assembly was debating the invasion and occupation of Western Sahara by Morocco and Mauritania, Koh voted against them. His step was different from the position of most of his other ASEAN colleagues as well as the US, who all voted for Morocco, a friendly state. Koh justified his position on two principles. The first was the principle of self-determination, which he considered to be a sacred and necessary ingredient of international order. But there was a more pragmatic consideration as well. Voting for self-determination would earn Singapore the goodwill of Algeria, which had strongly backed the Polisario, and secure for ASEAN Algeria's vote against Vietnam (on the question of Vietnam's invasion of Cambodia) in the UN General Assembly. Algeria was a key country with influence in the Non-Aligned Movement. So there was a trade-off. By voting for self-determination, Koh was able to deliver Algeria from the pro-Vietnam camp among the NAM members. A supposedly principled stand was consistent with the interest of Singapore and ASEAN.

To be sure, Koh has faced moral dilemmas, especially when he has had to function within a policy context that is less given to the optimism, trust and positive interaction that his own idealist inclinations would desire. He has been able to operate within the Singapore foreign policy framework because his idealism has carried with it a strong pragmatic streak. However, throughout his career, Koh has remained something of an iconoclast within the Singapore government, sometimes holding views that are different from mainstream official thinking.

I have already noted that Koh's pragmatic idealism is linked to his conception of human nature. Idealists assume that human nature is inherently good, while Realists take the opposite and distinctly Hobbesian view of human beings as selfish, egotistic and conflict-prone. Typically, Koh takes a middle ground. As he puts it, "human beings are neither angels nor devils". No society exhibits pure good or pure evil. People are capable of being both evil and self-centred on the one hand, and generous and altruistic on the other. A society needs laws because human beings are not always altruistic. But neither are people so evil as to violate the law all the time. In a similar vein, the international system comprises both peaceful and law-abiding states as well as those who see conflict as the natural order of things and who would not hesitate to use force to advance their interests. International law and institutions are needed to cope with conflictual behaviour of states just as states need law to maintain domestic peace and order among their citizens. Koh's view of human nature, society and the world is more benign than that of most Singaporean leaders, who continue to display greater pessimism and cynicism.

Koh realizes and accepts that the world can never be a perfect place. One can never rule out self-seeking and aggressive behaviour by states. But international relations can be ordered on the basis of certain basic and universal moral principles. Conflict and war may be realities, but need not be inevitable. Mutual accommodation of interests is possible. Countries will co-operate for mutual benefit, over issues of trade, global commons and even the arms trade. For example, on the issue of environment and development, one of the most complex and controversial areas in international relations today, Koh believes that the wealthier countries of the world should and can be persuaded to accept lower consumption levels without sacrificing material sufficiency. In return, the poorer countries can be persuaded to accept the notion of sustainable development.

If pragmatic idealism has been the hallmark of Koh's conceptual vision, his practical approach to diplomacy has been marked by a relentless search for the common ground. Most good diplomats are expected to be conciliators, but few make it so central to their approach, still fewer do it so well. His "Twelve Rules of Negotiations" are suggestive in this regard. Take, for example, Rule 5 which asserts that a negotiator should try to put himself "in the position of the person on the other side of the negotiating table". Or Rule 6 which advises the negotiator to "look for a formula for agreement that encompasses the other party's needs as well as your own". This is necessary not for the sake of "being nice" to the other side, but is critical to reaching an agreement. In a similar vein, he points out that that success in negotiations depends on the willingness of negotiators to "try to design a proposal (or proposals) which, while advancing your interests, also accommodates the irreducible minimum interests of your negotiating counterpart". (See "The Practice of Negotiations: Lessons from the UN".)

What makes Koh different? Several factors are worth noting. The first is his background and training in law. This underlies his strong belief in the desirability and need for international law and norms. A second factor has to do with the fact that he has never held an administrative position in the Singapore Foreign Ministry. He was brought into the foreign service from his academic position at the Law Faculty of the University of Singapore (later the National University of Singapore). He did not see this as a permanent move and often considered returning to academia. In a sense, he has always regarded himself as a "scholar in residence".

Koh's identification with the larger issues of world order is also linked to the fact that he has spent more time in the world of multilateral diplomacy than in handling Singapore's sensitive bilateral relations. Unlike most of his colleagues in the foreign service, he was assigned many multilateral responsibilities in the UN system. Singapore's leaders saw him as an asset in this role. While serving long stints abroad, he had the opportunity to interact with and be influenced by leaders with a commitment to world order issues. U Thant was such an inspiration. Koh was much impressed by his sincerity and devotion to a just world order. U Thant's pragmatism was similar to his own; both accepted the principle that "one should always have ideals, but be prepared to adjust to reality". Others whom Koh admires and who have influenced his world view as well as his approach to diplomacy include Brian Urquhart, a former British Under Secretary-General of the UN; Elliot Richardson, a former US Attorney-General; and Carlos P. Romulo, the legendary Foreign Minister of the Philippines.

Finally, family and upbringing have been major factors in shaping Koh's outlook toward life and international affairs. Koh attributes his optimism to his father. He was a businessman who did not complete university, but made up with hard work, resourcefulness and perseverance.

Koh was much inspired by his father's ability to bounce back after business failures to take up new challenges until he was successful. Scouting is another major factor which has shaped Koh's personality and professionalism. Scouting taught him multiculturalism and the importance of team work, qualities which served him well in handling negotiations at the UN, at the Law of the Sea Conference, and at the Earth Summit. It also inspired his avowed opposition to prejudice and bigotry in all forms. His love of nature was another lasting legacy of his years in scouting. Most importantly, scouting taught him the principle that "Few human beings could be completely happy if they only work for their own interests and those of their families".[4] This philosophy applies not just to individual citizens in relation to their countries, but also to diplomats operating in a world of states. It formed the basis of his view that while the tradecraft of a diplomat is to protect and promote his or her country's interests, this also requires attention to the interests of other countries, and a willingness to make adjustments and compromises in order to accommodate those interests. Without this, international relations will be conflictual and regressive.

Koh's pragmatic idealism has not only shaped his handling of Singapore's foreign policy concerns, but also of such world order issues as UN reform and North-South relations. He recognizes the limitations of the UN, but believes strongly in its value:

The UN is admittedly an imperfect institution. However, would the world be better off if there were no UN? I do not think so. I think that on balance, the UN has done more good than harm for the world in the last 50 years. However imperfectly, the UN has tried to create a world which is governed by the rule of law rather than by the law of the jungle.

("The United Nations at Fifty: Time for Renewal")

His advice to the Non-Aligned Movement (NAM), the once-influential international coalition of developing countries which opposed Cold War geopolitics and demanded a redistribution of the world's wealth between the developed (the North) and the developing (the South) countries, illustrated his rejection of extremist bargaining positions. He felt that NAM had little to gain by adopting the sweeping demands of some of its more radical members and advised the coalition to refrain from putting forward demands which did not make economic sense or which required the North to make unilateral concessions. (See "How the Non-Aligned Countries Can Strengthen the United Nations".) He asked both the South and the

North to adopt a conciliatory and pragmatic posture in dealing with each other. He saw no future in North-South confrontation. Subsequent developments in North-South relations, especially the collapse of the South's demands for a New International Economic Order and the resultant ideological pragmatism of the NAM, have vindicated Koh's position. As an Asian, he believed in the Golden Mean and in the virtue of balance and moderation.

"A Lilliputian in the Land of the Giants"

Apart from being an Idealist in a realistic world, another challenge facing Koh on the international stage was how to rise above the "Lilliputian syndrome", a mentality associated with representatives of small states operating in a world dominated by large and powerful states. The foreign policy of newly-independent Singapore was a foreign policy of survival. Singapore's small size, population, lack of physical resources, and its highly sensitive relations with its two larger Malay neighbours (Indonesia and Malaysia), meant that ensuring its continued physical and economic survival was more important than developing an active and high profile role in the global arena. To be sure, small states view the principle of collective security as an important means of ensuring their survival, and participate in the UN and other multilateral institutions in order to compensate for their lack of national power. Singapore was no exception. But Singapore's leaders were too aware of their position on the "totem pole", as Koh likes to call it, to aspire for a leadership role in international affairs.

Koh took a different view. For him, while size and firepower are important, they are not the only source of influence in international relations. More important is soft power, the ability to set the agenda and come up with new ideas and initiatives. From the very outset of his diplomatic career, Koh firmly rejected the view that size is the destiny of small states. One of his greatest contributions to Singapore was to demonstrate through his own actions, that Singapore can play an effective and significant role in shaping the global agenda on issues ranging from collective security to sustainable development.

As with his belief in international law and institutions, Koh's rejection of the "size is destiny" thesis comes from his years of work in the world of multilateral diplomacy. The multilateral arena is very different from other theatres of diplomacy. Here, the size and power of one's country becomes less important than his or her negotiating and mediating skills. One is less concerned about one's place on the totem pole. Koh's 13 years in multilateral diplomacy gave him a different world view and a sense of leadership and power quite out of proportion to the size and population of the country he represented. At the UN, he was always part of the inner circle of negotiators. It is here that representatives from small states can excel.

One may ask if Koh's instincts and approach would work equally well in handling sensitive bilateral relations as it did in the multilateral arena. Perhaps not. Yet, his grooming in the art of multilateralism did not make him less suitable for the conduct of bilateral diplomacy. When Koh arrived in Washington from New York, he was reminded by the departing Singaporean Ambassador, Punch Coomarasamy, of the differences between the UN system and the American capital as diplomatic environments. In Washington, said Coomarasamy, there was a totem pole, but Koh felt otherwise. He recalls the very useful advice he received from Allan Gottlieb, the then Canadian Ambassador in Washington. Gottlieb told him: "In Washington, if you are not seen, you don't exist. If you are not heard from, your interests will not be taken into account. Consequently, it is necessary for an embassy, no matter how powerful the country or how powerless the country it represents, to try to assume a high profile, to be assertive of its interests and to first, build and then massage your network of allies and friends, both inside and outside of government". (See "A Lilliputian in the Land of the Giants: The Work of the Singapore Embassy in Washington".)

Koh took the advice to heart. It was consistent with his own thinking, and appealed greatly to his positive and optimistic mindset. He believed that the rest of the world was interested in his way, not who he represented. Within a short time, he did succeed in turning the Singapore Embassy in Washington into one of the most informed and dynamic diplomatic missions in the capital of the world's most powerful state.

As he sees it, being influential demands being pro-active and hardworking. He values the power of information. The ability to collect and provide information for others is important to one's ability to receive information from them. For Koh, work is power. He recognizes Singapore's strengths as well as vulnerabilities. Though a small state, Singapore is one of the world's largest trading nations. What it lacks in natural resources can be made up for with the development of human resources, by being able to send capable people who can make their views count in international organizations and multilateral negotiations. Koh's experience in Washington suggests that with extensive contacts and a deep knowledge of the American system, Singapore's representatives in the US can develop a relationship of mutual respect and mutual benefit with the United States. With adequate preparation and the right attitude, a small state need not feel overwhelmed by the size and might of a big power.

Contributions to World Order

Although he has every reason to look back with satisfaction on his stint in Washington, Koh's main strength and contribution has been in the area of multilateral diplomacy. It is here that he pursued his vision of a world order founded upon a network of international legal norms, global regimes and multilateral institutions. It is here that he sought to use diplomacy not just in the services of his own country, but also to promote a peaceful and just world order.

Koh's contribution to global issues has been recognized not just by policy-makers and leaders, but by academic scholars of international relations. In a study of the role of leadership in the building of international regimes and institutions, Oran Young, a prominent scholar of international relations, puts him in a select list of leaders whose "interplay of bargaining leverage, negotiating skill and intellectual innovation" made an important contribution to the global regime and institution-building process. He identifies Koh, along with Hamilton Amerasinghe and Christopher Beebe, as an "entrepreneurial leader", defined as "an individual who relies on negotiating skill to frame issues in ways that foster integrative bargaining and to put together deals that would otherwise elude participants endeavouring to form international regimes through institutional bargaining". Such a leader "makes use of negotiating skills to frame issues at stake, devise mutually acceptable formulas, and broker the interest of key players in building support for these formulas". They are also "expert brokers of the interests of numerous states in their roles as custodians and refiners of the key negotiating texts" in multilateral negotiations such as the Law of the Sea. This type of leaders are different from "structural leaders" (representatives of major powers), who conduct themselves by translating their tremendous "power resources into bargaining leverage in an effort to bring pressure to bear on others to assent to the terms of proposed constitutional contracts".[5]

It is especially noteworthy that the issue areas in which Koh has made his major contribution to international co-operation are not directly related to power and security, the staple of traditional diplomacy. Instead, he has involved himself in such global issue areas as the Law of the Sea and the environment. As President of the Third United Nations Conference on the Law of the Sea (1981–1982) and as Chairman of the Preparatory Committee and Chairman of the Main Committee of the United Nations Conference on Environment and Development (1990–1992), Koh made a major contribution to the success of these highly complex and contentious negotiations. What is particularly significant is that he carried out these functions while serving as the representative of a small state, without being aided by the substantial home country resources and leverage which diplomats from major or middle powers can bring to these negotiations. For such a person to be effective, what counts most is the qualities of his or her leadership, negotiating skills and ability to establish the common ground. Moreover, both the Law of the Sea and the environment are issues marked by significant North-South divisions, a major fault line of post-Cold War international relations. Koh's ability to narrow the North-South gap in these vital issue areas is a significant contribution to world order. His role in building global environmental regimes was recognized, among other things, by the awarding of the 1996 Elizabeth Haub Prize for Environmental Law. The prize is awarded annually for "exceptional achievements in the field of environmental law" by the Free University of Brussels and the International Council on Environmental Law.

Although he has spent much of his professional life dealing with people of high status and influence, Koh believes that the ultimate goal of diplomacy must be to promote the well-being of common people. For example, he considers the years spent in the Cambodian peace negotiations to be well worth it because they were part of an effort to give ordinary Cambodians a chance to live a normal life. Similarly, he is an enthusiastic supporter of UN peacekeeping efforts and humanitarian operations, which despite their failures and limitation, deserve widespread support from the international community because they save lives. As the Director of The Institute of Policy Studies in Singapore, he organized several joint seminars on UN peacekeeping operations. Koh is a strong believer in global governance. To him, the World Trade Organization (WTO) is part of the emerging global governance regime; like the Law of the Sea, it affects the livelihood of common people. In bringing a successful end to global forums such as the UNCLOS and UNCED conferences, he was inspired by a belief that these are not short-term or one-time events, but part of a larger picture of building world order with a view to enhancing the security and well-being of people around the globe.

Avoiding a Clash of Cultures

When Koh returned to Singapore after 19 years of overseas postings, he continued as Ambassador-at-Large, but was also appointed as the Director of The Institute of Policy Studies. In addition, he was also given other responsibilities, among them the Chair of the National Council for the Arts. For the first time, he was concerned professionally not just with foreign policy and international relations, but also with issues that were important in Singapore's domestic context, including the subject of "Asian values".

He added to an international debate already simmering on this subject, especially with the publication of an article in the *International Herald Tribune* entitled "The Ten Values that Undergird East Asian Strength and Success".[6] (The title was not his, however. When submitted, the manuscript had the title "Does East Asia Stand for Any Positive Values?", which is how it appears in this volume.) The article was a reactive piece, written in direct response to an earlier article in the same newspaper by columnist George Hicks, who had argued that despite their economic success, East Asians had little to offer to the world in terms of positive values. It was not an assertion of the superiority of Asian values, but a call on the West "to drop its stance of moral superiority", and to recognize that East Asia stood for some positive values.

Koh's position did not go down well with a number of Western scholars and commentators. *The Economist* magazine found his list of Asian values superficial or "vapid".[7] Critics argued that what passed as Asian values were in no way special or unique to Asian societies, and that the sheer political and cultural diversity of Asia could permit no such generalization about a set of commonly held values across the region. Worse still, critics saw the talk of Asian values as a justification for Asian authoritarianism.

But Koh's thinking on Asian values is more complex than is realized by his critics. To be sure, he recognizes the salience of certain personal and societal traits throughout Asia. These include "the importance of the family, the reverence for education, the virtues of saving, frugality and hard work, the concern for others and the importance of team work". (See "Revisiting the 'Asian Values' Debate".) None the less, he concedes that these values are not "uniquely Asian", but "are probably of a universal character". He allows that these have also been the dominant values of Western societies, although they have suffered a great deal of erosion in recent years.

In "Revisiting the 'Asian Values' Debate", Koh refers to his "evolving thinking on the debate concerning our moral values". This suggests that his position on this subject is not final or dogmatic. His comments on Asian values are contributions to a debate, not the enunciation of a moral or philosophical doctrine. Koh concedes that he might have somewhat overstated the case for Asian values. But cultural differences do exist and matter greatly in how societies behave and perform.

It is worth noting that Koh's assertion that culture matters in international life comes at a time when an increasingly influential body of Western international relations theory has "rediscovered" the importance of cultural identity as a determinant of how states conduct their foreign policy and international security behaviour.[8] It is fair to see Koh's position on Asian values as an intellectual plea to recognize culture as a factor in international relations, and not as an arrogant sermon to the West to acknowledge Asian superiority and change its ways accordingly.

Indeed, while asserting that East-West cultural differences matter, Koh refrains from making any judgement on the respective superiority of the two cultures. He remains an admirer of America, listing the many reasons for his admiration (including the American passion for volunteer and community work, which, ironically enough, is deeply ingrained despite the emphasis on personal achievement and individualism in American culture). At the same time, he recognizes that there are many aspects of Asian culture and belief systems which are unappealing. Examples of "bad Asian values" include the caste system in Hindu culture, the subjugation of women, nepotism, authoritarianism and the negative attitude toward people with physical and mental disability.

Most importantly, Koh believes that cultural differences should not become an excuse for East Asia's failure to promote human dignity. Without sacrificing values such as family, hard work, thrift, respect for education, and respect for elders, etc., East Asian governments, he believes, need to show greater respect for the rights of their citizens and to provide greater scope for opposition parties in national politics. Although Koh is identified with the so-called "Singapore school", which is seen as challenging the universality of human rights and projecting the superiority of Asian values, in reality, he takes a much more moderate and balanced view. This is hardly surprising, considering his general streak of idealism and pragmatism, and his tendency to search for the middle ground.

It is worth noting that Koh is not an unqualified "culturalist" when it comes to the practical world of diplomacy. His essay, "Negotiating with America" provides a good indication of this. This essay is something of a primer to diplomats who are newly posted to the US or who are likely to negotiate with the Americans. In this essay, he advises America's interlocutors to be aware of the cultural idiosyncracies of the American diplomat, such as impatience and pragmatism. But he cautions that "Good and effective negotiators, irrespective of their national and cultural background, have certain common skills and aptitudes". Moreover, he asserts that any generalization about national negotiating styles is necessarily impressionistic; the actual negotiating process and outcome depends a lot on the character and temperament of the individuals rather than cultures.

Neither does Koh see a clash of cultures and civilizations resulting from differences in values. The fact that Asian values exist does not mean that they will conflict with the values of others. For one thing, relations between countries are not necessarily determined by values. "My relations with friends in the West are not determined by values", he says. He rejects the "clash of civilizations" thesis advanced by Samuel Huntington. He regards some of Huntington's arguments, such as those positing a Sinic-Islamic alliance, as being based on "flimsy evidence". Moreover, Huntington's thesis runs counter to the spread of democratic ideologies around the world, which suggests an increasing convergence of values across nations. He regards the 21st century political order as one very much shaped by the values and norms, such as the rule of law, transparency and accountability, which have historically had their origins in the West, but which have been modified and accepted by the world community. Looking at the relationship between the US and East Asia, he sees an increasing trend toward mutual learning, mutual understanding and mutual benefit, rather than toward a conflict over culture and values. Certainly, there are more areas of convergence than of conflict. Here, his quintessential moderation and optimism militate against accepting conflict, cultural or otherwise, as the inevitable fact of international life.

Neither does Koh regard cultural differences among nations to be necessarily permanent. In his essay, "The East and the West: Towards a Convergence of Values", he outlines three scenarios of a world grappling with the rise of East Asia – the "clash of civilizations" scenario of Huntington, "a world order based on universal values" and "a community of nations based on a partial convergence of universal values". He views the first as the least likely of the three, the second as too unrealistic, but the third to be the most logical and realistic. The essay reflects Koh's innate and cautious optimism, the essence of a pragmatic idealist.

The so-called "West versus the Rest" debate of recent years has tended to degenerate into an unproductive exchange of polemics and mutual recrimination. Koh's approach calls for moderation and compromise, based on a recognition of their mutual dependence and of the need to deal constructively with each other.

Pragmatism with Principle

Koh's career attests to the possibility of conceptualizing international relations as an arena for pragmatic but principled diplomacy, rather than as blind realpolitik and raw geopolitics. It offers a firm challenge to the constraint of size and the iron law of geography. It shows that hard-working and dynamic individuals with an aptitude for international negotiations can contribute a great deal to making the world a less dangerous and more just place.

Koh's most important contribution is to demonstrate that idealism and pragmatism are not irreconcilable attributes in international relations. Leaders, especially those involved in developing international co-operation, need not choose one over the other. The lesson of his extensive role in global negotiations on the Law of the Sea and the environment is that the supposedly "idealistic" qualities of honesty, openness and willingness to recognize the other side's fundamental interests, are more effective in producing results than the qualities associated with a realpolitik approach, such as self-interest, secrecy, deception and power orientation.

This brings us back to the question as to whether pragmatic idealism is an oxymoron. Koh's answer to this question, as presented through the essays in this collection, is clear. For any state, whether small or large, weak or powerful, idealistic pursuits such as building international regimes and institutions and securing respect for international norms are but effective ways of ensuring survival and progress. To be sure, the "hard realities" of international life, such as the disparities of power between states, and the constraints imposed on states by size and location, must be part of the diplomatic calculus. In some situations, their effect on foreign policy and diplomacy may be inescapable. But they need not prevent or constrain states and leaders from seeking peace and development through co-operation and compromise.

While Koh's diplomatic career is devoted to promoting Singapore's interests abroad, and his involvement in global negotiations is a major contribution to Singapore's foreign policy goals, he has, at the same time, been able to use his skills and experience to advance the cause of peace and justice at the global level. While defending Singapore's foreign policy interests, he has not found it difficult to transcend the national level to make a contribution to world order. His ability to reconcile and synthesize the two roles is a testimony to his skills and strong beliefs. It has earned him the admiration not only of the people of his own country, but of the international community as well.

NOTES

1. S. Rajaratnam, "Evolving a Foreign Policy for Singapore", Lecture at The Institute of Policy Studies, Singapore, 12 July 1988, p. 6.
2. S. Dhanabalan, Talk given at the National University of Singapore Forum, 27 November 1981, p. 8.
3. Hugh Grotius (1583–1644) was a Dutch scholar on international law and international relations, whose views have had a major impact on the theory of international relations. The Groatian tradition provides a middle ground between Realist and Liberal-Idealist positions. It accepts the sovereignty of states and their right to wage war under certain circumstances. But it also stresses the need for international norms and the existence of shared values. The Groatian tradition assumes an "international society of states" in which international rules and international law can be constructed and employed to regulate the use of force. The tradition underlies much of contemporary theorizing about the importance of international regimes, such as the Law of the Sea. It has been revived in the work of scholars such as Martin Wight, Hedley Bull, Adam Roberts and others, an approach which has been referred to variously as the "English school" or the "international society" perspective.
4. "What Scouting Has Taught Me", Speech before the International Commissioners' Gathering, 22 June 1995, Singapore.
5. A third kind of leader identified by Young is the intellectual leader, who "relies on the power of ideas to shape the thinking of the principals in processes of institutional bargaining". See Oran R. Young, "Political Leadership and Regime Formation: On the Development of Institutions in International Society", *International Organization*, Vol. 45, No. 3, Summer 1991.
6. "The Ten Values That Undergird East Asian Strength and Success", *International Herald Tribune*, 11-12 December 1993.
7. "Asian Values", *The Economist*, 28 May 1994, pp.13-14.
8. See, for example, Yosef Lapid and Friedrich Kratochwil (eds.), *The Return of Culture and Identity in IR Theory* (Boulder: Lynne Rienner, 1997); Peter Katzenstein, *Cultural Norms and National Security: Police and Military in Post-War Japan* (Ithaca: Cornell University Press, 1996); Peter Katzenstein (ed.), *The Culture of National Security: Norms and Identity in World Politics* (New York: Columbia University Press, 1996).

A VISION OF WORLD ORDER

Can Any Country Afford a Moral Foreign Policy?

Let me begin with a caveat and a confession. The caveat is that the views I am about to express are my own and do not necessarily reflect those of my government. The confession is that although I have spent more than 16 years in the foreign service of my country, I regard myself as an amateur in diplomacy. My formal education was in law, a fact which some adherents of the Realist school of foreign policy would regard as a disqualification rather than a qualification. I did not have the benefit of having attended a school of foreign service, such as this, or of having studied political science or international relations. I did not work my way up the ladder of my country's foreign service. Instead, I was helicoptered to the top of the ladder at a comparatively young age. I have been learning on the job. What follows is an account of a personal odyssey; the reflections of an untutored practitioner of the craft of diplomacy and an attempt to develop a framework encompassing the role of power and force, of morality and law, of conflict and negotiation in the conduct of foreign policy.

> *It is necessary ... to be a great pretender and dissembler ... he who seeks to deceive always find some one who will allow himself to be deceived.*
> (Machiavelli)

I arrived at the United Nations in New York in August 1968. A few days after my arrival, Soviet and other Warsaw Pact forces invaded Czechoslovakia and put an end to Alexander Dubcek's reform movement. On the instructions of his government, the head of the Czechoslovak delegation requested an urgent meeting of the UN Security Council and demanded the immediate withdrawal of the invading forces. During the meetings of the Security Council, the Soviet Ambassador first denied that his country had invaded Czechoslovakia. I was astonished both by his ability to tell a pack of lies with apparent sincerity and by the stupidity of his action. No one in the UN was taken in by his deceit. In December 1978, Vietnam invaded Cambodia. At first, the Vietnamese Ambassador also sought to deny that his country had invaded Cambodia. In December 1979, the Soviet Union invaded Afghanistan. Initially, the Soviet Ambassador attempted to deny the invasion. The propensity by governments and their diplomatic agents to lie is not confined to the communist countries. In my 13 years at the UN, I was appalled by the duplicitous conduct of colleagues from all parts of the world. Is it any wonder that jokesters like to say that diplomats are individuals who are sent abroad to lie for their country?

Machiavelli, in his classic work, *The Prince*, said that "he who seeks to deceive will always find some one who will allow himself to be deceived."[1] In my experience, Machiavelli's assertion is untrue. No one at the UN was deceived by the lies of my errant colleagues. In the contemporary world of instantaneous communication, of an alert and probing world press, of satellite monitoring, it is futile to lie. The truth will prevail over falsehood. Apart from a few gullible people and those who wear ideological blinkers, most people are not easily deceived.

Machiavelli also advised the prince that "It is necessary to be a great pretender and dissembler".[2] In my experience, this is bad advice. In the community of nations, some governments and diplomats acquire a reputation for duplicity and dishonesty. Is a government or a diplomat with a reputation for veracity and integrity more likely to succeed in promoting the country's interests than one with a reputation for duplicity? I think the answer is yes. I have witnessed at the UN that governments and diplomats with a reputation for veracity and integrity tend to enjoy more influence and stature and are more likely to be entrusted with leadership positions than governments and diplomats with dubious reputations. Sissela Bok was right to have pointed out in her book, *Lying: Moral Choice In Pubic And Private Life*, that "Trust and integrity are precious resources."[3]

> *Whether, to consummate their enterprise, have they to use prayers or can they use force? In the first instance they always succeed badly, and never compass anything; but when they can rely on themselves and use force, then they are rarely endangered.*[4]
>
> (Machiavelli)

The Nuremburg Trials have made the waging of wars of aggression a crime against humanity. The Charter of the United Nations has prohibited the use of force except in self-defence. Notwithstanding these achievements in international law and in the evolving international consensus on the norms applicable to relations between states, violence and conflict are the ugly realities of our contemporary world. In view of this, it could be asked whether Machiavelli's advice to the prince to use force to consummate his enterprise is as valid today as it was 500 years ago?

Are there any limits to the efficiency of the use of force in the modern world? Let us examine this question in respect of the relations between the two superpowers, between a nuclear power and a non-nuclear power and between two non-nuclear powers. In the relations between the two superpowers, the doctrine of mutual assured destruction has practically precluded either power from resorting to force in settling disputes with the other. Both President Reagan and General Secretary Gorbachev agree that nuclear wars cannot be won and must never be fought. It is unlikely for either power to start a conventional war against the other because such a war is likely to escalate into a nuclear war.

Let us turn to look at the conflict in Afghanistan as an example of a nuclear power using force to subjugate a non-nuclear power. In spite of the Soviet Union's preponderance in firepower, it has been unable to subjugate the guerrilla forces of the Mujahideen. What lessons can one learn from Afghanistan regarding the efficacy of the use of force? First, that a tenacious guerrilla army can neutralize, to some extent, the difference in the firepower of the armies of a nuclear power and a non-nuclear power. Second, that although the international system is too weak to prevent aggression, it is capable of inflicting political and economic costs on the aggressor. The invasion of Afghanistan has diminished the influence of the Soviet Union with the members of the Non-Aligned Movement and the Organization of Islamic Conference (OIC). At the current session of the UN General Assembly, 123 states voted against the Soviet Union on Afghanistan. Third, that even a totalitarian state which professes to be unaffected by the opinion of mankind must be concerned by its standing in the eyes of the other states in the international community. General Secretary Gorbachev is reported to be anxious to find a diplomatic formula which would enable him to pull Soviet troops out of Afghanistan.

The same lessons are applicable to the case of Vietnam's invasion of Cambodia, an example of a non-nuclear power resorting to force to subjugate another non-nuclear power. The tenacity of the resistance plus the political and economic isolation of Vietnam are beginning to have an impact on the policy-makers in Hanoi. Between 1975 and 1978, Vietnam was treated like a heroic nation, especially by the non-aligned countries.

Today, Vietnam is an isolated nation. I do not believe that this dramatic change in the standing of Vietnam in the world community has had no effect on the leaders of the politburo in Hanoi. Indeed, there are signs to suggest that Vietnam's leaders may soon be ready to consider non-military options to end the conflict in Cambodia.

The purpose of this excursus is not to assert the proposition that in the modern world states can never succeed in using force to achieve their ends. The Soviet Union has, for example, succeeded in subjugating Hungary and Czechoslovakia. Other states have also succeeded in using force to occupy parts of their neighbours' territories and in incorporating foreign territories and peoples within their boundaries. The purpose of this excursus is to question the Machiavellian thesis that a state can always rely upon its superior force to consummate its enterprise. There are clearly limits to the efficacy of the use of force in the contemporary world, limits imposed by the nature of nuclear war, by the character of guerrilla war, by the political and economic costs which the international system, weak as it is, is capable of inflicting on the aggressor and, in the case of democratic societies, by domestic public opinion.

> *Saints can be pure, but statesmen must be responsible. As trustees for others, they must defend interests and compromise principles.*[5]
>
> (Arthur Schlesinger)

In his celebrated book, *Moral Man and Immoral Society*, the Christian theologian, Reinhold Niebuhr, wrote that "Perhaps the most significant moral characteristic of a nation is its hypocrisy."[6] In *The Cycles of American History,* Arthur Schlesinger said that "Saints can be pure, but statesmen must be responsible. As trustees of others, they must defend interests and compromise principles".[7] Both Niebuhr and Schlesinger belong to the Realist school of foreign policy. They believe that the lodestar which guides a state in the conduct of its foreign policy is its national interest. But, does it follow that in pursuing its national interest, a state must be hypocritical, that it must compromise its principles? Let me explore these questions by reference to the following examples.

The first example revolves around the principle of self-determination. Spanish Sahara was a Spanish colony in North-West Africa, situated between Morocco and Mauritania. In order to pressurize Spain into decolonizing the territory, the African group at the UN asked the International Court of Justice for an advisory opinion on the right of the people of Spanish Sahara to self-determination. The court upheld the right of the people of the Spanish colony to freedom and independence. Acting contrary to the opinion of the court, Morocco and Mauritania occupied the colony and divided it between them. (Mauritania later gave up its share of the territory.) When the question came before the UN General Assembly, the then US Ambassador to the UN lobbied me to support Morocco, arguing that Morocco had always supported Singapore's and ASEAN's interests whereas Algeria (which supported the pro-independence movement in Spanish Sahara – Polisario) had not always done so. The argument was factually correct. I pointed out, however, that what was at issue was not whether Algeria or Morocco was a better friend of Singapore, but the principle of self-determination which was important to small countries such as Singapore. I explained that it was contrary to Singapore's national interest to undermine that principle. I argued that Singapore's credibility would be eroded if it failed to stand up for the principle against all violations. Therefore, I concluded that Singapore's long-term national interest was better served by supporting the principle of self-determination than by supporting a friend. I appreciate that the yardstick of national interest is imprecise and reasonable people can disagree as to what course of action is most consonant with a country's interest.

My next example concerns the US intervention in Grenada. For small countries such as Singapore, one of the most precise principles of international law and international relations is the principle of non-interference in the internal affairs of other states. The intervention by the United States, Barbados, Jamaica and the members of the Organization of Eastern Caribbean States (OECS) in Grenada posed a dilemma for me. On the one hand, I appreciated that the motive which led those states to intervene was a benign one, i.e. to rescue the people of Grenada from an oppressive communist regime and to return the country to democracy. On the other hand, the intervention was contrary to the Charter of the United Nations and to international law. I also realized that if I had not protested against the intervention in Grenada, it would have undermined my moral credibility in leading the opposition to the Soviet intervention in Afghanistan and the Vietnamese intervention in Cambodia. After wrestling with the dilemma, I came to the conclusion that the national interest of Singapore required that I put principle ahead of friendship. This is what I said to the Security Council:

> *Mr President, it is easy enough for us to demonstrate our adherence to principle when to do so is convenient and advantageous and costs us nothing. The test of a country's adherence to principle is when it is inconvenient to do so. I find myself in such a situation*

today. Barbados, Jamaica, the United States and the member states of the OECS are friends of my country. It is extremely convenient for me to acquiesce in what they have done or to remain silent. To do so, however, will, in the long run, undermine the moral and legal significance of the principles which my country regards as a shield. This is why we must put our adherence to principle above friendship. This is why we cannot condone the action of our friends in Grenada. The stand which my country has taken in this case is consistent with the stand which we have taken in other cases where the principle of non-interference in the international affairs of states was also violated.

Let me bring this discussion to a close. What is my lodestar? Do I subscribe to the Realist or the Moralist school of foreign policy? I reject the Realist school not because of its moral cynicism but because it does not reflect the world in which we live. The Realists believe that the only standard by which a state should conduct its foreign policy is its national interest. They believe that in pursuit of its national interest, it is necessary for a state to be hypocritical and to compromise its principles. They reject any consideration of ethics or morality in the conduct of foreign policy as being irrelevant. Although they do not say so expressly, the logical implication of the Realist stand is that we live in a world of anomie, that is to say, in a condition of lawlessness, in the absence of any governing structure, in a situation in which there are no laws, principles, rules to govern the conduct between nations. Is this an accurate description of the world in which we live?

In my view it is not. We live in an imperfect world. It is not, however, a lawless world. The world community has evolved by custom, and adopted by treaty, a very considerable body of laws, principles and rules to govern the conduct between states as well as between states and their citizens. This body of international law deals with almost every area of international relations, including the recognition of states and their admission to international organizations; trade and foreign investment; diplomatic protection of nationals; nationality; war; human rights; boundaries; territorial acquisition; the law of the oceans. There are therefore universally accepted criteria by which the conduct of a state may be judged to be lawful or unlawful, right or wrong. The Realists will say, at this point, that there is a big difference between international law and domestic law. Domestic law works because it is a command backed up by force. There is no force behind the decisions of the International Court of Justice or the UN Security

Council. In his book, *International Conflict for Beginners,* Roger Fisher answered the argument in the following way:

> *The [US] Supreme Court had no regiments at its command. It had no greater force vis-à-vis the government than does the International Court of Justice sitting at the Hague.*[8]
>
> *Law enforcement against a government involves not a command backed up by force. Rather it involves so changing the choice with which the government is confronted that their long-range interest in orderly settlement of disputes outweighs their short-run interest in winning this particular dispute.*[9]

I agree with Roger Fisher that the Realist tends to exaggerate the difference between domestic law and international law. However, I concede that international law does not have the same efficacy as domestic law in a well-ordered society. Although the international legal system is weak, it is not totally ineffective. I also feel that the Realist view that in the conduct of its foreign policy, a state should act exclusively on the basis of its national interest is flawed because, in reality, no state, no matter how powerful, can entirely ignore the interests of other states, the rules of international law and international relations, the decisions and recommendations of international, regional and binational institutions and the opinion of mankind.

However, my rejection of the Realist school does not lead me to embrace the Moralist school. What is the Moralist view of foreign policy? The Moralist believes that moral values should control foreign policy. He believes that no matter how noble and virtuous the end, it never justifies the use of means that violate moral or ethical standards. Some moralists have argued that states should behave in accordance with the same high standards of morality that apply to individuals in a good society.

I have a major problem with the Moralist school. The Moralist fails to appreciate that the primary purpose of a government is to protect the independence, sovereignty and territorial integrity of the state and to promote the welfare of its people. In pursuing these objectives, a government ought to employ means which are lawful and moral. However, there will be situations, hopefully rare, when a government will be confronted by conflicts between its national interest and its fidelity to law and morality. In such situations, a government may feel compelled to subordinate considerations of law and morality to its national interest. In extreme cases, when the very survival of a state is in question, a government may even feel justified in acting beyond the law. In such situations, it is important for the politician or diplomat to have a bad conscience, to be aware of the damage that his action will inflict on the international system, so that the moral values will survive their violation.[10]

If I am neither a Realist nor a Moralist, what am I? If I have to stick a label on myself, I would quote U Thant and call myself a practical Idealist. I believe that as a Singaporean diplomat, my primary purpose is to protect the independence, sovereignty, territorial integrity and economic well-being of the state of Singapore. I believe that I ought to pursue these objectives by means which are lawful and moral. On the rare occasions when the pursuit of my country's vital national interest compels me to do things which are legally or morally dubious, I ought to have a bad conscience and be aware of the damage which I have done to the principle I have violated and to the reputation of my country. I believe that I must always consider the interests of other states and have a decent regard for the opinion of others. I believe that it is in Singapore's long-term interest to strengthen international law and morality, the international system for curbing the use of force and the institutions for the pacific settlement of disputes. Finally, I believe that it is in the interests of all nations to strengthen international co-operation and to make the world's political and economic order more stable, effective and equitable.

Speech given to the School of Foreign Service, Georgetown University, on being presented with the 1987 Jit Trainor Award for Distinction in the Conduct of Diplomacy, 18 November 1987.

NOTES

1. Nicolo Machiavelli, *The Prince*, Everyman's Library, Ernst Page (ed.)(New York: E.P. Dutton & Co., 1952), p. 143.
2. Ibid, p. 142.
3. Sissela Bok, *Lying: Moral Choice in Public and Private Life* (New York: Pantheon Books, 1978), p. 249.
4. *Supra*, Note 1, p. 48.
5. Arthur M. Schlesinger, *The Cycles of American History* (Boston: Houghton Mifflin, 1986), p. 72.
6. Reinhold Niebuhr, *Moral Man and Immoral Society* (New York: Charles Scribner & Sons, 1932), p. 95.
7. *Supra*, Note 5.

8. Roger Fisher, *International Conflict for Beginners* (London: Allen Lane, 1971), p. 155.
9. Ibid, p. 156.
10. See Gordon A. Craig and Alexander L. George, *Force and Statecraft, Diplomatic Problems of Our Time* (New York: Oxford University Press, 1983), p. 278.

The United Nations and the Quest for World Order

The quest for an international order is as old as the advent of nation-states. However, in the old days, relations between states were governed less by law than by might. Small nations were often preyed upon by militarily more powerful nations. Even during the 19th century in Europe, small nations were often sacrificed to maintained peace among the more powerful states. Lord Castlereagh, one of the architects of the Concert of Europe, which resulted from the Congress of Vienna, frankly stated that he "could not harbour any moral or political repugnance" against the act of handing Saxony over to Prussia, since the King of Saxony had "put himself in the position of having to be sacrificed to the future tranquillity of Europe".[1]

The League of Nations

The first major attempt to create a world order was made immediately following the end of the First World War. Although the US President, Woodrow Wilson, was an ardent advocate of the League of Nations, the United States failed to join the new world organization because of the isolationist sentiments in the US Congress and because of the uncompromising attitude adopted by President Wilson towards his domestic critics. The failure of the United States to join the League of Nations is thought by some to be one of the reasons for its eventual failure.

The Principle of Collective Security

The League of Nations had been created to implement the principle of collective security. The idea was that wherever an act of aggression occurred, the whole international community would combine to defend the victim. By doing so, the League would be defending not only the victim of aggression, but peace itself. Article 11 of the League's Covenant declared that "any war or threat of war, whether immediately affecting any of the members of the League or not, is hereby declared a matter of concern to the whole League". When an act of aggression took place, the League's Council was to "advise upon the means by which this obligation should be fulfilled". Under Article 16, members were under an absolute obligation to apply economic and communications sanctions against another member which had gone to war in disregard of its Covenant. But they were under no obligation to take any stronger action. If economic sanctions were to fail, the Council might recommend armed action to defend the victim. But no member was automatically obliged to respond.

An Epidemic of Lawlessness

When put to the test, the League of Nations failed to defend the victims of aggression against their aggressors. Italy attacked and colonized Ethiopia. Japan conquered Manchuria. Germany annexed the Rhineland, Austria and Czechoslovakia. In none of these cases did the League impose economic sanctions against the aggressor or recommend armed action to defend the victim. In 1939, when Russia attacked Finland, the League finally acted to expel the former from its membership. But, as George Scott commented, "... when viewed against the omissions, the erosions, the failures of the past, and the reality of the world scene at that moment, the incident (of expelling Russia from the League) must seem like no more than an irrelevant piece of play-acting".[2]

Causes of the League's Failure

Why did the League of Nations fail?

Evan Luard, the author of *A History of the UN*, has suggested the following reasons for the failure of the League. First, "A purely voluntary commitment to go to the defence of other states if they were attacked was far too feeble to be of any value ... Clearly, a far more specific obligation, based on collective and not individual judgment, would be required".[3] Second, "The League had collapsed because it had no 'teeth'".[4] "It was thus almost universally concluded that, to be effective, any subsequent organization must be equipped with some more substantial military power to implement its decisions".[5] Third, "Most of the disputes of the time were essentially political rather than legal in character; and it was political procedures rather than legal which were required to resolve them effectively. International law, and the legal procedures which applied it, might have their part to play in resolving certain kinds of international disputes, though usually not the major ones. But they were unlikely to be able to maintain for long a peaceful and harmonious order unless they were supplemented by procedures which were political rather than legal in style".[6]

The Second Try at World Order

While the Second World War was still raging, the leaders of the three principal allies – Roosevelt, Churchill and Stalin – were already planning to set up a new world organization after the war. Their representatives met at Dumbarton Oaks, in Washington, D.C., to hammer out the salient features of the new organization. The Charter of the UN, approved in San Francisco, was based essentially upon the accord reached at Dumbarton Oaks.

The UN's Collective System

There were certain similarities and differences between the UN and the League of Nations. Like the League, the UN would have an Assembly consisting of all its members, a smaller council, a secretariat and a court. The Charter of the UN was designed to avoid some of the defects of the League's Covenant. For example, the League had to make all its decisions by unanimity, thus giving every member a veto. In the UN, the General Assembly would decide by either a simple majority or, on important questions, a two-thirds majority. In the Security Council, the five great powers, which were allies in the Second World War – the United States, USSR, UK, France and China – were members from the beginning and were pledged to work together in maintaining the peace of the world.

The UN Paralysed by the Cold War

The efficacy of the collective security system of the UN was based upon the assumption that the wartime allies would continue to work together after the war. This assumption proved fallacious as the alliance between the Western powers and the Soviet Union broke down as soon as the war ended and the era of the Cold War began. The polarization between the East and West became so pervasive and intense that almost every dispute or conflict, anywhere in the world, became tainted by the East-West confrontation. As a result, with rare exceptions, the collective security system enshrined in the UN Charter was paralysed.

Is the Cold War Over?

Both President Mikhail Gorbachev of the Soviet Union and President George Bush of the United States have declared that the Cold War is over. Their words have been backed up by deeds. The first achievement was the INF Treaty which, for the first time in the history of disarmament, wiped out a whole class of intermediate-range nuclear weapons. The two superpowers have resumed their Strategic Arms Reduction Talks (START) in Geneva.

The two sides are also engaged in a series of confidence-building measures as well as in the reconsideration of defence doctrines and defence postures. Their mutual goal seems to be to achieve security at vastly reduced numbers.

Impact on Regional Conflicts in the Third World

Have the positive developments between the two superpowers and their respective military alliances in Europe had a beneficial impact on the regional conflicts in the Third World? The answer is yes. The two superpowers are seeking to extricate themselves from such conflicts and are even co-operating to resolve them. Let me just cite a few examples. The Soviet Union has withdrawn its troops from Afghanistan. The United States and the Soviet Union co-operated to negotiate the implementation of Security Council Resolution 435, which would enable Namibia to accede to independence and which led to the withdrawal of Cuban troops from Angola. The influence of the Soviet Union was probably one of the factors which led Vietnam to decide to withdraw its troops from Cambodia by the end of September this year. The Soviet Union has informed the United States that it has stopped the supply of arms to the Sandinista Government in Nicaragua and was prepared to work with the United States to bring peace to Central America. Even in the Middle East, the Bush Administration has expressed its willingness to work with the Soviet Union to resolve the Arab-Israeli conflict.

Regional Conflicts Likely to Continue

I would like, however, to strike a note of warning. One should not assume that regional conflicts in the Third World will disappear just because the two superpowers will cease to inject their rivalry into them. The fact is that most of the conflicts in the Third World have indigenous causes – tribal, racial, religious and linguistic conflicts, disputes over boundaries and the hegemonic ambitions of regional powers. Superpower involvement has often exacerbated these conflicts but it was seldom the cause of the conflicts. As one of my esteemed African friends said to me recently: "Very soon, we will not have the excuse of blaming our conflicts on the two superpowers. We will have to confront the unpleasant reality that most of the conflicts in the Third World are of our own making".

Strengthen Regional Unity

If I am correct in predicting that regional conflicts are likely to endure, is there anything that can be done about them? I would like to suggest one possible approach. Let us use Southeast Asia as an example. During the past 22 years, one of the most remarkable achievements in Southeast Asia has been the formation and progressive strengthening of ASEAN. The six member states of ASEAN have woven a tapestry of co-operative arrangements which bind them. They have developed a habit of consulting one another and of taking the others' interests into account when deciding on a policy. Because of ASEAN, bilateral differences between member states have either been resolved or tranquilized. Because of the progress which ASEAN has made these past 22 years, mutual confidence has increased, mistrust and misunderstanding have dissipated, and the danger of conflict has grown more remote.

Southeast Asia

In September this year, Vietnam has pledged to withdraw its troops from Cambodia. If the Vietnamese withdrawal is accompanied by an internationally acceptable comprehensive political solution, leading to a quadripartite interim coalition, a credible international peacekeeping force and free elections to enable the Khmers to exercise their right to self-determination, the principal source of tension in Southeast Asia for the past ten years will disappear. I can then foresee the normalization of relations between ASEAN and the states of Indochina. In time, as mutual confidence grows and trade and investment expand, the countries of Southeast Asia could learn to live with one another as good neighbours. When that happens, a Southeast Asian forum, like the CSCE[7] in Europe, consisting of all ten states of the region, could well be a helpful development which would enable the countries of Southeast Asia to enhance their co-operation and reduce misunderstanding through the process of dialogue and conciliation.

The Third Try at World Order

The end of the Cold War and the emergence of Mikhail Gorbachev as the new Soviet leader have raised the tantalizing thought that the UN may be about to enter into a new and creative phase of life. New Soviet thinking about the UN began on 17 September 1987 with the publication of an article by Gorbachev in Pravda. In it, Gorbachev embraced Hammarskjold's vision of the UN as a "place for the mutual search for a balance of differing, contradictory, yet real, interests of the contemporary community of states and nations". He called for "drastic intensification and expansion of the co-operation of states in uprooting international terrorism" and proposed the creation under the UN aegis of a tribunal to investigate acts of international terrorism. He indicated agreement with the proposition that "the world cannot be considered secure if human rights are violated in it" and held it "necessary that national legislation and administrative rule in the humanitarian sphere everywhere be brought in accordance with international obligations and standards". He observed that one "should not forget the capacities of the International Court either" and proposed that the General Assembly and the Security Council ... approach it more often "for consultative opinions on international disputes". "Its mandatory jurisdiction", he added, "should be recognized by all on mutually agreed upon conditions. The permanent members of the Council, taking into account special responsibility, are to make the first step in that direction".

Soviet Proposals to Strengthen the UN

One year later, on 22 September 1988, the Soviet Union circulated an *aide-mémoire* entitled "Towards Comprehensive Security through the

Enhancement of the Role of the United Nations". The *aide-mémoire* proposed the "extensive use of UN peacekeeping operations" and the affirmation of the primacy of international law in interstate relations". The memorandum also proposed that UN observers could be stationed along "frontiers within the territory of a country that seeks to protect itself from outside interference at the request of that country alone". The memorandum proposed granting the Secretary-General the right, without further authorization, to dispatch military observer missions and fact-finding missions to a state or states where a conflict, or outside interference, threatens the peace. It also envisaged fact-finding and truce observation on the authority of the General Assembly with the consent of the state or states on whose territory these activities are to be carried out. As an onus of its good faith, the Soviet Union has begun to pay, in convertible currency, its UN budget arrears and even to pay for UN peacekeeping operations.

Will the West and the NAM Respond?

The new proposals and suggestions of the Soviet Union to strengthen the UN are nothing short of revolutionary. They represent a complete reversal of the policies and postures which the Soviet Union had pursued in the past. How will the West, especially the United States, respond? According to Thomas M. Franck, the United States has accepted the challenge presented by these Soviet initiatives and the State department is authorized to prepare counter proposals.[8] Franck is also of the view that the new mood in Moscow and Washington is generally viewed by the governments of the Third World as being beneficial to them.[9]

A Unique Moment in History

I agree with Professor Franck when he wrote:

> *There thus exists at this moment a unique opportunity, a rare conjunction of the principal tendencies in the international system. For the first time since the creation of the United Nations, the United States, the Soviets and the Non-Aligned Movement appear able to form a common view of the organization's systematic capabilities: a view neither excessively optimistic nor mired in cynical pessimism. Moreover, all three groupings are moving away from fear-based, or ideology-driven, policies toward pragmatic politics of overlapping*

national self-interest. Above all, the three principal tendencies appear to understand that the system offers sound machinery ... for negotiating and administering agreed responses to humanity's recognized common enemies of poverty, illness and environmental degradation.[10]

Conclusion

We are living in a unique moment of world history. Man's first try for a world order, the League of Nations, foundered in an epidemic of lawlessness which led to the Second World War. At the end of the Second World War, the international community made a second try at world order by establishing the United Nations. The Charter of the UN was intended to cure the deficiencies of the League's Covenant. The Charter envisaged a system of collective security to maintain world peace and gave the Security Council the teeth to enforce its decisions. The Charter was not drawn up by a group of utopianists, but by Roosevelt, Churchill and Stalin. The UN has not, however, been able to function effectively because of the Cold War and, less importantly, the occasionally irresponsible behaviour of the Third World majority in the General Assembly. Now that the Cold War is coming to an end, we are faced with a new opportunity to breathe life into the provisions of the UN Charter. Let us, the East, the West and the non-aligned, seize this opportunity to make the third try at world order a success. History may not present us with another opportunity.

An edited version of the Inaugural Tun Mohamed Suffian Public Lecture, delivered at the Institute Pengajian Tinggi, University of Malaya, 20 July 1989.

NOTES

1. Guglielmo Ferrero, *The Reconstruction of Europe: Tallyrand and the Congress of Vienna, 1814–1815*, translated by Theodore R. Jaeckel (New York: G.P. Putnam & Sons, 1941), p. 178.
2. George Scott, *The Rise and Fall of the League of Nations* (New York: Macmillan, 1974), p. 398.
3. Evan Luard, *A History of the UN*, Vol. 1 (New York: St. Martin's Press, 1982), p. 6.
4. Ibid.
5. Ibid, p. 8.
6. Ibid, p. 10.
7. Conference on Security and Cooperation in Europe. This regional group was later renamed the Organization for Security and Cooperation in Europe (OSCE).

8. Thomas M. Franck, Vol. 83, *American Journal of International Law* (1989), p. 540.
9. Ibid.
10. Ibid.

THE UNITED NATIONS: REFORM AND RENEWAL

The United Nations and Small States: The Singapore Experience

Let me begin by telling you a story. A UN Ambassador was invited to give a lecture at an American university. He took the invitation very seriously and prepared a long and closely reasoned lecture on the assigned topic. He was warmly applauded when he completed his lecture. Afterwards, several members of the faculty and a few students came and shook his hand. They were effusive in their compliments. He felt rather pleased with himself until a student approached him and whispered in his ear: "You spoke too long". The Ambassador was rather taken aback at first but soon forgot the incident as others approached him to congratulate him. Much to his consternation, however, he saw that student joining the queue again. When the student shook his hand the second time, he whispered in his ear: "And your speech was too long".

When it was all over, the President of the University escorted the Ambassador to his car. On their way, the President said to the Ambassador that it was a splendid speech and he was very grateful. He added that he had noticed that a certain student had approached him twice. He said, "He does this to all our speakers. I don't know what he said to you but please don't take it seriously. Besides, he was only repeating what the others are saying".

I promise not to speak too long. I will also try not to be too boring.

The question which I will try to answer is: In what ways has Singapore benefited from its membership of and participation in the United Nations?

How Singapore Has Benefited from Its Participation in the United Nations

First, by joining the UN in 1965, Singapore obtained the imprimatur of legitimacy from the international community. Why was it important for Singapore to have obtained the recognition and acceptance of the international community as a sovereign and independent country? It was important because when Singapore separated from Malaysia in 1965, the Malayan Communist Party (MCP) and its front organizations denounced the separation as an imperialist plot and refused to recognize an independent Singapore. Obviously, the MCP and its front organizations could not sustain their position for long when the whole world, including the Soviet Union and its allies, recognized the independence of Singapore.

Looking around Singapore today, a visitor is struck by its prosperity, its cleanliness, its stability and order. The Singapore of the 1950s and 1960s was quite a different place. Unemployment was high, the birth-rate was among the highest in the world, housing conditions were deplorable, the place was filthy and prone to riots and strikes. Although the transformation was accomplished primarily through our own efforts, we did receive valuable help from others. This leads me to the second benefit we have derived from our membership of the UN, i.e. the help we obtained from the UN during the critical years of the 1960s. Let me just mention a few examples.

The UN helped us in the establishment of the Economic Development Board (EDB) and the training of some of its pioneers such as Chan Chin Bock, the alternate Chairman of the EDB. The UN sent us many advisers and experts. Some of these, such as Dr Albert Winsemius and I.F. Tang, have become familiar figures to many Singaporeans. The UN sent many missions to Singapore, to study the feasibility of various industrial projects and to advise on how such projects should be implemented. One such mission led to the establishment of the Singapore National Iron and Steel Industry. The valuable contributions of the UN Development Programme (UNDP), the UN Department of Technical Cooperation for Development (UNDTCD), the UN Industrial Development Organization (UNIDO) and of the World Bank (IBRD) should be acknowledged. The UN, through UNICEF and the UN Fund For Population Activities (UNFPA), helped us with advice and with funds in the fields of family planning and in child care and maternal health. A UN team, working with a Singaporean counterpart, updated our master plan and recommended the building of Changi Airport. It is not necessary for me to go on because I think I have given enough examples of the valuable help we obtained from the UN, in a variety of fields, during the past 25 years, especially during the critical years of the 1960s.

Third, the UN has been useful to us in our efforts to oppose protectionism, both in trade and in the service sector. A few years ago, when the tide of protectionism in the industrialized countries was running very strong, Singapore decided to take the issue to the UN General Assembly. We succeeded in getting the Group of 77, the group to which all developing countries belong, to endorse a draft resolution we had prepared. Having obtained the endorsement of the Group of 77, we then negotiated the text of the draft resolution with Group B, consisting of the developed market-economy countries. The negotiation failed to reach an agreement because the developed countries were unyielding. The Singapore delegation then put the draft resolution to the vote and it was, of course, adopted with an overwhelming majority.

On another occasion, we took the issue of Australia's discriminatory international civil aviation policy (ICAP) to UNCTAD V, which was held in Manila in 1979. The Australian Government had adopted a new policy in which a passenger travelling on an ASEAN airline between Australia and Europe could not make a free stopover in one of the ASEAN countries; if he or she did make such a stopover, the passenger had to pay an exorbitant sum. The ASEAN countries, in general, and Singapore, in particular, felt that the Australian policy was discriminatory and protectionist. When negotiations failed to yield satisfactory results, we decided to take the dispute to UNCTAD. We had to convince, first of all, the Asian members of the Group of 77 to support us. This we succeeded in doing. Then we had to convince the whole of the Group of 77 to endorse our position. That took a considerable amount of effort because some of the Latin American countries were not sympathetic. We succeeded in overcoming their reluctance. Through a stroke of good luck and the successful lobbying of our current Permanent Representative to the UN in Geneva, Ambassador Chew Tai Soo, I was appointed the spokesman of the Group of 77 on the question of protectionism in the service sector. The spokesman for Group B was an official, English by nationality, of the European Economic Community in Brussels. I can still remember the marathon sessions of negotiations between us, some lasting till the early hours of the morning. In the end, we failed to agree and we put our draft resolution to the vote. Since our position had been endorsed by the Group of 77, the draft resolution was adopted by an overwhelming majority.

You may ask, what is the use of a General Assembly resolution or an UNCTAD resolution since neither body has the power to enforce its decisions? Their utility lies in the fact that the UN reflects the public opinion of the world and a resolution of the UN General Assembly and of UNCTAD exerts moral pressure on the state or states to which it is addressed. I believe that no country is immune from the pressure of world public opinion, although I recognize that some governments are more concerned about their self-respect and how others regard them than others.

Singapore is an island country. It is a great entrepôt port. Our security and economic well-being are therefore very much dependent upon the freedom of navigation and the maintenance of the rule of law at sea. For this reason, we viewed with great concern the erosion of the traditional Law of the Sea during the decades of the 1950s and 1960s and the proliferation of unilateral clams by coastal states. By the late 1960s, the legal order which had lasted over 100 years had suffered a fatal blow and the international community was confronted with the challenge of either negotiating a new legal order or of chaos. Singapore participated actively in the preparations for, as well as in the work of, the Third UN Conference on the Law of the Sea. The Conference, which began in 1974, concluded its work in 1982 with the adoption of the UN Convention on the Law of the Sea. Whatever the merits and demerits of that treaty, one thing is indisputable. The treaty has put a stop to the creeping jurisdiction of the coastal states. The treaty has replaced a state of legal chaos with a new international legal order in which the rights and duties of coastal states and of other states are clearly spelt out. It is a significant contribution to the rule of law. The treaty protects our navigational, strategic and economic interests. I would point to this and other law-making activities of the UN as the fourth benefit which Singapore derives from its membership in the UN. The point is, I think, reasonably clear. As a small country, our security interests are enhanced when the rule of law prevails and contrariwise, our security interests are jeopardized when the rule of might replaces the rule of law.

The fifth and perhaps the most dramatic occasion on which Singapore took an issue to the UN and obtained the desired outcome was the Vietnamese invasion and occupation of Cambodia in December 1978 and January 1979. Why did the ASEAN countries, in general, and Singapore, in particular, oppose the action of Vietnam? Wasn't the Pol Pot regime a blood-thirsty and barbarous regime? Why then did we condemn rather than applaud the overthrow of that odious regime?

The ASEAN countries had never approved or supported the Pol Pot regime. On the contrary, it was Vietnam, the Soviet Union and its allies which had nurtured and supported the Pol Pot regime and shielded it against criticism in the UN Human Rights Commission. Therefore, Vietnam's intention for intervening was not humanitarian but hegemonistic.

The ASEAN countries believed that if we had acquiesced in Vietnam's action, we would have allowed a bad precedent to be set. Militarily weak states would be exposed to the so-called "humanitarian intervention" of their militarily more powerful neighbours. The ASEAN countries felt that the principle of respect for the sovereignty, independence and territorial integrity of states and the principle of non-interference in the internal affairs of states – two of the cardinal principles of the UN Charter – must be maintained because they protected weaker states against their more powerful neighbours. Although ASEAN acknowledged that Vietnam had legitimate security interests in respect of Cambodia, such interests could not detract from the right of the Khmer people to determine their own destiny.

At the UN General Assembly in 1979, ASEAN was by no means sure that it had the necessary support to retain the seat of Democratic Kampuchea. We faced a formidable array of adversaries consisting of Vietnam and its Third World allies, the Soviet Union and its East European allies, and India. Our arguments prevailed and a majority of the UN's member states, including many of the Non-Aligned countries, supported ASEAN's stand. Between 1979 and 1982, Vietnam's challenge to the credentials of Democratic Kampuchea received less and less support and was faced with mounting opposition. In 1983, Vietnam made no challenge to the credentials of Democratic Kampuchea. Each year, since 1979, ASEAN has also presented to the UN General Assembly a resolution on Kampuchea which, *inter alia*, called upon Vietnam to come to the negotiating table and urged a political solution which would include the total withdrawal of Vietnamese forces from Cambodia and the holding of free elections under international supervision. During the last two years, 105 countries have voted for the ASEAN resolution.

A cynic may ask what is the use of these resolutions when the reality is that five years and five resolutions later, Vietnam is still occupying Cambodia. The cynic, of course, has a point. The sanctions against violations of international law are usually weak. But the resolutions of the General Assembly are not without effect. They have boosted the morale of the nationalist forces fighting against the Vietnamese in Cambodia. The ASEAN countries have been largely successful in persuading the Western countries and Japan to withhold their bilateral economic assistance to Vietnam until the problem of Cambodia is resolved. Vietnam has been seriously embarrassed. From 1975 to 1978, Vietnam was seen by the Third World as a heroic country, having defeated, first, the French and then, the United States. Today, Vietnam is viewed by most of the countries of the Third World as an aggressive and expansionist state. I cannot believe that however stoical the Vietnamese may be, it does not hurt.

Although the Vietnamese have not yet agreed to sit at the negotiating table, they have progressively shifted their position. Vietnam has stopped saying that the situation in Cambodia is irreversible. It has stopped insisting that any negotiation on Cambodia must simultaneously take up other issues which the Vietnamese wished to raise, such as American bases in the Philippines and East Timor. Lately, Vietnam has even stopped saying that it will only withdraw its troops from Cambodia when the Chinese threat has been eliminated. I am aware of the fact that these changes in the Vietnamese tune may be tactical rather than real, but I am also fairly confident that ASEAN's three-prong policy on Cambodia has a better than 50 per cent chance of success.

The Three Prongs of ASEAN's Policy

First, to support the nationalist forces, especially the two non-communist forces, in order to maintain the military pressure on the ground. Second, to isolate Vietnam and thereby exert political, diplomatic and economic pressure on her to come to the negotiating table. Third, to offer Vietnam an honourable political settlement which will restore Cambodia as a sovereign and independent state and which will, at the same time, safeguard the legitimate security interests of Cambodia's neighbours, including Vietnam.

Let me now turn to the sixth instance in which Singapore took an issue to the UN and secured positive results. Most of you will, I am sure, remember the period of 1979–1980, when Vietnam either expelled or encouraged large numbers of its unwanted citizens to leave the country by boat, often unseaworthy ones at that. The exodus of the "boat people", as the media came to call them, reached alarming proportions. The ASEAN countries were concerned for three reasons. First, the arrival of large numbers of Vietnamese refugees, many of whom were of Chinese ethnicity, posed a threat to the internal social order of some of the ASEAN countries. Second, as the number of new arrivals exceeded the number of refugees who were accepted by the countries of final refuge, mainly in the West, ASEAN was afraid to be stuck with a residue. Third, the financial resources to care for the refugees in the places of temporary refuge in the ASEAN countries were rapidly dwindling. Confronted with this situation, the ASEAN countries requested the then Secretary-General of the UN, Kurt Waldheim, to hold a high-level conference on Indochinese refugees in Geneva.

The Geneva Conference proved extremely productive. First, the Western countries agreed to increase their intake of the Indochinese refugees. Second, owing largely to a very generous contribution from Japan, the Conference raised a very large sum of money to care for the refugees. Third and most important of all, Secretary-General Kurt Waldheim managed to negotiate an agreement with the Vietnamese Deputy Foreign Minister, Phan Hien, whereby Vietnam agreed to discourage the exodus of the "boat people" and agreed to allow the UNHCR to establish an office in Vietnam in order to arrange for the orderly departure of the Vietnamese who wished to leave their country. The agreement has been observed by Vietnam and the latest figures show that the number of orderly departures, over 2,000 per month, exceeds the number of "boat people".

Let me turn to the seventh case. In 1979, the Western mass media reported that famine had struck Cambodia. At first, the authorities in Phnom Penh denounced such reports as falsehood, characterizing them as imperialist propaganda. Heng Samrin and his colleagues had to stop denying the undeniable when thousands of Khmers, men, women and children arrived at the Thai-Cambodian border, many of them literally dying in front of our eyes, on our television screens, from hunger and disease. Much to Kurt Waldheim's credit, the Secretary-General took the initiative to convene in New York, in November 1979, a conference to raise funds and material contributions, for the humanitarian relief of the Cambodians, both those inside Cambodia as well as those encamped along the Thai-Cambodian border and inside Thailand. The conference initiated a process which continues today. If the Cambodian people did not perish from famine and disease, the UN and its specialized agencies as well as the Swiss International Committee of the Red Cross (ICRC), must be given much of the credit. The survival of the Cambodian people is important to ASEAN and to the world because had they perished there would be nothing to fight for.

The eighth and last utility of the UN to Singapore which I wish to discuss is that it is the concourse of the world. This is important to a small country such as Singapore because we have no diplomatic missions in Africa, in the Caribbean and in Latin America. The UN is a convenient forum in which we transact some of our bilateral business with these countries. The UN also serves us as a listening post as well as a window on the world. Each year, when our Deputy Prime Minister and Foreign Minister come to New York, they meet 20 or more of their counterparts from various regions of the world. If the Ministers had to travel to their countries to meet them it would probably take up several months of their valuable time.

Excerpt of a speech delivered to the Alpha Society, the UN Association of Singapore and the faculty and students of the National University of Singapore (NUS), at the Public Utilities Board (PUB) Auditorium, Singapore, 12 July 1984.

THE UNITED NATIONS: REFORM AND RENEWAL

Can the United Nations Be Reformed ?

Can the United Nations be reformed? I would answer the question in the affirmative but with two major caveats. My first caveat is that no amount of reforming can realize the two central goals of 1945 which are enshrined in the UN Charter, i.e. that disputes between states would be settled by peaceful means and that international peace and security would be maintained by the Security Council. The fact that more than 20 million persons have been killed in armed conflicts since 1945 is horrible but irrefutable evidence of the failure of those goals. The reality of international politics leads me to the conclusion that those goals cannot be realistically achieved in the future. My second caveat is that we should have no illusions about the formidable vested interests, both in the Secretariat and in the delegations of member states, which will oppose any reform which impinges on their interests. This unholy alliance has succeeded in defeating all previous attempts at reforming the United Nations.

The following is a highly subjective and selective agenda of reforms which I would like to see implemented at the UN.

Personnel Policy and Management

The strength of the UN depends upon two factors. First, it can only be as strong as its member states will allow it to be. Second, its strength and effectiveness depend upon the competence and integrity of the men and women who make up the Secretariat. My first cluster of suggestions relate to the reform of personnel policy and management. Over the past 41 years, the concept of the international civil service has been progressively eroded. No region or group can be exempted from blame. However, the worst offenders are the communist countries who have never accepted the concept. Their nationals are not permitted to become international career civil servants. They are seconded to the Secretariat and a portion of their salaries is siphoned off by their governments. I support Ambassador Charles Lichenstein's proposal that not more than 50 per cent of the nationals of any communist country should be allowed to serve in the UN Secretariat on secondment. I object equally to the practice of the communist countries in siphoning off a portion of the salaries of their nationals in the Secretariat and to the practice of some Western countries in paying a supplement to their nationals in the Secretariat.

The process of recruitment and promotion has become highly politicized. This has two deleterious consequences. First, the UN is not always recruiting the best and brightest. Second, it has a demoralizing effect on the staff. Both the delegations and the Secretariat are to be blamed for this deplorable state of affairs. The Secretary-General must insulate his personal office from pressure from the delegations. He should let the missions know that he is not prepared to receive any ambassador if the purpose of his visit is to lobby for the recruitment or promotion of a national from his country or region. The Secretary-General should back the substantive heads of the various departments and the Office of Personnel Services. My third suggestion is that a Search Committee should be established to assist the Secretary-General in shortlisting qualified candidates for each vacancy at the level of D2[1] and above. The members of the Search Committee should be recruited from outside the UN system. The purpose of the Search Committee is not to take away the Secretary-General's prerogative of selecting his senior staff. It is to assist him by presenting him with the most qualified candidates.

My fourth suggestion is to stop the wasteful duplication of resources in the Secretariat. Let me give you one simple example. At present, there are two offices within the Secretariat working in the field of the Law of the Sea. They are the Office of the Special Representative of the Secretary-General on the Law of the Sea and the Office of Ocean Economics and Technology, which belongs to the Department of International Economic and Social Affairs. In order to maximize economy and efficiency, the two offices should be merged. My fifth suggestion is that the Secretary-General should redeploy staff from "sunset" departments of the Secretariat, for example, the Department of Decolonization, to "sunrise" departments. My sixth suggestion is that the Secretary-General should improve the morale of his staff by rewarding good work and by punishing incompetence. The Secretary-General should be given enhanced power to get rid of dead wood in the Secretariat.

The Budget

The UN budget, like the US federal budget, has a lot of fat in it which can be cut. One way to do this is to strengthen the powers of the Advisory Committee on Administrative and Budgetary Questions (ACABQ) which has a good track record of fiscal responsibility. My second suggestion is to bring Secretariat salaries into line with those of the US federal civil service. This is in accordance with the Noblemaire principle which states that an international organization must be prepared to pay enough to attract the citizens of the countries with the best paid national civil service. At present, UN salaries are about 20 per cent higher than US salaries. My third suggestion is to stop, or at least to reduce substantially, the junkets and needless conferences which the UN has become addicted to. Let me give you two examples. I see no justification for allowing members of the UN Council on Namibia to go on junkets to preach the gospel of a free Namibia to those who are already converted to the cause. I also see no justification for allowing the members of the Economic and Social Council (ECOSOC) to hold their summer meetings in Geneva just because the weather is more pleasant in Geneva during the summer than in New York. My fourth suggestion is to create a procedure to discourage the creation of new committees. Very often, when a delegation runs out of ideas on an item which it has inscribed on the agenda, it resorts to the expedience of proposing the creation of a committee to examine the question. The UN has literally hundreds of such committees, many of which have overlapping jurisdiction. My suggestion is that before any resolution which contains a proposal to create a new committee is adopted, the Secretary-General should be required to submit a report containing his observations on whether there are existing committees which could look into the question, and on the usefulness of creating a new committee.

The Non-Aligned Movement and the Group of 77

The key to the revitalization of the United Nations lies not in amending its Charter, its institutions and its procedures, but in the attitudes and policies which its members adopt towards the organization and towards the subjects and questions which appear on the global agenda. In the political field, the member states of the UN which belong to the Non-Aligned Movement, now numbering 99, can play a vital role in the revitalization of the UN. However, if the Movement is to play such a role it must first set its house in order. If the Non-Aligned Movement can act objectively and impartially between the two superpowers and their respective alliances; if the

Movement will uphold and apply its principles uniformly and not on a selective basis; if it will exercise its majoritarian power in the General Assembly with wisdom and with prudence; and if it will put forward realistic and imaginative proposals on the whole range of subjects and issues on the global agenda, the Non-Aligned Movement will have made an important contribution towards the revitalization of the UN.

In the economic field, the Group of 77 must alter its agenda, its posture and its rhetoric if it is to be taken seriously, and if the UN is to become an important forum for the North-South dialogue. The Group, like the Non-Aligned Movement, has come to be dominated by a hard core of unrepresentative and radical countries. Economically speaking, most of the leaders of the Group of 77 are countries which have failed to make economic progress. Their attitude is therefore to blame the "inequitable international economic order" for their failures. They are basically hostile to free enterprise and to multinational corporations. They seek confrontation instead of accommodation, they demand the transfer of resources from the rich to the poor instead of seeking mutual benefits. If the Group of 77 is to be taken seriously by the industrialized countries, a change of attitude, of tone and of rhetoric would be helpful. The groups should put forward proposals which are economically sound and which will bring about mutual benefits to the developed as well as the developing countries.

The Responsibility of the West

At present, the West tends to play a defensive and reactive role at the United Nations. One of my good friends from a Western delegation has told me that his objective at the UN is damage limitation. This is a very negative and defeatist attitude. The West should play a more active and positive role at the UN. It should have an agenda of problems and questions which it is willing to discuss or negotiate with the developing countries at the UN. The West should learn how to play the game at the UN and adopt a more skilful and muscular strategy in furthering its foreign policy objectives through the UN. When the West has nothing to offer, the moderate leadership in the Third World is weakened and the radical leadership is strengthened. The West should not abandon the UN because of a mistaken perception that the UN has already been captured by the Soviets and is therefore a forum in which the West cannot win. The defeat of the Soviet Union on Afghanistan, the defeat of Vietnam on Cambodia and the victories of the US on the status of Puerto Rico and the right of Israel to remain in the UN are ample proof of my assertion that the UN is a forum which the West can win. The UN is an important forum for winning the hearts and minds of the peoples of the world. Through a combination of skilful diplomacy and a positive agenda, the West can beat its principal ideological adversary at the UN.

I cannot leave the subject of the responsibility of the West without commenting on two recent actions of the United States. First, after years of condemning the Soviet Union and others for illegally withholding their assessed contributions to the UN, the United States has, in recent years, joined the delinquents. Second, the US Congress has unilaterally decided to reduce the assessed contributions of this country to the UN budget, in clear violation of US treaty obligations and of the due process of law. Actions such as these not only undermine the financial integrity of the UN but they also cause many of your friends to wonder whether your real intention is to reform the UN or to emasculate it.

Conclusion

Let me conclude by asking the two questions which are in the minds of many people. First, will the UN survive? Second, what kind of a UN will it be? I think the UN will survive. Although it has many flaws and shortcomings, on balance, it does more good than harm. If the UN does not exist, the imperative of global interdependence will compel us to create an organization very much like the UN. The UN is particularly important for small countries such as Singapore because, in spite of all its inadequacies, the UN does provide us with some protection against the law of the jungle. Whether the UN of the future will become a stronger and more effective organization will depend primarily on the policies and practices of its member states. The answer does not lie in tinkering with the Charter or in institutional reform.

Remarks prepared for an Ambassadors' Round Table at the Heritage Foundation, 7 August 1986.

NOTES
1. A position just below the rank of an Assistant Secretary-General.

THE UNITED NATIONS: REFORM AND RENEWAL

The United Nations: Is There Life after Forty?

Forty years ago, the UN was born in the city of San Francisco. Under more auspicious circumstances we should be celebrating the UN's 40th anniversary. Instead of doing that, I have asked whether the UN is going to survive. I have done so because the prestige of the United Nations today is at an all-time low. It is perceived as an organization which has failed to maintain world peace and security. It is perceived as an organization which is drowning in a sea of words and suffocating under an avalanche of paper. The United Nations is seen as an organization which practises double standards. The General Assembly is seen less and less as a forum which expresses the decent opinion of mankind. In the light of these widely held perceptions of the United Nations, one must wonder whether the organization is going to survive.

If it is going to survive, will it be a stronger and more effective institution? To answer these questions, let us begin with a retrospective look at the last 40 years. Let us examine both the UN's successes and failures, its strengths and weaknesses.

"To Save Succeeding Generations from the Scourge of War"

The preamble to the Charter of the United Nations begins with these words: "We, the peoples of the United Nations determined to save succeeding generations from the scourge of war, which twice in our lifetime has brought untold sorrow to mankind ..." The first article of the Charter prescribes the maintenance of international peace and security as the first purpose of the UN. How did the founding fathers envision the organization carrying out this important task?

At their meeting in Moscow in October 1943, President Roosevelt, Prime Minister Churchill and Marshall Stalin decided that it was necessary to establish at the earliest practical date "a general international organization based on the principle of the sovereign equality of all peace-loving states and open to membership by all such states, large or small, for the maintenance of international peace and security". Representatives of the United States, the United Kingdom and the Soviet Union met in August 1944 at Dumbarton Oaks, in Washington, D.C., to draw up more detailed and comprehensive plans for the organization which would be called the United Nations. The Dumbarton Oaks' proposals included the following two elements. One of the principal organs of the United Nations would be called the Security Council and it would be given primary responsibility for the maintenance of peace and security. The five Great Powers, i.e., the United States, the United Kingdom, the Soviet Union, France and China would be permanent members of the Security Council and they would have the power to veto any substantive decisions in matters to which they were not a party. As envisioned by the founding fathers, the Security Council was to be the centrepiece of the UN's collective security system.

Has the UN's collective security system succeeded in maintaining international peace and security? The answer is obviously "No". According to the Stockholm International Peace Research Institute, more than 100 armed conflicts have taken place since the UN was founded. Twenty-six million people have perished in those conflicts. Why has the UN's collective security system, as conceived by Roosevelt, Churchill and Stalin, failed to live up to its mandate?

I would like to draw an analogy between the UN's collective security system and the legal system of a state. The Charter of the United Nations, like the legal codes of a country, contains rules prohibiting certain types of conduct by states. The Security Council is expected to function very much like a court of law in a national legal system. States which have disputes with other states, where the disputes threaten a breach of international peace, may bring their disputes to the Security Council. In theory, the Security Council would make a determination of the facts of a case; it would apply the relevant rules, either from the UN Charter or from the general body of international law, and it would then make a determination and recommend appropriate measures. If the offending party refuses to comply with the decision of the Security Council, the Council is empowered to take appropriate measures, including the use of force.

The collective security system has not worked for several reasons. First, it has not worked because many of the member states of the organization have flagrantly violated the principles of the UN Charter even though every member country has committed itself to adhere to those principles. It is often said that member states have violated the Charter principles because there are no effective sanctions against such violations. Although there is no doubt some truth in this proposition, I have never been prepared to accept it as a justification for the conduct of states. After all, in most societies good citizens obey the law not only because of their fear of the sanctions but because it is in their enlightened self-interest to do so. As someone else has remarked, the degree of civilization of a people can, in part, be measured by the extent to which they comply to what is unenforceable. Judged by that standard, we must come to the regrettable conclusion that the international community in which we live is not a very civilized one and that we have a long way to go before we can outlaw the use of force.

The second reason for the failure of the collective security system is that the 15 members of the security council seldom act in an impartial and judicial manner. Although judges are not free from personal prejudices, by and large, they attempt to ascertain the facts of a case in an objective manner and apply the relevant rules of law to the facts. In the case of the Security Council, the determination of the facts of a dispute by the Council members is inevitably affected by such extraneous considerations as the relationship between each council member and the parties to the dispute. The identification and application of the relevant rules are similarly affected by such extraneous considerations. The result is that the members of the Council are often unable to agree on who is the aggressor and who is the victim, and what measures should be adopted to redress the situation.

The last and most important reason for the failure of the collective security system is the inability of the five permanent members, especially the United States and the Soviet Union, to work together. The Security Council can only work on the assumption of great power unanimity. In the current state of international relations, it is clear that that assumption does not exist. There are, in fact, very few instances in which the five great powers have a congruence of interests and are therefore able to work together. Some of the members of the Non-Aligned Movement have sought to overcome this problem by suggesting that the veto power should be abolished. This is not a very realistic proposal because four of the five permanent members are opposed to such an amendment and because the great powers would not have agreed, in 1945, to invest the Security Council with such extensive powers if they did not have the veto power to protect their national interests. I fear that there are no realistic prospects of making the collective security system work better until the United States and the Soviet Union come to the conclusion that the absence of more effective means of maintaining international peace is creating unacceptable risks for their national interests.

If I have been critical of the UN's failure to prevent armed conflicts in the past 40 years, I think it is incumbent upon me to balance the picture by pointing to some of the UN's success stories. In some cases, the UN has played a helpful role in preventing the escalation of wars, in ending wars, in preventing the recurrence of fighting or in offering an agreed framework for the settlement of a political conflict.

The Arab-Israeli War of 1948

During the Arab-Israeli War of 1948, the United Nations called twice for cease-fires and was obeyed each time. Although the attempt to establish a peace agreement between the Arabs and the Israelis was not successful, the Special Representative of the Secretary-General, Ralph Bunche, (an American) succeeded in negotiating armistice agreements which held for many years.

Indonesia

The United Nations played a helpful role in the armed conflict which took place between the Dutch government and Indonesian nationalists. The UN called for two cease-fires which were very rapidly implemented. It also set in motion a conciliation process which eventually led to the independence of Indonesia.

Azerbaijan

The Iranian province of Azerbaijan was occupied by Soviet troops in 1946. The repeated consideration of the question by the Security Council was probably one of the factors which led eventually to the withdrawal of the Soviet forces from that province.

Lebanon and Syria

After the fall of France in 1940, Lebanon and Syria were, for a year, controlled by the Vichy government. In 1941, the two countries were invaded and occupied by the British and the free French. After the war, the British and French forces remained. The governments of Lebanon and Syria wanted them to leave and when negotiations for a date for their withdrawal were inconclusive, the issue was brought to the Security Council by Lebanon and Syria. Although the Security Council was unable to adopt a resolution, the issue was fairly quickly resolved when France and Britain agreed to withdraw their forces.

Greece

Following the end of the Second World War, a civil war broke out in Greece. The United Nations sent a commission to observe the civil war and to investigate the alleged involvement of external powers in it. By focusing public attention on the area, and by publicizing evidence of foreign activities against the Greek borders, the UN probably helped deter or restrict such activities. The actions taken by the UN, together with the change in the political situation of Yugoslavia and the subsequent closure of its borders with Greece, were probably the two most important factors responsible for the termination of the Greek Civil War.

Korea

In protest against the fact that the Chinese seat in the Security Council was occupied by the Government of Taiwan, the Soviet Union walked out of the Council on 13 January 1950. On 24 June 1950, North Korea invaded South Korea. On 25 June, the UN Security Council ordered a cease-fire, which was ignored by North Korea. On 27 June, the Security Council, in the absence of the Soviet Union, which would otherwise have vetoed the resolution, voted for collective armed action by the UN. Sixteen countries contributed troops which fought under the UN flag against the North Koreans and, subsequently, also the Chinese. Although the war ended in a truce, the intervention by the UN succeeded in repelling the invasion by North Korea.

The Arab-Israeli War of 1956

The United Nations played a very important role in ending the Arab-Israeli War of 1956. With the Security Council blocked by British and French vetoes, the question was taken to the General Assembly. In a rare display of co-operation, the United States, the Soviet Union and the Non-Aligned countries succeeded in ending the conflict and establishing a UN peacekeeping force which helped to maintain the peace in the Middle East from 1956 to 1967.

Crisis in the Congo

The UN's Congo operation from 1960 to 1963 must be viewed as one of its success stories. The Congo, now known as Zaire, attained its independence from Belgium on 30 June 1960. On 5 July, the Congolese army mutinied. On 10 July, Belgian troops intervened and occupied Leopoldville and Elizabethville. The next day, 11 July, Tshombe, the President of the province of Katanga, proclaimed the secession of his province from the Republic. On 12 July, the Republic of the Congo requested the UN's help. The UN's operation in the Congo was an extremely complex one. It had to maintain law and order, prevent the secession of Katanga and secure the withdrawal of the Belgians and of foreign mercenaries. At its peak, the UN had only 18,000 troops and 1,300 civilians in a territory of more than 900,000 square miles. The UN succeeded in its mandate and in keeping the great powers out of the conflict. In the process, the second Secretary-General of the UN, Dag Hammarskjold, lost his life in a plane crash.

The Arab-Israeli War of 1973

On 6 October 1973, Egypt and Syria launched a co-ordinated attack against Israel. By taking the Israelis by surprise, the Egyptians forces rapidly crossed the Suez Canal and President Sadat was able to achieve his fundamental objective of shattering the belief in Israel's invincibility and Arab impotence. In order to buy time to enable the Israelis to recover the offensive, the United States opposed early action by the Security Council. A cease-fire agreement was finally negotiated in Moscow between Kissinger and Brezhnev on 21 October and was adopted by the Security Council on 22 October as the famous Resolution 338. The cease-fire did not, however, last long. Egypt and Israel accused each other of violating the cease-fire. The Israeli forces advanced and succeeded in encircling the Egyptian Third Army which was on the eastern bank of the Suez. On 24 October, the Soviet Union informed the United States that it would support a resolution calling for the despatch of American and Soviet troops to the Middle East. Later, the Soviet Union threatened that if the United States rejected its proposal, it would send its troops unilaterally. This led to a major confrontation between the two superpowers which was only defused when the non-aligned members of the Security Council tabled a resolution on 25 October asking the Secretary-General to increase the number of UN observers and to set up a UN peacekeeping force immediately. The force established by this resolution continues to keep the peace between Egypt and Israel.

UN Peacekeeping Forces

I have already alluded to the UN peacekeeping force which helps to keep the peace between Egypt and Israel. There are, in fact, four other peacekeeping forces. They help to keep the peace between Israel and Syria in the Golan Heights, between Israel and the Palestinians in southern Lebanon, between Greek Cypriots and Turkish Cypriots in Cyprus, and between India and Pakistan in Kashmir. The United Nations' peacekeeping forces must certainly be considered as one of the success stories of the United Nations.

The Secretary-General and Quiet Diplomacy

The popular perception of the UN Secretary-General is that he is a powerless moralist whose sermons to member states to conduct themselves in conformity with the UN Charter are largely ignored. Although there are some elements of truth in this perception, it ignores the many other roles which the Secretary-General performs, for example, as mediator, as arbitrator, as a negotiator and as a catalyst. Because much of the Secretary-General's work is performed in private, away from the glare of publicity, in what is sometimes called "quiet diplomacy", the world is often unaware of his achievements. I would like to give a few examples of actions taken by each of the five Secretaries-General of the United Nations which had productive results.

Trygvie Lie

During the Berlin crisis of 1948, the Security Council tried repeatedly but without success, to find a way of defusing the crisis. A compromise introduced by the six non-aligned members of the Security Council on 22 October 1948 calling for the removal of the Soviet restrictions and for an immediate meeting of the four military governors to arrange for a unified currency throughout Berlin based on the Soviet Zone currency, was vetoed by the Soviet Union. Secretary-General Trygvie Lie then took the personal initiative of bringing together the chief delegates of the United States and the Soviet Union for private discussions. The representatives of Britain and France were later invited to join these talks. On 4 May 1949, it was announced that agreement had finally been reached on all major questions affecting Berlin. Although it is impossible to prove, I suspect that the initiative exercised by Trygvie Lie helped to pave the way towards a solution.

Dag Hammarskjold

The second Secretary-General of the United Nations, Dag Hammarskjold, was an extremely intelligent and courageous person. During his tenure, he did not shrink from exercising his good offices in many difficult situations, often with helpful results. One of his many triumphs was a trip to China in 1954 to secure that release of 15 US airmen who had been captured in 1952 by China in Korea. Hammarskjold held four meetings with Chou En-Lai between 6 January and 10 January 1955 in Peking. On 29 May, the Chinese government announced that it had decided to release four of the US airmen. The rest were released on 4 August.

U Thant

In October 1962, the world came very close to the nuclear brink. The crisis began on 15 October when President Kennedy told the American people that the Soviet Union, despite assurances to the contrary, was building offensive missile bases in Cuba. He announced that, with immediate effect, he had imposed a naval and air quarantine on the shipment of offensive military equipment to Cuba.

At that time, 25 Soviet ships were steaming toward Cuba. Of these, 12 turned back. The remaining 13 ships continued steaming towards Cuba, thus bringing the confrontation between the two superpowers closer with every passing hour. At this critical moment, U Thant, the third Secretary-General, issued an appeal to Khrushchev asking that Soviet ships keep out of the United States interception area for a limited time in order to promote discussion of the modalities of a possible agreement. U Thant also sent a letter to Kennedy asking that instructions be issued to United States vessels to do everything possible to avoid a direct confrontation with Soviet ships in the next few days in order to minimize the risk of any untoward incident.

Kennedy replied that if the Soviet ships were to stay away from the interception area for the limited time required for preliminary discussion, U Thant could be assured that US vessels would abide by his request. Khrushchev also advised U Thant that the Soviets would abide by his request.

Thus, the timely appeal by U Thant helped to defuse the confrontation between the two superpowers by allowing Khrushchev to back down without losing face.

Kurt Waldheim

I would like to give two examples of the initiatives taken by the fourth Secretary-General, Kurt Waldheim of Austria, which led to beneficial results. Many of us will remember the period of 1979–1980 when Vietnam expelled or encouraged large numbers of its unwanted citizens to leave the country by boat, often unseaworthy ones. The exodus of the "boat people", as the media came to call them, reached alarming proportions. Secretary General Waldheim subsequently convened a high-level conference on Indochinese refugees in Geneva.

The Geneva Conference proved to be extremely productive. First, the Western countries agreed to increase their intake of Indochinese refugees. Second, the conference raised a very large sum of money for the care of the refugees. Third, Waldheim successfully negotiated an agreement with the Vietnamese Deputy Foreign Minister, Phan Hien, whereby Vietnam agreed to discourage the exodus of "boat people", and agreed to allow the UN High Commissioner for Refugees to establish an office in Vietnam in order to arrange for the orderly departure of the Vietnamese who wished to leave. Although the number of orderly departures has been relatively small, over two thousand per month, the agreement has been sucessful in that the number exceeds that leaving by boat.

In 1979, the Western media began to report that famine had struck that tragic country, Cambodia. At first, the authorities in Phnom Penh denounced such reports as falsehoods, characterizing them as imperialist propaganda. Heng Samrin and his colleagues had to stop denying the undeniable when thousands of Cambodians arrived at the Thai-Cambodian border, many of them literally dying in front of our eyes, on our television screens. Much to Waldheim's credit, he took the personal initiative to convene in November 1979, in New York, a conference to raise funds and material contributions for the humanitarian relief of the Cambodians inside Cambodia, as well as those encamped along the Thai-Cambodian border and inside Thailand. That conference initiated a rescue operation which continues today. If the Cambodian people have not perished from famine and disease, the UN and its specialized agencies, the Swiss ICRC and many non-governmental organizations must be given much of the credit.

Javier Perez de Cuellar

I would also like to give two instances in which the current Secretary-General, Javier Perez de Cuellar of Peru, was successful in the exercise of his good offices. There has been a long-standing territorial dispute between Guyana and Venezuela. A few years ago, the dispute became very heated and there was a very real prospect that the dispute would escalate into an armed conflict. Fortunately, the two parties invited the Secretary-General to exercise his good offices and he was able to tranquilize the dispute and to bring the two parties to the conference table.

The cruel and dangerous war between Iran and Iraq has been going on for several years. In early 1984, Iran accused Iraq of using chemical weapons in violation of international law. Iran requested the Secretary-General to verify its accusation. Acting without any legislative mandate, the Secretary-General despatched a fact-finding mission to investigate the Iranian claim. The mission reported unanimously that it had found evidence of the use of chemical weapons. Upon the receipt of the Secretary-General's report, the Security Council adopted a joint statement condemning the use of chemical weapons. Since that time, Iraq has desisted from using such weapons. In another move, the Secretary-General negotiated an understanding with both Iran and Iraq that they would refrain from bombarding each other's civilian populations. The Secretary-General has sent observers to both countries to monitor the agreement.

The General Assembly: The Common Jury of the World

The General Assembly is the plenary body of the UN in which every member state is represented and every state has one vote. What are the functions and utilities of the General Assembly? The General Assembly has a residual responsibility for the maintenance of international peace and security. When the Security Council is paralysed by the veto power of one or more of the permanent members, a question may be taken from the Council to the Assembly under a procedure which has come to be known as the "Uniting for Peace Resolution". This procedure was successfully invoked in the case of Korea when the Soviet Union ended its boycott and returned to the Security Council. It was also invoked during the Suez crisis when the Security Council was paralysed by the vetoes of France and the United Kingdom. The procedure was also used during the

Congo crisis when action in the Security Council was blocked by the Soviet Union.

The General Assembly can generate new international norms and, in exceptional cases, even new principles of international law. The Universal Declaration of Human Rights is an example of a document adopted by the General Assembly which has created new norms. Last fall, the General Assembly adopted a new Convention against Torture.

Another utility of the General Assembly is that it can function as a negotiating forum. Given the necessary political will on the part of the member states and wise management by the UN's leaders, the General Assembly can be used as a negotiating forum. It is unfortunate that the member states have seldom used the General Assembly for this purpose. Instead, it is normally used by member states as a debating forum in which to berate one's opponent and to score a victory on paper.

The fourth and perhaps most important function of the General Assembly is that of the common jury of the world. It is a forum which seeks to express the decent opinion of mankind. The record of the General Assembly in this respect is a mixed one. It is sometimes capable of acting in a reasonably objective and fair-minded manner. For example, one of the objectives of the UN Charter is to outlaw the use of force in international relations. In 1983, the General Assembly adopted several resolutions which reflect a fairly consistent adherence to that principle. For example, 105 members of the Assembly voted for a resolution asking for the withdrawal of all foreign forces from Afghanistan, while 108 members voted for a resolution asking for the withdrawal of all foreign forces from Grenada.

The General Assembly does not, however, always act in such an exemplary manner, partly due to the conflicting postures of the Western and non-aligned countries. (See "How the Non-Aligned Countries Can Strengthen the United Nations".)

Human Rights

What contributions has the UN made to the field of human rights over the last 40 years? The UN has developed an impressive body of international human rights law. It has promulgated the Universal Declaration of Human Rights, the International Covenant on Civil and Political Rights, the International Covenant on Social, Economic and Cultural Rights, the

Convention against Torture, and many other legal instruments. The UN has also progressively, although somewhat erratically, pioneered the view that a government which mistreats its citizens cannot take shelter behind the legal doctrine that what it does to its citizens is a matter which falls exclusively within its domestic jurisdiction. The emergent norm is that human rights is a proper concern of the international community. These are considerable achievements.

The weakness of the UN system is in the application of the principles, standards and norms which have been promulgated. The Secretary-General plays a quiet but helpful role in this field. He often intercedes with the governments of member states on behalf of individuals whose human rights have been violated. Under the two International Covenants, there is a Human Rights Committee which periodically reviews the compliance by states parties with their obligations under those convenants. On the whole, the Human Rights Committees perform a useful function. The same cannot be said in respect of the work of either the UN Commission on Human Rights or the UN General Assembly. Up until recently, the consideration of human rights questions by those two bodies was highly politicized. There was a tendency to pick on a few victims such as South Africa, Israel, Chile, El Salvador and Guatemala. There was a failure to apply the human rights principles and norms in a uniform manner. There has been, however, some improvement in the work of the UN Commission on Human Rights in the last few years. The Commission has, for example, investigated the alleged violations of human rights in Poland and in Afghanistan.

The International Civil Service

You may have heard of the story of a father who took his son on a visit to the United Nations. The young man was very impressed by the size of the Secretariat building. He asked his father, "Daddy, how many people work at the United Nations?" The father replied, "Son, about half". I suspect that the proportions between the outstanding, the average and the incompetent in the UN Secretariat are probably not very different from those of an average national civil service. What is, however, so demoralizing at the UN is that sometimes, the incompetent, who should be gotten rid of, are instead promoted because they have political pull, and the bright young men and women are bypassed.

When the United Nations Secretariat was established, it was based upon the concept of an independent international civil service. Every member state has assumed the obligation to respect the exclusively international character of the responsibilities of the Secretariat and not to seek to influence it in the discharge of its responsibilities. The communist countries have, however, never accepted the concept of an independent international civil service. They do not allow their nationals to become career officials of the Secretariat. Instead, their nationals serve secondments to the Secretariat for limited periods. The result is that the Secretariat officials from the communist countries owe their first loyalty to their own governments rather than to the organization. The problem is not, however, confined to the communist countries. In recent years, I have noticed a steady erosion of the concept of an independent international civil service. If this trend is not checked, we will end up by having a multinational Secretariat instead of an international one.

The Charter of the United Nations prescribes competence and geographical distribution as the two principles which govern the recruitment of staff. Over the years, the process of recruitment as well as the process of promotion have become highly politicized. The fault for this state of affairs lies both with the member states and with the Secretariat. The governments of many member states are guilty of putting pressure on the Secretariat to recruit their candidates as well as to promote their nationals. The Secretariat is often guilty of yielding to such pressure.

If it is true that the United Nations can only be as strong as its member states will allow it to be, it is also true that the UN can only be as effective as the competence and integrity of the Secretariat will enable it to be. Since the Third World needs the UN more than the great powers, it should therefore take the lead in checking the present abuses which go on in the field of UN personnel policies and practice, and not be among the main perpetrators of those abuses. The politicization of the process of recruitment and promotion should be stopped. The UN should recruit only the best and the brightest. Those who are competent and productive should be rewarded. Those who are lazy or incompetent should be gotten rid of. The independence of the Secretariat and the concept of an independent international civil service should be strengthened.

Conclusion

I now return to the question I started my lecture with: Will the UN survive? I think the answer is yes. Although it has many flaws and shortcomings, on balance, it probably does more good than harm. If the UN does not exist, the imperative of global interdependence will probably compel us to create an organization very much like the UN. This is not to say, however, that we should be satisfied with the current condition of the United Nations. A wise American, John Gardner, who served in the Kennedy administration as the Secretary of Health, Education and Welfare, once said that institutions languish when their lovers are uncritical and their critics are unloving. Those of us who support the UN must not do so blindly. We must have the courage to point out its shortcomings and demand that they be corrected.

If the UN is likely to survive, is it likely to get any better? I am reminded of an occasion when someone asked a former British Ambassador to the UN, Lord Caradon, what was wrong with the United Nations. He replied, "Nothing is wrong with the UN except its members". I think Lord Caradon was essentially right. What the UN badly needs is a core group of countries, from the West, from the South and from the East, who share a common commitment to the revitalization of the UN. Such a group of countries could develop an agenda of questions which are ripe and suitable for negotiation at the UN; it could serve as a bridge linking the different constituent groups and it could provide the UN train, which is now stuck in its track, with the intellectual and moral steam to drive it forward.

Excerpts from the First Jackson H. Ralston Lecture, 7 February 1985.

THE UNITED NATIONS: REFORM AND RENEWAL

A New Era in Peacekeeping

Professor Tham Seong Chee, Your Excellencies, Ladies and Gentlemen, we have gathered here this evening to celebrate the 43rd anniversary of the founding of the United Nations. During the past decade or so, the UN has gone through a bad period during which it suffered from declining public esteem and increasing doubts about its usefulness and relevance. I am happy to note that that period seems to be over.

Solving Regional Conflicts

This year, the UN has played a significant role in helping to bring a number of regional conflicts to an end. In April, the Geneva Accords on Afghanistan were signed in Geneva. The Special Representative of the UN Secretary-General, Diego Cordorvez, played a crucial role in forging those agreements. In August, a cease-fire was secured in the eight-year-old Iran-Iraq War. In the case of Namibia, I note with interest that the representatives of the United States, South Africa, Angola and Cuba have been meeting to discuss independence for Namibia and the simultaneous withdrawal of Cuban troops from Angola. Sources close to the parties seem optimistic that an agreement may soon be reached for the implementation of Security Council Resolution 435 (1978).

On Cyprus, the Secretary-General has made a new initiative which has been well received by the leaders of the Greek-Cypriot and the Turkish-Cypriot communities. At their meeting with the Secretary-General, they expressed their willingness to meet without any prior conditions and to attempt to achieve by 1 June 1989, a negotiated settlement on all aspects of the Cyprus problem. The talks with the Secretary-General began on 15 September 1988.

In the case of Western Sahara, the Secretary-General, along with the Chairman of the Organization of African Unity (OAU), has submitted a proposal to the parties concerned. They conveyed their acceptance with some comments and remarks on 30 August 1988. The Secretary-General is working with the parties towards a final settlement.

With respect to Cambodia, the Secretary-General has presented to the parties a number of specific ideas intended to facilitate the elaboration of a framework for a comprehensive political settlement. He stands ready to help the parties bring the process to fruition.

The UN, in general, and the Secretary-General, in particular, are therefore very actively engaged in the process of peacemaking around the world. This year, the Nobel Peace Prize has been awarded to the UN Peacekeeping Forces. Not many people know what is a UN Peacekeeping Force, how it is different from a national force, what are its functions, and where such forces are deployed.

The UN Peacekeeping Forces

The concept of a UN Peacekeeping Operation is to use a multinational force, under the UN command, to keep disputing countries or communities from fighting while efforts are made to help them negotiate a solution. UN Peacekeeping Operations take two forms. First, there are the military observer missions whose members are unarmed. Second, there are the Peacekeeping Forces whose members are lightly armed.

Functions of UN Peacekeeping Operations

What functions and tasks are carried out by the UN Peacekeeping Operations? They carry out a variety of tasks and functions. First, they observe a situation and report on it to the Secretary-General. Second, they investigate incidents and negotiate with the parties to avoid a resumption of fighting. Third, they take physical control of buffer zones. Fourth, they control the movement of armed personnel and weapons into sensitive areas. Fifth, they verify compliance with agreements. Sixth, they help the local government to restore normal conditions in an area where fighting has taken place. Seventh, they provide humanitarian support to the local population.

Characteristics of UN Peacekeeping Operations

What are some of the essential characteristics of a UN Peacekeeping Operation?

First, it must have the consent of the parties involved. The UN cannot impose peacekeeping upon two unwilling parties. It has to wait until they are ready for it. Another problem is that consent can be withdrawn. This happened in 1967 when President Nasser of Egypt requested the UN Peacekeeping Force to leave Sinai. The removal of the UN Peacekeeping Force was one of the principal factors which brought about the Arab-Israeli War of 1967.

Second, a UN Peacekeeping Operation must enjoy the support of the international community. This is required at the beginning when the force is established. The mandate to establish the force must have the support of the five permanent members of the Security Council as well as at least four of the remaining ten non-permanent members.

Third, the troops of the UN Peacekeeping Operations are provided voluntarily by the member states to the Secretary-General. During the last 40 years, over 400,000 soldiers have served in the various Peacekeeping Operations of the United Nations. I should, in this context, say a word about the costs of Peacekeeping Operations. In principle, the costs are to be shared by the member states. In practice, however, many of the member states have not honoured their obligation under the Charter to pay their share of the cost of Peacekeeping Operations. The result is that the Secretary-General often lacks the financial resources needed to reimburse the countries contributing troop. This situation is extremely unfair and must be rectified.

Fourth, a Peacekeeping Operation is under the command of the Secretary-General, who is, in turn, accountable to the Security Council. This means that the troops receive their operational orders from the Secretary-General and not from their national authorities. This is an important principle because if Peacekeeping troops are thought to be serving their countries' interests, they will lose the impartiality which must be at the heart of peacekeeping.

Fifth, the UN Peacekeeping Operations must be strictly impartial. If a Peacekeeping Operation appears to take sides, it is bound to lose acceptability and to run the risk of its becoming a party to the conflict. Unfortunately, that was what befell the US-sponsored Multinational Force in Beirut a few years ago.

Sixth, the Peacekeeping Force should use force only to the minimum extent possible. In fact, the military observer groups are unarmed and therefore the question of force does not arise. The Security Council has, however, decided to set up armed forces in two situations. The first is where the Peacekeeping Operation is required to take physical control of territory and deny its access to the combatants. The second is when law and order has broken down and the Peacekeeping Force is required to restore normal conditions. The rule to use minimum force follows naturally from the facts that peacekeeping is accepted voluntarily by the parties and not imposed on them, and that the peacekeepers must, at all cost, remain impartial. It is, nevertheless, a rule which could place heavy demands on the troops. Peacekeeping Operations do, unfortunately, sometimes come under attack and nearly 300 UN soldiers have died from hostile actions directed against them.

The Three UN Peacekeeping Forces

How many UN Peacekeeping Forces are there today? Where are they deployed? There are three UN Peacekeeping Forces in the world today. The first is the UN Force in Cyprus (UNFICYP). This force was first established in 1964 to stop inter-communal fighting. Since 1974, it has controlled the buffer zone between the two sides. The force is made up by 2,100 soldiers from eight countries.

The second is the UN Disengagement Observer Force (UNDOF). This force was set up in 1974 to monitor compliance with a disengagement agreement between Israel and Syria on the Golan Heights. The force consists of 1,300 soldiers from four countries. The third force is the UN Interim Force in Lebanon (UNIFIL). This force was set up in 1978 to confirm the withdrawal of Israeli troops from Lebanon, to restore international peace and security between the two countries, and to help restore the central government's authority. The force consists of 5,800 soldiers from nine countries.

The Four UN Observer Missions

How many UN Observer Missions are there in the world? Where are they deployed? The first is the UN TRUCE Supervision Organization (UNTSO). This Observer Mission was established in 1948 and is deployed on various points of conflicts between Israel and its Arab neighbours. The Mission consists of 30 officers from 17 countries.

The second Observer Mission is called the UN Military Observer Group in India and Pakistan (UNMOGIP). This Observer Mission was set up in 1949 to monitor a cease-fire between India and Pakistan in Kashmir. The force consists of 36 officers from nine countries.

The third Observer Mission is the UN Good Offices Missions in Afghanistan and Pakistan (UNGOMAP). This Observer Force was established in May 1988 to assist in the implementation of certain aspects of the Geneva Accords relating to Afghanistan. The Mission consists of 51 officers from nine countries.

The fourth Observer Mission is the UN Iran-Iraq Military Observer Group (UNIIMOG). This Observer Mission was set up in August 1988 to monitor the cease-fire and withdrawal of troops demanded by UN Security Council Resolution 598 (1987). The Mission consists of 350 officers and about 500 military support staff drawn from 26 countries.

Conclusion

The term "peacekeeping" is nowhere to be found in the UN Charter. It is an instrument which has evolved, over time, and in answer to a felt need. Peacekeeping is generally acknowledged to have been one of the UN's success stories. There is now a greater degree of international consensus than ever before on the need to maintain and strengthen this function of the United Nations. In recent months, the Secretary-General's successes in mediating various international conflicts have led to a revival of confidence in the UN's peacekeeping and peacemaking roles. There is much talk of new Peacekeeping Operations. Two such Operations, in Namibia and Western Sahara, are actively being planned. If a political settlement on Cambodia is arrived at, there will most certainly be a need for an international Peacekeeping Force, whether constituted within or outside the framework of the UN.

We should, however, avoid making exaggerated claims for Peacekeeping Operations. They cannot, by themselves, resolve conflicts. What they can do is to create conditions which make peacemaking possible. Peacekeeping must therefore go hand in hand with peacemaking. As a small country, it is in Singapore's national interests to strengthen the UN's peacemaking and peacekeeping capacities.

Remarks prepared for the UN Day Dinner organized by the UN Association of Singapore, 22 October 1988, Singapore.

THE UNITED NATIONS: REFORM AND RENEWAL

An Iconoclastic View of the United Nations' Disarmament Activities

No one can reasonably accuse the United Nations of inactivity in the field of disarmament. The General Assembly has held two special sessions on disarmament. At each regular session of the General Assembly, the First (Political) Committee devotes about two months to the discussion of disarmament. At the last session, the Assembly adopted approximately 60 resolutions on disarmament. Between sessions of the General Assembly, there are meetings of the UN Disarmament Commission. The United Nations negotiating forum on disarmament, the Conference on Disarmament, meets around the year in Geneva. In addition, the UN has an Institute of Disarmament Studies and a host of expert groups dealing with different aspects of arms control and disarmament.

The question is: Why has so much activity produced so little by way of results? Why is there such a stark contrast between what nations say at the United Nations and what they do at home? As I pointed out at the United Nations' first special session on disarmament, if every member state is against the arms race, who is responsible for it? The truth is that, with the few exceptions of countries such as Costa Rica (which has no army), all of us are participating, to varying degrees, in the arms race. One must not forget that there is both a nuclear arms race and a conventional arms race. Whilst the first have only five participants, with the two superpowers in a special league by themselves, the second includes many of the developing countries.

There are several reasons which explain why so much activity produces so little result. First, the representatives of member states have fallen into the bad habit of verbalizing support at the United Nations for all sorts of lofty ideals, such as general and complete disarmament, which have no relevance to the reality external to the United Nations. Second, some member states put forward proposals at the United Nations which are not serious, but which are merely intended as propaganda or to score a point against their adversaries. Third, in the field of arms control and disarmament, there is very little congruence between what member states say they support at the United Nations and what they actually do. Fourth, the prospects for arms control and disarmament are dependent upon the state of relations between the great powers, especially the two superpowers. In the present political climate, there is probably not very much that the member states can do at the United Nations to break the impasse between the two superpowers and to move things forward. Fifth, there is a need for UN activities to be infused by a greater sense of realism and priority. The United Nations should concentrate on the real and critical issues instead of going off in so many directions.

The Real Issues

What are some of the real questions which the United Nations should be addressing? Between the United States and the Soviet Union and between NATO and the Warsaw Pact countries, the critical question is how to achieve the goal of parity at lower numbers. At present, the two superpowers and their respective military alliances regard the question as being essentially a bilateral one. However, since the bilateral negotiations are deadlocked, other countries should encourage the two superpowers to examine the possibility of using the multilateral forums, such as the Conference of Disarmament, to bring about progress. The Non-Aligned Movement can be more effective than it now is in interposing between the two giants and in acting as a bridge-builder, provided that the group sets its own house in order. It should be truly objective and impartial, and not be tilted in favour of one superpower or the other. Secondly, the members of the Non-Aligned group must start to practise what they preach. They must have the courage to address the issue of the conventional arms race taking place between certain regional rivals in the Third World. The group must also insist that its own members adhere to the principles of the movement, and it must have the courage to censure violations of those principles by its members.

The Threat to Small Third World Countries

For many people in the West, their greatest fear is the fear of nuclear war. This is not, however, the main preoccupation of the countries and peoples of the Third World. The fact is that, during the past 39 years, no one has been killed by a nuclear weapon, but 26 million people have lost their lives in conventional wars in the Third World. Small countries in the Third World feel threatened by the breakdown of the rule of law in the world and the increasing resort to violence.

When the victims of aggression have taken their complaints to the United Nations Security Council, their pleas for help have largely gone unanswered. The sad fact is that the UN collective security system, as contained in its Charter, does not work because of the differences among the great powers, and is therefore incapable, in most cases, of protecting small states against aggression by their militarily more powerful neighbours. In such circumstances, does it make any sense for the governments of the member states to ask themselves to consider reducing their military budgets or their armed forces? There is an inextricable link between international security and disarmament. Until we make progress in the first area, there can be no meaningful progress in the other. The only aspect of the United Nations which could be realistically strengthened and which could play a more effective role in world peace and security is the office of the Secretary-General. I attach great importance to the Secretary-General's role in diplomatic mediation. We should do everything we can to strengthen the capacity of his office to detect incipient disputes between states, to prevent disputes from becoming conflicts and to prevent conflicts from escalating out of control. The UN is not very good at settling armed conflicts. It is better at preventing them. We should, therefore, enhance the role of the United Nations, especially that of the Secretary-General, in preventive diplomacy.

Commentary first published in **Disarmament: A Periodic Review by the United Nations**, *Vol. VII, No. 3, Autumn 1984.*

THE UNITED NATIONS: REFORM AND RENEWAL

The United Nations at Fifty: Time for Renewal

This year, the United Nations (UN) is celebrating its 50th anniversary. On 24 October, many of the world's leaders will gather at the UN in New York to mark this important milestone in the UN's history. However, not every one at the party will be in a celebratory mood. Indeed, the Prime Minister of one of our neighbouring countries has gone so far as to say that it is an occasion not for celebration but for mourning.

Why is the celebration of the UN's 50th anniversary marked by controversy? I think for four reasons. First, because the UN is faced with a financial crisis which is so acute that the organization is on the brink of bankruptcy. Second, because of the failures of the UN's peacekeeping operations in Somalia and in Bosnia-Herzegovina. Third, because of the perception that the UN system has a bloated, inefficient and wasteful bureaucracy. Fourth, because there is no consensus at the UN on how to respond to the new post-Cold War challenges of intra-state conflicts and of failed states.

Why is the UN faced with a serious financial crisis? Because 70 member states owe the UN a total of S$5,200 million (US$3.7 billion). The biggest debtor, the United States, owes the UN over US$1 billion. What is the solution to the UN's financial crisis? First, it should insist that every member state must pay its dues on time. Second, those who do not do so should be charged with interest on their arrears. Third, those whose arrears exceed two times the amount of their annual contributions should be deprived of their right to vote in the General Assembly, in accordance with Article 19 of the UN Charter. Fourth, the UN should consider lowering the percentage of the US's contributions to the UN's budget from the present 25 per cent to 20 per cent, to reflect the decline of the US's share of world GNP. Fifth, the UN should consider how it could raise funds by privatizing and commercializing some of its activities. Some of the ideas often proposed for raising money for the UN, for example, by imposing a tax on international travel, or imposing a tax on the consumption of fuel oil, are unlikely to gain consensus among member states.

Is it true that the UN system's bureaucracy is bloated, inefficient and wasteful? It is true that there is too much duplication in the UN system. It is also true that there is a lot of inefficiency. There are two basic problems. One is that the UN has failed to recruit and promote its staff exclusively on the basis of merit. Patronage, pressure from influential member states and regional groups have corrupted the UN's meritocratic system. To restore confidence in the UN, the UN Secretary-General should run the UN bureaucracy strictly as a meritocracy. The other problem is that over the past 50 years, the system has grown in an unplanned and often chaotic manner. As a result, there is a great deal of duplication and waste. So far, the vested interests in the *status quo* have succeeded in blocking reform. A way must be found by the Secretary-General and the member states to defeat the vested interests and streamline the organization.

Because of Somalia and Bosnia-Herzegovina, there is a growing impression that the UN's peacekeeping operations have been unsuccessful. This is an unfair view. If we look at the historical record, we will find many more cases of success, such as Namibia, Cambodia and Haiti, than of failures. It was not for nothing that the UN's peacekeeping forces were awarded the Nobel Peace Prize a few years ago.

The UN failed in Somalia because it was dealing with an internal conflict with many complex ethnic and religious divisions. The UN's mandate in Somalia was also unclear. I have learnt four lessons from the failure of the UN's peacekeeping operation in Somalia. First, every peacekeeping operation should have a clear mandate. Second, the mandate should be achievable. Third, the UN does not have the expertise or the financial means to take over the administration of a failed state and to restore it to a state of normalcy. Fourth, the UN should not get involved in an intra-state conflict unless there is an agreement by all the parties to invite the intervention of the UN.

The failure of the UN in Bosnia-Herzegovina was due to two factors. First, there were differences of opinion among the five permanent members of the Security Council. Russia, because of its ethnic ties, has been partial to Serbia. It also feels that it had not been sufficiently consulted by the

West. Second, as for the three Western permanent members of the Security Council – the US, UK and France – until the last two months, they had shown a conspicuous lack of political will and willingness to commit sufficient resources to help the UN succeed in Bosnia. For example, when the UN safe areas in Bosnia were conceived, UN military experts estimated that their protection would require at least 34,000 troops. The Security Council only agreed to send 7,000; in actual fact, fewer than 7,000 were sent. My conclusion is that the West has used the UN as a scapegoat for its unwillingness to deter and punish aggression in Bosnia.

I shall conclude by asking a very simple question. The UN is admittedly an imperfect institution. However, would the world be better off if there were no UN? I do not think so. I think that, on balance, the UN has done more good than harm for the world in the last 50 years. However imperfectly, the UN has tried to create a world which is governed by the rule of law rather than by the law of the jungle. For all states, but especially for small states like Singapore, a world without the UN would be a more dangerous world. George Shultz, the former US Secretary of State, has said recently that if the UN did not exist, we would be busy trying to invent it. I therefore regard 24 October as neither a day for thoughtless celebration nor one for mourning. It is a day for stocktaking and reflection. We should use this historic occasion to marshall the necessary political goodwill to renew the organization, to consolidate its strengths and rectify its shortcomings, to re-engineer the organization so that it will be ready to meet the challenges of the 21st century.

Article first published in ***Lianhe Zaobao****, 24 October 1995.*

NORTH-SOUTH RELATIONS: CONFLICT AND CO-OPERATION

Beyond the North-South Divide

Until about ten years ago, international relations was dominated by the East-West confrontation. Over the past decade, a different confrontation has emerged. The relationship between the developing countries and the developed countries had become increasingly acrimonious. The dialogue between the North, representing the developed countries and the South, representing the developing countries is often confrontational. The purpose of my talk tonight is to try to explain the political and economic significance of the negotiations between these two groups of countries.

A witty friend of mine has compared the relationship between the developing countries and the Western industrialized countries to the relationship between a certain man and his wife. This man complained to his friend that his wife never stops asking him for money. He said, "Last Monday, my wife asked me for $100. On Tuesday, she asked me for $50. On Wednesday, she asked me for another $100 and today she asked me for another $50". The friend interrupted him and asked "What does your wife do with all the money you give her?" He replied "I don't know. I never give her any". There is another story which quite accurately represents the attitude of the Soviet Union and her East European allies towards the developing countries. One day, a visitor to the Soviet Union was walking along in the dark and fell into a ditch. The sides of the ditch were steep and slippery and he couldn't climb out of it. The poor man spent a cold and lonely night in the ditch. In the morning, he was very happy to see a passer-by. He waved to him and shouted "Please help me out of the ditch". The passer-by replied "Why should I? I was not responsible for your falling into it in the first place".

The Developing Countries

There are about 110 developing countries. They vary considerably in size, in wealth and in the levels of their economic development. A handful of developing countries, i.e. some of the oil-exporting countries, are extremely rich. The three countries with the highest GNP per capita income in the world are Kuwait, Qatar and the United Arab Emirates. There is another group of countries which have made considerable strides in their economic development. These include Brazil, Argentina, Mexico, South Korea, Taiwan, Malaysia, the Philippines, Thailand and Singapore. The great majority of the developing countries are, however, extremely poor. There are 19 countries whose GNP per capita income is between US$500 and US$875. There are 30 countries whose per capita income is between US$875 and US$1,425. The great majority of the people in the majority of the developing countries live in dire poverty. They have barely enough food to eat. They rarely have enough potable water. Health conditions are extremely inadequate. When work is available, the pay is usually low and the conditions are often deplorable. Malnutrition, illiteracy, disease, a high birth rate, employment, underdevelopment and low income are their constant companions.

Human Solidarity

Do the richer people in your society and mine have a duty to help those who are poorer? The answer, undoubtedly, is "Yes". What is the moral basis of this duty? The moral basis of this duty is human solidarity. In the same way, I would argue, that because of human solidarity, the richer nations have a moral duty to help the poorer nations. I cannot, therefore, accept the argument of the Soviet Union and her East European allies that because they did not exploit the developing countries in the past, they therefore do not have a duty to help them.

Apart from the human solidarity, there are other sound economic reasons for helping the developing countries. In the last few years, the world economy has been in a slump due to rampant inflation and to the slowdown in or stagnation of the economies of the West. If the developed countries can inject more dynamism into the economies of the developing countries, this will increase their purchasing power which will have a tonic effect on the economies in the West and on the world economy. Secondly, some of the causes of the present economic crisis stem from structural deficiencies. In order to cure these structural deficiencies in the world economic system, it is necessary for the developed and the developing countries to work together. This is the rationale for the proposed global economic negotiations.

I would now like to say a few words about the agenda of the global economic negotiations currently under discussion at the UN. The agenda will consist of five major areas. These are raw materials, trade, development, energy, money and finance.

Global Economic Negotiations at the UN

Raw Materials

In the area of raw materials, the North-South negotiations have led to some concrete achievements in the last few years. At the Fourth UN Conference on Trade and Development, held in Nairobi in 1976, the developing countries proposed an Integrated Programme for Commodities. The purpose of an integrated programme was to strengthen the markets, as well as to stabilize the prices, of 26 commodities of interest to the developing countries. The way in which this would be done would be to maintain buffer stocks of the 16 commodities. By selling the buffer stocks when prices are going up and buying them when prices are going down, it is hoped that the fluctuation of commodity prices will stabilize. A Common Fund of about US$6 billion was proposed as the centrepiece of the Integrated Programme for Commodities. The idea was that the Common Fund would lend money to enable the managers of the 16 commodity buffer stocks to buy when the prices of the commodities are falling. The loans from the Common Fund would be offset by income derived from the sale of buffer stocks.

After more than four years of intensive negotiations, the articles of agreement on the Common Fund were adopted in June 1980. The negotiations on the Common Fund were closely linked to the negotiation of a series of individual commodity agreements or arrangements. So far, commodity agreements have been concluded on tin, coffee, cocoa, sugar and rubber. Preparatory meetings have been held on copper, cotton, tea, jute, hard fibres, vegetable oils, bananas, meat and tropical timber.

The dialogue between the developed and developing countries in the area of raw materials includes the question of the participation of developing countries in the trade, transportation, marketing and distribution of their commodities and raw materials. It also includes the question of local processing and storage of commodities and raw materials produced by developing countries.

Trade

Turning from raw materials to trade, the questions for negotiation include access for the exports of developing countries to markets in the developed countries and the twin problems of protectionism and structural adjustment.

Development

In the area of development, several specific questions are involved. First, there is the question of what positive adjustment policies and incentives the developed countries can adopt to facilitate the industrialization of the developing countries. What we mean by "positive adjustment policies and incentives" is that the developed countries would adopt policies to phase out their obsolete and uncompetitive industries; that they would help the affected industries to diversify to or to specialize in areas in which the developed countries maintain a comparative economic advantage over the developing countries, as well as to adopt programmes to retrain the affected workers and to cushion the adverse social consequences resulting from the restructuring of their industries. The second question is what measure can be adopted to support the transfer of technology to developing from developed countries, including the adaptation and application of such technology. The third question concerns measures to enhance and improve the transfer of resources from developed to developing countries for the purpose of promoting economic development.

Energy, Money and Finance

The areas of energy, on the one hand, and money and finance, on the other, are closely inter-related. The industrialized countries wish to have assurances of regular and adequate supplies of energy at predictable prices. The developed countries also wish to minimize disruptive movements in financial markets. The oil-exporting countries wish to safeguard the real value of their exports and their financial reserves. They also wish to avoid an excessively rapid depletion of their non-renewable resources.

Thirdly, the oil-exporting countries wish to have technological support for their economic development from the developed countries, particularly in sectors of their economy which are based upon hydrocarbons. Finally, all countries, whether oil-exporting or oil-importing, whether developed or developing, have an interest in ensuring that the financial balances generated in the energy sector help to stabilize and not disrupt the international financial and monetary system.

Conclusion

I shall conclude my remarks on the North-South dialogue by asserting the following propositions. First, human solidarity requires that the richer nations should help poorer nations just as in our individual nations, the rich are required to help the poor through progressive income tax and other social measure. Secondly, I cannot accept the thesis of the Soviet Union that it has no moral duty to help the developing countries because it did not exploit them in the past. Since the duty to help is based upon human solidarity, I would like to see the communist countries of Eastern Europe participate more actively in the process of re-ordering international economic relations. Thirdly, by helping the developing countries, the developed countries are indirectly helping themselves because if the developing countries have greater purchasing power, this would be used to purchase technology, food and brain services from the developed countries.

Fourthly, if the developing countries succeed in growing at a more rapid pace, this will have a positive effect on the expansion of the world economy which will benefit all countries, including the developed countries. Fifthly, the present world economic crisis is due, in part, to structural deficiencies in the world economic system. To cure these structural deficiencies, it is necessary for developed and developing countries to work together. This is the logic behind the proposal of the developing countries for global economic negotiations. These negotiations should adopt an integrated approach as opposed to a sectoral approach. The negotiations should look at the measures which are necessary in the short term, in the medium term and in the long term. The negotiations should focus on specific issues and problems in five broad areas: raw materials, trade, development, energy, money and finance. The negotiations should avoid polemics and rhetorics, and should focus on finding solutions to problems which are economically sound and morally equitable.

Finally, I think I should say a word about the duty of the developing countries in the context of the New International Economic Order. I believe that the primary responsibility for their economic development rests upon the developing countries themselves. No amount of external assistance can transform a developing country into a developed country if it is not prepared to help itself. What do I mean by a developing country helping itself? By this, I mean several things. A developing country should inculcate in its population the values and social attitudes which will promote economic development. For example, the government should inculcate in its people the values of hard work and thrift. The government should have the political courage to ensure that the growth of its population does not exceed the growth of its economy. It must channel its resources into productive rather than consumptive ends, and practise fiscal responsibility and live within its means. The government must ensure that the fruits of economic development are equitably distributed to all sections of the population. Politicians and civil servants should be free of corruption. If a developing country follows this recipe, it will have a good chance of succeeding in its economic development.

The goal of building a New International Economic Order can only be achieved through action at the international and at the national level. Developing countries must avoid the mistake of thinking that co-operation at the international level can substitute for the needed sacrifices and hard work at the national level. It cannot be done. Our dream of a more prosperous and more equitable world can only be realized if all of us are prepared to work hard at home and to develop the habit of consultation and co-operation at the international level. The growing inter-dependence of our economies makes global economic co-operation an imperative of our time.

Statement given at the Annual Meeting of the UN Association of Minnesota at Minneapolis, 20 May 1981.

NORTH-SOUTH RELATIONS: CONFLICT AND CO-OPERATION

How the Non-Aligned Countries Can Strengthen the United Nations

Introduction

The beginning of wisdom about the United Nations is to recognize clearly that the United Nations is only the sum of its parts; in other words, the United Nations is the collectivity of its member states. The United Nations does not exist apart from its members. It can only be as strong or as weak as its member states allow or make it.

The prestige of the United Nations today is at a very low point. It is perceived as an organization which has failed to maintain international peace and security. It is perceived as an organization which is like a paper mill, churning out reams of declarations, plans of actions, resolutions and decisions which are seldom implemented and which have little or no impact on the external realities to which they are purportedly addressed. The United Nations is seen as an organization which practises double standards. The General Assembly is seen, less and less, as a forum which expresses the decent opinion of mankind. In the light of this appraisal of the present weaknesses and deficiencies of the United Nations, it is highly pertinent to ask what the member states which belong to the Non-Aligned Movement can do to strengthen the United Nations.

The Maintenance of International Peace and Security

According to the Stockholm International Peace Research Institute (SIPRI), in the 39 years since the United Nations was founded, over 100 armed conflicts have occurred and more than 26 million people have perished in such conflicts. It is no wonder that people in all our countries ask what the United Nations is doing to prevent armed conflicts from occurring. What is the United Nations doing to stop armed conflicts which are going on, or to persuade the belligerents to make peace?

Although the principal reason for the failure of the United Nations collective security system to function more effectively is the absence of consensus among the five great powers, some of the blame must be attributed to the non-aligned countries. After all, nearly all of the armed conflicts which have occurred since 1945 have occurred between countries in the Third World, many of which are members of the Non-Aligned Movement. As Rikhi Jaipal has pointed out in his book, *Non-Alignment: Origins, Growth and Potential for World Peace,* "There are on record, some 37 disputed borders concerning non-aligned countries ... In addition, there are some 20 non-aligned countries now engaged in hostilities or subjected to foreign occupation in Africa, Asia and Latin America, where the great powers are also involved directly or indirectly".[1]

What can the Non-Aligned Movement do to strengthen the United Nations in the maintenance of international peace and security? First, the Non-Aligned Movement should insist that its members should adhere strictly to the principles of the Movement, the principles of the United Nations Charter and the principles of international law governing relations between states. In the past, the Non-Aligned Movement has been more conscientious in demanding that countries outside the movement should adhere to these principles and less conscientious in making the same demand of its own members. Second, the Non-Aligned Movement must have the courage to stand up to the regional bullies in the Third World. The reality in the world today is that the sovereignty, independence and territorial integrity of small countries are threatened not only by the great powers, but also by the regional bullies of the Third World. The credibility of the Non-Aligned Movement was seriously undermined when it failed, for example, to censure Vietnam for its invasion of Cambodia.

Third, the Non-Aligned Movement must defend the rule of law against all those who violate it, no matter whether the violator is from the East or from the West, or whether it is a member of the Movement. The failure, for example, of the Non-Aligned Movement to condemn the Soviet invasion of Afghanistan robs the Movement of its moral integrity. Fourth, it is time for the Non-Aligned Movement to establish some kind of negotiating process for resolving disputes among its members. Fifth, the Non-Aligned Movement should support the role of the United Nations Secretary-General in the exercise of his good offices and in his efforts to mediate disputes and conflicts between states more energetically.

The Prestige and Credibility of the General Assembly

The General Assembly is the plenary body in which all member states are represented and in which all states, irrespective of their size and weight, have one vote. The General Assembly is a forum which gives nations which would otherwise be voiceless, a voice in the world. It is a forum which should express the decent opinion of mankind. Although the General Assembly can, in rare instances, be used as a negotiating forum, its major role is to function as the court of world public opinion.

Over the years, the prestige and credibility of the General Assembly have been seriously undermined by certain actions of non-aligned countries. Since they command a majority in the Assembly, they can easily push a resolution through. On some occasions, non-aligned countries have pushed through the Assembly resolutions which contain accusations not based upon facts, resolutions which are not consistent with the principles which the Movement purports to uphold, resolutions which are biased and one-sided, and which are couched in inflammatory and intemperate language. The result of such behaviour on the part of the non-aligned countries is to reduce the credibility and importance of the General Assembly in the eyes of world public opinion. If this tendency is not checked, the world may one day stop taking the General Assembly seriously. When that happens, it is we, the small non-aligned countries, which will have the most to lose. Therefore, the non-aligned countries must exercise their majoritarian power in the General Assembly with more wisdom and prudence. We must ensure that the resolutions we put forward are grounded on solid facts. We must ensure that these resolutions are consistent with the principles which we profess to uphold, that they are fair and balanced, and couched in dignified and temperate language.

Arms Control and Disarmament

The world is engaged in a dangerous and potentially self-destroying arms race. It is futile to argue whether the nuclear arms race or the conventional arms race is the more dangerous. Clearly, the two are related and both are dangerous. Although a nuclear war will very likely destroy much if not the whole of mankind, it is also a fact that since Hiroshima and Nagasaki, no one has been killed by a nuclear bomb whereas 26 million people have been killed in conventional wars.

The Non-Aligned Movement is not using the United Nations as effectively as it could to bring about greater progress in the field of arms control and disarmament. There are several reasons which account for this. First, the Non-Aligned Movement does not today enjoy the same prestige and stature which it had when the Movement was led by such statesmen as Nehru, Tito and Nasser. The leaders of the Non-Aligned Movement today are men and women of a much lower stature. Second, the Non-Aligned Movement does not have the unity which the Movement enjoyed during its early formative years. The main reason for this is the infiltration of the movement by a group of countries such as Cuba, Vietnam, Democratic Yemen, Ethiopia, Syria, Mozambique, Angola and others which are not Non-Aligned, but which are allies of the Soviet Union. The presence within the Movement of this group of countries is a constant source of friction and disunity because they try, at every turn, to hitch the Non-Aligned train to the Soviet locomotive.

Third, because of the presence within the Non-Aligned Movement of the pro-Soviet faction, the Movement is neither objective nor impartial in its dealings with the two superpowers. As a result, the Movement is unable to interpose itself and act as a bridge between the two superpowers. Fourth, very few non-aligned countries have been prepared to assign high-calibre representatives to work, on a full-time basis, in the field of arms control and disarmament. Thus, there are very few representatives of non-aligned countries who have the expertise and the imagination to make proposals which could help to break the impasse in the negotiations between the two superpowers and their respective military alliances. Fifth, the Non-Aligned Movement has never had the courage to face up to the difficult issue of the conventional arms race. The conventional arms race is taking place not only between NATO and the Warsaw Pact. It is also occurring between certain regional rivals in the Third World. Until we have the courage to face up to this issue, we have very little moral standing to preach sermons at others.

Development and the World Economy

In the economic field, the developing countries are represented by both the Non-Aligned Movement and by the larger Group of 77. Reading the communiques issued by both groups, one gets the impression that because of the unjust international economic order and the exploitative policies and practices of the developed countries, the developing countries have been growing poorer with the passing years. This impression may be true for some developing countries. It is certainly not true for others, such as the ASEAN countries, which have made great strides in their development during the past decade.

Both the Non-Aligned Movement and the Group of 77 serve the useful purpose of enabling the developing countries to unify their ranks and, thereby, to negotiate more effectively with the developed countries. One can point to some of the concrete achievements resulting from the North-South negotiations, such as the Generalized System of Preferences (GSP) and the Common Fund Agreement. However, much of the time and effort devoted by representatives of developing countries to their dialogue with the North is wasted on questions which are philosophical or conceptual in nature, or on questions and issues which are not ripe for negotiations. The Non-Aligned Movement as well as the Group of 77 should change its attitude towards the North-South dialogue (The North should also change its attitude and policies towards the North-South dialogue.) The Non-Aligned group should stop insisting that any North-South negotiation must be conducted on the basis of an agenda which resembles a laundry list. The group should accept that not all the issues on such an agenda are ripe for negotiation. It should, therefore, focus its negotiating energy only on those issues on which there are realistic prospects of achieving a breakthrough. The group should also refrain from putting forward demands which do not make economic sense or which require the North to make unilateral concessions. The South should only put forward proposals to the North which are economically sound and which will bring about benefits to both the North and the South.

Conclusion

The member states of the United Nations which belong to the Non-Aligned Movement can play a vital role in the revitalization of the United Nations. However, if the Non-Aligned Movement is to play such a role, it must first set its house in order and restore to itself some of the glory and prrestige which it once enjoyed. Speaking about the Non-Aligned Movement in March 1983, S. Rajaratnam, the Second Deputy Prime Minister of Singapore, said, "Its past is one of which we can be justly proud, its present condition does it no credit, and finally, if it persists in its present course, its future will be one of shameful oblivion".

Article first published in "The Non-Aligned and the United Nations", M.S. Rajan, V.S. Mani, C.S.R. Murthy (eds.) (New Delhi: South Asian Publishers, 1987).

NOTES

1. Rikhi Jaipal, *Non-Alignment: Origins, Growth and Potential for World Peace* (New Delhi: Allied Publishers, 1983), p. 178.

NORTH-SOUTH RELATIONS: CONFLICT AND CO-OPERATION

The Western Mass Media and the Third World

The Western Mass Media

The terms "Western mass media" and "Third World" need elucidation. The two terms suggest a homogeneity which does not accord with reality. There is a need to disaggregate the content of the two concepts. For example, the media in the different Western democracies are not alike. The media in each country is the product of its history, culture, legal system and experience. Let me illustrate my point by comparing the media in two societies, the United Kingdom and the United States, which are very similar in many ways. The parameters of press freedom are wider in the United States than in the United Kingdom. The media in Britain has to operate within the constraints contained in the British legal system, including the Official Secrets Act, the doctrine of contempt of court, the laws of sedition and defamation. In the United States, the law against the disclosure of official secrets is seldom, if ever, enforced. Martin Linsky, in his recent book, *Impact: How the Press Affects Federal Policymaking*,[1] discovered that over 40 per cent of the officials he interviewed for his book admitted to having leaked information to the media. Likewise, the media in the United States is seldom subject to sanction for scandalizing the courts or for commenting on matters which are *sub judice*.

The Third World

In the same way, the term "the Third World" embraces a large family of 133 countries which share very few common characteristics. Some countries in the Third World have modelled themselves after the Soviet Union. A larger number has followed the Western model of democracy. Many countries in the Third World are trying to find a third alternative, to evolve political institutions which are responsive to their particular history, culture and circumstances. It follows from this that the governments of the Third World do not have a common attitude towards either their own mass media or the mass media of the West.

The Communist Countries of the Third World

The attitude of the governments of the communist countries in the Third World towards the mass media, domestic or foreign, is no different from the attitude of the Soviet Union towards the media. In a communist country, the media is an extension of the party and the State. Its role is to help the party consolidate its hold on power, put down its class enemies, make propaganda for the party, the State and the socialist cause. The rulers of some of the communist countries in the Third World have proven to be very skilful in manipulating the Western mass media. Witness, for example, the success of the Vietnamese in using the American mass media in order to foment anti-war sentiments in the United States during the Vietnam War. Another example is the ruler of Cuba, Fidel Castro. Until very recently, Castro enjoyed a rather good press in the West. The double standards by which some members of the Western mass media judge communist rulers in the Third World – such as Fidel Castro – and non-communist rulers has always puzzled me.

In the rest of my lecture, I will be excluding the communist countries when I use the term "the Third World". I will confine myself to the non-communist countries of the Third World. I will further exclude from the concept, countries whose governments are dictatorial in nature. In other words, I will restrict myself to discussing the relationship between the "good guys" in the Third World and the Western mass media. By the "good guys", I mean countries which are non-communist, which have representative institutions of government and which are democracies or moving in the direction of democracy.

A Rocky and Confrontational Relationship

The relationship between the Western mass media and the Third World is rocky and often confrontational. Let me give you two recent examples from Southeast Asia. On 27 September 1986, the government of Malaysia banned the *Asian Wall Street Journal* for a period of three months and expelled its two correspondents. On 15 October 1986, the Singapore government required *Time* Magazine to reduce its circulation in Singapore in two steps, from 18,000 to 9,000 on 19 October 1986, and from 9,000 to 2,000 on 1 January 1987.

The Role of Media in Society

Why is the relationship between the Western media and the Third World charged with tension and conflict? There are many reasons which account for this state of affairs. The first and most important reason is the differing views of the West and the Third World regarding the role of the media in society. There was a time in the past when the media in the West saw its role as the disseminators of facts. During that epoch, journalists in the West were content to report the facts and to leave the judgement to the public. This view of the media's role in society has evolved over time and was greatly influenced by such momentous events as the Vietnam War and Watergate. As a result, many journalists in the contemporary West, especially in the United States, regard themselves as guardians of the public interest and the natural adversary to the government. They go in for what are called investigative reporting and advocacy journalism. In the United States, the media regards the freedom of the press and the public's right to know as absolute values. These values are not subordinated to or mediated by such considerations as the national interest. Thus, newspapers in this country publish official secrets without the slightest hesitation. Members of the media also feel that they have a right, indeed a duty, to publish a story regardless of its impact on the relations of the United States with a third country.

The Media's Role in Nation Building

The view of the Third World regarding the role of the media in society is somewhat different. Many governments in the Third World feel that the media has a duty to support the process of nation building. They expect journalists in the Third World to practise what is sometimes described as development journalism. Let me try to explain what this means. Most of the countries in the Third World, with the exception of those in Latin America, are newly independent countries. Upon their accession to independence, the governments of these countries were confronted with many challenges: the challenge of maintaining unity in a pluralistic society; of containing the divisive forces of racism, tribalism, linguistic chauvinism and religious intolerance; of overcoming social and economic backwardness; and of modernization. Faced with these challenges, the governments of the Third World expect the media to play a supportive role in the development process. For example, they expect the media to speak and write in favour of national unity and against racism, tribalism and religious fanaticism. They expect the media to combat social attitudes and values which are obsolete and which impede modernization. They expect the media to help the government in inculcating in the people the values which would support the development process, such as hard work, thrift, discipline, devotion to learning and the willingness to adapt to change.

Do the governments of the Third World have a legitimate case in requiring the media to support the process of nation building? I believe that they do. Is there a danger that some governments in the Third World will use this as a pretext to silence the press? There is indeed such a danger. One very distinguished Asian journalist has said, "In the name of 'development', regimes in many developing countries have become repressive, oppressive and corrupt". However, the fact that the concept is subject to abuse does not invalidate it. I think it is possible to reconcile the duty of the media to participate in the process of nation building and the freedom of the press. However, most governments in the Third World would have difficulties in accepting the role which the media plays in the contemporary West, especially the United States. Most political leaders in the Third World would maintain that the freedom of the press and the public's right to know are not absolute values. They would argue that these values must be subordinated to the overriding needs and integrity of the country. They would also not accept the view that it is the role of the media to be an adversary to government. Let me refer to my own country, Singapore, to illustrate my point.

The Example of Singapore

Singapore is a multiracial, multilingual and multireligious society. It is a very young country and national unity remains a fragile commodity. Race, language and religion are potentially explosive issues. In such a situation, the government expects the Singapore media to refrain from saying or publishing anything which could inflame racial, religious or linguistic feelings. The government would also expect the media to refrain from publishing stories which, though true, could cause serious damage to Singapore's relations with its immediate neighbours.

If members of the Western media working in Singapore were to assume an adversarial attitude towards the Singapore Government, a posture which they very often assume towards their governments at home, this would not be countenanced. The Singapore Government expects the media, both domestic and foreign, to be an impartial observer of but not a participant in the political process. The Singapore Government expects the media to be non-partisan. It should report the facts fairly and accurately but not take sides. A few Western correspondents in Singapore have got into trouble with the Singapore Government because their reporting shows a pattern of support for the opposition and hostility towards the government. Another area in which a collision between a Western correspondent and the Singapore Government could occur is if the correspondent were to write or broadcast reports which have the effect of stirring up emotions on the sensitive issues of race, religion and language.

Extrapolating from the West to the Third World

Another reason which accounts for the acrimonious relationship between the Western media and the Third World is that representatives of the Western media often expect the same ground rules to apply in the Third World as in their own countries. This is often an unrealistic and unreasonable demand. One has to remember that it has taken the Americans more than 200 years of independence to arrive at the state they are in. It has taken the Europeans even longer. Most of the countries of the Third World have been self-governing only in the last 20 to 30 years. Most of them have been subjugated under long periods of colonial rule. During the colonial era, even under the most benign of colonial rulers, freedom of the press was seldom, if ever, practised. There has, therefore, been no tradition of press freedom during the years leading up to independence. The West cannot reasonably expect that following independence, the flower of democracy would suddenly burst into full bloom. It takes time for the institutions of a free society, such as free elections, an independent judiciary, a free press, to take root and to grow in strength. Therefore, if the governments of the Third World do not immediately accord the same degree of freedom of expression to the domestic and foreign media, there are often understandable historical, cultural, political and economic explanations for this state of affairs. Representatives of the Western media working in the Third World, must therefore recognize this reality and be prepared to make some allowance for the difference between their own society and the conditions in the Third World.

The Third World's Complaints against the Western Mass Media

First, the governments of the Third World often complain that they do not receive a fair press in the West because their achievements and successes are seldom, if ever, reported and because the Western mass media is primarily interested in reporting sensational stories on disasters, coups and corruption in their countries. Is this a valid complaint? There is validity in this complaint. The media in the West, not unlike its counterpart in the Third World, seems to work on the assumption that good news is no news and bad news is good news. I think the media all over the world, except in the communist countries, suffer from this affliction which I have sometimes described as a pathological syndrome. I guess the reason why the media tends to concentrate on stories about disasters, coups and scandals, is because they sell papers and attract a larger audience. In other words, the media is catering to what the reading, viewing and listening public wants to read, see or hear. This is a rather sad commentary on the human condition but it is unfortunately a reality. In defence of the Western media, I should point out that some of the better newspapers and magazines do, from time to time, publish articles of a positive cast showing trends or achievements in the Third World.

Second, governments of the Third World often complain that some of the Western correspondents who visit and write about their countries are ignorant of their history, culture, languages and special circumstances. As a result, their articles are either inaccurate or are culturally insensitive. Is this a valid complaint? There is undoubtedly some truth in this complaint but it should not be overstated. Some Western correspondents in the Third World are extremely well qualified. They know a great deal about the countries they are reporting on. There are, unfortunately, some Western correspondents who have no prior knowledge of a country in the Third World, go out on a brief visit and return to pontificate on the most complex problems in that country as if they had become experts on that country. Such correspondents, which I believe to be a small minority, give their profession a bad name. It would be a good thing if media organizations were to prepare their correspondents before sending them out on foreign assignments. The correspondents should be required to learn the history, culture, language and special circumstances of the country to which they will be assigned.

Third, the governments of the Third World complain that some Western correspondents go to the Third World countries, not with an open mind but with preconceptions. The Third World governments complain that such correspondents do not report objectively because they are only interested in finding evidence which confirms their preconceptions and prejudices. Is this a valid complaint? There is some validity in this compliant, but again, I would have to say that in my experience such correspondents are in the minority. The overwhelming majority of Western correspondents are fair-minded individuals who try their best to report the facts objectively. As in any profession, there is minority of black sheep, comprising correspondents who are sloppy or who allow their preconceptions to colour their reporting or who are plain dishonest. We should not, however, mistake the minority of black sheep for the majority who are intelligent, hard-working, honest and fair-minded.

Fourth, the governments of the Third World often complain that Western publications are unwilling to publish their replies to articles in the publications. Is there validity in this complaint? Yes. The quarrel between the Singapore Government and *Time* Magazine is a case in point. In the Asia/Pacific edition of 8 September 1986, *Time* Magazine published an article on Singapore which contained what the Singapore Government considered to be several important errors of fact. On 3 September, the Press Secretary to the Prime Minister of Singapore wrote to *Time* Magazine requesting that it publish his correction of these errors. He received no reply. On 24 September, he again wrote to the magazine, reminding it of his earlier letter. On 30 September, the Press Secretary at last received a letter dated 23 September from the New York Office of *Time* Magazine. Although the letter acknowledged that *Time* might have made errors, it did not offer to publish the corrections. On 2 October, the Press Secretary again wrote to *Time* Magazine. On 3 October, *Time* Magazine called our Permanent Representative to the UN to negotiate the printing of the letter. *Time* wanted to edit the letter before publication. It was requested to publish the letter unaltered. On 10 October, *Time* submitted another edited version of the letter. The second edited version omitted an important point of substance and was therefore rejected by the Singapore Government. *Time* Magazine only agreed to publish the letter in full after the Singapore Government had decided to reduce its circulation. In order to avoid such confrontations, it is essential for Western publications to acknowledge that the freedom of the press is a two-way street. This means that the Western media must give a reasonable opportunity to the governments of the Third World to rebut its reports of their countries. If the Western media does not give the governments of the Third World an opportunity to do so, then they will have no alternative but to consider other means of asserting their right to reply.

Complaints of the Western Mass Media against Third World Governments

Let me turn to examine some of the major complaints of the Western mass media against the governments of the Third World.

First, the Western mass media complains that Third World governments often attack its reporting not because the stories are untrue or inaccurate, but because they reveal too accurately the corruption, nepotism and mismanagement which take place in their respective countries. Is this a valid complaint? In the case of some Third World countries, this complaint is undoubtedly true. There are, unfortunately, too many governments in the Third World which are corrupt, which practise nepotism and are guilty of the wholesale mismanagement of their countries. Such governments would, of course, bristle with anger when the Western media reports the truth about the conditions in their countries. Not all the governments in the Third World, however, are corrupt or practise nepotism or mismanage their countries. Some have as high an ethical standard as the governments in the West. In the case of Singapore, where corruption and nepotism are not tolerated, I am quite confident that if either the local or foreign media were to discover and report that a certain politician or an official were corrupt, the government would feel indebted to the media for having discovered the wrongdoing.

Second, the Western media often complains that many governments in the Third World are intolerant of criticism. They point to the deplorable condition of the local media as evidence to support their complain. Is this a valid complaint? I think there is some validity in this complaint. With very few exceptions, governments in the Third World are not as tolerant of dissent and criticism as the governments in the West. I have already tried to explain the reasons why it is unrealistic to expect that governments in the Third World would behave in exactly the same way as their counterparts in the West. The extent to which dissent and criticism can be tolerated is dependent, in part, on the stability of the country. The more stable the country, the more tolerant it should be of dissent and criticism. The degree of tolerance is also dependent upon the maturity of the political system. Most of the countries of the Third World are infants compared to the Western democracies. One cannot reasonably expect that the institutions of democracy in a nation which is 20 years old would be as mature and as strong as those in a 200-year-old country.

Third, the Western media often complains that many governments in the Third World adopt an uncooperative attitude towards them and refuse to give them timely access to information. Is this a valid complaint? Yes. Some of the governments in the Third World are very secretive and have a suspicious attitude towards the foreign media. They are often unwilling to brief the foreign media and to give them timely access to accurate information. I have always thought that this is a counterproductive attitude for Third World governments to adopt towards the Western media. If a government is unwilling to tell a foreign correspondent what the facts are, he or she is compelled to look elsewhere for the facts. If the report turns out to be not fully accurate, the government is as much to blame as the foreign correspondents. It is far better for the governments of the Third World to adopt a positive and co-operative attitude towards the Western media.

Conclusion

In conclusion, let me try to summarize the main points which I have made in this lecture.

First, I have pointed out that the terms "the Western mass media" and "the Third World" imply a greater homogeneity than exists in reality. The media in the different countries of the West have their own traditions and operate under different legal constraints. For the purpose of this lecture, I have arbitrarily defined the term "the Third World" to mean countries which are non-communist, which have representative institutions of governments and which are democracies or moving in the direction of democracy.

Second, I have described the relationship between the Western mass media and the Third World as being rocky and often confrontational. One of the reasons for this is the differing views of the West and the Third

World regarding the role of the media in society. In the United States, for example, the media regards itself as a guardian of the public interest and the natural adversary to the government. The media regards the freedom of the press and the public's right to know as absolute values which are not subordinated to or mediated by such considerations as the national interest. In the Third World, governments expect their media to play a role in nation building. Such governments would maintain that freedom of the press and the public's right to know must be subordinated to the overriding needs and integrity of the country. They would also not accept the view that it is the role of the media to be an adversary to government.

Third, another reason which accounts for the acrimonious relationship between the Western media and the Third World is that representatives of the Western media often expect the same ground rules to apply in the Third World as in their own countries. I have described this expectation as being unrealistic because there has been no tradition of press freedom in most of the countries of the Third World, and because they are infant democracies.

Fourth, I have discussed the complaint of governments of the Third World that they do not receive a fair press in the West because their achievements and successes are seldom, if ever, reported and because the Western media is primarily interested in reporting sensational stories of disasters, coups, corruption and scandals in the Third World. I have come to the sad conclusion that since most of the reading, listening and viewing public are primarily interested in such stories, and since the media in the non-communist world is interested in increasing its circulation or listening or viewing audience, it is difficult, if not impossible, to rise above the saying that good news is no news and bad news is good news.

Fifth, I have examined the complaint of the governments of the Third World that some of the Western correspondents who visit and write about their countries are ignorant of their history, culture, languages and special circumstances, and as a result, their stories are either inaccurate or culturally insensitive. I have come to the conclusion that this complaint is true of the minority but not of the majority. It would, however, be a very good thing if media organizations were to prepare their correspondents before sending them out on foreign assignments.

Sixth, I have considered the complaint of governments of the Third World that some Western correspondents come to report on their countries not with an open mind but with preconceptions. In my view, such correspondents are also in the minority. In my experience, the overwhelming majority of Western correspondents are fair-minded individuals who try their best to report the facts objectively.

Seventh, I have discussed the complaint of governments of the Third World that some Western publications are often unwilling to publish their replies to articles which criticize them. In my view, the Western media must accept that the freedom of the press is a two-way street. They must give a reasonable opportunity for the governments of the Third World to respond to reports of their countries.

Eighth, I have considered the complaint of the Western media that it is often attacked by governments in the Third World not because the stories are untrue or inaccurate, but because they reveal the corruption, nepotism and mismanagement which occur in their countries. I have come to the conclusion that this is often a valid complaint.

Ninth, I have examined the complaint of the Western media that many governments in the Third World are intolerant of criticism. I have concluded that with few exceptions, governments in the Third World are not as tolerant of criticism and dissent as governments in the West. I have gone on to explain why governments in the Third World are often unable or unwilling to accept the same degree of criticism and dissent as in the West.

Tenth, and finally, I have discussed the complaint of the Western media that many governments in the Third World adopt an uncooperative attitude towards them and refuse to give them timely access to information. I have come to the conclusion that there is validity in this complaint and that it is counterproductive for governments in the Third World to adopt such an attitude. In my view, it is far better for the governments of the Third World to adopt a positive and co-operative attitude towards the Western media.

The 1986 Brendan Brown Lecture, delivered at the Catholic University of America, Washington, D.C., 13 November 1986.

NOTES
1. Martin Linsky, *Impact: How the Press Affects Federal Policymaking* (New York: W.W. Norton, 1986).

NEGOTIATIONS, BARGAINING AND THE CONDUCT OF DIPLOMACY

Negotiating with America

Two caveats are appropriate for any discussion of national negotiating styles. First, there may not necessarily be a definable negotiating style for each country or people. Good and effective negotiators, irrespective of their national or cultural background, have certain common skills and aptitudes. Second, although it is probably possible to say impressionistically that the American people possess certain character and personality traits, there are many exceptions to the rule, and a person's negotiating style is inevitably affected by his character, temperament, and attitude toward people.

American Strengths and Qualities

American negotiators have many strengths and qualities. If distance makes the heart grow fonder, my perception of Americans may be unrealistically favourable and idealized, since Singapore is located 12,000 miles away from the United States.

First, US negotiators are usually well prepared. They arrive at negotiations with their homework completed, and they are armed with facts, figures, maps and charts. They usually know what their national interests and negotiating objectives are. This is not always the case among Third World negotiators.

Second, American negotiators tend to speak clearly and plainly. As someone who was educated in the Anglo-Saxon legal tradition, I regard this as a virtue, not a liability. However, the American preference for plain speaking can sometimes cause unintended offence to other negotiators whose national culture prefers indirectness, subtlety and avoidance of confrontation. There are, of course, exceptions to this rule, and some Americans can be as obtuse and inscrutable as Orientals.

Third, US negotiators tend to be more pragmatic than doctrinaire. They focus on advancing their country's interests rather than on principles which they cherish. The Reagan Administration, however, was a clear exception to this rule, and at the Third UN Conference on the Law of the Sea, decided, for rational and arguable reasons, that principles were more important than interest.

Fourth, American negotiators generally do not regard negotiations as a zero-sum game. A good US negotiator is even prepared to put himself in the place of his negotiating adversary. He or she is prepared to admit that his adversary, like himself, has certain irreducible, minimum national interests. A good US negotiator is prepared to engage in a process of give and take, and he believes that the successful outcome of a negotiation is not one in which he wins everything and his adversary loses everything, but rather one in which there is a mutuality of benefits and losses, in which each side has a stake in honouring and maintaining the agreement.

Fifth, a US negotiator's opening position is never his final position. He expects his opponent to make a counter-proposal or a counter-offer. He is anxious to reach an agreement and will, therefore, make concessions to his opponent, expecting – not unreasonably – that his adversary will behave in like manner. Americans are sometimes completely exasperated at international forums when their adversaries do not behave as they do.

Sixth, the American people are very candid and straightforward, and this is reflected in their negotiating style. Americans are not usually perceived as cunning or devious. In only one incident have I found American negotiators to be devious, and that was shocking. This incident occurred in July 1981 when the United Nations sponsored an international conference on Cambodia. The conference was initiated by the ASEAN countries, which proposed a framework for the resolution of the Cambodian situation. All Cambodian factions were invited to participate in the conference, including, of course, the Khmer Rouge. Vietnam was invited, but boycotted the meeting. At the conference, General Alexander Haig, the then US Secretary of State staged a dramatic walkout, accompanied by the entire US delegation, when the Khmer Rouge leader approached the rostrum to speak. The picture of this walkout appeared on the front page of the *New York Times*.

On a subsequent day, the ASEAN countries and the People's Republic of China (PRC) were locked in a ferocious confrontation over the future role of the Khmer Rouge in any post-settlement Cambodia. The ASEAN countries argued that in light of the massacres and atrocities that the Khmer Rouge had committed, it would be morally and legally impermissible to allow them to return to power. We demanded a public election to be organized and supervised by the United Nations. To ensure free elections, we insisted that all armed elements be disarmed or sequestered in camp. The Chinese fought against all these points. The negotiating group was composed of 25 delegations, but the dynamics of the discussions revolved around the PRC, the ASEAN countries and Pakistan as a middleman. Pakistan, however, was not an honest broker and basically submitted a series of amendments to dilute the ASEAN position. I assumed that Pakistan, because of its proximity to the PRC, was "fronting" for the Chinese, and was shocked to learn later that they were actually fronting for the Americans. Although the American delegation had publicly walked out of the negotiations, they were privately supporting China for geo-strategic reasons. This is the only example of devious behaviour by American negotiators of which I am aware, but I will remember it.

Weaknesses and Idiosyncracies

One problem in negotiating with Americans is that American delegations usually suffer from serious inter-agency rivalries. During the UN Law of the Sea Conference, the American delegation met every morning and sometimes their internal meetings lasted longer than the other meetings in the Conference.

A second problem in negotiating with the United States is the separation of power between the administration and Congress. One has to be very careful if one is negotiating an agreement that is subject to ratification by the US Senate. It is important to always keep in touch with Us senators as the negotiating process continues in order to obtain their independent inputs, to be aware of their sensitivities, and to recognize vested domestic interests and blocking constituencies.

A third special characteristic is the influence of the US private sector and private interest groups on negotiations. During the Law of the Sea Conference, I made it a point to meet not only with the official US delegation and members of the Congress, but also to meet with representatives from the sea-bed mining industry, the petroleum industry, fishing industry, the marine scientific community, the environmental lobby and individuals who have an affection for marine mammals. The reality of political life in America is that even one of these many lobbies can block the ratification of a treaty. Foreign negotiators must understand the domestic political process in the United States and must, in some way, interfere in American internal affairs to ensure the success of their mission.

A fourth problem – the role of the US media – is a problem more for US negotiators than for their counterparts. This is a problem because the good nature of Americans and their propensity for candour somehow makes it very difficult even for negotiators to keep confidences. And, in the midst of a sensitive negotiation it is sometimes very counterproductive for the media to report on issues that are under negotiation. In a recent speech to the House Foreign Affairs Committee, Secretary of State George Shultz recounted with great frustration an occasion when the US and USSR were engaged in bilateral negotiations. The negotiation had reached a critical point and he had that day drafted a cable giving his final instructions. He said he found to his horror at breakfast the next morning that the *New York Times* had reported the contents of his cable. Members of the US media should be asked whether they should exercise more discretion and self-restraint. Do they not feel an allegiance as American citizens to the advancement and protection of American national interests? Should not the right of the public to know and the freedom of the press sometimes be modulated by larger and competing interests? The extent to which the US exposes its flank makes it easier for others to win at the negotiating table.

A fifth weakness is impatience. Americans suffer from an "instant-coffee complex". They do not have time, as Europeans and Asians do, to buy coffee beans, grind them every day, brew the coffee, enjoy the aroma, and savour every sip. Americans are always in a rush and are extremely frustrated when there is a lack of progress. Americans are result-orientated. Jeane Kirkpatrick had a shock several years ago when she visited the ASEAN capitals and met the Foreign Ministers of the six ASEAN countries. To each she asked, "Do you think there are prospects for settling the Cambodian conflict?" All six ASEAN Foreign Ministers said "Yes". She said, "Do you think it will be soon?" They all said, "Oh yes, very soon". She said, "Well, how soon?" They said, "Oh, about five years' time". She was shocked because to an American "five years' time" is certainly not too soon.

A sixth weakness is cultural insensitivity. Everyone is guilty of this, not only Americans. Everyone assumes that others have similar cultures, customs and manners. Singaporeans are on occasion referred to as "the barbarians of Southeast Asia", and are often considered "the least sensitive and least subtle people in the region". But, if one is a professional negotiator, then part of the preparation for an effective negotiation is to learn enough about the culture of one's adversary to at least avoid simple errors of behaviour, attribution and body language.

Finally, it is surprising that in many recent multilateral forums, the United States has been represented by amateur rather than professional negotiators. Given that the United States is so rich in human resources and has a foreign service studded by superstars, it is amazing how inadequately the US is represented at important international negotiations.

Conclusion

In conclusion, a good negotiator, whether Indian, American, Canadian, English, Ghanaian, or whoever, is a person with certain definable skills, aptitudes and temperaments. His character and personality have an impact on his effectiveness. Some American negotiators put people off; others readily win people's confidence. In choosing a negotiator, select someone who does not bristle like a porcupine but who can win the trust and confidence of his negotiating partners. What are these qualities that attract people's confidence and trust? These are moral qualities, qualities of leadership. If a negotiator is a leader, a person who acquires a reputation for competence, reliability and trustworthiness, than others will trust him with leadership roles. The word "charisma" is not useful because it does not accurately portray the quality that bestows leadership on certain negotiators and not others. For instance, Henry Kissinger is not charismatic; he is dominating and impassive and has an exceptional intellect and a monotonous voice. In 1976, when the Law of the Sea Conference was deadlocked between industrialized and developing countries, Kissinger, who was then Secretary of State and had no background in the Law of the Sea and knew nothing about sea-bed mining, spent one morning in New York meeting with the US delegation. In the afternoon, he met with other leaders of the Group of 77, and by the end of the day presented an innovative scheme for reconciling the competing ambitions and claims of the different countries.

There probably is an American negotiating style, and this partakes of the qualities, attitudes, customs, conventions and reflexes that have come down through US history, culture and political institutions. On the whole,

American negotiators have very positive qualities, being well prepared, reasonable, competent and honourable. Even more than this, some, like Ambassador Elliot Richardson,[1] will take it upon themselves to be an honest broker and help to settle a conflict between two other groups in which they are a totally disinterested party. This graciousness and willingness to help is a positive attribute as well.

Article first published in **International Negotiation: A Journal of Theory and Practice**, *Vol. 1, No. 2, 1996, pp. 313-317.*

NOTES

1. Ambassador Elliot Richardson headed the US delegation at the Law of the Sea Conference.

NEGOTIATIONS, BARGAINING AND THE CONDUCT OF DIPLOMACY

The Paris Conference on Cambodia: An Example of a Multilateral Negotiation

Introduction

In this paper I will attempt to examine the International Conference on Cambodia (ICC) from the point of view of one seeking knowledge about the process rather than the substance of the Cambodian conflict. In other words, the emphasis will be on the institutional and procedural aspects of the Conference. The purpose is to compare this multilateral negotiation with others and to see what lessons or insights we can learn from it. However, in order to understand the process, it shall be necessary to begin with some background on Cambodia and to refer, from time to time, to the relationship between substance and procedure.

Background

In 1970, Prince Norodom Sihanouk was overthrown by his Prime Minister, General Lon Nol, in a *coup d'état*. Sihanouk sought refuge in China. He entered into an alliance with the Khmer Rouge to fight Lon Nol. At the same time, Sihanouk gave his support to North Vietnam and the Vietcong in the Vietnam War. In April 1975, the Khmer Rouge, with the help of the Vietnamese, defeated Lon Nol and seized power. It styled itself as the Government of Democratic Kampuchea.

The Khmer Rouge sought to build a new communist society in Cambodia. In order to achieve this goal, it sought to exterminate all those associated with the old regime as well as members of the intelligentsia, the clergy and the minorities. During the years when these massacres were taking place, neither Vietnam nor the members of the Soviet bloc protested against them. On the contrary, they protected the Khmer Rouge and characterized Western criticisms as lies fabricated by the imperialists. On 25 December 1978, Vietnam invaded Cambodia, overthrew the Khmer Rouge regime and imposed, in its place, a puppet government comprising mostly former members of the Khmer Rouge. The regime style itself the People's Republic of Kampuchea (PRK).

Since 1979, three guerrilla forces, the Khmer Rouge, the FUNCINPEC[1] led by Prince Sihanouk and the Khmer People's National Liberation Front (KPNLF) led by Son Sann, have been fighting against Vietnam and the PRK regime. Although the Khmer Rouge regime was overthrown by Vietnam in December 1978, Cambodia's seat at the United Nations was occupied by the Khmer Rouge from 1975 to 1981. In 1982, a coalition government was formed – the Coalition Government of Democratic Kampuchea (CGDK) – comprising the Khmer Rouge, Sihanouk and Son Sann. Cambodia's seat at the UN has since been occupied by the Coalition Government. Vietnam has been unable to exterminate the resistance on the battlefield or to win international recognition for its puppet regime. Vietnam had earlier announced that it would pull its troops out of Cambodia by 1990. It subsequently revised the timetable and announced that all its troops would leave Cambodia by 26 September 1989. In the absence of international verification, we do not know whether all of Vietnam's troops have left Cambodia.

The International Conference on Cambodia

The Government of France convened the International Conference on Cambodia (ICC) in Paris from 30 July to 30 August 1989. Why was the Conference convened by France and not by the UN? It was convened by France for the following reasons. First, the Conference could not have been convened by the United Nations because Vietnam and the PRK regime had stated that they would not attend such a conference. They had two objections to attending a conference convened by the United Nations. The first objection was that the United Nations was not an impartial forum as the General Assembly has, since 1979, annually adopted a Resolution on Cambodia critical of Vietnam. The second objection was that Cambodia's seat at the United Nations has been occupied by the Coalition Government opposed to Vietnam, instead of by the PRK regime. Second, France has historical links with Vietnam, Laos and Cambodia and is acceptable to Vietnam and the four Cambodian parties. According to various sources, both Vietnam and Sihanouk appealed to France to convene the Conference. Third, France has good relations with the other countries in Southeast Asia as well as with China, the Soviet Union, the United States and the United Kingdom.

The Co-Presidency of the Conference

Although the ICC was convened by France, it was co-chaired by France and Indonesia. Why did France invite Indonesia to co-chair the Conference? The reason was that Indonesia had convened two rounds of meetings, each of which is referred to as the Jakarta Informal Meeting or JIM in short. JIM I and JIM II were attended by representatives of the four Cambodian parties, Vietnam, Laos and the ASEAN countries. The two meetings had succeeded, to some extent, in defining the issues and in narrowing the gap between the two sides. Because of the contributions which Indonesia had made to the Cambodian peace process, France invited Indonesia to be the Co-President of the ICC. Did the two Co-Presidents succeed in working in tandem? On the whole, the two Co-Presidents appeared to have been able to work harmoniously. There were occasions, however, when France acted unilaterally and caused considerable embarrassment to Indonesia. On one such occasion, the Indonesian Embassy in Paris went to the extent of issuing a statement to explain that a proposal put forward by France was a French proposal and not a proposal of the two Co-Presidents.

Participation in the Conference

Who was invited to attend the ICC? How was the troublesome question of the participation of the four Cambodian parties resolved? After much wrangling and negotiation, the Co-Presidents decided to seat the four Cambodian delegations in the following manner. They were seated side by side behind a large nameplate bearing the word "Cambodia". Each delegation was referred to as the delegation of its leader by name. Thus, we had the delegation of Son Sann, the delegation of Prince Sihanouk, the delegation of Khieu Samphan (the Khmer Rouge) and the delegation of Hun Sen (PRK). Apart from the four Cambodian parties, the Co-Presidents invited the following. First, Vietnam and Laos. Second, the six ASEAN countries. Third, the other four permanent members of the Security Council. Fourth, Australia, Canada, India and Japan. Fifth, Zimbabwe as the Chairman of the Non-Aligned Movement. Sixth, the Secretary-General of the United Nations.

It was, of course, essential to have all the four Cambodian parties at the Conference. It was also vital to have Vietnam's presence because the Cambodian conflict is essentially a conflict between Vietnam and Cambodia. The ASEAN countries were invited because they are the countries of the region and because ASEAN had taken the lead in the quest for a comprehensive political settlement to the conflict, and to oppose Vietnam's intervention in Cambodia. It was wise to invite the five permanent members of the Security Council because the Soviet Union has substantial leverage with Vietnam; because China, the Soviet Union and the US have influence with the Cambodian parties; and because if the Paris Conference had succeeded, the Security Council would have had to be involved in the implementation of the Paris Agreement. Canada and India were invited because they were the Co-Chairmen of the International Control Commission under the 1954 Geneva Agreement on Indochina. Australia and Japan were included because they are in the region, had taken an active interest in the Cambodian peace diplomacy and could assist in financing the UN peacekeeping force in Cambodia and in the reconstruction of Cambodia. The Chairman of the Non-Aligned Movement was invited because the group has a Standing Committee on Cambodia. Zimbabwe did not, however, play an active part in the Conference. In contrast, the delegation of the UN Secretary-General, ably led by Rafeeuddin Ahmed, played a very active part in the Conference and submitted a number of very helpful papers.

The Absence of a Preparatory Meeting

An unusual feature of the ICC was that it was not preceded by a preparatory meeting of officials. The Co-Presidents had also not circulated any draft texts or the draft rules of procedure before the Conference. The question of whether the failure of the Conference could have been avoided if it had been better prepared for will be discussed later.

The Structure of the Conference

The ICC began with a short Ministerial Meeting during which the attending Foreign Ministers made their general statements, adopted the rules of procedure of the Conference and a paper containing the organization of work. After the departure of the Ministers, the Conference continued its work in four Committees. The Ministers returned to Paris for the concluding phase of the Conference.

The First Committee of the Conference was given the mandate of defining the modalities of a cease-fire and the terms of reference, as well as the principles which should guide the creation and operation of an effective International Control Mechanism. The Second Committee was given the mandate of defining the commitments which states participating in the Conference should undertake to guarantee the independence, sovereignty, territorial integrity and neutrality of Cambodia; to ensure the cessation and non-recurrence of all foreign interference and external arms supplies; and to prevent the recurrence of genocidal policies and practices and the return and introduction of foreign forces. The Third Committee was given the mandate to define the conditions which would enable refugees and displaced persons to return home, if they so desired, and to prepare the main elements of a national plan for the reconstruction of Cambodia.

The Ad Hoc Committee

A fourth Committee, called the Ad Hoc Committee, was also established. The Committee consisted of the four Cambodian parties and was co-chaired by France and Indonesia. The Co-Chairmen, in consultation with the Cambodian parties, could invite other participants of the Conference to join the Committee. One meeting of the Ad Hoc Committee was held which included all the five permanent members of the Security Council, Thailand and Vietnam. The mandate of the Ad Hoc committee was to examine questions regarding the implementation of national reconciliation and the setting up of a quadripartite interim authority under the leadership of Prince Norodom Sihanouk, which would be responsible for, among other duties, organizing internationally supervised free elections within a reasonable period of time.

It is clear that of all the four Committees, the Ad Hoc Committee was by far the most important. Failure on the part of the Ad Hoc Committee to arrive at an agreement on the internal aspects of the Cambodian conflict would doom the Conference to failure. After several meetings of the Ad Hoc Committee, it was clear to many of us that, left to themselves, the four Cambodian parties were unable to arrive at a compromise. We therefore welcomed the decision of the Co-Presidents and the Cambodian parties to include Vietnam, Thailand, China, the Soviet Union, the United States and the United Kingdom. Although the Co-Presidents considered this expanded meeting a success, they never explained why they did not invite these additional members to subsequent meetings of the Ad Hoc Committee. In my view, this was a mistake because there could be no agreement either on the external or the internal aspects of the Cambodian conflict without the active participation and agreement of Vietnam, China, the Soviet Union and the United States.

Rules of Procedure

There are a number of interesting features of the rules of procedure of the ICC. Let me identify a few of them. First, the concept of Co-Presidency was extended to each of the Committees. Thus, the First Committee was co-chaired by Canada and India, the Second Committee by Laos and Malaysia and the Third Committee by Australia and Japan. Why did the Conference choose to have a system of Co-Chairmanship rather than a single Chairman for the committees? The reason was the desire, especially on the part of Vietnam and her allies, to maintain a political balance in the leadership of each of the Committees. Of the two Co-Chairmen of the First Committee, Canada opposed Vietnam's invasion and occupation of Cambodia whereas India recognized the PRK regime. Of the Co-Chairmen of the Second Committee, Laos was an ally of Vietnam whereas Malaysia opposed Vietnam's intervention in Cambodia. In the Third Committee, the Co-Chairmen were Australia and Japan. Did the system of Co-Chairmanship work in the ICC? In general, my experience is that it is better to have a single Chairman than to have two Co-Chairmen. Having two Co-Chairmen can sometimes lead to deadlock and paralysis. In the ICC, the system of Co-Chairmanship worked reasonably well in the First, Third and Ad Hoc Committees. The Canadian and Indian Co-Chairmen of the First Committee, the Australian and Japanese Co-Chairmen of the Third Committee and the French and Indonesian Co-Chairmen of the Ad Hoc Committee were able to work with a reasonable degree of harmony and efficiency. In the Second Committee, however, progress was impeded by the refusal of the Laotian Chairman to acquiesce to the wishes of the overwhelming majority in that Committee.

Second, decisions of the Conference were made by unanimity. Why did the Conference adopt the French proposal for unanimity rather than other options such as consensus or a majority? I think the French felt, and the Conference agreed, that if the decisions of the Conference were taken by a majority, it would be impossible to impose them on those who had opposed the decision. The issues on the agenda of the Conference were of such grave importance to the Cambodians and to some of the participating states that they needed their concurrence if the agreements arrived at in Paris were to have any prospect of being implemented. The unanimity rule means that every delegation has the right of veto. The power to veto was sometimes used in a rather cavalier fashion, especially by the Cambodian parties, in considering amendments submitted by various delegations to the proposals of the Co-Chairmen of the First Committee. The option of taking decisions by consensus was not seriously considered because the consensus rule is susceptible to abuse.

Third, the draft rules of the procedure submitted by France to the Conference proposed the establishment of a Conference Bureau consisting of the Co-Presidents of the Conference, the Co-Chairmen of the Committees and the Secretary-General of the Conference. This proposal was rejected because many delegations feared that the Conference Bureau might abuse its power and seek to impose its views on the Conference. In the absence of a Conference Bureau, the function of co-ordinating the work of the Conference was given to the Co-ordinating Committee which consisted of all members of the Conference. This alternative worked reasonably well because of the limited size of the Conference. If the ICC had had a much larger membership, a smaller Bureau or Steering Committee would probably have been required.

The Role of the Five Great Powers

It is my impression that the five permanent members of the Security Council – China, France, the Soviet Union, the United States and the United Kingdom – wanted to resolve the Cambodian conflict. Prior to the Paris Conference, the representatives of the five great powers had conducted a series of meetings at the United Nations. In a remarkable show of unanimity, the five permanent members adopted a paper on the mandate of the International Control Mechanism. This paper was submitted by the French delegation, on behalf of the five, to the First Committee. During the Paris Conference, the representatives of the five met regularly. They did not, however, produce any texts or solutions to the outstanding problems. However, in spite of the collective desire of the five great powers to settle the Cambodian conflict, the first Paris Conference failed.[2] The lesson which I learnt from this experience is that the agreement of the five great powers is a necessary, but not a sufficient condition for the resolution of regional conflicts.

Why the Paris Conference Failed

The Conference failed because Vietnam and the four Cambodian parties could not agree on five core issues. These were first, power sharing in the quadripartite interim authority pending free elections; second, the auspices under which the International Control Mechanism would be established; third, the use of the term "genocide" to describe the atrocities committed by the Khmer Rouge; fourth, the question of Vietnamese settlers in Cambodia and fifth, the modalities of a cease-fire. Of these five core issues, the most important was the question of power sharing. Once this issue was resolved, the others would have fallen into place.

The Conference therefore broke down because of the failure to arrive at a compromise on power sharing in the interim authority prior to the holding of free elections. Hun Sen was not prepared to give Sihanouk substantive executive powers. This was amply demonstrated by the fact that he rejected a French proposal of 19 August which named him as the Prime Minister of an interim coalition government and gave him substantially greater powers than Sihanouk. Hun Sen was only prepared to accept Sihanouk as a figurehead. Vietnam and Hun Sen also backtracked from an earlier agreement to consider the inclusion of the Khmer Rouge in an interim coalition authority as contained in the paper on the organization of work adopted at the Conference.

The Timing of the Conference

The judgement as to when to convene a Conference is often critical. The Convenor must be satisfied that the problem is ripe and the parties are ready to seek a solution before calling a Conference. Was the French Government mistaken in convening the Conference on 30 July? I do not think it would be fair to blame France for mistiming the Conference. Like France, I thought we had a 50 per cent chance of achieving a breakthrough. I was encouraged by the following factors. First, it was my impression that China and the Soviet Union wanted to settle the conflict. Second, I was impressed by the fact that the five permanent members of the Security Council were able to adopt a common paper on the mandate of the International Control Mechanism. I inferred that the five great powers wanted a solution to the Cambodian conflict. Third, the two superpowers wish to extricate themselves from the regional conflicts in the Third World and have co-operated to resolve some of them. Fourth, I thought Vietnam wanted a settlement because it would end her international isolation, lift the barrier blocking the flow of Western aid and give Vietnam a chance to resuscitate her stagnant economy. Fifth, I also thought that the four Cambodian parties wanted a settlement. Sixth, the Jakarta Informal Meetings (JIM I and JIM II) had improved the atmospherics and appeared to have narrowed the gap between the adversaries.

Why did Vietnam and Hun Sen harden their positions at the Paris Conference? It appears that in the midst of the Conference, from 14 to 21 August, the Politburo and the Central Committee met in Hanoi. According to various reports, the hardliners prevailed and the Vietnamese leadership retreated into ideological orthodoxy. They decided to make no concessions in Paris. The survival of Najibullah in Kabul may also have encouraged Vietnam to believe that Hun Sen could survive against his opponents. Hun Sen could count upon the massive supply of arms by Vietnam and the Soviet Union. Vietnam has also announced, on two occasion, that, if necessary, it would re-intervene in Cambodia.

Conclusion

What lessons can we learn from the ICC about multilateral negotiations? First, it is always helpful, perhaps necessary, to prepare carefully before convening an international conference. If France had held preparatory meetings at the level of senior officials, it would either have improved the prospects of the Conference or convinced France that Vietnam was not ready to strike a compromise. Second, in the case of regional conflicts in the Third World, the agreement of the five permanent members of the Security Council is a necessary but not a sufficient reason for success. The Soviet Union was either unwilling or unable to persuade Vietnam to seek a compromise in Paris. Third, in the case of regional conflicts in the Third World, the key to the solution is often held, not by the great powers alone, but in concert with the regional players. Fourth, although it is preferable to have a single Chairman to two Co-Chairmen preside over a conference or committee, the system of Co-Chairmanship can sometimes work if the Co-Chairmen are carefully chosen and if they are able to work in tandem. Fifth, timing is of the utmost importance. In the case of the Cambodian conflict, the Vietnamese had not yet given up their aspiration for hegemony over Cambodia. This is why Vietnam and its surrogate, Hun Sen, rejected compromise at the Conference table.

Remarks delivered to the American Academy of Diplomacy and the School of Advanced International Studies, 1 November 1989.

NOTES:

1. An acronym derived from *Front Uni National pour un Cambodge Indepéndant Neutre, Pacifique et Coopératif*, the French term for the National United Front for an Independent, Neutral, Peaceful and Cooperative Cambodia, established in March 1981 by Prince Sihanouk.
2. The reference here is to the first sitting of the Paris Conference from 30 July to 30 August 1989, which did not produce an agreement. The conference was subsequently reconvened in 1991 after further internationally-mediated negotiations among the Cambodian factions, and resulted in the Paris Peace Agreement on Cambodia.

NEGOTIATIONS, BARGAINING AND THE CONDUCT OF DIPLOMACY

The Earth Summit's Negotiating Process: Some Reflections on the Art and Science of Negotiation

Mr Chairman, distinguished guests, ladies and gentlemen, I must begin by thanking the editors of the Singapore Law Review for inviting me to deliver this prestigious lecture. The six lecturers who preceded me are good friends, all of whom I have enormous respect for. They have set a high standard. I hope I will not let them and you down by my lecture today.

Next, I want to use this occasion to thank the members of the Singapore delegation to the Earth Summit and its Preparatory Committee. Without their help and support, I could not have succeeded in carrying out my duties as Chairman of the Main Committee at the Earth Summit and as Chairman of the Preparatory Committee.

Finally, I want to acknowledge my intellectual debt to the following friends who have made seminal contributions to the fields of conference diplomacy and negotiations:

(a) Dutch Ambassador Johan Kaufmann's 1968 book entitled *Conference Diplomacy*;
(b) Johns Hopkins University Professor, William Zartnam's 1982 book, *The Practical Negotiator*;
(c) Harvard Business School Professor, Howard Raiffa's 1982 book entitled *The Art and Science of Negotiation*;
(d) Harvard Law School Professor, Roger Fisher's two books entitled *International Conflict for Beginners* and *Getting to Yes*; and
(e) Harvard Kennedy School Professor, James Sebenius' two books entitled *Negotiating the Law of the Sea* (1984) and *The Manager as Negotiator* (1986).

A Brief Background

Let me now provide you with a few salient facts about the UN Conference on Environment and Development (hereinafter referred to as the Earth Summit) and its preparatory process. In 1989, the UN General Assembly decided to convene the Earth Summit in 1992, 20 years after the Stockholm Conference on the Human Environment. I have said, only half in jest, to the *New York Times* that the UN should learn not to hold a major international conference during a US Presidential Election year. There is no doubt in my mind that his preoccupation with winning the election was a factor which caused President Bush to adopt a defensive rather than a pro-active role. The decision to convene the Earth Summit was contained in Resolution 44/228. Some Arab colleagues referred to it as our Koran. The text contained in that resolution soon came to be regarded as sacred.

The Size of the Preparatory Committee

In order to prepare for the Earth Summit, the UN decided to set up a Preparatory Committee. Because of the great interest in the Conference, the committee was enormous in size. It consisted of all the member states of the UN as well as non-member states such as Switzerland. The size of the Committee made negotiation difficult. One of my challenges was how to gradually reduce the size of negotiating groups. I will return to this later.

The PrepCom, as it came to be known, was mandated by our Koran to hold an organizational session in New York, from 5 to 16 March 1990, and four substantive sessions in Nairobi, Geneva, Geneva and New York respectively, in 1991 and 1992. You may wonder why the four substantive sessions were held in three different cities on three continents. Was this an example of the UN diplomats awarding themselves junkets at the expense of their tax payers? It wasn't. It was an example of the kind of compromises that had to be struck in order to achieve consensus. The New York-based diplomats, who were the most politicized, wanted all the sessions to be held in New York. The Geneva-based diplomats argued that they should be held in Geneva, the home of the UNCED Secretariat. The supporters of UNEP, which is based in Nairobi, argued that they should be held in Nairobi.

The Organizational Session

The organizational session of the PrepCom was two weeks long. It was held in New York from 5 to 16 March 1990. What were the objectives of the organizational session? It had five objectives. First, to elect its Chairman. Second, to decide on the size of the Bureau and the distribution of the number agreed upon among the five regional groups. Third, to decide how many working groups to establish and which regional groups would provide candidates for their Chairs. Fourth, to adopt a provisional agenda for the Earth Summit. Fifth, to adopt its rules of procedure.

Any reasonable person would think that you would need only one or two days, not two weeks, to agree on five such seemingly simple tasks. This was not the case and the two weeks were barely enough to complete our tasks. Of the five tasks, the only simple one was electing me. All the other candidates wisely withdrew when they realized the pain and suffering which the Chairman would have to endure for the next two years and three months! The first thing I did on assuming the Chair was to propose that we should refrain from polluting the air in our meeting rooms by prohibiting smoking at all our meetings. Before the nicotine addicts could rally their forces, I asked if there was any objection. Seeing none, I banged the gavel and pronounced that there was a consensus in favour of my proposal. The former Secretary-General of the UN, Javier Perez de Cuellar, watched in surprise because no UN Chairman had succeeded in defeating the tobacco lobby at the UN before.

Any Objections?

The speed with which I used my gavel would later give rise to some unhappiness. As a result, I would count to five before banging my gavel. On one occasion, the Chairman of the Group of 77, a wonderful man from Pakistan, Ambassador Jamshid Marker, remarked that my counting of 1, 2, 3, 4, 5 became faster and faster the longer the meeting lasted.

The Size of the Bureau

I failed, however, to persuade my colleagues to accept a relatively small Bureau. For a Bureau to be efficient, it has to be representative but small. Many delegations wanted to be in the Bureau because they thought that it might become a negotiating forum. In the end, I had to accept a Bureau of 42 members. A Bureau of 42 is too big to be useful. I will tell you later of the steps I took to invent a smaller but more efficient group to help me manage the negotiating process.

The Politics of Drafting the Agenda

The PrepCom agreed to establish two working groups which would be chaired respectively by a West European and an African. There was, however, no agreement to establish a third working group to deal with questions relating to law and institutions. The third working group was established at the beginning of the second substantive session in Geneva. The most difficult task was in drafting the agenda. Why? Because delegations feared that the wording of an agenda item could tilt the balance in favour of their adversaries.

To return to my story. On the last day of the organizational session, 16 March 1990, there was still no agreement on the agenda. I was determined to get one. I instructed the Secretariat to arrange for interpreters to be available so that I could go through the night until 6.00 am the next morning. The Secretariat did not believe me and I had no interpreters after midnight. I had to persuade the non-Anglophones to work in English. This was by no means an easy task, especially with the Francophone group.

Maintain the Pressure

My strategy was to maintain the pressure on the delegates until they agreed to compromise. By 4.30 am, the delegates were so exhausted that they asked me to draft a compromise. I called for a short recess, and with the help of about a dozen colleagues representing the various interest groups, succeeded in crafting a compromise. I got my agenda. The meeting adjourned at 6.00 am on St Patrick's Day. I felt exhausted but vindicated in my determination not to adjourn the meeting until I had secured an agreement. If I had adjourned the meeting, the pressure would have eased and delegations would again dig in their heels. I also wanted to make the point to delegates and the Secretariat that when I set a deadline, I meant to keep it. The Secretariat never doubted my resolve again. At all subsequent session of the PrepCom and the Main Committee, I had teams of interpreters ready to serve the meeting through the night and into the morning of the next day on the final day of each session. On two subsequent occasions, I went through the night – until 4.30 am on the last day of the fourth substantive session in New York, and 6.00 am on the last day of the Main Committee at the Earth Summit in Rio.

Managing the Negotiating Process

Managing a complex negotiating process requires both leadership and team work. I worked closely with the Secretary-General of the Conference, Maurice Strong, and the various members of the Secretariat. Twenty years earlier, he was the Secretary-General of the Stockholm Conference on the Human Environment. I had worked closely with him in preparing for the Stockholm Conference. The fact that our friendship went back 20 years helped us to forge a good working partnership. I kept no secrets from him and his deputy, Nitin Desai.

The Collegium

I expanded the collective leadership or Collegium to include the Chairman of Working Group I, Ambassador Bo Kjellen of Sweden; the Chairman of Working Group II, Bukar Shaib of Nigeria; the Chairman of Working Group III, Bedrich Moldan of Czechoslovakia; and the Rapporteur, Ahmad Djoghlaf of Algeria. I institutionalized the collective management of the negotiating process by holding meetings every morning at 9.00 am with this group and the senior members of the UNCED Secretariat. This would be followed by a daily meeting at 9.30 am with the representatives of all the UN agencies. The purpose of the second meeting was to bring all the members of the UN family together and to prevent turf fights and misunderstandings. It was also to tap the expertise and inputs of the various agencies.

The Delegation of Power

The work of the PrepCom was carried out in four principal forums: the plenary of the PrepCom and the three working groups. The agenda of the plenary was long and complex. It included the difficult questions of financing sustainable development and the transfer of technology from developed to developing countries. It also included such questions as the relationship between the environment, on the one hand, and poverty, population, the international economic order and human settlements, on the other.

A good Chairman must avoid the temptation of keeping everything under his wings. He must learn to delegate. He must choose able men and women to delegate responsibility to. When it becomes clear that a delegatee is unable to deliver, a chairman must do the very unpleasant job of replacing him with someone else.

Open-Ended Negotiating Groups

At the second substantive session held in Geneva in the spring of 1991, I established a number of open-ended negotiating groups in the plenary. I appointed Ambassador Bjorner Utheim of Norway to chair the one on technology; Deputy Foreign Minister John Muliro of Kenya to chair the one on the poverty-population-health cluster; Ambassador Enrique Penalosa of Colombia to chair the one on human settlements and Ahmad Djoghlaf of Algeria to chair the one on the international economic order. I co-opted the chairmen of the negotiating groups into the Collegium.

A Painful Duty

At the fourth substantive session, I replaced Ambassador John Bell with Deputy Foreign Minister Andres Rozental of Mexico. At the Summit, I replaced Rozental with Ambassador Ricupero of Brazil. Also, at the Summit, I replaced Utheim with the Dutch Minister of the Environment, J.G.M. Alders. As one who attaches great value to loyalty and friendship, I have always found it very difficult to abandon a colleague. However, I felt duty-bound to put the best interests of the Conference before friendship and loyalty. The fact that both Ricupero and Alders succeeded in their work showed that I was right to make the personnel changes.

The Elephantine Bureau

The Bureau of a committee or conference is supposed to act as its steering committee. The Bureau of the PrepCom and the Earth Summit was unable to play this role effectively because of its size: 42 members. It was almost as difficult to reach a consensus among the 42 members of the Bureau as among the 150-plus members of the PrepCom and the 170-plus members of the Summit. I had to invent another body to act as the steering committee.

De Facto Steering Committee

I convened twice weekly meetings of a group consisting of the Chairmen of the five groups; the Chairman of the Group of 77 (representing the developing countries); the chairman of the EC; the Chairman of the Nordic Group; the Chairman of CANZ (representing Canada, Australia and New Zealand) and the three countries which do not belong to any interest group: China, Japan and the US. This group of 12 countries and the Collegium functioned as the steering committee of the PrepCom and Summit. It proved to be a very effective body. During critical periods of the PrepCom and Summit, I would convene daily meetings of this group. In order to pacify the members of the Bureau, who quite rightly felt by-passed, I would convene meetings of the Bureau from time to time.

The Importance of Timing

In negotiation, timing is very important. A chairman who acts prematurely risks being rebuffed. A chairman who acts too slowly loses the opportunity to clinch a deal. I have observed that multilateral negotiations often pass through three phases: confrontation, crisis and resolution. A good chairman must not be unnerved by the phase of confrontation. He must wait for the period of crisis which often follows confrontation. It is at this maximum hour of danger and opportunity that he must strike and bring about a resolution.

Let me illustrate these general observations with the following concrete example. Working Group III, on law and institutions, was established at the beginning of the second substantive session in Geneva. It elected Bedrich Moldan of Czechoslovakia as its Chairman. One of the items on its agenda was the drafting of the Rio Declaration on the Environment and Development, popularly referred to as the Earth Charter. At the beginning of the fourth substantive session, Moldan offered a compromise draft consisting of ten principles and three prerequisites. He moved too soon. Also, his draft was viewed, rightly or wrongly, by the developing countries as favouring the viewpoint of the developed countries. Because of this, the developing countries refused to continue to negotiate under his chairmanship. Instead, an informal contact group was established under the Co-Chairmanship of Mukul Sanwal of India and Ole Holthe of Norway.

Going from 150 to 16

On the morning of 31 March 1992, three days before the end of that session, Sanwal and Holthe asked for permission to speak to our daily meeting at 9.00 am. They reported that they had gone as far as they could and were unable to make any further progress. They requested me to take over the negotiations. The meeting supported their request. I then convened a meeting of the *de facto* steering committee. I said I would be prepared to chair the negotiation provided they agreed to establish a small, closed, representative group of 16, eight to represent the North and eight to represent the South. The meeting agreed. The North was represented by the US; Portugal, Netherlands and Germany (EC); Australia (CANZ); Norway (alternating with Sweden); Japan and Russia. The South was represented by Pakistan, India, Iran, Brazil, Mexico, Nigeria, Tanzania and China.

Preparing a Negotiating Text

I made another request. I requested Sanwal and Holthe to produce a negotiating text by 6.30 pm on 1 April 1992. They did so and the group of 16 began its work at 8.00 pm of the same evening. It adjourned before midnight and continued the next morning. A clean text, containing 27 principles was agreed upon, *ad referendum*, at 6.15 pm on 2 April 1992 (A/CONF.151/PC/WGIII/L33/Rev.1). This text would eventually be adopted by the Earth Summit as the Rio Declaration on Environment and Development.

The Negotiating Process in Rio

Apart from the clean text of the Rio Declaration, the other documents submitted to Rio contained 350 bracketed or disputed language. We had only one week in the Main Committee to remove these brackets and to find acceptable language. I was not at all sure that the job could be done.

Procedural Decisions

I persuaded the Committee to adopt a number of procedural decisions. First, that the negotiation would focus entirely on the bracketed language. I ruled out of order any delegate who tried to re-open discussion on unbracketed language (i.e. language which had been agreed upon). I also rebuffed the attempts by several delegations to insert new brackets on the ground that they had been inadvertently omitted by the Secretariat. Fortunately, we had brought along the authoritative documents of the PrepCom. Upon verification, we found no merit in any of the requests. Second, I refused to allow any delegation to make a new proposal if it met with a single objection. The reason is that any new proposal must advance the prospect of achieving consensus. Third, I asked the

Committee to allow me to establish nine open-ended negotiating groups on the understanding that not more than three would meet concurrently. Fourth, I persuaded the Committee to work from Monday to Saturday and to meet morning, afternoon and evening. Fifth, I imposed a strict time-limit on the length of statements. Sixth, whenever the negotiation got stuck on a point, I would set up an *ad hoc* open-ended negotiating group to deal with it and appoint an able colleague to chair the group. In this way, I was able to keep the negotiation moving at a steady pace.

A Long Day's Night

The final meeting of the Main Committee began at 8.00 pm on 10 June 1992. It continued through the night and ended at 6.00 am the next morning. I did take one short break. At 4.00 am, after eight hours in the chair, I was desperate to go to the toilet. I also sensed that there was a lot of tension in the room. I announced that we would recess the meeting for five minutes in order to enable me to make a discharge of non-toxic waste. I promised to do it in an environmentally safe and sound manner. The delegates brought into laughter and the meeting resumed in a better mood. All bracketed language, excepting those relating to finance and forest, was resolved. Those two issues were referred to ministerial-level negotiations chaired by Brazil and Germany respectively. The Brazilians had consulted me on who to appoint to chair the difficult negotiation on forest. I recommended the German Minister for the Environment, Klaus Toepfer. Consensus was achieved on those two issues on 12 June. The Summit was therefore able to adopt, on 14 June, the Rio Declaration, Agenda 21 and the Statement of Principles on Forests by consensus. Thus ended the largest conference the UN had ever held. It was attended by 116 Heads of State or Government, 172 states, 8,000 delegates, 9,000 members of the press and 3,000 accredited representatives of non-governmental organizations.

The Seventh Singapore Law Review Lecture, delivered to the Faculty of Law, National University of Singapore, 15 December 1992.

NEGOTIATIONS, BARGAINING AND THE CONDUCT OF DIPLOMACY

Working the Hill : Getting Your Country's Interests across to Congress

Introduction

Some newly-arrived diplomats in Washington, D.C., especially those who have had no prior exposure to the United States, and most especially those from relatively small countries, are bewildered and intimidated by the size and complexity of the US Congress. There are 435 members in the House of Representatives, 100 members in the Senate, over a hundred committees and subcommittees, and thousands of congressional staffers. How do you work the Congress? How do you put across your country's interests to Congress?

Define Your Agenda

First, you must define your agenda. What is it that you want the Congress to do or to refrain from doing? Every mission, every diplomat must be guided by a clear set of objectives. A few years ago, I asked a colleague who had also been transferred to Washington from New York what his agenda was. In reply to my question, he said he had no agenda. I was shocked. I believe that if you think carefully about your country's interests, you will be able to come up with a list of things which you would like the Congress to do and a list of congressional actions which you would oppose. Let me just give a few random examples. If your country is a recipient of US military or economic assistance, your objective would be either to increase the volume of such assistance or to maintain its present level. If your country exports textile or garments to the United States, one of your objectives would be to defeat the Textile Bill. If your country is opposed to the Administration's decision to reduce the refugee quota from Southeast

Asia, you may wish to encourage the relevant congressional committee or subcommittee to hold a hearing on the question in order to persuade the Administration to reconsider its decision.

Create Your Network

Second, you must identify the names of the congressional committees and subcommittees, the senators, congressmen or congresswomen, and the congressional staffers who could help you achieve your objectives. The size of your target network depends upon the length of your agenda. The total number of persons which your mission needs to cultivate could easily number more than 50. This could be true even for a small mission with a modest agenda.

The size of the network is the result of the following factors. In order for a proposal to become law, it has to be approved, both in the Senate and the House, by two sets of committees: the authorizing committees (which approve the proposal) and the appropriation committees (which appropriate the money for the proposal). Another complication is the fact that a proposal may be subject to the jurisdiction of more than one committee. Trade is an excellent example. There are constant battles for turf between the Senate Finance Committee and Senate Commerce Committee and between the House Ways and Means Committee and House Commerce Committee. During the process of formulating the 1988 Omnibus Trade and Competitiveness Act, the total number of committees and subcommittees which were involved was 23!

Having identified the committees and subcommittees which are relevant to your country's interests, you must draw up a list of its key members. You should start with the Chairman. But, unlike the old days, when the Chairman of a committee or subcommittee could tell his colleagues what to do, this is no longer true today. It is therefore not enough to cultivate the Chairman. You should also cultivate other members of the committee or subcommittee, especially those who are movers and shakers and potential troublemakers. You should not ignore the representatives of the minority party in the committee or subcommittee.

Finally, the congressional staffers. There are thousands of these highly intelligent, extremely hardworking and very knowledgeable persons working on Capitol Hill. Most of them are young, ranging in age from the 20s to the 40s. Some of them work for congressional committees or subcommittees. Others are on the staff of senators and congressmen. The congressional staffers are a very important part of your network. Why? Because they, not their bosses, are the real experts of the particular subject they deal with; because of the tremendous influence they wield over the senators, congressmen and the committees they serve; and because they could serve as your conduit to the senators, congressmen and the committees.

How to Put Your Case across?

Third, having defined your agenda and identified your network, you must now put across your case to Congress. If I want to meet the Chairman of a committee or subcommittee, I have always found it useful to begin by talking to his Staff Director or another committee staffer who looks after the particular subject. If you make a good impression on the staffer and succeed in winning his sympathy, he will be glad to arrange for you to meet his Chairman. In the same way, if you want to meet a senator or congressman, you will find it useful to talk first to the staffer who deals with the subject. Normally, it should not be a problem getting an appointment to see a senator or congressman. In the rare case when it is a problem, you could seek the help of a friend who can open the door for you. I remember the case of a particular senator I had wanted to meet without success. I finally managed to see him, not in Washington, but in his constituency, through the good offices of a friend who is a heavy contributor to the senator's campaigns. Thereafter, I never had any problems getting an appointment to see him.

After you have obtained an appointment to see a senator or congressman, you should prepare carefully for the meeting. There are several rules which I follow. My first is never to take more than ten minutes to put across my case. Senators and congressmen are extremely busy people. Don't abuse their time. My second rule is to try to link the interests of my country or my cause to those of his constituents. A senator or congressman is most likely to help you if you can show him that by doing so, he is also helping his constituents. My third rule is to leave behind, at the end of the meeting, a short paper containing my talking points. This will serve to refresh his memory. It will also enable his staffer to follow up on your request.

How to Build a Winning Coalition?

Whether your objective is to encourage Congress to pass a legislation favourable to your country's interests or to defeat a bill which is damaging to your country's interests, the challenge is to put together a winning coalition. How to build such a coalition? I suggest five rules. First, create bipartisan support for your cause. Do not allow your country or your cause to become a political football between the Democrats and Republicans in Congress. Contrast the fortunes of the Mujahideen in Afghanistan with the Contras in Nicaragua. Second, divide the members of Congress into three lists: those who support your cause, those who are opposed, and the waverers. Write or visit those who support your cause. Call personally on all the waverers and anyone in the opposed column who could be persuaded to shift his position. Third, work with other like-minded countries. In the case of Singapore, we work very closely with our ASEAN partners. Fourth, co-ordinate with interest groups, trade associations, and other organizations which support your cause. Fifth, enlist, where possible, the support of the American media.

Remarks prepared for presentation at a Panel Discussion organized by the Executive Council on Foreign Diplomats, Washington, D.C., 24 February 1989.

NEGOTIATIONS, BARGAINING AND THE CONDUCT OF DIPLOMACY

The Practice of Negotiations: Lessons from the UN

Rule 1

Invest both in serious preparation of the technical aspects of the problem and in an understanding of one's interests and of the other party's interests.

Example

At the beginning of UNCLOS III (the Third UN Conference on the Law of the Sea), many developing countries from Africa and Asia did not know what their interests were. They were therefore swayed by the emotional anti-colonial, anti-imperialistic rhetorics of the Latin American coastal states into supporting the latter's claims for extensive fishing zones and extensions of their continental shelves. It was not until the geographer of the US Department of State published a series of maps showing how a 200 mile Exclusive Economic Zone (EEZ) and extensions of the continental shelf to the continental margin would affect the various countries that they woke up to the fact that their national interests were different from those of the Latin American coastal states. This led to the formation of the Group of Land-locked and Geographically Disadvantaged States.

Rule 2

Use occasions for joint study and problem-solving exercises to lay the basis for a common approach.

Example

During UNCLOS III, I used universities and other non-governmental organizations to organize weekend retreats, seminars, to listen to the views of independent experts and to brainstorm. They served many useful purposes. First, they got the delegates away from the politicized atmosphere of the conference to a more informal and relaxed environment. Second, I encouraged participants to speak freely as they were invited in their individual capacities, not as representatives of their governments, and as no record was made of the statements. Third, it increased the knowledge of the delegates and closed the knowledge gap between the developed and the developing countries. Fourth, it threw up new ideas and options. Fifth, it helped to evolve a common approach.

Rule 3

Try to get the parties to agree on a common basis of facts.

Example

One of the most difficult areas of negotiations in UNCLOS III was in determining the financial terms of contracts to mine the manganese nodules in the deep sea-bed. Ideally, the financial terms of mining contracts should not be in the treaty. Why? Because we were dealing with an industry which does not yet exist and whose economics are very uncertain. However, because the US did not have confidence in the impartiality of the yet-to-be established International Sea-bed Authority, the US insisted that the financial terms of mining contracts had to be negotiated at the Conference and form part of the treaty.

The prospect looked daunting because there was no agreement on what the development costs of a mining project would be or the annual operating costs; there was also no agreement on what the revenues from the sale of the metals would be. Without agreement on these three basic parameters, it was not possible to even begin to negotiate. At this critical point, I chanced upon Professor Dan Nyhart's MIT Computer Model on the Economics of Ocean Mining.

First, I succeeded in winning the delegates' confidence in the objectivity of the MIT scholars.

Second, I persuaded the delegates to accept the parameters, viz. development costs, operating costs, revenues, in the MIT model.

Third, I succeeded in persuading the delegates in using the MIT computer model as an aid to our negotiations and to test various proposals in determining their effect on the investor's Internal Rate of Return (IROR).

Fourth, the computer model helped me to persuade the Conference to write a tax code which was flexible and progressive.

Rule 4

Focus on interests rather than on positions.

Example 1

During the course of UNCLOS III, the Soviet Union would often say that their position was based upon ideology and principle and was non-negotiable. My response was to avoid discussing their ideological position and to redirect the discussion to their interests. On all such occasions, we were able to find a compromise which accommodated their interests.

Example 2

On the composition of the Council of the International Sea-bed Authority and on its decision-making powers, the African Summit adopted a decision containing three "Nos" – no veto, no weighted voting and no guaranteed seat for the great powers. To overcome the three "Nos", I managed to persuade the Africans to give a guaranteed seat on the Council for the largest consumer of the metals, i.e. the US. I also succeeded in persuading them to accept consensus as the method of decision-making for the most critical list of questions. This meant that any one country, including the US, could block a consensus.

Example 3

This is an example of the triumph of position or ideology or principle over interests. In 1981 and 1982, after a change of government took place in the US, the new government (the Reagan Administration) demanded changes based upon both ideology and interests. The changes based upon interests were mostly taken care of but the changes that were demanded on the basis of free market principles were more difficult because not all members of the international community subscribe to those principles.

Rule 5

Try to put yourself in the position of the person on the other side of the negotiating table.

Rule 6

Look for a formula for agreement that encompasses the other party's needs as well as your own.

Rule 7

Don't make your negotiating adversary lose face.

Examples

These three rules are so axiomatic that they do not really need examples. If the purpose of a negotiation is to arrive at an agreement, there is no point in putting forward a proposal which does not encompass the other party's interests. The best way to understand what the interests of the other party are is to put yourself in his position. Ask yourself what your irreducible minimum interests are. Having understood that, try to design a proposal (or proposals) which, while advancing your interests, also accommodates the irreducible minimum of your negotiating counterpart.

Rule 8

Vary your negotiating tactics depending upon who your negotiating adversary is, what his negotiating style is, and what his opening position is. Ask yourself, is he taking a confrontational attitude or is he being flexible?

Rule 9

Never start out with your bottom line. Always leave room for concessions and trade-offs.

Rule 10

It is a good tactic to ask someone else to put forward your fall-back position as a compromise proposal.

Example

At the 1981 International Conference on Kampuchea, China began by adopting a confrontational attitude towards the ASEAN countries. We decided that on the first day of the negotiating session, we would hit the Chinese very hard in order to soften them up, before moving to a more compromising position on the second day.

At the same conference, the ASEAN side had worked out two fall-back positions. We gave them to two other delegations and requested them to put them forward as their own compromise proposals. They agreed to do so and appealed to China and ASEAN to accept the compromises. After asking for a recess to consult among ourselves, we went back to the negotiation and accepted the compromises.

Rule 11

Use constructive ambiguity only as a last resort. Why? Because it does not really settle the problem. It only postpones the disagreement to another day.

Example

At the 1981 International Conference on Kampuchea, one of the most contentious issues was between the PRC and ASEAN. In the event that Vietnam agreed to withdraw its troops from Cambodia, and prior to the holding of free elections under international supervision, the question was what to do with the armed Cambodians belonging to the different factions. In order to prevent the armed men from intimidating the voters and in order to prevent the Khmer Rouge from seizing power, ASEAN proposed that all armed Cambodians should either be disarmed or sequestered in camps. The PRC would have none of it. It argued that since the Khmer Rouge was the legitimate government of Cambodia at the time of the Vietnamese invasion, the Khmer Rouge forces should be allowed to retain their guns and remain at large. The issue was deadlocked. The final compromise was an example of "constructive ambiguity". It speaks of agreeing on modalities to ensure that the voters would be free of intimidation by armed men. Both ASEAN and China interpreted the compromise as a victory for their point of view.

Rule 12

Timing is essential. As the Bible says, there is a right time and a wrong time for everything. When the moment is ripe, exploit it to the full. Do not let the momentum fade away.

Example

In the negotiations of the financial terms of mining contracts, in the negotiations on the decision-making process in the Council of the International Sea-bed Authority and in the negotiations on the protection of preparatory investments in the deep sea-bed, a magical moment was reached when I could feel that matters were ripe for resolution and the timing was right. I chaired the negotiations around the clock, day after day, until all the loose ends were tied up and we were able to wrap up the package. It is difficult to anticipate when that magical moment will arrive. It could be triggered off by a whole variety of things – an approaching deadline, a new compromise proposal, a change in the atmospherics or for no apparent reason.

Talk given to the Law School of UCLA, 28 April 1986.

NEGOTIATIONS, BARGAINING AND THE CONDUCT OF DIPLOMACY

What Can We Learn from the Law of the Sea Conference?

The LOS Conference was not, exclusively, a North-South negotiation. In most areas, the negotiations were conducted between opposing groups which comprise both developed and developing countries. Geography, not ideology or development status, was the primary determinant of a country's interests in the Law of the Sea.

The only exception to the above was the negotiation on Part XI of the Convention. This part of the Convention deals with the mining of the mineral resources of the international area of the sea-bed and ocean floor. In this one area of the conference, the developing countries were able to harmonize their negotiating position through the Group of 77 (G77). The East European (Socialist) countries were also able to negotiate with a unified position. Group B, consisting of the developed market-economy countries, was unable to function in the LOS Conference. Instead, we found the following coalitions of developed countries. First, the five major industrialized countries, namely the US, UK, France, the Federal Republic of Germany (FRG) and Japan, closely co-ordinated their negotiating position. Secondly, although the EEC countries caucus regularly, they were not able to harmonize their differing views in this area of the work of the Conference. Thirdly, a group of small and medium-sized industrialized countries, viz. Australia, Canada, New Zealand, Denmark, Norway, Iceland, Sweden, Finland, Ireland, Austria and Switzerland, got together and at a critical point in the final session of the Conference, tried to act as a bridge-builder between the Group of 77 and the United States. Fourthly, two of the industrialized countries, Australia and Canada, which are land-based producers of the metals which are contained in manganese nodules, worked closely with the developing land-based producers. An interesting question is whether the absence of Group B was a help or a hindrance to the progress of the negotiations. My guess is that it was probably a help because it enabled the small and medium-sized industrialized countries to play an independent and constructive role.

Various attempts were made to miniaturize the negotiating forum. At the second session of the Conference, a negotiating forum consisting of 54 delegations was established. The meetings were, however, open-ended. After several sessions, this was not found to be an effective negotiating forum and was abandoned. In its place, the Conference established three negotiating groups, each of which was assigned a hard-core issue. When the three negotiating groups failed to find acceptable compromises to the three hard-core issues, the G77 made a bold proposal. The Group reasoned that since the three issues were closely inter-related, they should be negotiated in a single forum rather than in three fora. The Group also proposed the establishment of a small but representative negotiating forum, consisting of 21 members: ten from the Group of 77, eight from the West European and Others Group, two from the East European Group and China. The Working Group of 21 became the principal negotiating forum. The "real" negotiations did not, however, take place in the Working Group of 21.

When the moment was ripe, the President of the Conference conducted negotiations among a much smaller group of delegations. On the difficult issue of the financial terms of mining contracts, I conducted two rounds of negotiations. The first round was between three representatives of the G77, one from each of the three regional groups, and Ambassador Elliot Richardson of the United States, who had to represent all the industrialized market-economy countries. The second round was a negotiation I conducted personally with the Soviet Union. On the equally difficult issue of the decision-making producers of the Council of the International Seabed Authority, the G77 adopted a three-tier negotiating strategy. In the first round, six representatives of the Group negotiated only with the United States. Once agreement was reached, the Group of 77 invited the EEC and Japan to negotiate. Finally, the negotiation was between the Group of 77 and the Soviet Union. Although the outcome was successful and the strategy probably correct, France and the USSR objected strenuously to being relegated to the second and third tiers.

My observations on the question of the size of negotiating groups are as follows. First, it is not politically feasible, at the outset, to establish any negotiating forum of limited size. All delegations wish to have a sense of participation in the negotiating process. Those who have specific and concrete national interests at stake are reluctant to entrust them to others. Secondly, it is absolutely necessary when the time is ripe for the president of a conference, or the chairman of a negotiating group to select, on an *ad hoc* basis, a small number of delegates to carry out the negotiating process. In making such a selection, two criteria must be borne in mind. First, the group must be small enough to be effective. Secondly, it must include those delegates whose support for a compromise would ensure its ratification by the plenary. Thirdly, the negotiators must keep their constituent groups constantly informed on the state of the negotiations.

How did the Group of 77 perform during the LOS Conference? Given the diversity of interests which reside within the Group, it was remarkable that it was always able to reconcile the differences and to adopt a unified negotiating position. The manner in which the G77 worked in the LOS Conference differed slightly from the practices of the Group in Geneva and New York. In Geneva, the three regional sub-groups of G77 always caucus before the G77 meets in plenary. In New York, the three regional sub-groups do not meet. In the LOS Conference only the African Group insisted on caucusing before meetings of the Group of 77. Why did the African Group do so? It did so because the Organization of African Unity (OAU) Summits had adopted resolutions on the LOS Conference and the African delegations had to ensure that they did not deviate from such resolutions. The Group of 77 in the LOS Conference was therefore less rigid than the Group in Geneva and consequently, the representatives were able to negotiate with a higher degree of flexibility.

How did the G77 choose its leaders and negotiators? Formally, the group had a chairman and a co-ordinator in the Working Group of 21. The group did not choose a team of negotiators. What the chairman did, however, was to meet daily with a "cabinet" consisting of about 15 persons. How were they chosen? They were chosen on two bases. First, they were the veterans of the conference, persons with leadership qualities, with deep knowledge of the subject and demonstrated negotiating skills. Secondly, they included the troublemakers or extremists. By co-opting the second group, the chairman was able to compel them to moderate their views and to adopt a more positive and constructive attitude.

Another interesting feature of the LOS Conference was that although its rules of procedure envisaged voting when all efforts at achieving consensus have been exhausted, the Group of 77, which commanded a two-thirds majority in the conference, never asked for a vote on any substantive question. The Group of 77 understood that if it used its majoritarian power and imposed its views on an unwilling minority, the latter would walk away and the convention would be incapable of implementation. For this reason, the G77 behaved with admirable patience, moderation and accommodation. This should allay the fears of some industrialized countries who fear that the Group of 77 may impose its views on the minority in other fora.

A final word about the quality of delegates and the success of the Conference. There is an undeniable equation between the quality of the chairman of a conference, the quality of the delegates and the successful outcome of the conference. One cannot overemphasize the importance of choosing a chairman (or chairmen) who is knowledgeable, skilful and trusted by all delegations, and of having negotiators who possess the same qualities.

Remarks prepared on 20 May 1982.

NEGOTIATIONS, BARGAINING AND THE CONDUCT OF DIPLOMACY

The WTO's First Ministerial Conference: The Negotiating Process

Background

The dream of establishing a World Trade Organization (WTO) goes back to the 1940s when the victorious allies were planning the architecture of the post-Second World War world order. This resulted in the establishment of the United Nations and the Bretton Woods institutions. Because of some disagreement, the contracting parties were unable to agree on establishing the WTO. Instead, they adopted the General Agreement on Tariffs and Trade (GATT). The Uruguay Round of multilateral trade negotiations resurrected the dream and made it a reality.

The WTO consists of 127 contracting parties. As agreed to in Article IV of the agreement establishing the WTO, a ministerial meeting will be held once every two years. The first meeting was held in Singapore from 9 to 13 December 1996 (hereinafter referred to as "the Singapore Conference").

Agenda

What was the agenda of the Singapore Conference? The Singapore Conference had a four-point agenda:

(a) To assess the implementation of commitments under the WTO agreements and decisions;
(b) To review the ongoing negotiations and work programmes;
(c) To examine developments in world trade;
(d) To address the challenges of an evolving world economy.

For the US delegation, its most important agenda in Singapore was to negotiate an agreement to eliminate tariff for trade in information technology products. Miraculously, an Information Technology Agreement (ITA) was adopted in Singapore.

Negotiating Text

Every negotiating conference should begin with a negotiating text or texts. We need a text or texts to focus our minds and to ascertain the points of convergence and divergence. Did the Singapore Conference begin with a single negotiating text?

The answer was technically, "no", but substantively, "yes". Let me explain. For many months, the Director-General of the WTO, Renato Ruggiero, had been holding consultations with the representatives of the contracting parties in Geneva. The purpose of the consultations was to agree on the text of a draft ministerial declaration for Singapore. Although the negotiators worked very hard, even through several all-night meetings, they were unable to agree on a clean text to send to Singapore. The most difficult issues were left unresolved. In view of this development, the Singapore team shifted from a partying mode to a work mode! We prepared ourselves, intellectually and psychologically, for our rendezvous with history.

On 29 November 1996, Renato Ruggiero wrote a long letter to the Trade Ministers of the 127 contracting parties. His letter contained an account of the negotiations in Geneva. It also contained the texts on which there was agreement, the texts on which there was no agreement, and the texts on which there was agreement in substance but which were being held up by some delegations for tactical reasons.

There were 12 clean paragraphs. There were four other paragraphs on which there was no disagreement on substance, but which were being held up for tactical reasons. Two paragraphs, on agriculture and information technology, were pending. Finally, there were four issues on which the positions of the delegations were far apart. These were:

(a) Trade and transparency in government procurement;
(b) Trade and investment;
(c) Trade and competition policy;
(d) Trade and core labour standards.

The first question which the Chairman and the WTO Director-General had to decide on was whether to re-issue the latter's letter of 29 November 1996, either in its original, or in a modified form, as the single negotiating text of the Singapore Conference. It was decided against doing so because, technically, the Director-General's letter had never been approved by the contracting parties. It was, however, agreed that it was essential to protect against amendment the 12 clean paragraphs and the four paragraphs which were being held up for tactical reasons. Therefore, at the first informal meeting of the Heads of Delegations, held on Monday, 9 December 1996, the Chairman proposed and the meeting agreed not to re-open any paragraph or text on which there was agreement in Geneva. The Chairman gavelled this decision through so quickly that the meeting broke up in laughter. I subsequently advised the Chairman to count to five before bringing the gavel down! I wish, however, to reiterate an important point: in order to make progress and to prevent regress, it is essential for the chairman of a negotiation to focus the negotiation on disputed text and to prevent agreed text from being re-opened.

The Negotiating Process

The Singapore Conference had four and a half days, actually only four days, from Monday, 9 December, to Thursday, 12 December, to wrap up the negotiations. The Secretariat needed the morning of Friday, 13 December, to process the documents. The Singapore Conference was scheduled to adjourn by lunchtime on Friday, 13 December.

How did we do it? What was the nature of the negotiating process? Was it centralized or de-centralized? Was it transparent or opaque? How did we reconcile the conflict between the aspirations of the 127 delegations to participate in the negotiation and the reality that in order to negotiate fruitfully, we had to shrink the number to a manageable size? What was the division of labour between the Chairman and his team of advisers and the Director-General and his team? How did the Chairman decide when to go from a big group to a small group? What were the key constituencies? Who were their leaders? What lessons can we learn from the negotiating process of the Singapore Conference?

The Chairman and Secretariat

First, one of the positive features of the Singapore Conference was the ability of the Chairman, Yeo Cheow Tong, and the WTO Director-General, Renato Ruggiero, to work as a team. The good chemistry between the two leaders was transmitted down to their team of advisers. There were no ego problems. The Chairman's team and the Secretariat team worked very well together. We met several times a day, brainstorming on substance and strategy. We helped each other with the drafting.

The Conference Bureau

Second, the Chairman and his Vice-Chairmen also worked well as a team. The Chairman, the Director-General and the Vice-Chairmen met every morning to review the work of the previous day and to preview the programme of the day. This group performed the role of the Conference bureau. The Vice-Chairmen also helped the Chairman by taking turns to chair the Plenary, thereby freeing the Chairman from this responsibility. The Chairman was therefore able to devote himself to conducting the negotiations.

Bilateral Consultations

Third, the Chairman and the Director-General spent the whole weekend, Saturday, 7 December, and Sunday, 8 December, holding bilateral meetings with various Heads of Delegations. Some of these meetings were arranged at the request of the various Ministers. Others were arranged at the request of the Chairman and the Director-General. From Monday, 9 December, to Thursday, 12 December, there were also breakfast meetings with various delegations. Those bilateral meetings enabled the Chairman and the Director-General to accomplish several things:

(a) To touch base with the Ministers of influential delegations and to earn their goodwill;
(b) To listen to their concerns;
(c) To solicit their advice and help;
(d) To get a sense of the lay of the land.

Unitary Process

Fourth, in order to save time and to hold himself in reserve, the Chairman's thinking on the morning of Monday, 9 December, was to establish two parallel negotiating groups. Each group would be chaired by a Minister to be designated by the Chairman after consultation. The first group would deal with trade and core labour standards. The second group would deal with trade and investment. The feedback from delegations, especially from the developed countries, was unfavourable. They wanted a unitary process chaired by the Chairman. They argued that it would take too long to agree on who would chair the two negotiating groups. Therefore, it was decided to have a unitary negotiating process and not a decentralized one.

Conference Democracy

Fifth, a conference chairman has to reconcile two competing demands: the demand of democracy and the demand of realism. Conference democracy requires the chairman to design a transparent, inclusive, negotiating process in which all delegations can participate. In order to satisfy this demand, the Chairman convened regular, almost daily, informal meetings of all Heads of Delegations (HOD). Because of its size, the HOD meetings could not be used as a negotiating forum. The HOD meetings served three useful purposes:

(a) They enabled the Chairman to brief all delegations on the state of the negotiations;
(b) They were used by the Chairman to ratify the results of negotiations conducted elsewhere;
(c) They gave delegations an opportunity to hold the Conference leadership accountable.

The Green Room

Sixth, it was necessary to make a transition from the HOD meeting, involving 127 delegations, to a smaller negotiating group. How small? Who to include? When to make the transition? These were three of the important questions which the Chairman and the Director-General had to decide on. Fortunately, they did not have to start from scratch. There is a tradition in the GATT, which seems to have been transferred to the WTO, for about 35 key delegations to meet in the so-called "Green Room".[1] Contrary to the perceptions of some scholars and journalists, it is not true that the Green Room was dominated by the developed countries or the big countries. Of the 35 members, 26 belonged to the Group of 77. Indeed, of the 15 members of the Group of 15 (G15), 11 were in the Green Room. However, the least developed countries were under-represented. Only two of its 29 members, Bangladesh and Tanzania, were members of the Green Room.

The Green Room negotiating process began on Tuesday, 10 December. I remember that the Chairman and the Director-General discussed the question of timing. They decided that Monday would be too soon and Wednesday might be too late. We also took care to select a room big enough to accommodate 35 Ministers sitting at a conference table but not big enough to accommodate many more. Each Minister was allowed to bring one official who sat behind the Minister. A severe looking conference officer was stationed outside the door to keep out gatecrashers. Once the Green Room negotiating process began, the group acquired a life and momentum which carried us through Tuesday, Wednesday and Thursday. On two occasions, we met till the early hours of the morning. Most of the negotiation at the Singapore Conference took place in the Green Room.

Beyond the Green Room

Seventh, the two most difficult issues – trade and core labour standards, and trade and investment – were not negotiated in the Green Room. They were negotiated in even smaller fora. The eventual compromise on trade and investment was negotiated in a meeting between the European Union and India, chaired by the Chairman and the Director-General. The result of the negotiation was then ratified, in turn, by the Green Room negotiating group, the HOD and the Plenary. In a similar way, the issue of trade and core labour standards was substantially resolved in a negotiating group in the Chairman's office, which consisted of the United States, the European Communities, India, Pakistan, Egypt, South Africa, Chile and Morocco. The six developing countries were carefully chosen to represent three hardliners and three moderates. The Chairman could get away with such a process because it was done at the end of the Singapore Conference, when everyone was desperate for agreement; it was done with the knowledge and implicit approval of the Green Room; and the result was brought back to the Green Room.

Conclusion

As a student of the negotiating process, what lessons have I learned from the Singapore Conference? I should begin with a caveat. Every negotiation is, in some respects, unique. It is therefore not always possible to draw general lessons from one negotiation which can be applied to other negotiations. This does not, however, mean that there are no general lessons. Let me suggest a few which we can deduce from the Singapore Conference.

First, encourage the Chairman and the Secretariat to work as a team. Second, the Chairman should use the Secretariat and his Vice-Chairmen, as a collegium or bureau, to organize the conference. Third, preceding the start of a conference, as well as during it, the Chairman should hold extensive bilateral and multilateral consultations. Fourth, begin with a negotiating text or texts. Fifth, focus the negotiation on the disputed language in the text and prevent agreed text from being re-opened. Sixth, design a negotiating process which accommodates the demand for democracy, on the one hand, and the demands of realism, on the other. Seventh, judge the timing very carefully. When the time is ripe, move decisively from a big negotiating group to a small negotiating group and, if necessary, to an even smaller negotiating group. Eighth, earn the trust of your colleagues. If they trust you, they are more likely to accept the need to move from democracy to realism. If they do not trust you, they are less likely to accept such a necessity.

Speech given at the Book Launch of the Singapore Society of International Law, 19 March 1997.

NOTES

1. The "Green Room" negotiating process is an informal caucus of key negotiators at international meetings and conferences.

SETTING THE GLOBAL AGENDA: THE LAW OF THE SEA AND THE ENVIRONMENT

The Achievements and Implications of the Third UN Conference on the Law of the Sea

As I promised you yesterday, we have kept our rendezvous with history today. We have, after eight years of hard work, at last reached the mountain top.

The journey to the mountain top actually began not in 1973, when the Third United Nations Conference on the Law of the Sea commenced its work, but in 1967. In that year, the then Permanent Representative of Malta, Professor Arvid Pardo, made a historic statement in the First Committee of the UN General Assembly. That statement launched us on our journey. Professor Pardo is amongst us today and I take this opportunity to pay a well deserved tribute to him.

From 1967, when the Ad Hoc Committee on the Sea-bed and Ocean Floor beyond the Limits of National Jurisdiction was established, until his untimely death in 1980, the Captain of our ship was my beloved friend, Hamilton Shirley Amerasinghe. It is, I think, fitting on this historic day for us to remember him and to acknowledge our debt and gratitude to his contribution. As I have said before, let us make the new Convention on the Law of the Sea our lasting monument to our beloved late President, Hamilton Shirley Amerasinghe.

Dear colleagues,[1] you and I are like the proud parents of a newborn baby. It is natural for us to feel proud of our achievement. We are not, however, the most objective persons to evaluate the merits or demerits of the Convention which we have just adopted. Intellectual humility dictates that we be restrained in praising the product of our own work and that we let history vindicate or condemn us.

I hope that I am not departing from the tradition of intellectual humility in which all scholars are educated if I were to point out some of the unique feelings of this Convention, its importance to the international community and the unique methods of work of our Conference.

First, this is the first comprehensive Convention covering all aspects of the uses and resources of ocean space. In this respect, it is, therefore, different from the Geneva Conventions of 1958 which covered only limited aspects of the Law of the Sea.

Second, in this Convention we have not merely codified existing international law; we have also created many new and innovative concepts of international law, such as the Exclusive Economic Zone (EEZ) and the common heritage of mankind. The new and innovative concepts of international law contained in our Convention were negotiated and agreed upon in response to the advancement of technology, to the demands for greater international equity, especially by the new nations, and by new uses of the sea and its resources.

Third, the Convention contains important and agreed limits on different maritime zones of coastal states, agreed regimes of passage for ships through and aircraft over the critical sea-lanes of the world and clearly established rights and obligations of coastal states and third states in the territorial sea, in the exclusive economic zone and in the continental shelf. In this way, the Convention will have made a significant contribution to the promotion of peace and security and to law and order in the ocean space.

Fourth, for many developing land-locked states, one of the most important benefits of this Convention is the agreement it contains on the freedom of transit and the right of access of land-locked states to and from the sea.

Fifth, the Convention contains important provisions on the protection and preservation of the marine environment. In their totality, these provisions represent a significant advance in our common struggle to prevent, reduce and control pollution of the marine environment.

Sixth, this Convention has made a significant contribution to the elaboration of a comprehensive set of rules on marine scientific research and the promotion of international co-operation in the field of marine technology.

Seventh, unlike most other treaties under which there are no mandatory provisions on the settlement of disputes, a unique feature of our Convention is that it does contain mandatory provisions on the settlement of disputes. This is another contribution to the pacific settlement of disputes between States and the promotion of the concept of world peace through law.

Eighth, for those of us who feel deeply for the preservation of marine mammals, especially whales and dolphins, our Convention does enjoin States to co-operate, through appropriate international organizations, for their conservation, management and study. It is true that this is only a small step but it is a step in the right direction.

Finally, I wish to make a brief reference to Part XI of the Convention dealing with the exploration and exploitation of the resources of the international area of the sea-bed and ocean floor. This part of the Convention was essentially negotiated between the developing countries on one side, the Western industrialized countries on the second, and the Socialist states of Eastern Europe on the third. The relatively successful outcome of the negotiations on Part XI demonstrates that it is possible for North and South, East and West to co-operate with one another, to acknowledge each other's interests and to seek mutually acceptable solutions. In a world which is often marked by confrontation, misunderstanding and even by violence, it is no exaggeration for me to say that at least in this particular Conference, nations from every ideological and geographical group have eschewed the path of confrontation in favour of co-operation. The majority at the Conference, i.e. the developing countries, have not imposed their majoritarian power on the minority, and the minority of powerful states have tried to accommodate the legitimate interests of the less powerful states. This has been, if I may say so, a very successful exercise of North-South negotiations, in spite of the fact that we were unable to adopt the Convention by consensus, as was the fervent wish of all delegations.

The successful outcome of this Conference is important for the prestige and credibility of the UN. It shows that the United Nations can be an effective forum for important multilateral negotiations on issues of vital importance to all states and to the international community as a whole.

In conclusion, I would like to acknowledge my debt to my colleagues in the Collegium with whom I have always worked as a united team. I wish also to express the appreciation of the Conference to the Chairmen of all the negotiating groups and to all members of the Secretariat under the able and effective leadership of my dear friend, Bernardo Zuleta.

Now that we have adopted our Convention, we must go back to our respective countries and promote public understanding of its importance so that our governments and our parliaments will be convinced to sign and ratify it in a timely manner. I hope that the delegations which voted against and abstained on the Convention will, after further reflection, find it possible to support the Convention.

Statement delivered at the Third United Nations Conference on the Law of the Sea, 30 April 1982.

NOTES

1. Ambassador Koh made these remarks in his capacity as President of the Third United Nations Conference on the Law of the Sea (UNCLOS III) at the close of the Conference.

SETTING THE GLOBAL AGENDA: THE LAW OF THE SEA AND THE ENVIRONMENT

Negotiating a New World Order for the Sea

The UN Convention on the Law of the Sea (1982) took almost nine years to negotiate. The opposition of the United States notwithstanding, the treaty represents one of the major achievements of the UN during the past decade. During the last two years of the Third UN Conference on the Law of the Sea (UNCLOS III), I was privileged to serve as its President. In what follows, I shall attempt to tell the remarkable story of negotiating a new world order for more than two-thirds of the surface of the earth.

I shall divide my lecture into five parts. In the first part, I shall trace briefly the evolution of the traditional law of the sea. In the second part, I shall discuss the different forces which eroded and finally brought about the collapse of the old legal order and the convening of the Third UN Conference on the Law of the Sea in December 1973. In the third part, I shall give some examples of the subjects and issues which were negotiated at that Conference. I shall discuss the nature of the competing interests which had to be reconciled and the mutual accommodations which were arrived at. In the fourth part, I shall discuss some of the more interesting, perhaps even unique, features of the negotiating process. In the fifth and final part of my lecture, I shall seek to answer the question: What is the significance of the new legal order governing the uses and resources of the world's oceans embodied in the 1982 UN Convention on the Law of the Sea?

The Evolution of the Traditional Law of the Sea

From the end of the 15th century to the beginning of the 19th century, the law concerning the uses and resources of the sea was unsettled. There were two contending schools of thought. The first school, Mare Clausum, believed that the sea and its resources were capable of being subject to appropriation and dominion.

The second school of thought, called Mare Liberum, was brilliantly expounded by Hugo Grotius in the legal opinion he wrote for the Dutch East India Company. He argued that things which cannot be seized or enclosed, cannot become property. According to Grotius, on the high seas, no one can claim dominion or exclusive fisheries rights or an exclusive right of navigation.

In the course of the 18th century, the Grotian view came gradually to predominate over the opposing view. Coastal states were permitted to claim a narrow belt of the sea off their coasts for the purpose of fishing, as well as for neutrality. Beyond that belt, the sea and its resources were *res communis* and subject to the freedom of the sea.

By the beginning of the 19th century, after the end of the Napoleonic Wars and the Congress of Vienna, the three-mile territorial sea became almost universally accepted. Great Britain, which emerged from the Napoleonic Wars as the world's greatest power, on land as well as at sea, became the champion for the three-mile territorial sea. It was logical for her to adopt such a position because, as Lord Strang has explained:

> *In manufacture, in merchant marine, in foreign trade, in international finance, we had no rival ... As we came, by deliberate act of policy, to adopt the practice of free trade and to apply the principle of all seas freely open to all, we moved towards Pax Britannica, using the Royal Navy to keep the seas open for the common benefit, to suppress piracy and the slave trade, and to prepare and publish charts of every ocean.*

The Collapse of the Old Legal Order

An American scholar, Sayre A. Swarztrauber, has suggested that the old legal order which prevailed for over 100 years, began its decline in 1930. In that year, under the auspices of the League of Nations, the Hague Codification Conference was held. The objective of the Conference was to codify the international law on the territorial sea. Forty-eight states attended the Conference. Of the 48 states, only ten favoured a three-mile territorial sea. Seven states favoured a three-mile territorial sea, provided a contiguous zone was added. Six states favoured a six-mile territorial sea. Six others wanted a six-mile territorial sea together with a contiguous zone. Because the views were so divergent, no formal vote was taken on any of the proposals. A possible compromise consisting of a three-mile territorial sea and a nine-mile contiguous zone was squashed by strong British opposition. The 1930 Conference, therefore, ended in failure. Swarztrauber has argued that by allowing the Conference to fail, "the great maritime powers ended their oligarchical maintenance of the maxim Mare Liverum. The Conference suggested to all that the great powers were no longer committed to the enforcement of the three-mile limit".

The second blow against the traditional law of the sea was struck, ironically, by the country which eclipsed Great Britain in both naval and land power following the Second World War. It should have been clear to the United States that the burden of defending the principle of the freedom of the seas, in general, and the three-mile territorial sea, in particular, could no longer be borne by the British. The mantle had passed from the British to the United States. However, instead of defending the traditional law, the United States led the way in changing the old legal order.

In 1945, President Truman issued two proclamations relating to the sea. In the first proclamation, the United States asserted its jurisdiction and control over the natural resources of the subsoil and sea-bed of the continental shelf contiguous to the United States coast. The term "continental shelf" was described as generally extending to the point where the waters reached a depth of 600 feet or 200 metres isobath. In the second proclamation, the world was informed that the United States "regards it as proper to establish conservation zones in those areas of the high seas contiguous to the coast of the United States wherein fishing activities have been or in future may be developed and maintained on a substantial scale ..." The proclamation provided that the conservation zones would be established and maintained through agreement with those states whose subjects traditionally fish the areas in question.

The unilateral actions of the United States were immediately emulated and exceeded by her regional neighbours. Mexico issued a similar proclamation one month after the United States. A year later, Argentina not only claimed sovereignty over her continental shelf but also to the water column above the shelf. Between 1946 and 1957, ten other states claimed sovereignty over their continental shelves and the superjacent waters. Between 1947 and 1955, five Latin American states declared 200-mile limits for exclusive fishing rights.

In 1958, the UN held its First Conference on the Law of the Sea. The Conference succeeded in adopting four conventions: the Convention on the Territorial Sea and the Contiguous Zone, the Convention on Fishing and Conservation of the Living Resources of the High Seas, the Convention on the High Seas, and the Convention on the Continental Shelf. The Conference, however, failed to arrive at agreed limits on the territorial sea and on the coastal states' exclusive fishing rights. In the case of the Convention on the Continental Shelf, the rights of the coastal state were to extend "to a depth of 200 metres or, beyond that limit, to where the depth of the superjacent waters admits the exploitation of the natural resources". The second of the two criteria, i.e. the exploitability criterion, was imprecise and would soon give rise to trouble. In 1960, the UN held its Second Conference on the Law of the Sea to attempt to find agreement on the limits of the territorial sea and fishing zone. The attempt failed.

In the decade of the 1960s, the British, Dutch and French colonial empires were broken up. Their former colonies in Asia, Africa and the Caribbean attained independence, joined the UN and became new members of the international community. Most of these newly independent countries had not participated in the 1958 UN Conference on the Law of the Sea. They also felt dissatisfied with the traditional law which they regarded as the product of European experience. They, therefore, wanted an opportunity to remould the international Law of the Sea to reflect their aspirations and their interests.

In the fall of 1967, the then Permanent Representative of Malta to the UN, Professor Arvid Pardo, drew the attention of the world to the immense resources of the sea-bed and ocean floor, beyond the limits of national jurisdiction. He proposed that the sea-bed and ocean floor should be used exclusively for peaceful purposes and the area and its resources should be considered the common heritage of mankind. The UN established a Sea-bed Committee to examine the question and to elaborate a legal regime for the exploration and exploitation of the resources of the area.

At about the same time, the Soviet Union approached the United States and other countries on the idea of recognizing a 12-mile territorial sea, provided that a high-seas corridor was preserved in international straits. In 1968 and 1969, the United States started sounding out the views of its NATO partners, the Soviet Union and other countries on the idea of conceding 12 miles as the maximum permissible breadth of the territorial sea in return for free navigation of warships and overflight of military aircraft in and over straits used for international navigation.

By 1970, it was clear to all that the old legal order had collapsed. Support for the convening of a Third UN Conference on the Law of the Sea therefore seemed logical and timely. It was needed to resolve the unfinished business of the First and Second UN Conferences, viz. the limit of the territorial sea, the limit of the fishing zone, and to replace the exploitability criterion by a more precise criterion. It was necessary to replace the chaos created by the unilateral and conflicting claims of coastal states with a new legal order. The great maritime powers, especially the two superpowers, felt the need for a new internationally agreed upon regime for the passage of ships and aircraft through and over straits used for international navigation. The newly independent countries of the Third World wanted a new conference so that they could participate in the progressive development of this branch of international law. The international community had to agree on rules, as well as institutions, for the exploitation of the mineral resources in the sea-bed and ocean floor beyond the limits of national jurisdiction. Finally, the historic Stockholm Conference on the Human Environment and a series of accidents involving oil tankers had raised the world's consciousness regarding the threat to the marine environment and there was a consequent desire to adopt new rules to protect and preserve that environment.

Issues Negotiated at the Third UN Conference on the Law of the Sea

The agenda of UNCLOS III consisted of 25 subjects and issues. It will not be possible for me to discuss each of these subjects and issues. What I intend to do is to pick a number of examples and to explain in each case what the competing interests were, and how those competing interests were reconciled.

Let me begin by discussing the related subjects of the maximum breadth of the territorial sea and the regime of passage through straits used for international navigation. I have already referred to the fact that at the 1930 Conference, as well as at the 1958 and 1960 Conferences, the international community was unable to agree on the maximum breadth of the territorial sea. By the time UNCLOS III convened, only a minority of states claimed a three-mile territorial sea. The majority claimed a territorial sea of 12 miles. The great powers could not accept 12 miles as the maximum permissible breadth of the territorial sea unless it was also agreed that there would be a special regime of passage for ships and aircraft through and over straits used for international navigation. This was because there are about 116 straits in the world whose breadths are between six and 24 miles. With the extension of the territorial sea from three to 12 miles, the waters in these straits would become territorial waters and the high seas corridor would be lost.

The United States and the Soviet Union are global powers with allies and interests in areas far from their shores. They need to use the seas and the air space above for the purpose of projecting their conventional military power. Freedom of navigation for their navy and overflight for their military aircraft is, therefore, a strategic imperative. Since the straits constitute choke points in the world's communications system, the question of passage through, over and under them is therefore critical. The nuclear arsenals of the two superpowers are based on land, and in aircraft and submarines. Each superpower keeps part of its stockpile of ballistic missiles in submarines at sea. It is important for each superpower not to know the precise location of its adversary's submarines because this works as a deterrent against either of them launching a first strike against the other. The theory is that if one superpower launches a first strike and succeeds in destroying part or substantially all of its adversary's land-based ballistic missiles, the victim will retaliate by launching its submarine-based ballistic missiles at the aggressor. As long as each superpower retains a second strike capability, this acts as a deterrence against the temptation of launching a sneak attack. Since secrecy and mobility of their respective submarine fleets are critical, the two superpowers have therefore demanded free and submerged passage through straits for their submarines.

The UN Convention has sought to reconcile the competing interests of coastal states, on the one hand, and of the great maritime powers, on the other. The Convention recognizes 12 miles as the maximum permissible breadth of the territorial sea. At the same time, it prescribes a special regime, called transit passage, for ships and aircraft through and over straits used for international navigation. The Convention uses the words "freedom of navigation and overflight" to describe the nature of transit passage. It is significant that these are words which are normally used in connection with the high seas. The regime of transit passage is applicable to warships as well as to military aircraft. Submarines may also transit a strait used for international navigation in submerged passage.

The second example I would like to discuss is fisheries. There were at least four competing interests which the Conference had to reconcile. First, there was mankind's interest in the conservation as well as optimum utilization of the fish resources of the world. Mankind's interest would be hurt if certain fish stocks were to be overexploited and to become extinct or dangerously depleted. At the same time, mankind has an interest in promoting the optimum utilization of the world's fish resources because they constitute the cheapest source of animal protein for many countries and peoples. The second interest was the interest of the coastal states. In many coastal countries, there are coastal communities which depend solely or mainly on fishing for their livelihood. Many of these coastal countries complained that the traditional law was unfair in several ways. It was unfair because these coastal countries, especially the developing coastal countries, were unable to compete with the technologically more advanced countries in catching the fish stocks which lie off their coasts. They complained that under the traditional law, beyond the narrow belt of the territorial sea, the fish stocks constitute a common property. Being a common property, many of the fish stocks have become dangerously depleted due to overfishing and the regional fisheries commissions have not been given sufficient powers to enforce conservation measures. For these reasons, the coastal states claimed the right to establish economic zones of up to 200 miles within which they would have sovereign rights to the resources. Thirdly, the Conference had to take into account the interest of land-locked and geographically disadvantaged states which would either have nothing to gain or would have something to lose, if such economic zones were established. Fourthly, the Conference had also to take into account the interest of distant-water fishing nations which had invested large sums of money in their fishing industries and which, in some cases, have been fishing in certain fishing grounds for a considerable length of time.

The provisions of the Convention on the Exclusive Economic Zone have sought to reconcile these competing interests. Every coastal state is entitled to establish an exclusive economic zone of up to 200 miles. Within such a zone, the coastal state has sovereign rights to its living resources. The coastal state is, however, under an obligation to the international community to undertake conservation measures in order to ensure that the living resources in its economic zone are not overexploited. At the same time, the coastal state is obliged to fix the total allowable catch of the different species in order to ensure the optimum utilization of the resources. If the coastal state is unable to harvest the entire allowable catch, it is under an obligation to allocate the surplus to third states. The first priority will go to land-locked and geographically disadvantaged states. The second priority will go to developing countries. The third priority will go to other countries, including the traditional fishing nations.

The third example which I would like to discuss concerns the mineral resources of the sea-bed and ocean floor outside the limits of national jurisdiction. The main form of the mineral resources are polymetallic nodules which are also known as manganese nodules. It will be recalled that in 1967, Professor Arvid Pardo of Malta called the world's attention to the existence of these resources and proposed that the sea-bed and ocean floor outside the then prevailing limits of national jurisdiction, as well as the resources, should be declared a common heritage of mankind. In 1970, the UN General Assembly adopted the declaration of principles governing the sea-bed and ocean floor, and the subsoil thereof, beyond the limits of national jurisdiction by a vote of 108 in favour (including the United States), none against, with 14 abstentions. Although the Soviet bloc abstained in the vote, they subsequently declared their support for the declaration. The declaration states, *inter alia*, that the area will not be subject to appropriation by states or by other entities and that no state shall claim or exercise sovereignty or sovereign rights over any part thereof. The declaration also states that no state or other entity shall claim, exercise or acquire rights with respect to the area or its resources incompatible with the international regime to be established and with the principles of the declaration. All activities regarding the exploration and exploitation of the resources of the area shall be governed by the international regime to be established.

In the negotiations on this question, the Conference had to reconcile the following competing interests. First, the interest of the international community in promoting the development of the sea-bed's resources. Secondly, the interest of those members of the international community which are the consumers of the metals which can be extracted from the polymetallic nodules. Thirdly, the interest of those countries which have invested funds or are planning to invest funds in developing the technical capability to mine the polymetallic nodules. Fourthly, the interest of the developing countries which, as co-owners of the resource, wish not only to share in the benefits of the exploitation of such resources, but also to participate in such exploitation. Fifthly, the interest of those countries which produce in their land territories, the metals which are contained in the polymetallic nodules.

The provisions of Part XI of the Convention, of Annex III and of Resolution II, taken together, contain compromises which seek to accommodate these competing interests. Under Resolution II, the consortia and states which have already invested research and development funds in the exploration of specific mine sites have been recognized as a pioneer investor. If the state to which a consortium belongs signs the Convention, the consortium may be registered as a pioneer investor. In the case of a consortium which is unincorporated and which consists of partners from a number of different countries, the consortium may be registered as a pioneer investor if only one of the countries to which the consortium partners belong signs the Convention. Upon being registered as a pioneer investor, the consortium acquires the exclusive right to explore the specific mine site. When the Convention comes into force, the registered pioneer investor, so long as it complies with the requirements of the Convention and so long as its sponsoring state becomes a party to the Convention, has an automatic right to a contract to mine that specific mine site. Thus, the troublesome question about guaranteed access to the resources of the deep sea-bed has been resolved by Resolution II.

In order to give land-based producers some protection against the possible adverse economic consequences of sea-bed exploitation, the Convention contains a formula for limiting the amounts of metals which can be produced from the sea-bed for a period of 25 years. Resolution II states that the pioneer investors shall have priority in the allocation of the production authorization calculated under the formula. According to the experts, the production limitation in the Convention poses more of an ideological than a pragmatic problem for the sea-bed miners. This is because, given the economic prospects of the mining industry in the foreseeable future and the limited number of actors which are likely to enter the industry, any reasonable projection will give us a number of mine sites which will be adequate to accommodate all those who are likely to want to enter this industry.

A sea-bed miner will have to pay to the International Sea-bed Authority either a royalty payment or a combination of a royalty payment and a share of his profits. The sea-bed miner may choose either one of the two schemes. If he chooses the latter, he will find a tax structure which is more progressive than any to be found in land-based mining contracts. The tax which a sea-bed miner pays to the International Sea-bed Authority will vary, depending upon the profitability of his project, and will be calculated annually, as well as over the lifespan of the project. The tax system uses the internal rate of return (IROR) as the measurement of the project's profitability.

Under the Convention, a sea-bed miner may be required by the International Sea-bed Authority to sell his technology to the Authority. This obligation has caused great concern to industrialized countries. It should be borne in mind, however, that the obligation cannot be invoked by the Authority unless the same or equivalent technology is not available in the open market. An internal study carried out by the US Department of Commerce shows that for every component of sea-bed mining technology, there are at least four sellers on the market. If this is true, then the precondition cannot be met and the obligation can never be invoked.

Some Unique Features of the Negotiating Process

The negotiating process of UNCLOS III contains many interesting, and even unique, features. Let me simply mention some of the highlights. The Conference committed itself from the very start to work by the procedure of consensus. An appendix to the Rules of Procedure states, "the Conference should make every effort to reach agreement on substantive matters by way of consensus and there should be no voting on such matters until all efforts at consensus have been exhausted". Why did the Conference place such an emphasis on consensus? It did so for two reasons. The Conference wanted to adopt a convention which would enjoy the widest possible support in the international community. The consensus procedure was intended to protect the interest and views of minorities in the Conference.

There were two other important procedural understandings. The Conference agreed to work on the package deal principle. This meant that the Conference would adopt one comprehensive convention instead of several conventions, as happened at the 1958 Conference. The other understanding was that the Convention would not permit any reservations.

The commitment of the Conference to the procedure of consensus was buttressed by its Rules of Procedure. The rules make it very difficult to vote on a proposal or an amendment. They also make it difficult for such a proposal or amendment to be adopted by vote. For example, when a matter of substance comes up for voting for the first time, either the President or 15 delegations may request a deferment of a vote for a period not exceeding 10 days. During this period, the President shall make every effort to facilitate the achievement of general agreement. At the end of the period, the President shall inform the Conference of the results of his efforts. A vote on a proposal may be taken only after the Conference has determined that all efforts at reaching agreement have been exhausted.

At the last session of the Conference, 30 amendments were submitted to the Draft Convention package. I ordered a cooling-off period of ten days. During this period, I found that there was general support for only four of the amendments. These were adopted by the Conference without a vote. I managed to persuade the proposers of the remaining amendments to withdraw, with the exception of three. All three amendments were put to the vote and rejected by the Conference. One of them obtained the required two-thirds majority of those present and voting but it failed to satisfy the second requirement of obtaining the support of a majority of the delegations attending that session of the Conference.

Another interesting feature of the Conference was the emergence of new interest groups. The traditional groups, such as regional groups, played a very minor role in the work of the Conference. Instead, groups were formed by countries which have kindred interests, such as the group of coastal states, the group of land-locked and geographically disadvantaged states, the group of straits states, the group of archipelagic states and many others. The group system at the Conference played both a positive and a negative role. On the positive side, it enabled countries to join forces with other countries with which they shared a common interest. In this way, a country would acquire a bargaining leverage which it would not have, if it were to operate alone. It was not possible to conduct serious negotiations at the Conference until these special interest groups were formed. It was only after their formation that the competing groups were able to formulate their positions in concrete texts and to appoint representatives to engage in negotiations. On the negative side, it must be admitted that once a group had adopted a common position, it was often difficult for the group to modify its position. This often meant that the negotiators were given a mandate, with little or no flexibility.

Yet another unique feature of the negotiating process was the fact that there were two parallel structures of negotiations at the Conference. On the one hand, there were the officially established committees and negotiating groups. Because there were generally forums of the whole, they were too large to function effectively as negotiating forums. The need for small but representative negotiating bodies was filled by the establishment of informal and unofficial negotiating groups. Most of these groups were established on the initiative of individuals. The Evensen Group of juridical experts was established at the personal initiative of Jens Evensen, the leader of the Norwegian delegation. The Evensen Group did extremely valuable work on the exclusive economic zone. The Castaneda Group, convened by the leader of the Mexican delegation, Jorge Castaneda, succeeded in resolving the controversial question of the legal status of the economic zone and related issues. There was also a private group on dispute settlement which was convened on the initiative of Professor Louis Sohn of the United States. Sometimes, an unofficial negotiating group was formed on the initiative of two competing groups. This happened when the group of coastal states and the group of land-locked and geographically disadvantaged states agreed to establish a negotiating group comprising ten representatives from each group and approached Ambassador Satya Nandan of Fiji to be its Chairman.

Towards the later stages of the Conference, the other presiding officers of the Conference and I gradually miniaturized the size of the official negotiating groups. It was absolutely essential to transform a large, unwieldy Conference of approximately 140 delegations into small, representative and efficient negotiating groups. Although the efforts to miniaturize the official negotiating forums encountered resistance, they were essential and were ultimately successful.

Another lesson which I have learnt is that a conference needs formal, informal and even privately convened negotiating groups. As a general rule, the more informal the nature of the group, the easier it is to resolve a problem. However, secrecy must be avoided and if the results of a negotiating group are to have any chance of winning the support of the conference, then the group must include all those who have a real interest at stake, as well as the conference leaders.

The Significance of the New Legal Order Embodied in the 1982 UN Convention on the Law of the Sea

What is the significance of the new Convention on the Law of the Sea? Its first significance is that it is the first comprehensive Convention governing all aspects of the uses and resources of the world's oceans. Unlike the four Geneva Conventions of 1958, the new Convention has tried to respect the inter-relationships between different aspects of the Law of the Sea. It has also tried to live up to Professor Arvid Pardo's exhortation to view ocean space as an ecological whole.

The second significance of the Convention is that it represents the most ambitious effort at the codification and progressive development of international law undertaken by the international community since the creation of the United Nations. The new Convention does not merely codify the pre-existing law. It contains many new and innovative concepts, such as the concept of transit passage through straits used for international navigation; the concept of archipelagic baselines and archipelagic sea-lanes passage; the concept of the exclusive economic zone; the fundamental change in the legal definition of the continental shelf; the explicit recognition of the freedom of scientific research and of the freedom to construct artificial islands and other installations as additional freedoms of the high seas; the duty of international co-operation in the development and transfer of marine science and technology; and the concept of a comprehensive environmental Law of the Sea based on the obligation of all states to protect and preserve the marine environment.

The third significance of the Convention is that it will contribute to the promotion of international peace. It will do this by replacing a plethora of conflicting claims by coastal states with universally agreed limits for the territorial sea, the contiguous zone, the exclusive economic zone and the continental shelf. Fourthly, the Convention represents a victory of the rule of law. It is the first major multilateral treaty which contains mandatory provisions for the settlement of disputes. Fifthly, the Convention affirms the possibility for countries of the North and South, East and West to co-operate for their mutual benefits. Finally, the successful outcome of UNCLOS III vindicates the United Nations as an institution which, given the necessary political will by its member states, can be used to conduct serious negotiations on matters of vital importance to the member states.

The William L. Clayton Lecture, delivered at the ASEAN Auditorium to the Fletcher School of Law and Diplomacy, Tufts University, 23 February 1984.

SETTING THE GLOBAL AGENDA: THE LAW OF THE SEA AND THE ENVIRONMENT

The UN Convention on the Law of the Sea: Implications for Singapore and the Region

Background

The date 16 November 1994 is a very significant date in the development of international law and in the history of the United Nations. On this date, exactly one year after the 60th state deposited an instrument of ratification or accession with the United Nations, the 1982 United Nations Convention on the Law of the Sea will enter into force.

The 1982 United Nations Convention on the Law of the Sea, commonly referred to as UNCLOS, is one of the most significant achievements of the international community since the founding of the United Nations. The 1982 Convention was the culmination of eight years of negotiations at the Third UN Conference on the Law of the Sea. More than 150 countries, representing all regions of the world, all political systems, and all degrees of socio-economic development participated in these negotiations. Never before had the international community taken on so monumental a challenge in international negotiation and law-making.

The 1982 Convention aimed to establised a "constitution for the oceans", that is, a comprehensive regime dealing with all matters relating to the Law of the Sea which would remain viable into the next century. Its text comprises 320 articles and nine annexes which were intended to establish the principles and rules governing the use of ocean space.

As the 1982 Convention will enter into force today, almost 12 years after it was completed for signature, it seems appropriate to undertake a review of the Convention, and assess the significance of its entry into force for Singapore and the region.

Major Provisions of the Convention

Certain portions of the 1982 Convention, such as those relating to the high seas, were a codification of existing rules of international law. Other provisions, however, were new. They were often the result of long and arduous negotiations among the various groups of states, such as the major coastal states (who were often most interested in extending their rights and jurisdiction over a larger area of ocean space) and the major maritime and naval powers (who were most interested in preserving traditional freedoms of navigation and overflight). Many provisions of the 1982 Convention reflect delicate compromises designed to protect the competing interests of various groups of states.

Expanded Rights of Coastal and Archipelagic States

The 1982 Convention resolved the existing controversies relating to the breadth of the territorial sea, the right of coastal states to claim an exclusive fishing zone or exclusive economic zone, and the right of mid-ocean archipelagic states to claim archipelagic waters. Under the 1982 Convention, coastal states can claim a 12 nautical mile territorial sea. They can also claim a 200 nautical mile exclusive economic zone, where they have sovereign rights over the living and non-living resources. The 1982 Convention also recognized that mid-ocean archipelagic states such as Indonesia and the Philippines can draw straight baselines connecting the outermost points of their outermost islands, and claim the waters within the baselines as their archipelagic waters.

Rights of Passage Made More Secure

At the same time as the 1982 Convention extends the rights and jurisdiction of the coastal states, it also protects the interests of other states by preserving their right to passage on routes used for international navigation and international aviation, even when such routes are through international straits, exclusive economic zones and archipelagoes. The provisions of the 1982 Convention on international straits, archipelagoes and the exclusive economic zone reflect this delicate balance between the interests of the coastal states and the interests of the user states.

Protection of the Marine Environment

Another major achievement of the Convention is that it is the first global convention which contains comprehensive provisions placing obligations on all states to take measures to prevent, reduce and control pollution of the marine environment. It also contains provisions designed to enhance the world community's interest in the conservation and optimum utilization of the living resources of the oceans.

Mandatory Settlement of Disputes

The 1982 Convention is also significant in that it contains the most sophisticated system ever devised for the mandatory settlement of disputes arising from the interpretation or application of its provisions.

Common Heritage of Mankind

Finally, the Convention provided that the resources of the deep sea-bed were the common heritage of mankind, and contained detailed provisions which attempted to establish principles, institutions and arrangements for a fair and workable system governing their exploitation.

Deep Sea-bed Provisions and the 1994 Amendment Agreement

Most of the 60 states which ratified the Convention prior to 1994 were developing countries from the African regional group or the Latin American/Caribbean regional group. Only one developed state from Western Europe – Iceland – was among the first 60. Indonesia and the Philippines were the only Asian countries among the first 60. Two other Asian states, Sri Lanka and Vietnam, ratified the Convention in 1994.

The major reason why more developed countries have not ratified the Convention is that the United States and many of its Western allies were unhappy with the provisions in Part XI relating to deep sea-bed mining. Because of this, the United States refused to sign the Convention in 1982, and most of the developed countries have refused to ratify it. This dispute between the First and Third world countries over Part XI threatened to prevent the Convention from ever becoming universally acceptable.

However, recent developments at the United Nations may result in the Convention becoming universally accepted in the near future. On 28 July 1994, the General Assembly adopted a resolution which contained an Agreement relating to the implementation of Part XI of the 1982 Convention by a vote of 121–0–7. The effect of this Agreement is to amend the deep sea-bed mining provisions in Part XI of the Convention. The resolution and the Agreement are the result of four years of informal consultations convened by the UN Secretary-General and conducted by Ambassador Satya Nandan of Fiji. The consultations were with a group of states representing all regions and interest groups, including the United States, Germany and the United Kingdom. The Agreement represents a compromise which was agreed to by representatives of the Group of 77, as well as the major OECD states.

The terms of the Agreement are ingeniously drafted to encourage states to become parties to the Agreement (and to the 1982 Convention) as soon as possible. The Agreement also contains a unique procedure to allow for its provisional application and for provisional membership of the Authority (the body charged with responsibility for administering Part XI on the deep sea-bed). Under the terms of the Agreement, all states which voted for its adoption in the General Assembly are to apply it provisionally from 16 November 1994. Also, until the Agreement enters into force, all states which are applying it provisionally automatically become provisional members of the Authority, with the same rights and obligations as full members. As of 7 November 1994, 65 states, including many OECD and developing countries, have signed the Agreement. In addition, two important developed states, Germany and Australia, ratified the Agreement in October, and thereby became parties to both the Convention and the Agreement.

Given these developments, it is likely that more developed countries will follow the lead of Germany and Australia, and that consequently, the 1982 Convention as amended by the 1994 Agreement, will become universally acceptable by the year 2000.

Matters Not Dealt with Adequately in the Convention

Though comprehensive, the 1982 Convention does not contain provisions which will resolve all of the important issues relating to the oceans. For example, the Convention has no provisions on the resolution of competing claims to sovereignty over disputed islands or territory such as the Spratly Islands in the South China Sea. Also, although the Convention contains a comprehensive system for the mandatory settlement of disputes, existing territorial disputes between states are not subject to the mandatory system of dispute settlement.

The provisions of the Convention governing the exploitation of fisheries resources on the high seas, as well as straddling stocks and highly migratory species, proved to be inadequate. As a consequence, a UN conference has been convened to supplement the Convention's provisions relating to these issues.

Significance of the Entry into Force for Parties

The Convention's entry into force on 16 November will be significant for states which have deposited instruments of ratification or accession in at least two respects. First, because the provisions in the Convention will be binding between parties, such states will finally have a comprehensive, clear and predictable set of principles and rules governing their conduct in ocean matters. Second, in most situations where there is a dispute between two such states as to the interpretation or application of the provisions of the Convention, the compulsory system for the settlement of disputes set out in Part XV of the Convention will be available as a means of resolving the dispute. A meeting is being convened in New York on 21 and 22 November to establish the International Tribunal for the Law of Sea, which is a special tribunal created under the 1982 Convention.

One impact of the coming into force of the 1982 Convention will be that states which are parties to the Convention are likely to undertake a review of their policies, practices and legislation relating to the Law of the Sea to determine whether they are consistent with their obligations under the 1982 Convention. For example, states which have issued maps or coordinates for their maritime boundaries which are based upon the use of straight baselines, such as Indonesia, are likely to review their method of drawing the straight baselines to determine whether they are in conformity with the provisions of the 1982 Convention. Also, parties to the Convention are likely to review their laws and practices to ensure that they are fulfilling their obligations relating to the protection and preservation of the marine environment and the conservation and management of living resources in their exclusive economic zones.

Significance of Entry into Force for Non-Parties

Although only parties to an international convention are strictly bound by its provisions, an international law-making treaty like the 1982 Convention has a significant impact on all states, even on those which are not parties. During the past 12 years, the 1982 Convention has become the primary source and pre-eminent authority for the modern Law of the Sea, and has had a dominant influence on the conduct of most states. Its influence can be seen in domestic legislation, in state practice, and in bilateral and regional arrangements and agreements.

It is generally agreed by international lawyers that many of the substantive provisions in the 1982 Convention are binding on states under customary international law, even if they have not become parties to it. This is because most of its provisions (except those relating to the deep sea-bed) reflect generally accepted principles and practices prior to the Convention or principles and practices which have become generally accepted since the Convention was adopted.

The entry into force of the 1982 Convention and the adoption of the 1994 Agreement relating to the implementation of Part XI is likely to induce most states to review their position on the 1982 Convention to determine whether it would be in their interests to ratify the 1994 Agreement and the 1982 Convention.

If the major OECD countries do ratify the 1982 Convention (as amended by the 1994 Agreement) and it becomes universally acceptable among all groups of states, the provisions of the 1982 Convention will have even greater force as the best evidence of existing rules of customary international law governing the Law of the Sea. The provisions of the 1982 Convention will therefore have great impact on all states, whether or not they have chosen to formally become parties to it. A major difference, however, will be that states which do not become parties will not be able to invoke the compulsory system of dispute settlement which is set out in the Convention.

Advantages of Ratification for Singapore and the Region

If all of the ASEAN countries and other states in the region were to ratify the 1982 Convention as amended by the 1994 Agreement, there would be several advantages for Singapore and the region. First, because there would be a clear set of legal rules governing the uses of the marine areas in the region, and setting out the rights, jurisdiction and obligations of states, misunderstandings or conflicts arising because of differing views as to what rules are applicable would be less likely. Second, if disputes do arise between states in the region as to the interpretation or application of the rules in the Convention, the states concerned will have the option of invoking the compulsory system of dispute settlement under the Convention. With a wider choice of means for resolving disputes by peaceful means, states are less likely to resort to other means.

A third advantage of ratification for Singapore and the region is that the 1982 Convention would serve as a framework for co-operation at the regional and subregional level. In many areas, such as the protection of the marine environment, the 1982 Convention merely provides the basic structure and framework. It envisages that states will co-operate at the regional and subregional level to fully address certain types of issues. An example in this region is the Straits of Malacca and Singapore. The problems of safety of navigation and protection of the marine environment cannot be resolved without the co-operative efforts of the three bordering states. If all three states were parties to the 1982 Convention, they would have agreed that the basic rules governing the Straits of Malacca and Singapore are those set out in the Convention on straits used for international navigation. It would then be easier for them to explore ways and means to co-operate to improve the safety of navigation and to protect the marine environment within the framework of the 1982 Convention. The provisions of the Convention do not allow the straits states to impose levies on ships passing through the straits. The Convention does, however, enjoin the straits states and the major user states to co-operate with one another. The International Maritime Organization (IMO) could play a helpful role by bringing the interested parties together.

Article (co-authored by Associate Professor Robert Beckman of the Faculty of Law, National University of Singapore) published in ***The Straits Times****, 12 November 1994.*

The Environment in Southeast Asia: Prospects for Co-operation and Conflict

I will divide my talk into three sections. First, I will update you on preparations for the 1992 UN Conference on Environment and Development. The popular media has referred to the Conference as the Earth Summit because the UN General Assembly has recommended that it be attended by Heads of States and Governments. The Summit will be held in Rio de Janeiro, Brazil, from 1 to 12 June this year. Second, I will discuss the prospects for co-operation and conflict between and among the countries of Southeast Asia. Third, I will discuss the prospects for co-operation and conflict between states within the region and those outside the region.

I

Twenty Years after Stockholm

The Earth Summit will be held 20 years after the historic UN Conference on the Human Environment, which was held in Stockholm, Sweden, from 5 to 16 June 1972. The Stockholm Conference was historic for several reasons. It was the first meeting of the governments of the world to consider what actions they should take, at the national, subregional, regional and global levels to preserve and enhance the human environment. The Conference raised the consciousness of the peoples and governments throughout the world. In one sense, the Conference was a success even before it was held. During the preparatory phase, many governments established, for the first time, ministries or departments on the environment or environment protection agencies. After Stockholm, the environment has become a permanent item on national, regional and global agendas.

Apart from consciousness-raising, the Stockholm Conference achieved three concrete results. It adopted a Declaration of Principles, a Plan of Action and created a new UN agency, the UN Environment Programme (UNEP). The Declaration contains 26 principles which, over time, have affected the behaviour of governments as well as contributed to the evolution of customary international law on the environment. One of these principles, No. 21, is perhaps worth recalling: "States have the responsibility to ensure that activities within their jurisdiction or control do not cause damage to the environment of other states or of areas beyond the limits of national jurisdiction". In other words, there is no such thing as absolute sovereignty over the use of your natural resources or environment. Your sovereignty is limited by your obligation not to cause damage to the environment of other states or areas beyond your national jurisdiction, such as the global commons.

Differences between Stockholm and Rio Conferences

There is a major difference between the Stockholm Conference and the Earth Summit. At Stockholm, the Conference had a single focus on how to preserve and enhance the human environment. In Rio, the Summit will have a double foci: environment and development and, specifically, on how to reconcile mankind's desire for economic progress on the one hand, with the need to protect our environment on the other. Because of its double foci, the Earth Summit is a more complex and difficult conference than the Stockholm Conference. Indeed, some sceptics believe that there is an inherent and irreconcilable conflict between the two objectives. I do not agree with this view. I believe that it is possible to strike a balance between environment and development. Experts call such development, which is environmentally friendly, "sustainable development". The experience of Singapore during the last 25 years suggests that sustainable development works; that concern for the environment does not have to impede a country's economic growth.

Possible Output of the Earth Summit

Two years ago, the UN General Assembly established a committee to prepare for the Earth Summit. I am the Chairman of the Preparatory Committee. The Committee has held an organizational session in New

York and three substantive sessions in Nairobi (once) and Geneva (twice). The last session of the Committee will be held in March in New York. Although the Committee has made steady progress, much remains to be done. There is still a considerable gulf between the developed and developing countries to be bridged. Success is therefore not assured. However, if the Earth Summit succeeds, it could be one of the most important conferences of this decade.

What can the Earth Summit achieve?

First, an "Earth Charter" containing the principles governing environmental and developmental relations between states, and between states and peoples to ensure our common security.

Second, two new conventions on climate change and biological diversity.

Third, a statement of principles on the management and conservation of all types of forests.

Fourth, "Agenda 21", which will contain the over 300 programmes which are currently being negotiated, including agreements on how the programmes will be financed and how the transfer of environmentally sound technology from developed to developing countries will be facilitated.

Fifth, agreement on institutional reform.

II

Intra-Regional Co-operation and Conflict

Within Southeast Asia, the six ASEAN countries have been co-operating in the field of the environment, both bilaterally and multilaterally. Let me briefly refer to four aspects of their co-operation.

ASEAN Environment Programme (ASEP)

The ASEAN Environment Programme (ASEP) was started in 1978. The objective of ASEP is to promote the proper management of the ASEAN environment so that it can sustain continued economic development while maintaining a high quality of life for the peoples of the ASEAN countries. The fourth meeting of the ASEAN Ministers for the Environment was held in Kuala Lumpur in June 1990. The meeting adopted an Accord on Environment and Development which reaffirmed ASEAN's commitment to the pursuit of sustainable development. ASEP is likely to be succeeded by an "ASEAN Common Plan for Environmentally Sound and Sustainable Development to Year 2000" (ASCEND 2000).

ASEAN Senior Officials on the Environment (ASOEN)

In June 1990, a committee consisting of the ASEAN Senior Officials on the Environment (ASOEN) was established. The Committee will report directly to the ASEAN Standing Committee (ASC). ASOEN has set up the following six working groups:

1. ASEAN Seas and Marine Environment chaired by Brunei;
2. Environmental Economics chaired by Indonesia;
3. Nature Conservation chaired by Malaysia;
4. Environmental Management chaired by the Philippines;
5. Transboundary Pollution chaired by Singapore; and
6. Environmental Information, Public Awareness and Education chaired by Thailand.

At the second ASOEN meeting in June 1991, the meeting accepted a proposal by the World Wildlife Fund (WWF) to establish an ASEAN Subregional Environmental Trust (ASSET), to serve as a new, assured and sustained financial mechanism for the implementation of ASEAN environmental programmes. The third meeting of ASOEN will be held later this month in the Philippines.

Co-ordinating Body on the Seas of East Asia (COBSEA)

Another form of regional co-operation relating to the environment is the Co-ordinating Body on the Seas of East Asia (COBSEA). Following UNEP's very successful initiative in bringing together the littoral states of the Mediterranean Sea to work together for the purpose of reducing marine pollution in the Mediterranean Sea, UNEP has launched a series of regional seas programmes. The East Asian Seas Action Plan is one such programme. Its objective is to promote the better management and protection of the region's marine environment through projects financed by the East Asian

Seas Trust Fund and the UNEP Environment Fund. The members of COBSEA are: Indonesia, Malaysia, Philippines, Singapore and Thailand. Brunei is an observer.

Bilateral Co-operation

Singapore has established joint committees on the environment with Malaysia and Indonesia. The Malaysia-Singapore Joint Committee on the Environment (MSJCE) was formed in 1990. Since its formation, the committee has met once in Malaysia and once in Singapore. The issues discussed at the first two meetings centred on emission standards for vehicles and control of fuel quality; improvement of water quality in the Straits of Johor; management of the movement of hazardous chemical and toxic wastes; and air quality monitoring and joint consultations on emission from industries.

The Indonesia-Singapore Joint Committee on the Environment (ISJCE) was established in November 1991. The first meeting of the joint committee is scheduled for March 1992. The meeting will discuss several proposed joint programmes and other bilateral environmental issues. The issues include joint environmental quality monitoring; standardization of environmental quality standards; development of land-use planning and resource conservation strategies; and management of hazardous materials and co-ordination of emergency response systems.

More Co-operation or Conflict?

Are the prospects for more co-operation or more conflict among the states of Southeast Asia? I think the prospects are for more co-operation, not conflict. The countries of ASEAN have already acquired the habit of consultation and the skill of problem-solving through mutual accommodation. I have every reason to believe that these habits and skills will be applied in the field of the environment. Two events in 1991 have reinforced the need for greater co-ordination and co-operation, both at the bilateral and subregional levels. The first was the eruption of Mount Pinatubo in the Philippines. The ashes from the eruption reached Malaysia and Singapore. The second was the forest fires in Indonesia. For several weeks, the skies over Singapore and peninsular Malaysia were darkened by a haze. These two incidents also explode the myth that transboundary air pollution is unknown between developing countries.

III

Relations between Intra and Extra-Regional States

Countries within Southeast Asia can have co-operation or conflicting relations with countries outside the region with respect to the environment. The ASEAN countries have worked closely with other developing countries in co-ordinating their positions on environmental issues in various international forums. In recent years, environmental movements in several developed countries in the West have mounted campaigns against the rate at which the rain forests in Southeast Asia, especially those in Indonesia and Malaysia, are being felled. The campaigns of the environmental lobbies have had varying degrees of impact on their governments. The Prime Minister of Malaysia has reacted strongly to such campaigns and charges. In my view, it is better for the developed countries and the developing countries of Southeast Asia to work together, on the basis of mutual respect, to help the latter pursue the path of sustainable development. Finger pointing and mutual recrimination are easy to do, but they are counterproductive. They raise the temperature but produce little light.

Let me suggest a few specific steps.

First, the developed countries should try to create a more supportive international economic environment which would reduce the burden of the developing countries as they embrace sustainable development.

Second, the developed countries should encourage the development of environmentally sound technologies and facilitate the flow of such technologies to the countries of Southeast Asia.

Third, the developed countries should ensure that there would be adequate financial resources and proper funding mechanisms to implement the various conventions and programmes being negotiated.

Fourth, the developed countries should refrain from translating their environmental concerns into new trade barriers.

Fifth, the developed countries should consider expanding the concept of foreign aid to include subsidizing the costs of environmental improvements by recipient countries.

Conclusion

The countries of Southeast Asia, especially ASEAN, have a bright economic future. They are in a good position to embrace sustainable development and to show other countries in the Third World that it is possible for developing countries to reconcile environment with development. To achieve this goal, the countries within Southeast Asia should co-operate with one another and with countries outside the region. The ASEAN countries have made a good beginning in environmental co-operation. I am confident that such co-operation will be broadened and deepened in the coming years. I would also urge ASEAN and her dialogue partners to eschew confrontation in favour of co-operation over the environment. Economic progress and care for the environment should unite, not divide us.

Talk given at the Fourth Southeast Asia Forum, Kuala Lumpur, 17 January 1992.

SETTING THE GLOBAL AGENDA: THE LAW OF THE SEA AND THE ENVIRONMENT

The Earth Summit: Success or Failure?

The Earth Summit is the child of the Stockholm Conference on the Human Environment. Twenty years ago, the leaders and peoples of the world met in Stockholm to call for a halt to environmental degradation. As a result of Stockholm, more than 100 countries established ministries of the environment or environmental protection agencies. The international community established the UN Environment Programme (UNEP), based in Nairobi, Kenya. Environment became an important item on the global agenda.

Growth in Harmony with Nature

However, the Stockholm Conference did not address the linkage between development and environment. The intellectual breakthrough in Rio is that we have a global consensus in favour of both development and environment. To put it simply, the consensus is that in order to alleviate poverty and to give people a better life, we must continue to achieve economic progress. We must, however, do so in harmony with nature. Henceforth, every economic or development policy or project will be subjected to an environmental policy or project will be subjected to an environmental cost/benefit analysis. Likewise, every environmental policy or project will be subjected to a development cost/benefit analysis.

New Global Partnership

The second breakthrough in Rio is of a political character. The end of the Cold War gives us an opportunity to overcome past divisions and to forge a new global partnership. The countries of Eastern Europe are going through a painful transition process. They are no longer in a position to give aid to the developing countries. Instead, they are competing with developing countries for aid from the West. This gave rise to a conflict in Rio between the Group of 77 and Eastern Europe. The Chairman of the Main Committee settled the conflict by maintaining the priority of developing countries but drawing special attention to the needs of the countries in Eastern Europe. With this conflict resolved, we can say that there is a new global partnership, embracing North and South, East and West, to achieve sustainable development. This global solidarity was evidenced by the fact that 172 countries attended the Summit, 116 countries were represented by their Heads of State or Government, and all the texts were adopted without a vote.

Rio's Achievements

What are the concrete achievements of the Earth Summit?

Convention on Climate Change

First, 154 states (including the European Community) signed the Framework Convention on Climate Change. The Convention has been severely criticized by many states as being weak and inadequate. The Convention sets no limits for the emission of greenhouse gases, especially carbon dioxide, and no time-frames for achieving such limits. Several delegations have proposed an early meeting of States Parties in order to consider the feasibility of taking the next step, i.e., to negotiate a protocol on carbon dioxide. At present, the United States and Saudi Arabia are opposed to taking such a step.

Convention on Biological Diversity

Second, 153 states (including the European Community) signed the Convention on Biological Diversity. President Bush's complaints against the Convention sounded hollow and he effectively isolated the United States when the EC, Japan and other developed countries decided not to follow the United States but to sign the Convention. The chapter in Agenda 21 on Biological Diversity contains agreed language on the fair and equitable sharing of benefits derived from research and development and use of biological and genetic resources; promotion of national registration related to biological resources; and technology transfer.

Rio Declaration on Environment and Development

Third, the Summit adopted the text of the Rio Declaration which was negotiated in New York at PrepCom IV. The Declaration contains 27 principles. The Rio Declaration is neither short nor inspirational. Those who want it to read like the ten commandments are naturally disappointed. They do not understand that the ten commandments cannot be negotiated by a UN committee. They have suggested that in 1995, when the UN will celebrate its 50th birthday, a fresh attempt be made to negotiate an "Earth Charter". Like the Universal Declaration of Human Rights, the Rio Declaration can, however, influence the evolution of customary international law on the environment and inspire the international community to negotiate legal instruments.

Agenda 21

Fourth, the Summit has adopted an ambitious plan of action called "Agenda 21". It contains 40 chapters and covers the whole range of environmental problems, such as atmosphere, deserts and forests, as well as cross-sectoral issues, such as finance and technology. The UNCED Secretariat has estimated that the annual cost to the international community of implementing Agenda 21 is US$125 billion. It is, of course, impossible to mobilize such resources at this time. The only sensible approach is to transmit these proposed programmes of activities to the relevant UN agencies for refinement and adoption, and to stagger their implementation in such a way as to reconcile programmes with resources.

Forests

One of the hard-core issues in Rio was the question of forests. The subject was inherently difficult because we have to balance the national interests of states to exploit their forests and the international community's interest to preserve forests as carbon sinks. The inherent difficulty of the question was compounded by the political agenda of President Bush and Prime Minister Mahathir. Under attack by the environmental community and the media, Bush tried to capture the moral high ground by proposing to protect the forests of other countries. He called for an international convention to promote the sustainable management of forests. Mahathir, on the other hand, accused the West of hypocrisy and opposed any reference to an international convention on forests. Both sides could, however, agree to adopt a statement of principles.

The Main Committee was unable to resolve this question. It was finally resolved, at the ministerial level, in a negotiation chaired by the German Minister for the Environment, Klaus Toepfer. The agreement was to adopt a non-legally binding but authoritative statement of principles and a chapter in Agenda 21 on forests. The US agreed to give up its insistence on a forest convention in return for agreement "to consider the need for and the feasibility of all kinds of appropriate internationally agreed arrangements to promote international co-operation on forest management ..."

To Combat Desertification

Of all the issues on the UNCED agenda, the most important to the Africans was the question of combating desertification. Desertification is a threat to the global environment. Its victims are primarily but not exclusively Africans. Some countries in Asia and Latin America are also affected by this phenomenon. The Africans had pleaded, for years, for an international convention to fight desertification. Their pleas had fallen on deaf ears. With the end of the Cold War, the Africans feel completely neglected.

The Chairman of the Main Committee decided that the plea of the Africans had merit. He managed to convince the United States to agree to request the 47th UN General Assembly to appoint an inter-governmental negotiating committee to negotiate an international convention to combat desertification. He resisted an attempt by the United Kingdom to link a desertification convention with a forestry convention.

Fishing on the High Seas

One of the unresolved issues in the law of the sea concerns the sustainable management of two kinds of fish stocks. The first is a fish stock which straddles the national jurisdiction of two or more states. The second is a highly migratory species such as tuna. If the international community does not co-operate, in accordance with the Law of the Sea Convention, to manage such fish stocks sustainably, there is a danger that they could be overfished. This is an issue which divides Canada and the coastal states from the EC, especially Spain.

The Chairman of the Main Committee requested Tucker Scully of the United States to chair an open-ended consultation on this and other issues relating to the chapter on the oceans. At the same time, he put public and private pressure on the EC to settle the dispute. Agreement was finally reached to convene an inter-governmental conference with a view to promoting the effective implementation of the provisions of the Law of the Sea Convention on straddling fish stocks and highly migratory fish stocks. Canada and the Latin Americans have requested Ambassador Koh to chair the said conference. He has declined.

Financial Resources

For the developing countries as a group, the most important chapter of Agenda 21, is Chapter 33 on finance. It is expected that developing countries would carry the primary burden of financing the programmes in Agenda 21. The developing countries, however, expect the developed countries to assist by providing about 20 per cent of the total costs. This must be new money and not money taken from existing programmes. The phrase, "new and additional resources" is intended to convey this meaning.

The negotiations on finance were particularly difficult because at the end of the PrepCom IV, there was not only no agreement but there was not even a common basis for negotiations. The Chairman of the Main Committee established a negotiation group on finance and appointed Ambassador Reubens Recupero of Brazil to chair the group. Recupero, assisted by Joe Wheeler from the Secretariat, did a wonderful job. At the completion of the work of the Main Committee, there were four paragraphs with bracketed language. These were referred to the plenary for further negotiations. The Dutch Minister for Development, Jan Pronk, helped to secure agreement on a paragraph referring to Official Development Assistance (ODA).

What is the final package on finance? The compromise contains three elements. The first element is that the developed countries committed themselves to providing "new and additional resources" for financing Agenda 21. The developed countries agreed to make known their plans at the forthcoming session of the UN General Assembly. It is difficult to compute the amounts which were announced in Rio because they were not symmetrical. The second element concerns the International Development Agency (IDA) of the World Bank. The compromise text refers to a statement which the President of the World Bank made to the Earth Summit. In his statement, Lewis Preston said that the tenth replenishment of the IDA should match the level of the ninth replenishment "in real terms". He also proposed creating an "Earth Increment" in the IDA. The third element is that the developing countries agreed to give up the idea of a "Green Fund" in return for a restructured Global Environment Facility (GEF), which is managed jointly by the World Bank, UNDP and UNEP.

Transfer of Technology

The transfer of environmentally sound technology from developed to developing countries was another of the hard-core issues. In Rio, the Chairman of the Main Committee appointed the Dutch Minister for the Environment, J.G.M. Alders, to chair a negotiating group on this chapter (Chapter 34). As a result of the negotiations, the developing countries agreed to give up their demand for the compulsory acquisition of privately-owned technology. It was also agreed that environmentally sound technology would be transferred:

> *... on favourable terms, including on concessional and preferential terms, as mutually agreed, taking into account the need to protect intellectual property rights as well as the special needs of developing countries for the implementation of Agenda 21.*

Israel versus the PLO

PrepCom IV adopted the text of the Rio Declaration on Environment and Development and transmitted it to Rio "for further consideration and finalization". During the interval between the end of PrepCom IV and Rio, the growing feeling among delegations was to adopt the text of the Declaration as negotiated in New York and not to re-open it. The United States and Israel could accept the Rio Declaration, including Principle 23, which refers to the environment and natural resources of people under occupation, provided that the words "people under occupation" and "organizations under occupation" were deleted from the text of Agenda 21.

The Chairman of the Main Committee personally conducted the consultations with the US and the PLO. He was assisted in these consultations by Algeria, Egypt, Iran, Jordan and Tunisia. Eventually, he succeeded in persuading the PLO to give up the two phrases in Agenda 21. In return, he gave them a phrase in the preamble of Agenda 21 which links the two documents. Both Israel and the PLO could live with this compromise.

Post-Rio Institutional Process

The road to Rio has been a very challenging one. The road from Rio is equally important because of the need to monitor the implementation of Agenda 21 and to promote the objective of sustainable development. The Earth Summit agreed to establish a new functional commission of the UN Economic and Social Council (ECOSOC) on sustainable development. The commission is described as "high-level", meaning that it will meet at the level of ministers. The decision to establish the commission will be taken at the 47th Session of the UN General Assembly. The UN Secretary-General intends to appoint a new Co-ordinator for Sustainable Development, at the level of Under-Secretary General. In Rio, he offered the job to Ambassador Koh, who turned it down.

Was Rio a Success or Failure?

In the coming days and months, the media will continue to ask, was the Earth Summit a success or failure? Was it merely a photo opportunity? Do the three documents adopted in Rio, namely, the Rio Declaration, Agenda 21 and the Statement of Principles on Forests, have any substantive content or are they only empty words? The final judgement can only be rendered by history. The view of the Singapore delegation is that Rio was a success and that the agreements and compromises adopted were substantive and the best that could be achieved under the contemporary circumstances of the world.

Singapore's Interests and Role

Singapore's chairmanship of the Preparatory Committee and the Main Committee of the Earth Summit has earned the country goodwill and credit. Singapore could continue to play a pro-active and leadership role in environmental diplomacy. In the decade of the 1970s, Singapore achieved prominence in the international community through its leadership role in the UN Conference on the Law of the Sea. In the decade of the 1980s, Singapore maintained a position of influence, far beyond its size, because of Cambodia. In the decade of the 1990s, Singapore has an opportunity to play an active role in sustainable development, helping to find consensus between the various actors in the international arena. Such a role would be consistent with our desire to be useful to others. It would also be consonant with our objective of presenting Singapore as an environment city to the world. The Singapore delegation to the UN in New York should therefore play an active and constructive role at the 47th Session of the UN General Assembly in the negotiations on the post-Rio institutional arrangements. Thereafter, Singapore should seek election to the Commission on Sustainable Development. This is one of those rare occasions when virtue is married to self-interest.

Overview of the UN Conference on Environment and Development prepared 15 June 1992.

SETTING THE GLOBAL AGENDA: THE LAW OF THE SEA AND THE ENVIRONMENT

The Challenge of Sustainable Development

Mr Chairman, colleagues and friends, I would like to thank the Chairman and members of the Commission on Sustainable Development (CSD) for inviting me to speak to you. Although I played a small part in the conception and birth of the CSD, this is the first time that I will have the pleasure of appearing before the Commission. The Chairman has allocated ten minutes to each of us. I wish to share five thoughts with you.

First, I think the most important environmental challenge facing humankind is the protection of the atmosphere. The Framework Convention on Climate Change which we signed in Rio and which has been ratified by over 150 states is an important first step. It is analogous to the Vienna Convention for the Protection of the Ozone Layer. Just as the Vienna Convention was followed by the Montreal Protocol, so must the Framework Convention be followed by additional agreements to limit the emission of greenhouse gases. A few months ago, scientists from over 120 countries met and agreed that, on the basis of the best scientific evidence, global warming has begun. If this is true it will have dire consequences for the whole human family but especially for the small island developing countries. This is not an issue which should divide North and South. To be sure, the North has generated the most greenhouse gases and must be willing to make the most sacrifice. However, it is also a problem for the South. Rapid economic growth and increased standards of living must lead inevitably to the higher consumption of energy. Let me cite China and India as two examples. Given the size of their countries, their demands for energy, and their reliance on coal, they have the potential to pollute the world. The developed world must help China and India to satisfy their demands for energy but to do so in an environmentally sound manner. Developed and developing countries must therefore join hands to reconcile, on the one hand, our need for energy, and, on the other hand, our need to protect the atmosphere.

Second, although the CSD is supposed to be cross-sectoral and holistic, it has largely ignored one of the greatest environmental challenges facing us, the deleterious consequences of rapid and unplanned urbanization. I am aware that the Centre for Human Settlements is organizing the Second World Conference on Human Settlements in Istanbul in June this year. However, given the fact that Chapter 7 is an integral part of Agenda 21, the CSD should be working closely with the Centre for Human Settlements to achieve the goal of sustainable human settlements. Let me take Asia as an example. By the year 2020, 36 of the world's 100 largest cities will be in Asia. Asia's cities and towns will have a combined population of 2,300 million people – approximately one quarter of the world's population. Without a dramatic improvement in their management, many of Asia's cities could become the most polluted human settlements in the world. Contaminated water is Asia's most serious health problem. Only five per cent of the municipal waste is treated before disposal. The rest is discharged into our rivers and the sea. One thousand million Asians do not have adequate shelter. Like New York and Los Angeles, most of Asia's booming cities are being strangled to death by motor vehicular traffic. The relationship between transportation and the environment must surely be one of the most important and difficult issues before us. It is one which the CSD has not focused on with the political courage and the intellectual rigour which it deserves.

Third, while we live on land, we should always remember that two-thirds of the earth is covered by water. In spite of the advance of civil aviation, the world's commerce is still largely conducted by sea. The largest source of protein for humankind – fish – lives primarily in the sea. There is also a close relationship between land and sea and between the ocean and the atmosphere. We have witnessed much progress in this area during the past four years. The 1982 UN Convention on the Law of the Sea came into force in 1995. Agenda 21 contains an integrated approach to ocean management. We have adopted the Washington Global Programme of Action for the Protection of the Maritime Environment from Land-Based Activities. An agreement has also been reached on the conservation and management of straddling fish stocks and highly migratory species of fish. The FAO has adopted a Code of Conduct for Responsible Fisheries. We also have the London Dumping Convention. We have therefore set in place an international framework for the sustainable management of the oceans and of marine ecosystems. Our collective challenge is to ensure the implementation of these agreements and to promote greater co-operation at the bilateral, subregional and regional levels. The circumstances are extremely propitious. We must not squander this golden opportunity.

Fourth, I want to talk about the role of the CSD. With due respect, I think the CSD needs to be better plugged into the real world. Like most UN bodies, the members of the CSD seem to be living in a world of their own. They do not act as bridges between the UN system and our scientists and other scholars, our business and industry, our non-governmental organizations and our mass media. The CSD needs to think of an outreach programme, a communication strategy and of the need to bring all the other actors into the work of the Commission. The CSD should also consider how it can play a catalytic role in bringing together the government, business, industry and all the other stakeholders in each of our societies, to work co-operatively for the achievement of sustainable development.

Fifth and finally, I want to make a more general point. With the end of the Cold War, with low rates of growth and high rates of unemployment in the West, with pressing domestic problems and budget deficits, there has been a dramatic decline in the West of the will for international co-operation. This trend is reflected in the sorry state of the UN today, in the reduction of ODA, in the marginalization of Africa and in the rise of isolationism. This development is ironic because the world has never been more interdependent and integrated. It is increasingly difficult to draw a line between what is domestic and what is international. Fewer and fewer problems are capable of being solved by a single country alone. The environment is a paradigmatic example. Yet, despite this reality, governments have grown increasingly self-centred and indifferent to the plight of others. My sad conclusion is that our moral development has not caught up with our economic and technological revolution. My other conclusion is that the world needs visionary and courageous leaders with the political will to reform and revitalize our international institutions and to mobilize domestic support for such an enterprise. Let us hope that the world will produce such leaders.

Statement made as Chairman, Preparatory Committee for UNCED, and as Chairman, Main Committee, UNCED, at the High Level Segment of the Fourth Session of the Commission on Sustainable Development, New York, 2 May 1996.

SETTING THE GLOBAL AGENDA: THE LAW OF THE SEA AND THE ENVIRONMENT

Five Years after Rio and Fifteen Years after Montego Bay: Some Personal Reflections

Mrs Helga Haub, Professor Nicholas Robinson, Ambassador Winfried Lang, Dr Wolfgang Burhenne, ladies and gentlemen. I would like to thank the German Minister for Construction, Professor Klaus Toepfer, for honouring us with his presence. He was one of the heroes of Rio. He broke the deadlock in the negotiation on forest.

I would like to express my gratitude to the Universite Libre de Bruxelles and the International Council on Environmental Law for honouring me with the 1996 Elizabeth Haub Prize.

I have looked at the list of the persons who have received the prize before me. I am in very distinguished company. I must, however, confess that I am the least learned of the laureates. I have therefore chosen a suitably unlearned topic for my remarks. I would like to share with you some personal reflections on the UN Convention on the Law of the Sea, 15 years after Montego Bay, and on the Earth Summit, five years after Rio. I hope you will forgive me if I am unable to match the high standard set by previous laureates.

UN Special Session

The UN is holding a Special Session in June this year to commemorate the fifth anniversary of the UN Conference on Environment and Development (the Earth Summit). I hope that one of the focal points of the Special Session will be on the sustainable use of the oceans and their resources. The UN has designated 1998 as the Year of the Ocean in recognition of the fact that 71 per cent of the earth's surface is covered by the sea. The sea is the origin of atmospheric water vapour and a heat accumulator. It is also a source of food, habitat and income for humans. The oceans are in great danger. Marine pollution, caused by the excessive use of fertilizers, the discharge of industrial waste and domestic effluent, is increasing. The seas are also being used by humans as dumping ground. In many parts of the world, fish stocks have also become depleted or extinct, due to overfishing. Marine ecosystems are being destroyed by dynamite and cyanide fishing.

The Earth Summit

In March 1990, I was elected to chair the Preparatory Committee for the Earth Summit in June 1992. I chaired the negotiations on the Rio Declaration of Principles on Environment and Development at the final session of the Preparatory Committee in New York. I am delighted that the soft law contained in the Declaration is being transformed into hard law in the form of an international convenant. I salute the good work done by the International Council on Environmental Law and the Commission on Environmental Law of the World Conservation Union (IUCN). In Rio, I had the agony and ecstasy of chairing the negotiations on Agenda 21. I have written elsewhere about the experience of chairing those negotiations and will not repeat it here. Instead, I will share with you a few of my reflections on the occasion of the fifth anniversary of the Rio Summit. Have we made progress? Have we moved closer to the goal of sustainable development in the last five years? Is the world better off today than it was five years ago? A pessimist will say that the glass is half empty. As an optimist, I prefer to say that the glass is half full. Let me count the main achievements.

Development and Environment

First, the Earth Summit has brought to a final resolution the age-old debate between economic development and protection of the environment. It used to be fashionable to argue in the developing countries that their priority should be economic development and that, if necessary, the environment should be sacrificed in order to achieve high economic growth. The sentiment was to get rich first and to clean up the environment later. Some leaders of the developing countries even accused the developed countries of using the environment as a weapon to retard their economic progress. Such rhetoric and mindset belong to the past. Today, developing countries understand the need to integrate environment into their development policies. At the same time, developed countries have become increasingly aware of the need to cut down on their wasteful consumption patterns. There is growing understanding between the environment community and the development community. They realize that they must seek mutual accommodation. The new wisdom is that we want economic progress, but we also want to live in harmony with nature. To be sure, governments have to make hard choices and there are trade-offs between the two objectives. But, since the Earth Summit, it is no longer possible to talk about development without considering its impact on the environment. Many countries have enacted legislation to provide for environmental impact assessment.

Empowering the Green Movement

Second, the Earth Summit has empowered the environmental movement. Within national governments, the ministries of environment and environmental protection agencies have become more important. The Non-Governmental Organizations (NGOs) community has gained in stature and influence. Many countries have established National Councils on Sustainable Development. Many companies have adopted mission statements which include environmental goals. They have reformed their businesses to reduce waste in production, consumption and disposal of their products. The ISO 14000 is being embraced by more and more companies. Business leaders have become aware that support for the environment is not inconsistent with profitability. Governments are more willing to listen to and co-operate with NGOs. The environmental ethic is increasingly popular with students and other young people. The progress is, of course, uneven. But, looking at the world as a whole, I have no doubt that the environmental movement is stronger today than it was five years ago.

Convention on Climate Change

Third, the Framework Convention on Climate Change has come into force. The States Parties are engaged in the difficult process of negotiating a Protocol which would contain legally binding limits on the emission of greenhouse gases. The next meeting will be held in Kyoto, Japan, in December 1997.

Convention on Biological Diversity

Fourth, the Convention on Biological Diversity has also come into force. States Parties are required to undertake inventories of their biological diversity. They are also required to publish Red Data Books containing their endangered species of flora and fauna. The IUCN and the World Wide Fund for Nature (WWF) have made major contributions to the conservation and sustainable use of biological diversity. The conservation and sustainable use of biological diversity could be one of the focal points of the UN's Special Session.

Convention to Combat Desertification

Fifth, in response to the urgent need of Africa, a Convention to Combat Desertification has been negotiated and adopted. It will enter into force in December 1997.

The Oceans and the Law of the Sea

Sixth, the 1982 UN Convention on the Law of the Sea has entered into force. In response to Rio's mandate, a conference was convened to deal with the difficult issue of straddling fish stocks and highly migratory fish stocks. This resulted in the 1995 Agreement. Another positive development was the Washington Conference on the Protection of the Marine Environment from Land-based Activities. The Conference adopted a declaration and a programme of action. This was an important development because about 75 per cent of marine pollution is caused by land-based activities. We also have a code of conduct on Responsible Fisheries. There is, however, much to be done. For example, we need to harmonize the chapter on marine pollution (Part XII) of the Law of the Sea Convention with Chapter 17 of Agenda 21 from Rio. In order to manage the oceans holistically, the UN should do a better job of bringing together the legal community with the expertise represented by the International Maritime Organization (IMO), the Food and Agriculture Organization (FAO), UN Environment Programme (UNEP), the International Oceangraphic Commission (IOC), etc.

Human Settlements

Seventh, the second UN Conference on Human Settlements was held in Istanbul in June 1996. The sustainable management of cities is a challenge which merits high priority, because by the year 2000, half the world's population will live in urban human settlements. I am very pleased that Germany will be hosting a conference on the future of cities in Berlin in the year 2000. During the past five years, the awareness of the problem has increased. In the cities of East Asia, a higher proportion of the urban population has access to drinking water, modern sanitation and housing compared to five years ago. The challenge of making our cities sustainable, however, remains formidable. Economic prosperity in East Asia has, in most cities, not been accompanied by an increase in the environmental quality of life of their citizens. There are two other questions which I would cluster with human settlements. They are energy and the environment, and transport and the environment. I would recommend making this cluster another focal point of the UN's Special Session.

Trade and the Environment

Eighth, progress has been made in elucidating the relationship between trade and environment. The WTO has a standing committee on trade and environment. Although the committee was unable to recommend specific actions for adoption by the WTO's Ministerial Conference in December 1996, a lot of valuable work has been accomplished. Ambassador Winfried Lang has submitted a very good paper on this subject to our colloquium.

Capacity Building

Ninth, progress has also been made in the field of capacity building. Many countries, both developed and developing, have implemented programmes to share their experiences and to train personnel from other countries. Several international organizations are also playing a constructive role in capacity building in the developing countries. Professor Nicholas Robinson, Dr Wolfgang Burhenne, Dr Francoise Burhenne-Guilmin and I are involved in a modest project. Together with colleagues from the Commission on Environmental Law of IUCN and in collaboration with the UN Environment Programme (UNEP), the Law Faculty of the National University of Singapore has established an Asia Pacific Centre for Environmental Law (APCEL) in Singapore. Beginning this June, APCEL will undertake training courses on environmental law for law teachers from the Asia Pacific region, with funding from the Asian Development Bank and support from the National University of Singapore.

Winning Hearts and Minds

Tenth, in the final analysis, the goal of sustainable development cannot be achieved by government, business, experts and NGOs alone. We have to win the hearts and minds of the citizens of the world. We have to inculcate in every child a love of nature. We have to influence the daily habits and lifestyles of peoples all over the world. We should aim to persuade every consumer to internalize the ethic of "reduce, re-use and recycle". In this respect, I greatly admire the decisions made by the Haub Group not to sell turtle soup, frog's legs, detergent containing phosphate, all products containing CFCs and batteries containing mercury. I believe that during the past five years we have made progress in raising consciousness, in reaching out to the young and in shaping attitudes.

Conclusion

I hope I have persuaded you that the glass is half full and that we have made some progress towards the goal of a more sustainable world. I would argue that the world is better off today than it was five years ago. I must, of course, acknowledge that the glass is also half empty. This is, therefore, not the time for complacency. For every achievement I have cited, I can point to a failure. Every day, some species of flora and fauna will become extinct. The deserts are expanding. Our oceans are becoming more polluted. Fish stocks are being overexploited. Many cities are turning into slums and are being strangled by traffic congestion. We must therefore use the occasion of the fifth anniversary of the Earth Summit to renew our faith and redouble our efforts. The Convention on the Law of the Sea and the Earth Summit were two important landmarks in our quest for legal order and sustainable development. I have had the unusual privilege of chairing both negotiations. I hope that I was able to make a modest contribution towards making this a better world.

Speech delivered at the Elizabeth Haub Prize Ceremony, Wiesbaden, Germany, 17 April 1997.

SINGAPORE'S ROLE IN THE REGION AND THE WORLD

Lee Kuan Yew's Foreign Policy Legacy

For the past 25 years, Lee Kuan Yew has personified Singapore to the world. He has been the principal architect of Singapore's foreign policy. He has also been Singapore's chief diplomat to the world. He hands over to his successor a principled and pragmatic foreign policy which has enabled Singapore to survive and prosper. This article will attempt briefly to assess Lee Kuan Yew's foreign policy achievements.

Mini in Size but Not Influence

With a population of 2.6 million and a physical area of only 626 square kilometres, Singapore is one of the world's smallest states. However, Singapore enjoys a role and influence in the world quite unlike those enjoyed by other countries of similar size. This is due to two factors: the stature of Singapore's Prime Minister and the country's record of achievements.

Lee Kuan Yew's Impact on Foreign Leaders

Why is Lee Kuan Yew so greatly admired by his peers abroad? Because of his intellectual brilliance, his political experience, extraordinary powers of analysis and judgment, his eloquence, his willingness to offer candid and disinterested advice and his domestic record of success. His political longevity places him in a very special category of elder statesmen in the world. He is the longest serving Prime Minister in the Commonwealth and the longest serving Head of Government in Asia. His address to the Joint Meeting of the US Congress on 9 October 1985 was a reflection of the esteem which US leaders of both parties have for him. In the same way, the fact that he had often been asked to be the keynote speaker at the biennial meeting of Commonwealth Heads of Government is an example of the respect he commands from the Prime Ministers of the Commonwealth countries. In Asia, his views on world affairs are sought and listened to with respect by the leaders of countries ranging from China and Japan to Hong Kong and Papua New Guinea.

Fellows of Harvard and Yale

Lee Kuan Yew has won the admiration of many foreign scholars. The many meetings between him and the professors of Harvard, Yale and other universities and think-tanks in America always produced intellectual discourse of the highest order. It is quite extraordinary for the Prime Minister of a Third World country to have held fellowships at both Harvard and Yale, and to have been conferred honorary doctoral degrees by three prestigious universities in the United States and two in the United Kingdom.

Relations with Foreign Media

Lee Kuan Yew has always had a love-hate relationship with the foreign, especially American and British, press. On the one hand, he enjoys his intellectual encounters with the more able and gifted members of the Western media. On the other hand, his sensitivity to criticism, his contempt for those who had not done their homework and his resentment against any attempt by the "whites" to preach at him, have given him and Singapore a rather bad press in the West in recent years. The fundamental cause of the disagreement is the Western media's insistence that Singapore should follow the principles of Western liberal democracy and Lee Kuan Yew's belief that such principles had to be adapted to the special circumstances of Singapore. However, even his critics admire his moral and intellectual courage in being willing to face them. He appeared before the International Press Institute in Helsinki (1971), the American Society of Newspaper Editors in Washington, D.C. (1988), the Commonwealth Press Union and the Foreign Correspondents' Club in Hong Kong (1990) and earned the respect if not the agreement of those audiences. From the point of view of the Third World, Lee Kuan Yew's willingness to stand up to the Western media has helped to strengthen Singapore's credentials as a country which is independent-minded, notwithstanding its general pro-Western foreign policy.

The Defects of Our Virtues

No human is perfect. Even a great man like Lee Kuan Yew is not without foibles. Indeed, we all suffer from the defects of our virtues. Thus, Lee Kuan Yew's brilliance sometimes causes him to appear arrogant, his single-mindedness can come across as dogmatism and his candour as indiscretion. I remember that I once urged the Prime Minister to be more discreet in his remarks about other countries. I think it was after a speech he made in Singapore during which he made some disparaging remarks about the Calypso culture of the Caribbean countries. The remark had been widely reported by the Caribbean media and had caused offence to our Caribbean friends. The Prime Minister replied that he was known for his candour and should not be expected to speak like a diplomat. He said that if he had ruffled any feathers, it was the job of our diplomats to smoothen those feathers. I protested that as our Prime Minister, he was our chief diplomat to the world.

The Seven Pillars of Singapore's Foreign Policy

What foreign policy legacy is Lee Kuan Yew leaving to his successor? What is his vision of Singapore's role in the region and the world? Below are seven pillars of Singapore's foreign policy which bear the imprint of Lee Kuan Yew.

First, we have a pragmatic foreign policy based not on any ideology or doctrine, but upon the fact that our foreign policy must be constantly guided by one lodestar – the security and prosperity of Singapore.

Second, we rely, first and foremost, on ourselves. Thus, believing that the world does not owe us a living, Singapore has never sought foreign aid from the developed countries. This belief in self-reliance has also led us to develop a capacity to deter aggression. To quote Lee Kuan Yew, "In a world where the big fish eat small fish and the small fish eat shrimps, Singapore must become a poisonous shrimp".

Third, we must accept the world as it is and not as we would like it to be. This has installed in us a pragmatic and hard-headed attitude towards realities. Our realism, however, is not a fatalistic attitude. We are constantly seeking to change the *status quo* for the better.

Fourth, Singapore is committed to making ASEAN work and to good relations with our five regional partners, especially our two immediate neighbours, Indonesia and Malaysia. Lee Kuan Yew's support for ASEAN and his personal rapport with President Soeharto and Prime Minister Mahathir are important assets.

Fifth, Singapore is a member of a larger, dynamic and increasingly prosperous Asia Pacific community. Singapore supported the creation of the Asia Pacific Economic Cooperation (APEC) grouping and is the location for the Secretariat of the Pacific Economic Cooperation Conference (PECC). Singapore has played and will continue to play a seminal role in the evolution of the Pacific community. Her commitment to ASEAN is not inconsistent with its support for the Pacific community.

Sixth, Singapore is a member of the world community and is a good citizen of the world. Singapore has supported the primacy of the principles of the UN Charter and the collective security system centred on the UN Security Council. As a small country, Singapore has a vested interest in ensuring respect by all states for the principles of international law governing relations among states. Singapore's free trade policy, its environmentally sensitive development policy, its strong support for the UN and GATT, and the role of her diplomats as neutral chairmen are some examples of Singapore's contributions to the world community.

Seventh, Singapore will work with other countries to ensure a stable and peaceful environment in our region. Singapore favours the continued presence of the United States in East and Southeast Asia and is against its precipitate withdrawal from the region. We favour a balance of power in Southeast Asia which produces a stable political order and are against an arms race by the regional powers, or any destabilizing changes. Singapore is not, however, against the need to re-assess existing security arrangements in the region in the light of the ending of the Cold War.

Conclusion

With the help of Goh Keng Swee, Toh Chin Chye and S. Rajaratnam in the earlier years, and S. Dhanabalan and Wong Kan Seng in more recent years, Lee Kuan Yew has masterminded Singapore's external relations. In 1965, Singapore's independence was questioned by some. Today, no one does. In 1965, Singapore's economic prospects looked dubious. Today,

Singapore's economy is one of the powerhouses of the dynamic Asia Pacific region. Singapore's place in Southeast Asia is secure because of ASEAN and because of Singapore's good relations with her neighbours. Singapore is plugged into the world grid of trade, investment and technology flows and is a good economic partner of the United States, Japan and the European Community. Singapore is viewed by others as a good citizen of the world community. In sum, Singapore's relations with other countries, both within and outside the region, are excellent. This happy state of affairs is due to the collective efforts of an extraordinary crew but, especially, to its illustrious captain, Lee Kuan Yew.

Article contributed to **Trends**, *a monthly publication of the Institute of Southeast Asian Studies (ISEAS) distributed with* **The Business Times**, *15 November 1990.*

SINGAPORE'S ROLE IN THE REGION AND THE WORLD

A Lilliputian in the Land of the Giants: The Work of the Singapore Embassy in Washington

I want to begin by asking the question: Do the conventional rules of diplomacy apply in Washington, D.C.? And if they don't, why not? I will then try to go on and answer a more intriguing question: In a town which according to its inhabitants, worships power, how does the embassy of a very tiny country which wields very little power in the real world, gain effectiveness? These are the two very basic questions I want to discuss with you.

When I first arrived in Washington, almost three years ago, one of my very good friends, the Ambassador of Canada, Allan Gottlieb, who is regarded by many as one of the most effective ambassadors in Washington, took me to lunch. And the first thing Allan said to me was, "Tommy, throw away all the books you have ever read on diplomacy". He said, "All the conventional rules don't apply in this town". I was of course quite startled and said, "Allan, what do you mean?" He said, "In Washington, if you are not seen you don't exist. If you are not heard from, your interests will not be taken into account. Consequently, it is necessary for an embassy, no matter how powerful the country or how powerless the country it represents, to try to assume a high profile, to be assertive of its interests and to first, build and then to massage your network of allies and friends, both inside and outside of government". This was very valuable advice from Allan and I took it to heart. I think there are also other reasons which make Washington, D.C., different from other capitals, such as our own, or London or Paris or Bonn, and this had to do with the special characteristics of the United States Federal Government. So, if you will permit me, I would like to say a few words about some of these special characteristics which make the work of a foreign embassy in Washington significantly different from the work of an embassy in other capitals of the world.

What are these special characteristics? Well, let me begin by mentioning two of them. First, unlike the situation in a parliamentary democracy, in the United States, there is quite a strict separation of powers between the three branches of government, between the Executive branch, the Legislative branch and the Judicial branch. In a parliamentary democracy, there is in fact no separation of powers between the Executive and Legislative. And as you know, the Executive would not be in power if it did not control a majority in Parliament. And if you have the commitment of the Cabinet to a piece of legislation or a policy, one can in almost all cases rely upon the Cabinet to deliver Parliament. Not so in Washington. So, the first special characteristic of the United States Federal Government is that it consists of three separate branches: the Executive, the Legislative and the Judiciary. And the second, which is the other side of this same coin, is that it is truly a system of checks and balances. The wisdom of the founding fathers, the inspiration driving them was to construct a system of governance that would minimize the accumulation of governmental power and the possibility of its abuse and maximize the protection of the liberty of the individual. If you don't understand this, then you cannot understand America. The very founding rock of America is this concept – the celebration of individual liberty and the deep-rooted suspicion of government which has been transmitted down the generations from the pioneers.

I want to tell you a story which gives an example of the kind of bewildering experience a foreign ambassador, unfamiliar with the American system, could have. The first Ambassador from the People's Republic of China arrived in Washington, D.C., soon after Congress had adopted and the President had signed into law the Taiwan Relations Act. At his first meeting with the State Department, he protested loudly against the Taiwan Relations Act. He said that the Taiwan Relations Act was inconsistent in letter and in spirit with the Shanghai Communique. Well, the State Department official was tactfully apologetic but suggested to the Chinese Ambassador that in the American system, unlike the Chinese, the Administration does not control the Congress, which I am sure the Chinese Ambassador did not believe. And the State Department official politely suggested that it would be a good idea if he were to travel up to the hill and speak directly to the members of the Congress to influence them. The Ambassador was shocked by this. He said, "But isn't that an interference in your internal affairs?" And the State Department official reflected for a moment and evaded an answer but said, "But Mr Ambassador, if you don't do that you will not be effective in this town". And that is the moral you must learn, that even with an overwhelmingly popular President, the President cannot dictate to Congress. Even in the rare circumstance when the President and the majority in both the Senate and the House come from the same party, the President cannot dictate to Congress. The senators, the members of the House may belong to the same party but they respond only in part to party loyalty. They respond, in my view, to a greater part, to constituent interests. And a senator or a congressman or congresswoman may be obliged to say to a President whom he or she greatly admires and with whose policy he or she is not in disagreement, "I am sorry Mr President, I cannot vote with you on this issue because it runs contrary to my constituent interests at home". This is the reality of American politics that we foreigners who work in Washington have to understand. As the former Speaker of the House of Representatives, Tip O'Neill once said, with only a slight bit of exaggeration, "All politics in America is local". This is, of course, an exaggeration and it would indeed be a very sad day if there were no member of the United States Congress who is capable of rising above local parochial interest to ask himself or herself what the national interest and what America's global interest are on an issue.

Let me now talk about the Executive branch. When I first arrived, I was also rather puzzled by the constant bickering in public between the Heads of the various departments and agencies of the Federal Government. I mean, it seems extraordinary to us in Singapore, to find ministers in the same cabinet publicly quarrelling over the policy, or quarrelling over how policy that was supposedly settled in cabinet is to be implemented. There is, in the American Executive branch, a certain leeway accorded to cabinet secretaries which is both good and bad. Good in the sense that sometimes out of this constructive tension, different points of view are considered, and reconciled, in a constructive compromise. Bad in the sense that it can sometimes paralyse the Executive branch and worse, confound America's allies and friends abroad as to who speaks for America.

So, one of the functions of a foreign embassy in Washington is to help the President co-ordinate his cabinet! And I am not joking. I am absolutely serious that when you have a cause, a proposal that you wish to achieve or to sell, you must identify the departments and agencies that have jurisdiction over the issue and you must then knock on all their doors. To take as an example, in dealing with an issue relating to Cambodia, you must make sure that the State Department, the Defence Department, the National Security Council (NSC), the White House, the CIA are all with you. And it is a considerable effort, you know, to do that. And many small embassies do not know that you have to do that because in most capitals, you limit your contact to the Foreign Office and suppose, not unreasonably, that since they all belong to the same government, serving one President, that the Foreign Minister speaks for the whole government. In Washington, however, Rule No. One is never to assume that to be the case. In fact, it is a rarity which we in ASEAN very fortunately enjoy, that on America's policy towards Southeast Asia, there is no difference of opinion between the State Department, Defence Department and the NSC. And it is a truly rare and happy exception to the general rule. If you do not believe me, read for example, Strobe Talbot's book on *Arms Control* to obtain an idea of the kind of bitter quarrels and disputes that went on during the first four years of the Reagan Administration between the State and Defence Departments over arms control policy. So, that is another characteristic of the Federal Government that makes the work of an embassy, especially a little Lilliputian like us, very challenging.

Now, I want to talk a little bit about working the Congress. I want to recall what I said earlier, which is that the Congress is independent of the Executive branch. And that even when the President, the majority in the Senate, the majority in the House, all come from the same party, the President cannot dictate and expect that they would follow his bidding. Now, the present situation of course is not so favourable to the President in the sense that the majorities in the Senate and the House are in the hands of the Democrats. This makes your work even harder than it would normally be the case. So, a foreign embassy must learn to work the Congress. What do I mean by working the Congress? What I mean is, first, a foreign embassy must cultivate the congressional leadership and I mean both the leadership of the majority party and the leadership of the minority party. Second, you must cultivate key members who may not be holding leadership positions, but who wield considerable influence in the Senate or the House. You would have to first identify these people and attempt, in one way or another, through your mutual friends or through your wives' machinations, to get to know them. And I should say a word about the wives' machinations.

You know, it is a fact of life that in Washington, on any one day, a senator or a congressman probably gets ten invitations to social functions. He would normally, of course, give priority to a constituent. A chairman or CEO of a major corporation in his district or state would have priority over almost everybody else. He would give priority to a leader of the media. If Ben Bradlee, the Executive Editor of the *Washington Post*, wishes to have dinner with him, I think that the Ambassador of Singapore can go and fly a kite. He will give priority to even representatives of interest groups and lobbies which have influence in his state or district, or whose interests are congruent with the interests of his constituents. So, you are competing with many people for valuable time. But I found my wife's contacts to be in fact extremely valuable. And let me briefly explain what I mean. There are in Washington, eight women's clubs, and these eight clubs consist of the wives of cabinet secretaries, wives of senators, wives of congressmen and wives of diplomats, as well as some prominent Washingtonians. By happenstance, my wife is the president of one of the eight clubs. And whenever I have a cabinet minister visiting Washington and I have to host a function at home for him, and I need people from the Hill, I find that my wife is much more effective than I am. If I call the appointments secretary of the senator or congressman, she will hold my invitation in abeyance to see what other invitations come along. And they are all highly protective of their bosses because it is important to their own job security, which would be threatened if he does not get re-elected two years or six years hence. Whereas my wife, having come to know the wife of the senator or congressman, can pick up the phone and call the wife and say, "Jean, we have Mr Dhanabalan coming to dinner two weeks hence, we would like you and your husband to come, can you do that?" And the wife, being the boss, of course, phones the husband and says, "Clayton, Siew Aing has invited us to dinner on 11 July and I have accepted, will you please tell your secretary?" So, the Foreign Office should, I think, recognize the fact that wives of diplomats in fact make a significant contribution to their husband's work. They give up their own careers. Instead of practising medicine, my wife is now my chief cook at home, works for various charities in Washington, and is the social escort of every visiting fireman from Singapore.

Let me now make a different point which is not often appreciated by embassies and especially by ambassadors because some ambassadors tend to be rather snobbish about their status. They have worked their way up the ladder, they have become ambassadors, they feel that, "You know, I am now a demi-god and I only shake hands with my equal, it is beneath my dignity to call upon these young people who work for senators and congressmen, and congressional committees". But, in fact, they are profoundly wrong in doing that. There are more than 10,000 congressional staffers on the Hill and it is naturally impossible to get to know all of them. Of the 300 congressional committees and subcomittees you have to identify, looking at your national agenda in Washington, what the committees and subcommittees which are important to Singapore are. You then find out who the key staff members of the chairman of the committee are, the ranking minority of the committee, and the most influential members of those committees. Then the committee also has professional staffers, so you must put them all on your list. These key congressional staffers are far more knowledgeable than their bosses about the specific issues and it has to be so. A senator or congressman has to deal with literally thousands of agenda items. He or she cannot be an expert on everything. He or she employs very bright, mostly very young congressional staffers who do the homework for them – position papers, draft bills, and in fact, advise them on how to vote. And cultivating these key congressional staffers is a very important priority, or ought to be, in the work of any embassy. And that is what I have tried to do in the last three years. First, I identified the key congressional staffers on foreign and defence policies. Then I tried to identify the key congressional staffers on trade and economic issues. I have gone up to the Hill, called on them individually, become their friends. We now have a monthly lunch. In order to make it easy for them to accept my invitation, I come up and have lunch with them on the Hill rather than expect them to travel half-way across the town to have lunch with you at your embassy or at your residence because they work extremely hard. Congress is a strange body which does not observe either a lunch or dinner break. They must always be on call and if the beeper goes, they have to rush back to work. So, cultivate congressional staffers.

Finally, one rule which I have tried to apply to my own work in Washington is, always try to get bipartisan support for your cause – whether it be trade or Cambodia. It is very dangerous if the support for your cause comes only from one of the two parties in Congress because it is then liable to become a political football. Contrast, for example, the bipartisan support for the Cambodian cause with the basically partisan support for the cause of the Contras in Nicaragua. And the moral I have drawn from that is, you must make sure that your foreign and security policies are broadly based. You have to work both sides of the House, you have to get the leadership of the Democratic and the Republicans parties on board. And if you don't, then don't push it. The lesson I administer to myself is, if I cannot carry the Democrats in Congress with me on ASEAN's Cambodian policy, then I will not push it. And in fact, since I knew that the Republicans would be more naturally sympathetic to my cause, I started by cultivating the liberal leaders of the Democratic Party and getting them on board. Once I got the liberal Democratic leaders supporting the non-communist Cambodian cause, it was relatively easy to get the moderate and conservative elements in the Democratic Party, and it became easier still to get the Republicans aboard. So, that was an important lesson which I hope the ASEAN countries never forget. That as your cause is never secure and Congress is a very whimsical animal, you must seek security by seeking bipartisan, broad-based support. It is also very important to work the private sector. And I think that unfortunately, ASEAN businessmen do not understand this. When an ambassador calls on a congressional leader, they see us in the personage of a government bureaucrat, government official. Sure, they listen to us politely, but we do not have the impact which an ASEAN business leader could have. The ASEAN business leaders, at the moment, are very unsophisticated and have no conception of how Washington works, unlike the Japanese, the Koreans and even the Taiwanese who are increasingly sophisticated, who spend money lobbying, come on regular visits, knock on doors on the Hill, and build up their own networks. The ASEAN business leaders' impact on the US Congress is zero.

The other thing is, the American private sector wields more influence in Congress than foreign governments. Why is that so? Because the foreign embassy doesn't contribute to its campaign and cannot vote. The people who have the greatest influence on senators and congressmen are the people back in his district who contribute to his campaign, vote for him, people who can mobilize media support for him and who are major employers of workers in his district. These are the people he listens to. And in fact, the ASEAN embassies in Washington are trying to mobilize the US-based MNCs in the six ASEAN countries to help us in our lobbying effort in Washington. I am absolutely certain that if the Chairman or CEO of General Electric makes a call to a senator or congressman, and I make the same call, I will not have one-tenth the influence that he will have. So, the private sector is very important. What we have done in Washington, not just Singapore alone, but ASEAN as a group, is to have an ongoing dialogue with the ASEAN-US Business Council, which consists of many of the largest American corporations that either have investments or very close trade relations with the ASEAN countries. And we seek to work very closely with these US-based MNCs in our activities on the Hill.

Next, work the media. At the moment, as you know, I am not in a very good position to have much influence with the media. I really regret this because for 16 years, I have systematically attempted to cultivate the American media, not only because I like media people; I prefer them to bureaucrats, frankly, but also because the US media enjoys a power and influence in their body politic which few foreigners realize and appreciate. And I am afraid, Singaporean leaders probably do not understand or appreciate this. The media in the US can make or break a government, it can make or break a candidate. It is a power, a very considerable power. As one congressman from Massachusetts warned me when I was involved in writing letters to the editors of several newspapers, he said, "Tommy, if you are a wise man you would observe a saying in Massachusetts". I said,

"What's that?" He said, "Never pick a fight with a man who orders his ink by the barrel".

Let me go on to the next two points I want to make and then I will conclude with two quick examples. There are two other interest groups or institutions I work very closely with, in order to increase my leverage. When you represent a tiny country, you have little or no leverage. And in fact, to be very frank, the trump card I have in Washington is Lee Kuan Yew. When that is gone, there will be a very considerable gap for me to fill, in terms of getting access to people, gaining influence, having a point of view to listen to. We have therefore to start building as extensive as possible a network for Singapore in America, which we can mobilize to support our interests and our causes.

First, interest groups and lobbies. In Washington, there are literally representatives of thousands of these groups. And some of them are extremely powerful on specific issues. If your cause touches or runs contrary to the interest of a group, you had better watch out and you had better win them over to your side. If that is not possible, then build countervailing power; identify countervailing pressure groups whose interests are identical to yours and opposed to that group's. So, in trade policy, for example, I have built a coalition with many pro-free trade interest groups and lobbies in Washington. Groups like the American Business Conference which consists of major US MNCs; the US Chamber of Commerce; the Wheat Growers; the Retail Trade Association; people who import goods from abroad and therefore are pro-free trade; the people who represent the services industry (because America is very big in the service sector and very competitive in the world in banking, insurance, consultancy services, it is therefore a natural ally); and consumer groups, a major one of which is led by a very good friend of mine, Doreen Brown, called Consumers for World Trade. So, I build coalitions with these people.

The point I was making is that you have to identify the interest groups on specific causes, and the lobbies that will support your position. If it is on trade, then you look for all the various associations, interest groups, lobbies which support free trade, you build coalitions with them, you meet them regularly, exchange notes, discuss strategies with them, sometimes even show them drafts of letters, and get their inputs on how to make it shorter, more liable to be read by their recipients and not to be thrown into the wastepaper basket, ask advice on who to speak to at the level of the staffers – they are invaluable as a resource.

Finally, the think-tanks and the universities. America, especially Washington, has many important think-tanks. In Washington alone, you have on the right the Heritage Foundation, then moving from right to left, the American Enterprise Institute, the Brookings Institution, the Carnegie Endowment for International Peace. There are many other smaller think-tanks. On economic matters, the most important think-tank in my view is the Institute for International Economics headed by a very brilliant economist called Fred Bergsten. Why are think-tanks important? Think-tanks are important for two reasons: one, they are not like universities that put out scholarly publications that nobody on the Hill reads. The think-tanks in Washington tend to be very policy and action-oriented. They are very topical, they attempt to answer the intellectual needs of people on the Hill. And if you can influence these people, if you can make inputs into the scholarly products, then you can indirectly influence opinion on the Hill, in the administration, in the media. They also have a multiplier effect. This is the reason why we all go round the country speaking to universities and other learned institutions. So, you have to build up that network too – the think-tanks, the learned society, the universities.

Let me give you just two quick examples and then I will answer your questions. From the way I have described the system, I may leave you with the unfortunate impression that the system is so bewildering, is so decentralized, is so uncoordinated that it is impossible to achieve anything. It is not so. In spite of its apparent lack of co-ordination, in spite of the fact that power is highly decentralized and dispersed, in spite of the fact that it is a system of tier upon tier of checks and balances, at critical moments, they are capable of coming together, arriving at a compromise and taking action. Sometimes, the action is very long in coming and you wish that this big elephant would move. But there is also a beauty in the system. The down side is that it is slow, it is uncoordinated, and that it sometimes sends very conflicting signals. For example, on the Persian Gulf, the administration is pushing one policy asserting that America has a strategic interest as the leader of the free world in preserving freedom of navigation in the Persian Gulf and that it must therefore be prepared, at the cost of US lives, to preserve that strategic interest. The Senate and the House seem to be sending different signals. It is very confusing for American allies and I suspect sometimes for American enemies as well in reading the American policy on an issue. But there is a beauty to this system and I would like to conclude on a positive note.

The beauty of the system is that the system is open, accessible and even though you may be small, if you work hard, if you build your network, it is possible to achieve things which would be impossible in other capitals. Let's take Cambodia as an example. Two years ago, the Administration was very much opposed to the idea that the United States should give overt aid to the non-Cambodian resistance forces – you know, they would rather give it under the table and very little at that. Singapore felt that there was no reason why America should not say publicly to the world that "we support the non-communist Cambodian forces", that "we give money publicly to this cause". And we, in fact, felt that the political signal of overt aid subordinates all the difficulties that the bureaucracy can think of. So, what did we do? Well, we looked for a champion and we found this champion in the person of a relatively young, very liberal congressman from the district of Brooklyn in New York City, Stephen Solarz, the Chairman of the House, Foreign Affairs Subcommittee on Asia and the Pacific.

The beauty of the system is that a man can, if he has a just cause, if he is persistent, if he is eloquent, and if other things come together, turn this huge supertanker around, and he did. Of course, he had help from all of us in the ASEAN Community. My colleagues and I in the Singapore Embassy, worked very hard to assist Steve. We called on every member of the House Subcommittee on Asia and the Pacific. We called on Democrats and Republicans. We called on all the members of the full Committee on Foreign Affairs. We mobilized our friends in the media to write editorials and articles supporting giving overt aid to the Cambodians. And when I visited people on the Hill and was able to give to each of them a dossier consisting of editorials, articles, from liberals as well as conservative papers – the *New York Times*, the *Washington Post*, the *Wall Street Journal*, *Los Angeles Times* – all urging support for the Cambodian cause, I knew that half the battle was won.

So, the beauty of the system is that a single person can, with a bit of luck and a good cause, persuade this supertanker to make a turn very slowly, as we did. Overt aid was appropriated and is being appropriated. The doubts of the Administration have been allayed. I want to conclude, therefore, on this positive note and say that sure, there is a down side to the American federal system of government because power is so decentralized and dispersed. It is so difficult for a President to achieve what he wants to achieve on his agenda because he has constantly to bargain, negotiate, compromise. Every individual member of the Senate and Congress can be a stumbling block and can actually stop legislation in its tracks. But there is also an up side to this system. And the up side is that it is open, it is accessible, it is truly democratic and if you have the right champion, with a little bit of luck, you can sometimes achieve an almost impossible turn in the policy of the Administration.

Speech delivered at the Institute of Southeast Asian Studies, Singapore, June 1987. The speech was followed by a question and answer session, an excerpt of which is reproduced below.

The Question and Answer Session

Question:

You talked earlier about how your Massachusetts friend advised you not to quarrel with friends. Now, in the light of what has happened between the Singapore Government and the *Asian Wall Street Journal*, do you think the Singapore Government has adopted the right approach in handling this issue ... On hindsight, do you think that there could have been a different approach?

Professor Tommy Koh:

Are you trying to get me into trouble? Well, let me put it this way. It is an issue on which there is, in my view, an unbridgeable gulf of political, cultural, historical attitudes. In America, the freedom of the press is protected by the First Amendment to the Constitution and it is an absolute right. The First Amendment says, in very simple language, that Congress shall make no law to abridge the freedom of the press and the courts have interpreted that very strictly and struck down laws which even I would feel are reasonable. Let me give you an example just to show the gulf that exists and why, for me, the mission is an impossible one. A few years ago, the state of Florida passed a law requiring the media to give politicians whom it attacks during the period leading to an election, during the pre-election period, a right to reply to that attack. And this is particularly important in a state where you have only one major newspaper, the *Miami Herald*. If the *Miami Herald* endorses you, it has tremendous impact on public opinion. If the *Miami Herald* says you are a bum, it is very difficult to reply to that if you can't get access to its columns. The traditional American belief is that we should trust in the multiplicity of tongues. If the *Miami Herald* attacks you, seek other vehicles to express your view. The Americans do not like the idea of imposing obligations upon the media because they see this as attempts by government to restrict the freedom of the press. So, this Florida law – which will, I think, win public approval in this country and possibly in America – was upheld by the Supreme Court of the state of Florida. The media in Florida appealed against the State Supreme Court to the US Supreme Court and the US Supreme Court struck it down as unconstitutional saying that the government has no business to be in the editor's office, and that to impose the right of reply is a first step towards giving the government a right to interfere. Now many people will disagree with the US Supreme Court. They would ask, what's happened to the fairness doctrine? If the media is free to attack governments, corporations and individuals, then fairness would seem to require that you give the victim of your attack the right to rebut. But in America, this is not the case because the court would strike down any law obligating a right to reply. If American public opinion was polled, the American public opinion will probably say, "Yes, I agree with you that the victim of an attack by the media ought to be given a right to reply". But when you take it to the next step and say, "Well, do you think it should be made obligatory?", I think the American public opinion will be divided. Some Americans will say yes, fairness requires that it should be so. The others will say, no, because we fear this may be the first step towards interference and the American public attitude would be that if we have to make a choice between an irresponsible press and an irresponsible government, it is better to have an irresponsible press which keeps in check an irresponsible or potentially irresponsible government. The gulf between our two societies on this issue is just unbridgeable. I can win public opinion in America on the first point: that victims who are attacked, whether the victim be a foreign government or the US Government itself, should be accorded a right of reply. I do not think I can win the approval of American public opinion when we restrict the circulation of a publication because of its failure to publish our reply. I regret what has happened because of the power of the US media and because we have enjoyed, for 20 years, a favourable press in America. And now, I suspect our image is turning increasingly negative.

Question:

As to your comment about the professional staff and so on in the Congress up on the Hill, I think it must be attracting the best brains in the country because of its glamour, the attraction to power and so on and so forth, and one would assume a certain uniformity of good government actions coming out of all these activities at the various levels. Do you get the impression that over the years, the American Government, whether on foreign policy or otherwise, whether it has been uniformly successful? If not, what is the positive side of this?

Professor Tommy Koh:

As I mentioned, in my view, some of the positive sides to this system are that it is open, it is accessible, it is truly democratic. Individuals and groups, who have interests can have those interests heard, considered, taken into account. So, in that sense it is very good system. It is not a good system for the number one superpower of the world and the leader of the free world. If America were a small little republic like Singapore, I would say it is a wonderful system. But when a superpower has to act decisively, you sometimes hold your breadth and ask yourself, when are these guys ever going to get together and agree on a policy? As to the congressional staffers, they are, by and large, young. They are mostly people out of graduate school, very bright, very dedicated men and women. Their pay is miserable, the working hours are impossible. They work around the clock, weekends. What are their rewards? Their rewards are one, it is a very good tutelage for entering politics if they want to become future politicians themselves; they build up such a terrific reservoir of knowledge about the specific area they are assigned to and of contacts that they become very marketable merchandise. So, they don't stay very long. Usually they stay a few years, they come out, either join a law firm, a consulting firm or open their own consulting firm. It is not fair to insist, as you seem to do, that a very intelligent, dedicated congressional staffer, who serves, for instance, a congressman representing a district, say in Pennsylvania or Michigan, that produces steel, should be able to rise above the parochial interest of his congressman and say, "Look, America should not adopt a protectionist policy on steel. If your steel mills are losing your competitive edge, well, it is partly your own fault. You've not been modernizing whilst the Japanese and the Koreans have been doing that, and your answer is either to allow obsolescent plants to die or modernize or innovate". Well, he can't take that position. The political imperatives compel him, in spite of his own instincts, to seek protection for an industry that is the major employer in his district. Now, that doesn't mean that you put him on your list of enemies and ignore him. No, no. In fact, I would also cultivate them and see if I can minimize the damage that he could do to me or perhaps, try to redirect his fire to the bad guys and say, "Look, I am such a good guy, you know, why do you want to cause damage to Singapore? We are one of the two free trading nations in the world. I will give you a list of bad guys you could attack".

Question:

Mr Ambassador, a few months ago, a *Straits Times* article mentioned the ... co-ordination of your own efforts with other Asian ambassadors in opposition to protectionist trade legislation. Would you care to comment on the joys and sorrows of co-ordinating this group on trade issues?

Professor Tommy Koh:

Actually, it is a typographical error. The co-ordination was with other ASEAN ambassadors. Americans have never heard of the term "ASEAN", so they always think it is a misspelling of the word "Asian". Really, if you write ASEAN, they will think it is an error, they will strike it out and put Asian. If you administer a questionnaire to the 100 members of the Senate and the 435 members of the House and say, "What is ASEAN and which countries make up ASEAN?", I would not be surprised if the majority failed those two tests.

Question:

Box Oxnam, President of the Asia Society, carried out a survey of taxi drivers and their knowledge of ASEAN. On a rainy day in New York, he asked one taxi driver: "Do you know where Indonesia is?" The driver replied, "Buddy, when it is raining, we don't go beyond city limits". Your comments?

Professor Tommy Koh:

Well, one would have thought given the size and in my view, inherent importance of Indonesia to America's global strategic and economic interests, that more Americans would know about Indonesia. But they don't. The only comfort I take about their ignorance of Singapore is that they are even more ignorant of this much larger country which should, in fact, feature prominently in the American consciousness. My Indonesian colleague is constantly frustrated that when he goes around the country, people will ask him, "Ambassador Soesilo, which part of Bali is Indonesia?" They have heard of Bali, fictional or otherwise, and they all know the song "Bali Hai". So they think that Indonesia is somewhere in Bali. Well, to come back to the earlier question. It is not Asian, just ASEAN, and we work very closely in Washington. We know that each of us wields little leverage. In fact, to be very frank, of the six ASEAN countries, the only one which has a natural lobby in Congress is the Philippines. And it is a great shame that for so long the Philippines had a very ineffective government of not good repute, and instead of being an asset to ASEAN, was in fact a liability. I am hoping that as President Aquino continues to make progress, we can in fact use the Philippines as our Trojan Horse to achieve the collective good that ASEAN wants. We work very closely, the six of us. For example, we lobby collectively, we have sent three letters to every member of the House of Representatives on trade issues in these last few months. We have written two letters to every member of the Senate. We have a monthly meeting of our own. We have a joint lunch every month with Americans and we rotate the American guests. Every month, we try and reach out to different networks, different sources of power and we travel the country in what I call road shows. We are about to go on a very extensive road show. It is impressive to Americans when they see six ambassadors from six different countries get along so well, able to speak on a subject with such coherence and uniformity that even the US administration is not capable of doing. So we put on very impressive road shows. We are about to take our road show this month to Los Angeles and then to Honolulu. And we do this partly because we feel we must bring the good word about ASEAN and about US-ASEAN relations to the rest of the country, but we also do it in an opportunistic way. We would ask, for example, the chairman of an important committee to sponsor our trip. Last year, we asked Richard Luger, Chairman of the Senate Foreign Relations Committee. We got to know Dick well and I asked his staff (and this is where the staff is important), I asked his key foreign policy staffer, "Fred, do me a favour. Can you persuade Dick Luger to invite the six ASEAN ambassadors and our wives to come and visit the state of Indiana and do a programme for us where we can meet the Mayors of the cities, the Governor, the Lieutenant-Governor, the academia, business leaders, farm groups". And our friend Fred did it. He delivered. This very important, because when you go to his district or state and cultivate people who are important to him, you actually gain influence with the senator or congressman back in Washington.

Question:

Why is Singapore that important to the US?

Professor Tommy Koh:

We are important to the United States for many reasons. One, because we are an exemplar the United States can hold out to the rest of the world. A developing country, one with no natural resources, that has a relatively clean, honest administration pursuing basically a free enterprise economic policy and which has made the jump from being a poor, backward society to being Number 19 now on the scale of per capita GNP. Two, because we offer a very hospitable business environment to American investors, and to the American service industries. The feedback from Americans in business and industry to America on Singapore is just fantastic. And third, because of the prestige of the Prime Minister. The Prime Minister is viewed even by those who are not in love with him, as an extraordinary man, a person whose comprehension of world affairs, and whose insights are valued by American leaders of both parties.

Question:

Your analysis seems to me to be almost that of an idealist. You say that if you have the right wife, if you mix with the right people, you can influence public opinion – almost a boy scout's attitude ...

Professor Tommy Koh:

I was a boy scout. And I resent your implied negatives on the Boy Scout. I spent ten very happy years of my life hiking around what was once rural Singapore. According to some politicians, it has done me irreparable harm. I hope you don't subscribe to that view.

Question:

As a loyal successful lobbyist, how do you then explain that other countries have had to hire professional lobbyists to do the job for them?

Professor Tommy Koh:

We have not hired a lobbyist and the matter is, in fact, being actively considered. Many people in Singapore feel that no matter how effective the embassy is, that it need to be backed up with additional professional resource. And many embassies spend big money – Japan spends about US$15 million in Washington; Canada which is a relatively small country but whose relations with the United States are very important, spends US$76 million hiring lobbyists, consultants, lawyers. We don't do that. But I am not ruling that out as a possibility. One must be very careful about hiring these people, because if you hire a big-name firm which has many clients, and you give them a general retainer, they'll probably charge you a huge fee. My assessment is that you do not get value for money because you cannot compete with big spenders like Japan, Korea, even Taiwan or Brazil or Canada. I have asked the Canadians why they need to have so many lobbyists and not just one when they are a next-door neighbour. I would have thought that the Canadian Ambassador would be able to pick up the phone and call anyone, or get an appointment to see anyone. He said, "You are mistaken. Even the Ambassador of Canada cannot get his phone calls returned by White House staff".

Question:

How do you see the balance between your task in promoting Singapore's causes versus defending actions at home. Is there a correlation that exists between what the government does here and you having to explain what the government does ... do you at some point say, "Listen, if you take this step, you are making my job harder in Washington".

Professor Tommy Koh:

I'm a very irreverent member of the civil service. I take advantage of the fact that I am untrained and that I don't belong to the career service. I argue with my government constantly on policy. I can't tell you what my positions are and show you correspondence, but let us take an example which we can talk about because it is now in the past. I may be very unpopular with my fellow Singaporeans because I have increased their cost of living to a very small degree. In 1984, even prior to my appointment, I came home and informed our government that in the field of trade, we were like an angel, but one with a very bad stain in the field of the protection of intellectual property rights. I also told the government that if this stain was not cleaned up, we were going to be hit by trade retaliatory action because it had become a very emotional issue in Washington, with industry and business, the Administration and also with the Congress. It was not easy to convince the bureaucracy because they felt that it meant penalizing Singapore consumers. But I could not accept a position in which questions like intellectual property were not straightened out. and I bothered the bureaucracy until action was in fact taken.

At this point, the discussion was brought to a close.

SINGAPORE'S ROLE IN THE REGION AND THE WORLD

Hong Kong and Singapore Are Hard Acts to Follow

The collapse of communism in the former Soviet Union and Eastern Europe has brought the model of the centrally planned or command economy into disrepute. Leaders in Russia, Eastern Europe, Africa, Latin America and elsewhere are looking for an economic model. There has been discussion about the paths Singapore and Hong Kong have followed to become newly industrializing economies.

Is there a Hong Kong or a Singapore model? Are their similarities greater than their differences? What conclusions can be drawn from the success of these two economies? Which is likely to do better in the next phase of development?

Hong Kong is a British colony. The colonial government had adopted a *laissez-faire* approach. With a small but efficient civil service, the Hong Kong government concentrates on effective control of a minimalist regulatory system and on the preservation of law and order. Defence and foreign affairs are the responsibilities of Britain, not of the government in Hong Kong.

The colony benefited from an influx of entrepreneurs and skilled workers from China after the victory of the Chinese Communist Party in 1949. Refugees from Shanghai transplanted cotton spinning and textile businesses to Hong Kong. The colony also benefits from its large hinterland of southern China, especially Guangzhou. Hong Kong enterprises today employ some three million workers in the Pearl River Delta of China, about four times the manufacturing work force in Hong Kong itself.

The Hong Kong model has worked for Hong Kong. The colony has a physical infrastructure that would make any city proud. It has three universities and provides decent health care and housing to a population of 5.7 million people.

Singapore did not, and could not, choose the Hong Kong model. It is an independent island-state and therefore had to create the capacity to defend itself. As a country with a parliamentary democracy and a government accountable to the people, Singapore had to be more attentive to the aspirations of its people. Thus, for example, it provides quality public housing for its people.

Because Singapore did not enjoy an influx of entrepreneurs and skilled workers, the government had no choice but to jump-start the economy by assuming the role of creator, entrepreneur and regulator. In addition, it encouraged multinational corporations to become major players so that the economy could achieve rapid industrialization and high rates of economic growth. For these reasons, the state in Singapore plays a bigger economic role than it does in Hong Kong.

Which of the two models is better? In terms of the government-private sector mix, Hong Kong and Singapore represent two ends of the spectrum. It is not possible to say that one is better than the other. Hong Kong and Singapore have taken different paths that have been equally successful. They have achieved per capita incomes of between US$13,000 and US$14,000.

An economy must choose a model appropriate to its historical and contemporary circumstances. The test is not the proportions of the government/private sector mix but the capacity of an economy or state to generate and apply the appropriate growth-oriented policies at the right time.

It is a mistake to emphasize differences between Hong Kong and Singapore; it is more important to see their similarities. Hong Kong and Singapore are two market economies that have embraced open trading, investment and financial systems. They have pursued export-oriented industrialization. Their prudent fiscal policies have resulted in budgetary surpluses in most years. They have competent and committed public administrators working in civil services that are based upon merit. Finally, both societies have shown a high degree of adaptability.

These shared economic fundamentals account for the success of Hong Kong and Singapore. Both approaches to governance are proven successes for transition to the status of newly industrializing economies in their respective sociopolitical contexts.

However, there is no guarantee that this will hold true for the transition to developed country status. Industrial restructuring requires massive public expenditures on human resource development, and on research and development. It also requires intellectual space for creativity and innovation to blossom. A more educated society can also be expected to want greater political participation.

Change is therefore certain. The country which adapts best to new demands will reap the fruits of continued prosperity. Although there is no guarantee, the capacity that Hong Kong and Singapore have shown for successful evolution in the past augurs well for their future.

*Commentary (co-authored by Lee Tsao Yuan, Director, The Institute of Policy Studies, Singapore) contributed to the **International Herald Tribune**, 29 July 1992.*

SINGAPORE'S ROLE IN THE REGION AND THE WORLD

Singapore's Regionalization Vision

Singapore is a nation of doers. We are good at doing things but, generally speaking, not good with words. It is therefore pertinent to ask why we need a regionalization vision. We need it because we need a clear statement of our goals and objectives. We need to be clear in our minds what it is that we are seeking to achieve through regionalization, as well as what it is not intended to achieve. We need a clear vision so that it will inspire and galvanize our people, the public sector, the private sector, the labour unions, as well as the ordinary citizens to work together to achieve that vision.

Why Regionalize?

Why do we need to regionalize? We need to regionalize because our economy is maturing and our future growth rates will be moderate compared to those in the past. This problem is compounded by our limitations of space, manpower and resources. In order to overcome these constraints, it is necessary, as our Senior Minister has said, for the Singapore economy to grow an external wing. In this respect, we should seek to emulate the examples of two medium-sized European countries, Switzerland and the Netherlands.

Regionalization and Globalization

Our regionalization thrust is only one facet of our objective of building an external economy. The Singapore economy is linked to the global economy. Our largest export market is not in East Asia, but in the United States. We must continue to solicit inward investments from all over the world. Our companies must continue to invest and enter into strategic alliances wherever the opportunities present themselves, whether they be in East Asia, North America, Europe, Australia, New Zealand or elsewhere. It is important for us to maintain the global outlook which has been Singapore's lodestar.

Why Emphasize Regionalization?

Why are we placing so much emphasis on our regionalization thrust? We do so for the following seven reasons. First, because of the proximity of Singapore to the countries in the region. Second, because of our familiarity with them. Third, because they are rapidly deregulating their economies and therefore present fresh opportunities. Fourth, because of their high growth rates. Fifth, because there is a good match between some of their needs and our strengths. Sixth, because they want to do business with Singapore because of our reputation for quality and integrity and our good track record in economic development. Seventh, because of our good relations with all the countries in the region.

Objective of Regionalization

It is important, as the Minister for Trade and Industry, Mr S. Dhanabalan, pointed out, to remember that the objective of investing our capital, expertise and capabilities in other countries in the region is to strengthen our domestic economy. Mr Dhanabalan said that the government will therefore only give assistance to outward investments which produce spin-offs for Singapore. We must be alert to the danger that the wholesale relocation of Singapore businesses and manufacturing activities overseas could lead to the hollowing out of the Singapore economy. The purpose of regionalization is to expand what Kenichi Ohmae has called our "natural economic zone" and to raise the standard of living of all our people.

The Prime Minister's Five Guidelines

In his opening address to the Regionalization Forum, the Prime Minister laid down five guidelines. I wish briefly to recapitulate them. First, for economic and political reasons, we should not put all our eggs in one basket. Second, we should consolidate our traditional ties with our ASEAN partners. Third, when we go into new markets, we should do so with a long-term view. Fourth, we must make sure that our investments not only benefit ourselves but also the host countries. Fifth, our corporations should try to be good citizens in the host countries.

The PM's Three-Pronged Approach

In the Prime Minister's address, he also suggested that we could adopt a three-pronged approach in our regionalization thrust. First, we could let the private sector take the initiative and the public sector should play a supportive role. Second, the public sector or a Singapore consortium could identify a few major projects. Third, we could have a few very large-scale projects, such as the proposal to link Singapore to Shandong Province in China.

Our Strengths and Weaknesses

We must have a realistic assessment of our strengths and weaknesses. We must avoid the twin dangers of euphoria and self-aggrandizement. We have strengths in trade; in the design, building and maintenance of infrastructure; in management, financial and professional services; in deal-making; as a value-added mode for the region and in reconciling economic growth with the protection of the environment. It is necessary for us to remember that we also have some weaknesses, for example, we lack indigenous technology and, apart from Singapore Airlines (SIA), we have no world-class companies.

Linkages between Domestic and External Economies

The linkages between our domestic and external economies can take many forms. We can provide, in appropriate cases, research and development (R & D), design, engineering and marketing functions. Our companies can be involved as contractors or sub-contractors in infrastructure projects. Singaporeans can manage projects overseas. Singapore companies can take equity stakes in regional projects. Where appropriate, we can build little Singapore in other cities, such as Suzhou.

Preparing Singapore for Regionalization

We must educate a new generation of Singaporeans who are able to speak the languages of the region, who are familiar with their cultures, and who have the ability to work in different business environments and possess the mindset which makes them welcome a foreign posting. As more and more of our talented people work and live abroad, it is important for us to create a quality of life in Singapore, a pride in our country and enduring family ties which will always make our overseas Singaporeans want to come home.

Conclusion

Going regional will not be painless. It will mean the need to restructure our economy. It will mean the need to retrain and upgrade our workers. We must, in this respect, pay particular attention to the approximately one-third of our work force which has less than a primary education. We must ensure that the fruits of regionalization are enjoyed by all Singaporeans and will not lead to a growing gap between the rich and the poor. Finally, we must ensure that the domestic economy remains vibrant. The experience of Hong Kong leads me to believe that it can be done. The rise of East Asia in the world economy is a quiet revolution which has escaped the notice of some of our friends in the West. We, in Singapore, know it because we are part of that revolution. We will ride this new wave to a brighter tomorrow for Singapore, for East Asia and for the world economy.

*Article first published in **The Business Times**, 24 May 1993.*

SINGAPORE'S ROLE IN THE REGION AND THE WORLD

Explaining the Singapore Miracle

The Singapore Miracle

I am a child of British colonial rule. If any one had asked me in 1965, the year Singapore became independent, whether I could conceive of a day when Singapore's per capita income would exceed that of the United Kingdom, I would have said, "Impossible". Well, the impossible has happened. In 1965, Singapore's and the UK's real GNP per capita were US$450 and US$1,550 respectively. In 1994, they were US$23,360 for Singapore, and US$18,410 for the UK.

In the same way, if someone had asked me in 1963, the year I went to study at Harvard University, whether I could foresee a day when Singapore's infant mortality rate would be lower than that in the United States, I would have said, "Not in my lifetime". In 1950, the infant mortality rate in Singapore was 82 per 1,000 live-births. Today, it is four, lower than that of the US which is eight. Singapore's maternal mortality rate of ten per 100,000 live-births is also lower than that of the US which is 12 per 100,000 live-births.

It is therefore not out of a sense of arrogance or boastfulness that I have described the transformation which has taken place in Singapore in the past 30 years as a miracle.

Explaining the Singapore Miracle

Is there a rational explanation for the Singapore Miracle?

In brief, Singapore's success is living proof of the theme of the 1996 Human Development Report, i.e. that human development can help economic growth and economic growth can help human development. In the words of the report, we have created a "virtuous circle" whereby economic growth and human development are mutually reinforcing. Let me briefly discuss five salient components of Singapore's development strategy.

Education

Singapore's only resource is human resource. This being the case, the government attaches the highest importance to education and training. In the 1960s, the emphasis was on universal primary education. The school leavers were able to find work in the labour-intensive industries which were being established then. Later, the education system was revamped. Technical subjects were introduced into the secondary schools to develop the manpower needed by a rapidly industrializing economy. More recently, as the economy has moved into higher technology and higher value-added industries, the government has rapidly expanded enrolment in tertiary education. In 1984, only 22 per cent of the Primary One cohort enrolled in tertiary education. In 1994, the percentage had risen to 54 (35 per cent to the polytechnics and 19 per cent to the two universities). These figures do not include the large number of students who study abroad. Singapore's education policy is marked by three characteristics:

(a) Close co-ordination between education and employment opportunities;
(b) A strong emphasis on the learning of mathematics, science and technology;
(c) High standards maintained at all levels of the educational system.

In addition, the government, employer and employee, have joined hands to create a culture and system which emphasizes the need for training, retraining and upgrading. Therefore, although the Singapore work force is by no means the best educated in the world, it has been consistently ranked number one by the Business Environment Risk Intelligence (BERI).

Unlike the OECD countries, which have experienced the phenomenon of "jobless growth", there is no unemployment in Singapore. On the contrary, the shortage of labour is so acute that there are over 300,000 foreign workers in Singapore. In contrast, there are 100 million unemployed people in the OECD countries, a fact which is not reflected in the high ranking of these countries in the Human Development Index (HDI).

The Right to Adequate Shelter

When the British left Singapore, the housing conditions were so bad that the landscape was dotted with slums and overcrowding was the norm. The housing shortage was so acute that the colonial government had declared it insoluble. The poor housing conditions had a negative impact on public health. Tuberculosis was rampant.

After independence, and 30 years before the Second UN Conference on Human Settlements, the Singapore government pledged to build affordable housing for all the people. Today, there are no homeless people in Singapore. There are five million homeless people in the OECD countries, another fact which is not reflected in the HDI. Over 90 per cent of the people in Singapore own their own homes. Housing estates are designed to include all the social amenities, such as transportation, schools, clinics, markets, libraries, parks and proximity to work.

The 1996 Human Development Report has correctly pointed out on page 24, that: "Adequate housing is strongly correlated with progress in health, literacy, longevity, and with the social stability of communities".

The Right to Affordable Health Care

Singapore has one of the best health care systems in the world. This is reflected in our rising life expectancy (77 years in 1995), our low infant mortality (four per 1,000 live-births), and maternal mortality rates (ten per 100,000 live-births). There is one doctor per 725 persons.

Childhood infectious diseases have been virtually eradicated through a systematic mass immunization programme. Environmental health measures through improvements in public housing, sanitation, clean water and food supply, have brought communicable diseases under control.

Every Singaporean has access to good and affordable health services. Despite a comprehensive and highly subsidized public health system, total health expenditure has remained at three per cent of GDP. This is due to the government's emphasis on cost-effective prevention and health promotion. Financing expensive high quality medical services has involved a greater degree of cost sharing through a mandatory medical savings scheme, instead of relying mainly on the state through taxation. Singapore's health care financing philosophy is based on individual and family responsibility, coupled with public subsidies to keep basic health care affordable.

Growth and Equity

Singapore believes in growth with equity. According to Table 17 of the Human Development Report, there are no Singaporeans living below the poverty line. Singapore affords all its citizens equal opportunities but not equal results. Thus, the top 20 per cent of households earn 9.6 times as much as the lowest 20 per cent. However, educational opportunities are available to all and success in education is the passport to upward mobility. In Singapore, there is neither a privileged class nor an underclass. There are no impediments to social mobility.

The philosophy of the government is to make every citizen a stakeholder. Thus, 90 per cent of the population own their own homes. Each year, a tripartite body called the National Wages Council – consisting of the government, employer and employee – sits to decide the percentage of wage increase. In addition, both the public and the private sector pay their employees an annual bonus depending on how well the company or the economy has performed. In a bumper year, an employee may get as much as six months wages as bonus. When economic growth hits ten per cent, all civil servants are paid a bonus equivalent to two and half months of wages.

The National Trades Union Congress owns an insurance company, the largest chain of supermarkets, the largest taxi fleet, a golf club and holiday resorts for workers. The purpose is to empower the workers and to maintain social cohesion.

The government forces every employee to save 20 per cent of his monthly income. This is matched by an equivalent contribution by his employers. Every employee therefore saves 40 per cent of his monthly salary for his retirement. The net result is that Singapore has the highest saving rate in the world – 46 per cent of GDP.

Finally, the government is helping all its citizens to own shares by subsidizing their purchases of shares in the privatized state enterprises, such as Singapore Telecom. About 54 per cent of the population owns shares. This is another means of making every Singaporean, no matter how humble his or her circumstances, a stakeholder.

I should, perhaps, touch on gender equity in Singapore. At the level of primary school and secondary school, women have achieved equality with men. At the tertiary level, in 1993, women accounted for 43 per cent of all enrolment, only 7 per cent below that of men. There are, however, some glass ceilings against women which have yet to be broken. For example, only four per cent of the Members of Parliament are women. There is no woman in the Cabinet. There is no woman Permanent Secretary in the civil service. Women account for only 34 per cent of administrative and managerial jobs, 16 per cent of professional and technical jobs, and 31 per cent of earned income. There is, however, one figure which reflects the rising status of women in Singapore. The birth rate has plummeted from 4.2 to 1.6. The best form of family planning is the empowerment of women.

Good Government

The single most important factor in the making of the Singapore miracle is good governance. What are the elements of good governance?

First, Singapore has a clean, highly competent and courageous political leadership. It is continuously replenished with new blood. In a developing country, the quality of a country's political leadership can literally make or break a country.

Second, Singapore has a highly educated, non-corrupt and efficient bureaucracy. Civil servants are highly paid, financially and psychologically. It recruits the best and brightest into its ranks. Morale is high.

Third, Singapore enjoys a tripartite, symbiotic relationship among government, labour and management. This ensures industrial peace. It also ensures that labour gets a fair share of growing prosperity. We have therefore avoided the evil of "voiceless growth".

Fourth, there is a culture favouring consensus-building through extensive community consultations rather than through pressure exerted by powerful groups or lobbies. This is a form of participatory democracy.

Fifth, the government has provided a framework of sound macroeconomic and fiscal policies. We have enjoyed sustained growth of about eight per cent per annum for 30 years. As a result, Singapore's foreign reserves have risen steadily from S$1,069 million in 1965 to S$100,610 million in 1996.

Sixth, Singapore has studiously avoided the evil of "futureless growth". Beginning in the 1960s, the government has ensured that economic growth and protection of the environment must go hand in hand. Long before the Earth Summit in Rio in 1992, the Singapore government recognized the right of its citizens to live in a clean and green environment. Our collective ambition is to make Singapore the first tropical Green City of the 21st century.

Conclusion

Thirty years ago, Singapore was a backward developing country with high unemployment, slums, poor public health, corrupt officials and industrial unrest. For a population of two million, living on a small island of only 225 square miles, the future looked bleak. Yet, in a short span of only 30 years or one generation, we have caught up with many of the OECD countries. What is the moral of my story? It is that with good governance, the right framework of macroeconomic and fiscal policies, high investment in education, housing and health, and with a people-centred economic strategy of growth with equity, you too can perform your miracle.[1]

*Article contributed to the **Cambodian Journal of International Studies**, 1996.*

NOTES

1. This paper was originally entitled: "The Singapore Miracle: Lessons for Cambodia". Although written for a Cambodian audience, it has considerable relevance for anyone interested in understanding the factors behind Singapore's economic success.

SINGAPORE'S ROLE IN THE REGION AND THE WORLD

The Relevance of Singapore's Foreign Policy Experience for Africa

A Small State

In physical size, Singapore is one of the smallest states in the world. Its total land area of 626 square kilometres or 225 square miles places Singapore at 172nd in the ranking of states. Our total population of three million is made up of 2.7 million Singaporeans and 300,000 non-Singaporeans. By population size, Singapore ranks 123rd in the world.

An Unusual Small State

Singapore is not, however, a typical small state. It is the world's 14th largest trading nation. Using GDP as the yardstick, Singapore ranks 48th in the world. If we use GDP per capita as the yardstick, Singapore's ranking rises to 24th. Singapore has the world's eighth largest foreign exchange reserves. It ranks number one if we use the yardstick of foreign reserves per capita. I have cited these facts and figures not to boast about our achievements, but to make the point that although Singapore is very small in size, it is not an insignificant player in the world economy.

The Quest for Legitimacy

Singapore was born under very unique circumstances. I can, in fact, think of no other state in the world which was born as a result of being expelled from a federation. In the beginning, Singapore had to respond to questions raised by some quarters concerning its legitimacy. It therefore joined the United Nations, the Commonwealth, the Non-Aligned

Movement and the Group of 77 in order to receive their imprimaturs of legitimacy. Today, Singapore's legitimacy as a sovereign and independent state is a non-issue.

The Quest for Security: Yin and Yang

Like all small states, one of Singapore's major preoccupations is the quest for security. Singapore's quest for security has two aspects; the yin and the yang. By "yang", I mean building a capacity to deter aggression. Singaporeans are very realistic by nature. Singapore spends 6 per cent of its GDP on defence. It has a modern, well-equipped, army, navy and air force. In Singapore, as in Switzerland, every male citizen, below the age of 45, is a member of its armed forces. At the age of 18, every male citizen has to undergo two to two and a half years of compulsory military service. Thereafter, he becomes a reservist until he reaches the age of 45. Each year, a reservist is called up for retraining with full pay. In case the nation is threatened, Singapore can mobilize 250,000 citizen soldiers, sailors and pilots for its armed forces.

The Five Power Defence Arrangements

Singapore has no military alliances. It does, however, have arrangements with Malaysia, the UK, Australia and New Zealand, called the Five Power Defence Arrangements (FPDA). At one time, New Zealand maintained a battalion in Singapore and Australia had a squadron of aircraft in Malaysia. These have been withdrawn. Nevertheless, both Singapore and Malaysia regard the FPDA as a useful arrangement which enables the armed forces of the five countries to conduct joint exercises. The principal utility of the FPDA for Singapore is psychological. It is perceived by Singaporeans and by others as having a deterrent value.

US Military Presence in the Asia Pacific

There are no foreign military bases in Singapore. However, Singapore regards the US as a benign superpower. We would like the US to maintain an adequate military presence in the Asia Pacific for as long as possible. We fear that a precipitate withdrawal by the US would destabilize the region and could lead to an arms race between China and Japan, and between Japan and a reunified Korea. For these reasons, Singapore has granted the US Navy and Air Force access to our facilities for repairs and servicing for their ships and aircraft. This arrangement has been accepted by our neighbours, some of whom have made similar offers to the US.

The Quest for Regional Peace and Order

I would now like to discuss the "yin" dimension of our quest for security. We pursue a pro-active foreign policy of peace. The first objective is to establish an environment of good neighbourliness with our three immediate neighbours, Malaysia, Indonesia and Brunei. Relations between Singapore and our three neighbours are excellent.

A Peaceful and Prosperous Southeast Asia

The second objective is to make Southeast Asia a region of peace and prosperity. In 1967, two years after Singapore's independence, Singapore joined Indonesia, Malaysia, Philippines and Thailand in forming the Association of Southeast Asian Nations (ASEAN). The Association was later expanded to include Brunei. ASEAN is one of the diplomatic wonders of the world. It has transformed Southeast Asia, which had been described as the "Balkans" of Asia, into an oasis of peace. ASEAN's prestige is so high that the Foreign Ministers of the United States, Japan, the EC, Canada, Australia, New Zealand and South Korea journey each July to meet with their ASEAN colleagues at one of the ASEAN capitals. During the last two years, ASEAN has also invited the Foreign Ministers of China, Russia, Vietnam, Laos and Papua New Guinea to their annual meeting.

ASEAN's Achievements

A sceptic may ask: What has ASEAN really achieved? I would point to four major achievements. The most important achievement is that peace has prevailed among its six members during the past 26 years. They have acquired a habit of consulting one another, a willingness to give and take, to forge consensus and avoid division, to support one another in international fora, and to settle differences amicably through dialogue and negotiations.

The next important achievement is ASEAN's success in mobilizing the support of the international community against Vietnam's attempt to impose a puppet regime in Cambodia and to incorporate Cambodia into her sphere of influence. ASEAN led the campaign to free Cambodia from Vietnamese colonialism and the terror of the Khmer Rouge, from December 1978 until the signature of the Paris Agreement in 1991. The success of the UN Transitional Authority's role in the political rehabilitation of Cambodia has vindicated ASEAN's stand on Cambodia, which is based upon the principle of non-interference in the internal affairs of other states, the principle against the acquisition of territory by use of force, and the principle of self-determination.

Another notable milestone is the agreement to establish the ASEAN Free Trade Area (AFTA) signed in Singapore in January 1992. Under this agreement, the six ASEAN countries have agreed to progressively reduce their tariff barriers and to establish a free trade area in 15 years. In adopting AFTA, ASEAN's leaders were responding to the growing complementarities among their economies as well as to two external stimuli: the Single European Market and the North American Free Trade Agreement. ASEAN's leaders realized that they had to unite their strength in order to compete against the rise of those large regional economies, otherwise they would be marginalized.

Finally, ASEAN has taken the lead to create a new forum to discuss issues pertaining to the security of the Asia Pacific region. With the end of the Cold War, the old security order has disappeared. A new order has not yet taken its place. In the meantime, things are in a state of flux. In this promising and yet uncertain moment, ASEAN's Foreign Ministers proposed, at their annual meeting, in Singapore in July 1993, the creation of an ASEAN Regional Forum (ARF). The proposal was welcomed by the US, Japan, China, Russia, South Korea, Vietnam, Laos, Australia, New Zealand and Canada, the EC and Papua New Guinea. The ARF will hold its first meeting in Bangkok in July 1994.

The Asia Pacific Region

The third objective is to anchor Singapore securely to the larger, dynamic and increasingly prosperous Asia Pacific region. Singapore supported the creation of the Asia Pacific Economic Cooperation (APEC) grouping. Singapore is the host of both the APEC Secretariat and the Secretariat of a sister organization called the Pacific Economic Cooperation Council (PECC). Singapore was one of the first countries to support President Clinton's proposal to hold an APEC Leaders Meeting in Seattle later this month. Singapore was the first country to support the Malaysian Prime Minister, Dr Mahathir's proposal to form an East Asian Economic Caucus (EAEC). We see ASEAN, EAEC and APEC as three intersecting circles and not as contradictory institutions.

The Singapore Government has encouraged our government-linked companies and other private companies to take advantage of investment opportunities in ASEAN, China, Vietnam and India. The Singapore Government has been working closely with the Government of Indonesia and the Government of the State of Johor (part of Malaysia) to create the Southern Growth Triangle. Because of the shortage of land and labour in Singapore, many Singapore companies and Singapore-based MNCs have started manufacturing facilities in Johor and on the Indonesian island of Batam. Singapore investment is also pouring into China and Vietnam and, to a lesser extent, India. There is also a significant flow of Singapore investment into Australia and New Zealand. These cross-border flows are part of the explosion in intra-regional trade and investment in East Asia. There is a reasonably good chance that the economies of East Asia will maintain the current growth spurt into the next century. If this scenario comes true, some time in the early part of the 21st Century, East Asia will surpass both Europe and North America as the world's largest regional economy.

A Good Citizen of the World

The fourth objective is to project Singapore as a useful member of the international community and a good citizen of the world. Towards this end, Singapore has played an active part in the United Nations. It has contributed soldiers, police officers, and electoral officers to UN peacekeeping operations in Namibia, Angola, Iraq-Kuwait and Cambodia, as well as to the Commonwealth Observer Mission in South Africa. Singapore's free trade policy and its stature as the world's 14th largest trading nation have enabled Singapore to play an important role in GATT. Her relative success in reconciling economic growth with protection of the environment led Singapore to play a leading role in the Earth Summit's negotiating process. Through the Singapore International Foundation, Singapore has sent volunteers to work in the Philippines, Indonesia, Sri

Lanka, Nepal, China and Botswana. The Ministry of Foreign Affairs coordinates a modest programme of technical assistance for developing countries.

Characteristics of Singapore's Foreign Policy

The first characteristic of Singapore's foreign policy is that it is pragmatic and free of ideology or dogma. We accept the world as it is rather than as what we would like it to be. We expect states to act in their self-interests. We therefore have an unsentimental and hard-headed view of the world. This does not mean that this is a cynical or fatalistic view. We are activists and we seek change where change is possible. For example, in order to give small states a bigger voice at the UN, we helped to establish the Forum of Small States.

The second characteristic is that we try to be agile and nimble. As a small state, we have to be alert to changes in the external environment and to stay ahead of the wave. Some of the major changes which Singapore has to respond to include, the end of the Cold War, the rise of East Asia in the world economy, the increase of protectionism in the West, the evolution of the Single European Market and NAFTA, and Singapore's own stage of economic development as a capital exporter.

The third characteristic is that we plan for the future. We do this not by predicting the future since the future is unpredictable but by scenario planning. The art of scenario planning has been pioneered by companies such as Shell. The idea is to work out two or more scenarios of the future and to position oneself in such a way as to survive even if the worst scenario were to come true. In other words, we hope for the best but we plan for the worst.

The fourth characteristic is to be frugal in the use of our scarce human resources and to borrow from the strength of others. Singapore has only 33 diplomatic missions in the world. We have 17 Honorary Consuls. The Honorary Consuls are foreign citizens. They help to promote our interests in countries or cities where we are not represented. In addition, we have five roving Ambassadors. These five roving Ambassadors are Singapore citizens who live and work in Singapore. They are accredited to foreign countries as our Ambassadors. They usually visit their host countries several times a year. This unusual arrangement has worked well. It is an example of how we have made a virtue out of our necessity.

Conclusion

I hope I have succeeded in conveying to you some salient points of how a small country in Southeast Asia has succeeded in using foreign policy to help establish its legitimacy, security and prosperity. Whether or not there are lessons in the Singapore story which are applicable to the countries of Africa, is something which I will leave you to judge.

Paper presented at the African Leadership Forum (ALF)-Singapore International Foundation (SIF) Conference on "The Relevance of Singapore's Experience for Africa: The External Dimension", 10 November 1993.

SINGAPORE'S ROLE IN THE REGION AND THE WORLD

Indonesia and Singapore: A Strong Partnership

Introduction

The month of August 1995 is a very propitious one for Indonesia and for Singapore. On 17 August 1995, Indonesia will celebrate the golden anniversary of its independence. On 9 August 1995, Singapore will celebrate the 30th anniversary of its independence. This is therefore a very opportune moment to highlight the major achievements of Indonesia-Singapore relations over the past 30 years. In this essay, I will focus on the following five points:

(a) The importance of Indonesia to the region of the world;
(b) Indonesia's achievement under the leadership of President Soeharto;
(c) Indonesia's contributions to the region and the world;
(d) Indonesia-Singapore bilateral relations;
(e) The prospects of Indonesia-Singapore relations in the coming years and decades.

The Importance of Indonesia

Indonesia is one of the largest countries in the world. By size of population, it ranks number four in the world. Its national territory stretches across more time zones than the United States of America. It is a country of great diversity, consisting of peoples with different ethnic, religious, linguistic and cultural affiliations. Indonesia is also a country blessed with natural resources and scenic beauty. It has a rich cultural heritage, especially in Java and Bali.

When I was based in Washington, D.C., my ASEAN colleagues and I would frequently go on speaking tours of the United States. I was often astonished by how little the American people know about Indonesia. One of my Indonesian colleagues, Minister Soesilo Soedarman, was once asked, "Which part of Bali is Indonesia?" Soesilo Soedarman did not know whether to laugh or to cry.

Indonesia's Achievements under President Soeharto

The 30 years since Singapore became independent in 1965 has coincided with the period of President Soeharto's leadership. Under his presidency, Indonesia has concentrated on its economic development. In order to achieve this goal, President Soeharto has pursued a foreign policy of co-operation, mutual understanding and friendly relations with all of Indonesia's neighbours. As a result, Indonesia has succeeded in achieving a stable and peaceful external environment to promote growth at home. President Soeharto's wise policies have also helped to allay some of the concerns of the region about Indonesia's regional ambitions, which arose from an earlier period of Indonesian history.

During the past 30 years, President Soeharto has contributed to two very major achievements. First, domestic peace and social harmony. Second, rapid economic development. Given that the great diversity which exists within Indonesia, the management of diversity is one of the great challenges facing the Indonesian nation. By emphasizing the principles of Pancasila, by practising tolerance, by sticking to the national motto of "Unity in Diversity", Indonesia is a remarkably cohesive and harmonious society. This stands in sharp contrast to some parts of the world where inter-ethnic, inter-tribal, inter-religious and inter-linguistic conflicts have led to civil war and the dismemberment of the state.

President Soeharto's second achievement is in fostering rapid economic development. By bringing some of Indonesia's ablest technocrats into his Government, by pursuing economic policies consonant with the market, by accepting fiscal discipline, and by incrementally deregulating the Indonesian economy, President Soeharto has succeeded in bringing Indonesia into the mainstream of the dynamic economies of East Asia. The World Bank paid Indonesia the tribute of including her as one of the eight so-called "miracle" economies of East Asia.

Indonesia's Contributions to the Region and the World

I would like to highlight six of the most significant contributions which Indonesia has made to the region and the world. First, Indonesia has been a staunch supporter of ASEAN. Being the biggest country in Southeast Asia, Indonesia's support for ASEAN has been absolutely critical. Over the past 27 years, Indonesia has made many contributions, at critical junctures in ASEAN's history, which have made ASEAN the most successful regional organization in the non-Western world.

Second, Indonesia made a pivotal contribution to the resolution of the tragic conflict in Cambodia. I wish to recall that ASEAN had appointed Indonesia as its interlocutor with Vietnam. Subsequently, when the negotiations appeared to have bogged down, Foreign Minister Mochtar Kusumaatmadja and his successor, Ali Alatas, launched a new initiative called the Jakarta Informal Meeting (JIM). This helped to pave the way for the convening in 1989 of the Paris International Conference on Cambodia. Indonesia and France were the Co-Chairmen of the Paris Conference. The success of the Paris Conference in 1991 was, in part, attributable to ASEAN's steadfastness and, in part, attributable to Indonesia's skilful diplomacy.

Third, the skilful and pro-active manner in which President Soeharto chaired the APEC Leaders Meeting in Bogor in November 1994, resulting in the adoption by consensus of the Bogor Declaration, was an important step forward by APEC towards the achievement of the APEC common vision of free trade and investment by the year 2020.

Fourth, Indonesia's election as Chairman of the Non-Aligned Movement and the constructive and responsible manner in which Indonesia led the Movement during the past three years have brought her great credit.

Fifth, Indonesia has played a constructive role in the United Nations and has frequently participated in UN peacekeeping operations.

Sixth, I would like to acknowledge and applaud Indonesia's leadership in seeking a peaceful solution to the conflicting claims to the Spratly Islands. Indonesia has led a series of workshops, involving all the six claimants, as well as other interested parties, to avoid the use of force and to seek a peaceful and amicable solution to this thorny problem.

Indonesia-Singapore Bilateral Relations

Today, Indonesia-Singapore bilateral relations are closer, warmer and more broad based than at any time during the past 30 years. This happy state of affairs is due to several factors.

The first factor is the very close rapport and friendship which have developed between President Soeharto and Senior Minister Lee Kuan Yew. The present Prime Minister of Singapore, Goh Chok Tong, has also developed a close personal relationship with President Soeharto. This was particularly evident in 1994 when Prime Minister Goh worked very closely with President Soeharto to ensure the success of the APEC Leaders Meeting in Bogor.

The second factor is the common understanding between Indonesia and Singapore, that in spite of our differences in size, factor endowment, stages of economic development, we should work together in order to take advantage of our economic complementarity. Thus, Indonesia has welcomed Singapore's investment in her economy. Today, Singapore is Indonesia's sixth largest cumulative investor, after Japan, Hong Kong, Taiwan, the US and UK. Singapore is also Indonesia's third largest trading partner, after Japan and the US. Singapore and Indonesia are co-operating closely in the development of Batam and Bintan under the Growth Triangle, comprising Singapore, Johor and the Riau archipelago. The two countries are also co-operating in the development of Karimum. Indonesia-Singapore economic co-operation will be further enhanced as a result of the signing, in 1994, of the Tourism Co-operation Agreement and the Air Services Agreement. The Tourism Co-operation Agreement will enable Singapore to divert a greater percentage of the seven million tourists who visit Singapore annually, to Indonesia. The Air Services Agreement will expand air links between Indonesia and Singapore, including such new destinations in Indonesia as Lombok, Solo and Ujung Panjang. The successful inaugural meeting of the Ministerial Committee on Indonesia-Singapore Tourism Co-operation held in Jakarta on 29 June 1995 has injected new momentum into this joint enterprise.

The third factor is the increasingly close ties between our two defence establishments. Some of the achievements in this field include the Joint

Co-ordinated Patrols in the Straits of Malacca, which have significantly reduced incidents of piracy and smuggling; and the establishment of the Air Combat Manoueuvring Range in Pekan Baru, Sumatra, which allows our two air forces to conduct effective training. The visits of senior military personnel from the two countries have also intensified.

The fourth factor is the growing network of contacts between Indonesia and Singapore, both in the public and the private sectors. These growing networks include government officials, business leaders, youth, journalists, intellectuals from our think-tanks and non-governmental organizations.

Conclusion

As I look forward to the future, I am confident that the strong bilateral relationship between Indonesia and Singapore will endure and prosper. Economically, I expect the two countries to draw closer in order to take advantage of the many complementaries which exist between them. This process will be greatly accelerated as Indonesia deregulates her economy even more and opens it to foreign participation. Politically, the two countries share a common world view and are committed to the maintenance of peace and stability in East Asia. I expect the two governments and countries to continue to work co-operatively to strength such important regional institutions as ASEAN, APEC and the ASEAN Regional Forum. Culturally, there is much that the two countries can learn from each other.

Singapore, in particular, should take advantage of Indonesia's cultural wealth and build upon the historical links which already exists between, for example, our visual artists and Bali. Through more bilateral cultural exchanges and the Festival of Asian Performing Arts, Singaporeans can learn to appreciate and enjoy the cultural wealth and diversity that Indonesia has to offer.

Finally, I wish to express the hope that Indonesia will continue to be inspired by the vision that it should build not only a better life for all Indonesians, but for all the peoples of ASEAN.

Article written for the 50th Indonesian Independence Day Commemorative Souvenir Book published by the Indonesian Embassy in Singapore, 30 June 1995.

SINGAPORE'S ROLE IN THE REGION AND THE WORLD

Singapore's External Relations: Laying the Foundation for the Post-Cold War Era

Introduction

For Singapore, as for the world, 1990 was a historic and eventful year. In Singapore's external relations, the following were the most significant events which took place during the past year:

1. The change of Prime Minister in Singapore;
2. The signing of the two agreements on economic co-operation in the Riaus and on the protection of investments between Indonesia and Singapore in August; and the signing of the agreements on water and natural gas between Malaysia and Singapore in November;
3. The 23rd ASEAN Ministerial Meeting and Post-Ministerial Conference in Jakarta;
4. The Cambodian endgame;
5. The second APEC Ministerial Meeting in Singapore;
6. The Uruguay Round of Multilateral Trade Negotiations;
7. The establishment of diplomatic relations with China;
8. The end of the Cold War;
9. The conclusion of a Memorandum of Understanding between Singapore and the United States on the enhanced use by the US of Singapore's military facilities;
10. Iraq's invasion of Kuwait.

The Change of Prime Minister

The change of Prime Minister, from Mr Lee Kuan Yew to Mr Goh Chok Tong, will not result in any shift in Singapore's foreign policy. Prior to taking office, Mr Goh had visited the leaders of ASEAN, the United States, the United Kingdom and other countries to assure them that there would not be any change in Singapore's relations with those countries. In return, he was assured by the foreign leaders that they looked forward to working as closely with him as they had with Mr Lee. This does not, of course, mean that there will be no change in Singapore's foreign policy resulting from the dramatic changes which have taken place in the world and in the region. Adjustments to Singapore's foreign policy will have to be made to respond to such changes.

Why will there be no change in Singapore's foreign policy because of the change of Prime Minister? Because Mr Goh and his team share the world view of Mr Lee and the old guard, and because there is a broad consensus in Singapore about what I referred to, in a recent article in *Trends* (No. 4, 27 December 1990), as the seven principles of Singapore's foreign policy. What are they?

First, we have a pragmatic foreign policy which is not based upon any ideology or doctrine. The overriding objective of our foreign policy is to promote the security and prosperity of Singapore.

Second, we rely, first and foremost, on ourselves. The belief in self-reliance should not, however, be confused with a policy of isolationism or autarchy.

Third, we accept the world as it is and not as we would like it to be. This has instilled in us a realistic and hard-headed attitude towards realities.

Fourth, Singapore is committed to ASEAN and a policy of good neighbourliness with our five regional partners, especially with our two closest neighbours, Malaysia and Indonesia.

Fifth, Singapore believes that its commitment to ASEAN is not inconsistent with its support for APEC and PECC. ASEAN, APEC and PECC can co-exist as expanding and intersecting circles. Singapore has played and will continue to play an active role in the evolution of the Pacific Community.

Sixth, Singapore will be a good citizen of the world community, by supporting the principles of the UN Charter and international law, by pursuing a policy of free trade and supporting the GATT, by pursuing an environmentally sensitive development policy, by helping other less developed countries and by supplying Singapore's diplomats as the chairmen of international diplomatic conferences and negotiations.

Seventh, Singapore will work with other countries to maintain a stable and peaceful environment in our region.

Closer Singapore-Indonesia-Malaysia Relations

In August, Singapore and Indonesia signed two agreements on economic co-operation in the Riaus archipelago and on the protection of investments (IGA). These agreements reflected the rapid progress in the implementation of the Growth Triangle concept, and most importantly, underscored the principle behind the concept, which is economic co-operation for mutual benefit. The booming economies of Batam and Johor show the benefits of such economic linkages and the synergies which result from the pooling of the resources and comparative advantages of the three economies. Imagine what a boon it would be for ASEAN if the concept underlying the Growth Triangle could be extended to the whole of ASEAN.

In November, Singapore and Malaysia signed two agreements on water and natural gas. The agreements were historic and reflected a new maturity in the relations between the two countries. This is a very positive development in the relations between Singapore and Malaysia.

The 23rd ASEAN Ministerial Meeting and the Future of ASEAN

The 23rd ASEAN Ministerial Meeting and the Post-Ministerial Conference were held in July in Jakarta. The two meetings concentrated on three questions: Cambodia, the implications for ASEAN of the ending of the Cold War and the future of ASEAN after Cambodia. The ASEAN Ministers made an assessment of the political and security implications for ASEAN and the region of the ending of the Cold War. They agreed to explore the feasibility of a more co-operative relationship with the Soviet Union and looked forward to welcoming Vietnam back to the fold of Southeast Asia once the Cambodian conflict has been settled. ASEAN was also conscious of the fact that it had been an underachiever in the field of economic co-operation and that its prestige and stature in the international community had been due largely to its cohesive and skilful diplomacy on the Cambodian question. With the Cambodian issue about to be resolved or marginalized, the question had often been asked whether ASEAN would wither away or find a new cause.

Some ASEAN leaders have suggested that ASEAN should return to its original *raison d'être* of economic co-operation and adopt an economic treaty along the line of the EC's Treaty of Rome. The proponents of this view argue that such a treaty is feasible if its implementation could be stretched out over several decades. Other ASEAN leaders have suggested that ASEAN should attempt to consummate its long-standing proposals to make Southeast Asia a Zone of Peace, Freedom and Neutrality (ZOPFAN), as well as a Nuclear Weapon Free Zone (SEANWFZ). Still other ASEAN leaders have argued that ZOPFAN and SEANWFZ are ideas whose time has passed and that it would be more relevant to examine whether ASEAN should be transformed into a security community and whether the time has come for the Asia Pacific region to have a forum like the Conference on Security and Cooperation in Europe (CSCE). No doubt these and other issues will be on the agenda of ASEAN's fourth summit meeting to be held in Singapore.

The Cambodian Endgame

The Cambodian tragedy is now 20 years old. Following the failure of the Paris International Conference on Cambodia, in the summer of 1989, the negotiations for a plan to end the conflict and to give the Cambodians the right to choose a government in a free and fair election, have been undertaken by the five permanent members of the UN Security Council. Reflecting the radically improved relationships between the West and the Soviet Union, and between the Soviet Union and China, and the increasing ability of the Big Five to work together, the Permanent Five have adopted a proposal which, in essence, will set up an UN interim administration to govern Cambodia and to prepare for free elections.

After initially accepting the proposal, Vietnam and Hun Sen have backtracked from their initial acceptance. Why have they done so? Perhaps it is because Hun Sen is not certain that he can beat Sihanouk in a free and fair election. Or perhaps Vietnam feels that there is no need to take the risk of putting its client regime to the test of a popular election because, by beating the drum of the possible return of the Khmer Rouge to Phnom Penh and opening its economy to foreign investments, an increasing number of countries will recognize the Hun Sen regime and normalize its relations with Vietnam. Vietnam could also have felt encouraged by the fact that ASEAN is no longer united on the Cambodian question. The tragedy is that if Vietnam and Hun Sen continue to block the acceptance of the Permanent Five's plan, the people of Cambodia will continue to suffer. The outcome will either be decided on the battlefield or, neither side will prevail, and the world will simply ignore the low-level of fighting which will continue indefinitely.

A New Regional Order

If the Cambodian conflict is resolved in accordance with the UN plan and Vietnam gives up its hegemonic ambitions, there is an opportunity for the countries of Southeast Asia to evolve a new regional order. There could be more economic contacts between ASEAN and the countries of Indonesia. In the political arena, consultations and confidence-building measures between ASEAN and the Indochinese countries could also be initiated. In time, as Vietnam restructures its economy into a more market-oriented one, and as mutual trust and confidence grow, the idea of expanding ASEAN to include the other four countries of Southeast Asia becomes not unthinkable.

The Second APEC Ministerial Meeting

Singapore hosted the Second APEC Ministerial Meeting in late July 1990. Prior to this meeting, on 15 February 1990, ASEAN Ministers held a special meeting in Kuching to discuss the issue of ASEAN's involvement in APEC and to agree on a common ASEAN position. The Second APEC Ministerial Meeting was highly successful and achieved five results. First, it adopted a strong declaration highlighting the commitment of the APEC participants to the success of the Uruguay Round. Second, it endorsed the offers by Thailand and the US to host the Fourth and Fifth Ministerial Meetings. Third, unlike the first meeting in Canberra which issued a joint statement and a Chairman's summary, the Singapore Meeting produced only one document agreed to by all the participants. Fourth, the meeting agreed that China, Taiwan and Hong Kong should join APEC at the same time. The Republic of Korea, as the host of the Third APEC Ministerial Meeting, was entrusted with the task of holding consultations with the representatives of the three economies. Fifth, the meeting endorsed the seven work projects which were drawn up by the senior officials.

The Uruguay Round

The Uruguay Round of multilateral trade negotiations was scheduled to end by December 1990. At the Ministerial Meeting in Brussels, the negotiations broke down. The collapse was due primarily to the refusal of the EC, Japan and Korea to accept, as the basis of negotiations, a text prepared by the chairman of the negotiating group on agriculture. The US and the Cairns Group would like to phase out, if possible, and if not, to substantially cut agricultural subsidies within an agreed time-frame. The EC agreed to cut such subsidies by 30 per cent in ten years, backdating the reduction to 1985. This meant that the prospective reduction would be only 15 per cent and not 30 per cent. The US demanded a reduction of 70 per cent. The failure of the US and the Cairns Group, on the one hand, and the EC, Japan and Korea, on the other, to agree caused the meeting to collapse.

The failure of the Brussels meetings was a great disappointment to all participants, especially to the developing countries. If the talks, which are expected to resume sometime during January 1991, did not achieve a breakthrough, this could have very serious implications for the open trading system under the GATT. Some feared that the collapse of the Uruguay Round could lead the world to evolve towards three rival trading blocs: an enlarged EC, a North American Free Trade Area which would be extended to South America and an Asia Pacific trading bloc.

The Malaysian Proposal

Following the failure of the Brussels meeting, the Prime Minister of Malaysia proposed the creation of an East Asian economic grouping. The group would consist of the countries and economies of East Asia. Therefore, the United States, Canada, Australia and New Zealand would not be included. Is the group intended to become a trading bloc? The Malaysians have said no. They have explained that the group would only act in conformity with the GATT. The group would not create unnecessary barriers to imports from third countries. It would not divert trade but would seek to enhance trade and investment.

What would the group do? First, it would enable the countries and economies of East Asia to concert their policies and positions and increase their leverage in the Uruguay Round negotiations. Second, it would seek to liberalize trade and investment between and among the countries of the region.

What would be the relationship between this proposed group and ASEAN and APEC? The new group would be an intermediate tier between ASEAN and APEC. To use another metaphor, they would be a series of expanding and intersecting circles. The Malaysians have explained that the East Asian economic community is not intended to detract from ASEAN's commitment to APEC or to the GATT.

Wouldn't the proposed group, which includes Japan but excludes the United States, run the danger of becoming dominated by Japan? Such a grouping will naturally give Japan a leadership role. Is Japan ready to assume such a role? Is Japan ready to open her economy to her neighbours in East Asia? These are some of the questions which must be convincingly answered if Malaysia's proposal is to take off.

The Establishment of Diplomatic Relations with China

Singapore has always said that it would establish diplomatic relations with the People's Republic of China after Indonesia normalized her relations with China. Indonesia and China resumed full diplomatic relations on 8 August 1990. On 3 October 1990, Singapore and the PRC established formal diplomatic relations.

The establishment of formal diplomatic relations between Singapore and the PRC was more a formality than a substantive change. Singapore had never recognized the Republic of China. Since 1974, the leaders of Singapore and China had frequently visited one another and were always accorded the normal diplomatic honours. In spite of the absence of formal relations, Singapore is China's sixth largest trading partner and fourth largest foreign investor. In establishing formal diplomatic relations with the PRC, Singapore has preserved the substance of its relations with Taiwan, which are very close and substantial. Singapore has therefore succeeded in maintaining a delicate balance in its relations with China and Taiwan.

The End of the Cold War

Singapore welcomes the end of the Cold War and looks forward to entering into new and more co-operative relations with the Soviet Union and

Vietnam. The visit to Singapore by the Soviet Prime Minister and the return visit by the former Prime Minister of Singapore to the Soviet Union are examples of this trend at work. The end of the Cold War requires every state, including Singapore, to re-adjust its world view.

The end of the Cold War does not, however, necessarily lead to a more peaceful world or a safer world for small nations. Many of the conflicts in the Third World have indigenous roots and are unlikely to go away. The withdrawal of the two superpowers from various regions of the world may bring about destabilizing changes. There may be a race by regional powers to fill the vacuum. For these reasons, Singapore favours the continued military presence of the United States in East and Southeast Asia. Singapore appreciates that the US will have to re-assess its strategy, force structure and force levels in the light of the changing circumstances.

Singapore also appreciates that US allies and friends will have to carry a more equitable share of the burden of collective security. Singapore's offer to the US of the increased use of its military facilities by the US air force and navy is intended, in part, to take some of the heat off President Aquino and, in part, as Singapore's contribution to burden sharing.

The Future of the World Order

Iraq's invasion and purported annexion of Kuwait is a clear example of aggression. It violates the principles of the UN Charter and of international law. If Iraq were allowed to benefit from its aggression, it would set a very dangerous precedent for all small countries. It would also be a very bad beginning for the post-Cold War world order. For these reasons, Singapore has joined the overwhelming majority of the international community in condemning Iraq and has scrupulously enforced the UN-mandated sanctions. Singapore hopes that Iraq will comply with the decisions of the UN Security Council and withdraw from Kuwait by 15 January. If Iraq continues to defy the international community, it must be compelled to leave Kuwait. We must hope and pray that war can be avoided. If, however, war cannot be avoided, let it not be said that this is a war between the United States and Iraq. It is a war between Iraq and the rest of the world. What is at stake in this conflict is not just the fate of a small country, Kuwait. What is at stake is nothing less than the future of the world order and the efficacy of the United Nations to deter aggression and to maintain international peace and security.

Conclusion

Singapore had a very successful year in 1990 in its external relations. The change of leadership will not affect the principles of our foreign policy. However, Singapore's world view has to be modified to take account of the ending of the Cold War. Singapore has to re-assess its preference for multipolarity in the region in the light of the new circumstances. Economic co-operation between Singapore and its two closest neighbours, Malaysia and Indonesia, rose to a new height with the implementation of the Growth Triangle and the signing of the water and natural gas agreements between Singapore and Malaysia. The question is whether the leaders of ASEAN are ready to make a quantum leap at their forthcoming fourth summit meeting in Singapore, by concluding an agreement or treaty to move ASEAN towards the goal of a borderless ASEAN economy. The success of the second APEC Ministerial Meeting strengthened the evolutionary process of building an Asia Pacific economic community. The Cambodian conflict is winding down and the region is enjoying the fruits of the ending of the Cold War. Depending on how the Cambodian conflict is settled and Vietnam's subsequent conduct, a new regional order in Southeast Asia may be feasible. The leaders of the Asia Pacific region should now consider whether it is time to create a consultative forum like APEC, but with a wider membership, to discuss political and security co-operation in the region.

Paper first published in **Singapore: The Year in Review 1990**, *Tan Teng Lang (ed.) (Singapore: The Institute of Policy Studies and Times Academic Press, 1991).*

SINGAPORE'S ROLE IN THE REGION AND THE WORLD

Singapore's External Relations: Six Years Later

Introduction

Six years have passed since I last reviewed Singapore's external relations in 1991. At that time, the Cold War had just ended and things were in a state of flux. The intellectual atmosphere contained two aromas, hope and uncertainty. The optimists predicted a new era of peace and prosperity. The pessimists feared that without the paradigm of the Cold War, the world could become a more chaotic place.

In January, 1991, the Cambodian conflict was still unresolved. The Uruguay Round of multilateral trade negotiations looked dangerously close to collapse. APEC had not yet held its first annual summit. In my 1991 essay, I raised the following questions:

(a) Will ASEAN find a new cause or will it wither away once the Cambodian conflict is resolved?
(b) Will the Fourth ASEAN Summit make a quantum leap by adopting an ASEAN Free Trade Agreement?
(c) Will ASEAN take the lead in building a new regional order in Southeast Asia?
(d) Will the Asia Pacific create a new forum to discuss political and security co-operation?
(e) Will the Uruguay Round be successfully completed or will the world's trading system splinter into a number of rival trading blocs?

When we reflect on those questions we are struck by the dramatic changes which have occurred in the past six years. We should also be grateful that, by a combination of wise initiative and good fortune, things have turned out extremely well for us in Southeast Asia and the Asia Pacific. In this essay, I will therefore review Singapore's external relations in 1996, against the backdrop of the dramatic developments which have taken place since 1990.

Building a New Regional Order in Southeast Asia

In 1991, some of our Western friends predicted the early demise of ASEAN. They mistakenly thought that ASEAN was a creature of the Cold War and would disappear with it. They thought that Cambodia was the only glue which kept ASEAN together and that once the Cambodian conflict was resolved, ASEAN would become unstuck.

The performance of ASEAN in the past six years has proven its sceptics wrong. Far from becoming defunct with the end of the Cold War, ASEAN has been charged with a new surge of energy. It can point to the following achievements.

ASEAN Free Trade Agreement (AFTA)

First, ASEAN has adopted and is implementing its Free Trade Agreement. By the year 2003, tariff levels on manufactures will drop to zero to five per cent. The ASEAN leaders have also agreed, in principle, to extend AFTA to trade in agriculture and services. They also announced the idea of an ASEAN Vision 2020 to focus on economic co-operation targets beyond 2003, reflecting ASEAN's forward looking approach to regional co-operation. In addition, the ASEAN countries are discussing with Australia and New Zealand, the possibility of linking AFTA with the Australia-New Zealand Closer Economic Relations Trade Agreement (ANZCERTA).

Towards One United Southeast Asia

Second, once the Cambodian conflict was resolved, ASEAN decided to put its differences with Vietnam behind them and to admit Vietnam into the family. The admission of Vietnam has put an end to the division of Southeast Asia into two blocs: a communist Southeast Asia and a non-communist Southeast Asia. The expansion of ASEAN to include Vietnam has been good for ASEAN and good for Vietnam. The Vietnamese economy has become more prosperous and Vietnam has been able to tap the experience of the other ASEAN countries. Politically, Vietnam's membership of ASEAN has added strength to the organization. ASEAN's leaders are determined to bring the remaining three countries of Southeast

Asia, namely, Cambodia, Laos and Myanmar, into the family. An ASEAN consisting of all the ten countries of Southeast Asia is the dream of ASEAN's founding fathers. Such an ASEAN would be a historical first because, never before, have the ten countries of Southeast Asia been united as one family.

The ASEAN Regional Forum (ARF)

Third, ASEAN took the initiative to create the ASEAN Regional Forum (ARF) in 1994. The ARF is the only forum in the Asia Pacific which discusses political and security issues. Its creation in 1994 filled an institutional void which other countries, such as, Australia, Canada, and Japan had tried unsuccessfully to fill. ASEAN had succeeded where others had failed because ASEAN got the timing right and because all countries, especially China, felt comfortable with ASEAN in the driver's seat. China has become so comfortable with the ARF that it is co-chairing with the Philippines an ARF meeting on Confidence-Building Measures, which will be held in Beijing in 1997. The most important development in the ARF in 1996 was the admission of India and Myanmar. The admission of India was important because of India's political weight. The admission of Myanmar was important because it was the last of the ten countries of Southeast Asia to join the ARF.

Asia-Europe Meeting (ASEM)

Fourth, in March 1996, ASEAN launched another history-making initiative. It convened the first summit meeting, in Bangkok, of the 16 Leaders of the European Union and Commission and the ten leaders of ASEAN, China, Japan and Korea. The First ASEM Summit in Bangkok was inspired by the new reality that the world economy is being powered by three approximately equal locomotives – North America, Western Europe and East Asia – and the realization that there is a paucity of institutional links between Western Europe and East Asia. In contrast, there is a rich network of ties between North America and Western Europe and a growing network between North America and East Asia. The summit was intended to complete the missing third leg of the triangle. The ASEM Summit succeeded beyond all expectations. It has given rise to a number of specific projects which are in various stages of implementation. One such project is the Asia-Europe Foundation which will be launched next month in Singapore.

Building the Pacific Community

The idea of building a Pacific Community has been around since the 1960s. In the beginning, it looked like an unachievable dream because the Pacific is such a big ocean and because there were few ties which bound the disparate group of countries which inhabit the ocean. However, as the decades passed, there were more and more networks formed by political leaders, officials, scholars, business leaders, between and among some of the countries of the Pacific rim. In more recent years, trans-Pacific trade and investment have grown astronomically. Institutions such as the Pacific Basin Economic Council (PBEC) and the Pacific Economic Cooperation Council (PECC) have also contributed to the growing Pacific consciousness.

The Founding of APEC

It was against this background that Australia convened the first Asia Pacific Economic Cooperation (APEC) meeting in Canberra in 1989. At that time, the attitude of the ASEAN countries was lukewarm and ambivalent. They were concerned that if APEC took off, it could be at the expense of ASEAN. The first significant breakthrough occurred when the majority in ASEAN, including Indonesia, decided to back APEC. The second breakthrough was the decision by President Clinton to convene the first APEC Economic Leaders Meeting in Seattle in 1993.

Turning Vision into Reality

The vision of a Pacific Community is being gradually transformed into reality by the APEC process. In 1993, in Blake Island, APEC Leaders articulated a common vision of a community of Asia Pacific economies. In 1994, at Bogor, APEC Leaders committed themselves to achieving free and open trade and investment by 2010 for industrialized economies and 2020 for developing economies. In 1995, in Osaka, APEC Leaders adopted an Action Agenda to implement their 1994 commitment. In 1996, at Subic Bay in the Philippines, APEC Leaders reviewed their Individual Action Plans as well as their Collective Action Plan. Although some of the Individual Action Plans were disappointing in that they did not go beyond their Uruguay Round commitments, they could be improved in Vancouver in 1997. At Subic Bay, APEC Leaders also met with the representatives of the APEC Business Advisory Council (ABAC), pledged their support for the success of the WTO's Ministerial Conference in Singapore, and gave their backing to the US initiative to negotiate an Information Technology

Agreement at the WTO's ministerial conference. The APEC process is therefore on track.

Singapore's Foreign Policy Achievements in 1996

How did Singapore perform in 1996 in the field of foreign policy? Unlike Singapore's economic performance, I can't quantify the result and reduce it to a figure. I will, however, say that Singapore's performance in the field of foreign policy in 1996 was "excellent". Can I justify the good grade I have given? I think so. I will point to the following achievements.

First, Prime Minister Goh's proposal to hold the first summit between the 16 Leaders of Western Europe and the ten Leaders of East Asia was implemented within the short span of 15 months. The Bangkok summit was a great success. Subsequently, Prime Minister Goh made two successful visits to Western Europe, covering Finland, Norway and Sweden; and Belgium, Luxembourg, the Netherlands and the European Commission. In 1996, Singapore had the great pleasure of hosting President Chirac of France, Prime Minister Dehaene of Belgium, Prime Minister Wim Kok of the Netherlands and Chancellor Vranitzky of Austria.

Second, Singapore successfully hosted the first Ministerial Conference (MC) of the World Trade Organization (WTO). The MC's success strengthened the credibility of the WTO and the multilateral trading system. It also succeeded in reconciling the competing views of developed and developing economies on such potentially divisive issues as trade and core labour standards, trade and investment, and transparency in government procurement. As a bonus, the MC adopted an Information Technology Agreement. The success of the WTO MC should contribute to Singapore's growing reputation as the "Geneva of the East".

Third, Singapore and Australia established a "new partnership" on 17 January 1996. The new partnership encompasses co-operation in political, security, economic and cultural matters. The partnership is also intended to be a step towards the development of a community of comprehensive co-operation between Southeast Asia, on the one hand and, Australia and New Zealand, on the other. A Joint Ministerial Committee (JMC), co-chaired by the two Foreign Ministers, was established to review the progress of co-operation between the two countries. The first meeting of the JMC was held in Canberra from 29 October to 1 November 1996 and was a success.

Fourth, the damage done by the Flor Contemplation controversy to Philippines-Singapore relations, was repaired in 1996. In April, 1996, the Philippines sent a new Ambassador, Alberto Encomienda, to Singapore. Singapore reciprocated by sending a new Ambassador, Simon de Cruz, to the Philippines. Bilateral relations between Philippines and Singapore are back on track.

Fifth, Singapore maintained good relations with all our ASEAN partners and with Cambodia, Laos and Myanmar. The close relationship between Indonesian and Singapore is a model for Southeast Asia of how a big and a small country can work together for their mutual benefit.

Sixth, Singapore recognizes the importance of the strategic triangle consisting of the United States, Japan and China. Stability in this relationship is critical to the future prospects of the Asia Pacific region. Singapore has tried to be relevant and useful to each of the three great powers. In 1996, Singapore enjoyed excellent relations with China and Japan. In the case of the United States, the second half of 1996 saw a warming of relations between the two countries. I hope this positive trend will not be reversed by the exchange of views between the US and Singapore over the conduct of the General Elections in Singapore.

Seventh, Singapore gave solid support to Indonesia, as Chairman of the ASEAN Ministerial Meeting (AMM), Post-Ministerial Conference (PMC), the Third ASEAN Regional Forum (ARF) and the First ASEAN Informal Summit. Singapore and the US co-chaired a successful ARF intersessional meeting on "Search and Rescue", and will be co-chairing a second meeting in Singapore in March 1997. Singapore also gave positive support to the Philippines as Chairman of APEC in 1996.

Eighth, Singapore and the Republic of Korea intensified their bilateral co-operation in 1996. In late February, President Kim Young Sam made a state visit to Singapore. During his visit, President Kim delivered a major policy address on Korea's relations with ASEAN. This was followed in July by the visit of the former Foreign Minister, Gong Ro-Myung.

Ninth, Singapore welcomed the Presidents of Chile and Mexico in November. The visits of the two Latin American Presidents have helped to remind Singapore of the vast economic opportunities which that continent offers. With political stability and economic openness, Latin America has the potential to become the fourth locomotive of the world economy.

Tenth, in 1996, Singapore's technical co-operation programme made a quantum leap forward. Singapore signed agreements to undertake joint training of personnel from developing countries with Norway, the Vatican, the World Bank, the Colombo Plan and the WTO. In a modest and practical way, Singapore is determined to be a good citizen of the world and share her experience and expertise with other developing countries. In 1996, 1145 trainees from 67 developing countries benefited from Singapore's technical assistance programme.

Conclusion

Let me conclude on a more philosophical note. In a recent issue (21 December 1996), *The Economist* referred to Singapore as follows: "Singapore's government is not often accused of lacking self-confidence. Abroad, it punches far above its weight in diplomacy". The reference was intended to be a compliment. It, however, raises the question as to what is the league in which Singapore should be punching. My colleagues in the Singapore foreign service, who had the benefit of an education in political science or international relations, have generally been indoctrinated by the theories of the Realist School. They believe that the weight and influence of a country in the world are dependent upon a number of objective indices, such as size of country, population, military and economy. The Realists often cite Stalin's question, "How many divisions does the Pope have?" They also cite Mao Zedong's famous saying that power flows from the barrel of a gun.

A Country Which Punches above Its Weight

Guided by the philosophy of the Realist School, most practitioners of diplomacy have a hierarchical world view. They believe that "geography is destiny" and that a country's place on the totem pole is determined by its size. I hold a contrary view. I do so because my experiences at the UN and in Washington have convinced me that geography is not destiny and that a small country can overcome the inherent disadvantage of size to acquire influence in international relations through the acquisition of economic power, moral power and intellectual power. Let me cite a few examples. Singapore may be small but it is the eighth largest export market of the United States. This gives us a relevance and leverage in Washington which other countries with a population of three million do not possess. The good reputation of a country and government can give them moral power. Singapore has a good brand name in the world. Other countries admire our achievements and wish to learn from our experience. This gives us a stature and a profile which other countries of equivalent size may not possess. Finally, Singapore's ability to come up with new ideas, to translate them into action, to set the agenda, to negotiate and mediate, also increases our standing in the world. As we move into the 21st century, brainpower is not only an economic resource but it is also a source of state power. Singapore is therefore a small country but an extraordinary small country. It has always punched above its weight. With a good record at home and skilful diplomacy abroad, we will continue to do so.

Paper first published in **Singapore: The Year in Review 1996**, *Gillian Koh (ed.) (Singapore: The Institute of Policy Studies and Times Academic Press, 1997).*

ASEAN AND REGIONAL ORDER: PAST AND FUTURE

The Neutralization of Southeast Asia

Introduction

General de Gaulle would appear to have been the first statesman to have proposed the neutralization of Southeast Asia. He did this during his state visit to Cambodia in September-October 1966. General de Gaulle had suggested neutralization as a means of ending the conflict in the former states of Indochina, and of preventing the spread of conflict to the rest of Southeast Asia.

Close to home, Tun Dr Ismail, the Malaysian Deputy Prime Minister, made the same proposal before the Malaysian Parliament in January 1968.[1] At that time, Dr Ismail was only a backbencher and his proposal met with a cold reception from the Government of Tengku Abdul Rahman. But since the change of leadership in Kuala Lumpur, the Malaysian Government has adopted the idea of neutralizing Southeast Asia as one of the pillars of its foreign policy.

In this paper, I intend to discuss the meaning and significance of the proposal to neutralize Southeast Asia, the merits and demerits of the proposal, including its feasibility or lack thereof. I do not intend to speculate on the reasons which led the Malaysian Government to embrace the proposal.

A Definition of the Concept

There is much confusion over the concept of neutralization. It is often confused with neutrality, with neutralism or non-alignment, and even with demilitarization. No less a person than Tan Sri Ghazali Shafie, the Malaysian

Minister with Special Functions and Minister of Information, and formerly Permanent Secretary of the Ministry of Foreign Affairs, would appear to have fallen victim to this conceptual confusion. In an article entitled, "The Neutralization of Southeast Asia" published in *Pacific Community,*[2] the Minister wrote:

> *Neutralization, on the other hand, refers to the act which brings about a state of neutralism, and neutralism refers to the foreign policy of a state, either alone or in concert with other states, in time of peace.*

In the passage quoted, the Malaysian Minister is saying that neutralization is the act which enables a state to adopt a foreign policy of neutralism. I shall demonstrate that this is erroneous and that neutralization and neutralism are not related in the manner suggested, but are two very different concepts.

What is Neutralization?

Neutralization is a process of international law whereby a state assumes the status of permanent or perpetual neutrality, both in times of peace and of war; a status which is recognized as such and guaranteed by certain other states. The neutralized state and its guarantor states are bound to each other by a web of reciprocal rights and duties.

Differences between Neutralization and Neutrality

Switzerland is the most famous example of a neutralized state. Sweden is an example of a neutral, *not* neutralized state. What is the difference between a neutralized state such as Switzerland and a neutral state such as Sweden?

There are three differences between the two. First, a state can only be neutralized as a result of an international agreement, whereas a neutral state could attain that status by unilateral declaration. Thus, the status of Switzerland as a neutralized state is derived from the Act of Parts of 20 November 1815, in which Austria, France, Great Britain, Prussia and Russia declared "their formal and authentic acknowledgement of the perpetual neutrality of Switzerland; and the guarantee to that country of the integrity and inviolability of its territory". The status of Swedish neutrality is self-assumed and does not derive from any international agreement.

The second difference is that the status of a neutralized state is permanent or perpetual and can only be terminated by the agreement of all the guarantor states as well as the neutralized state, whereas a neutral state can terminate its neutrality at any time. The third difference is that a neutralized state retains that status in times of peace as well as of war, and is a general position, whereas a neutral state is only neutral in wartime and its neutrality refers to specific conflicts and not necessarily to all conflicts.

Differences between Neutralization and Neutralism

The differences between neutralization and neutralism or non-alignment are easier to demarcate. Since the conclusion of the Second World War, a number of states have taken to characterizing their foreign policies as neutralist or non-aligned. What these synonyms mean is that the neutralist or non-aligned state represents itself as not being allied to any of the rival power blows or collective security systems. The differences between a neutralized state and a non-aligned or neutralist state should be obvious. First, the former's status is derived from an international agreement and is guaranteed by certain guarantor states. The latter's status is self-proclaimed. Second, the status of a neutralized state can only be terminated by agreement of all the guarantor powers and the neutralized state itself. In contrast, a state could discard a foreign policy of neutralism or non-alignment at will. Third, a neutralized state is obligated by an international legal agreement to refrain from certain acts, e.g. not to allow other states to use its territory for military purposes. A non-aligned or neutralist state is under no legal obligation to refrain from such an act. Its obligation is a moral one.

The differences between neutralization and neutralism being reasonably clear, it is therefore surprising to read Ghazali Shafie's above-quoted statement that neutralization is the act which enables a state to adopt a foreign policy of neutralism. A state assumes or discards a foreign policy of neutralism by its own act and not by an international neutralization agreement.

Difference between Neutralization and Demilitarization

A neutralized state may or may not also be demilitarized. Demilitarization is not, however, a necessary part of neutralization and countries such as Switzerland and Austria are neutralized but not demilitarized whereas Luxembourg, during the period of its neutralization, was also demilitarized.

The Purposes of Neutralization

What are the purposes of neutralization? It is impossible to give a single purpose for neutralization because the different parties to a neutralization agreement may have very different purposes toward it. The neutralized state will probably have a purpose different from the purposes of the guarantor states. And though to be successful, neutralization does assume a convergence of interests among the guarantor states, their purposes need not necessarily be identical. To answer this question at the highest level of generality, it could be said that neutralization is a method for the avoidance of conflict, and, where conflict has already taken place, for the moderation or termination of conflict. To put it in other words, it is to insulate a neutralized state against certain forms of international contention. But it shall be necessary to proceed from this generalization to analyse the advantages and disadvantages of neutralization from the points of view of the state-to-be-neutralized and of the guarantor states.

Rights and Duties of the Neutralized State

What rights are gained and what duties are assumed by a neutralized state? To deal first with its duties, a neutralized state undertakes the following duties. First, it is obligated to refrain from using its military forces for any purpose except self-defence and the maintenance of internal order. Second, it is obliged not to enter into any military alliances with other states and to withdraw from any such pre-existing alliances. Third, it is under a duty not to allow other states to use its territory for military purposes. In return for these three duties, a neutralized state gains two rights. The first right that a neutralized state derives from its status is the obligation of the guarantor states to forgo any coercive policy against the neutralized state. A guarantor state must, for example, refrain from supporting domestic revolutionaries against the governments of the neutralized state. Second, the neutralized state gains the right to demand of the guarantor states that they come to the aid of the neutralized state in the event that its status is violated.

Advantages and Disadvantages of Neutralization for the Neutralized State

What are the advantages and disadvantages of neutralization for the state-to-be-neutralized? Why would a state be attracted to neutralization? What are the alternatives to neutralization?

A state would presumably not be attracted to the idea of neutralization unless it finds its independence and national welfare to be in jeopardy. Neutralization is an attractive proposal only for states which find themselves to be bones of contention between outside actors for control. Unless these pre-conditions are present, a state would not be attracted to such a proposal.

The disadvantages of neutralization for a neutralized state are the following. First, it must renounce the practice of indirect aggression against other states. Second, it must break its military ties with allies. Third, in the event of civil war, its government must refrain from inviting a foreign power to suppress domestic rebels. Fourthly, it would impose various restrictions on its foreign policy. For example, Switzerland has refrained from joining the United Nations organization for fear of an incompatibility between such membership and its neutralized status. The Soviet Union has opposed Austrian aspirations to join the European Economic Community. Fifth, a neutralized state must give up any aspirations to great or middle power status. Sixth, and finally, some regard neutralization as a degrading status. The people of Switzerland are, however, proud of their neutralized status perhaps because the guarantee of the guarantor states has lost most of its meaning and their status is seen to rest principally on Swiss military preparedness.

The attractiveness of neutralization for a state-to-be-neutralized must obviously be compared with the attractiveness of the alternatives. The alternatives to neutralization are unilateral or collective military forces, alliance arrangements, quasi-Parliamentary diplomacy at the regional and global levels.

Rights and Duties of Guarantor States

What are the rights and duties of the guarantor states? A guarantor state assumes two duties. First, it is under a duty to respect the status and integrity of the neutralized state. Often, it also assumes a second duty under the international neutralization agreement, to come to the aid of the neutralized state in the event that its status and integrity are violated by another power. The correlative of this duty is the right, on the part of the guarantor state, to intervene either singly or collectively, depending upon the terms of the agreement, in the event that the status and integrity of the neutralized state are violated.

What are the advantages and disadvantages of neutralization for the guarantor states? Why would a state agree to guarantee the neutralization of another state? The specific advantages and disadvantages of neutralization for a prospective guarantor state must necessarily vary from case to case. In one case, a neutralization agreement may serve the purpose of preserving a balance of power. In another case, a neutralization agreement may be a face-saving device for ending a costly and futile conflict. In yet another case, it may be regarded as a temporary status which will eventually lead to the victory of one rival one another.

The Three Paths to Neutralization

There are three paths to the achievement of neutralization. The first, following the precedent of Switzerland, is for the neutralization of a state to be guaranteed by the great powers of the day and for this guarantee to be embodied in a binding multilateral treaty. The second approach is to enlarge the guarantor states to include, in addition to the great powers, some medium powers as well as the states neighbouring on the state-to-be-neutralized. This was the case with the neutralization of the Kingdom of Laos. The third approach, which however has been questioned by some international lawyers, is that adopted by Austria. The neutralization of Austria was achieved by (a) the signing of a bilateral treaty called The Austrian State Treaty on 15 May 1955 between Austria and the Soviet Union, (b) by the enactment by the Austrian Parliament of a constitutional federal statute on 26 October 1955 in which "Austria, of its own free will, declares herewith its permanent neutrality and will never in the future acceded to any multilateral alliances nor permit the establishment of military bases of foreign states on its territory". The Austrian self-declaration of neutrality was subsequently recognized by the Four Great Powers and by other states with which it maintains diplomatic relations. There is not, however, an international neutralization agreement pertaining to Austria to which the Big Four are signatories. It may be pointed out here that an act of self-declaration such as that of Austria could prove futile if it is not recognized by the great powers and other outside actors. For example, the Kingdom of Cambodia in 1957 wrote into its constitution that neutrality was a law of the land and that Cambodia was forbidden to enter into any military or ideological alliances. This self-declaration on the part of Cambodia never succeeded in obtaining the recognition of all the outside actors, especially the great powers and was therefore abortive.

Pre-Conditions for Successful Neutralization

There are certain essential pre-conditions which must be fulfilled if neutralization is to be successful. It should be borne in mind here that the success of neutralization does not end merely with the conclusion of an international neutralization agreement, its continued success depends on its subsequent stability and maintenance. The essential pre-conditions for neutralization are that compromise or the appearance of compromise must be an acceptable diplomatic outcome to all actors concerned and that there exists a sufficiently converging state of perceived interests to terminate, avoid, or postpone military forms of competition for the control of the neutralized unit. The acceptability of neutralization depends on the comparative merits of other diplomatic alternatives. The stability of neutralization depends on the congruence of the objectives of the guarantor powers *inter se* and *vis-à-vis* the neutralized state itself. The maintenance of neutralization rests on an accompaniment of many factors including the good faith of the guarantors, the capacity of the neutralized state for autonomy, the will and capability of the guarantor powers to take action if the terms of neutralization are brought into jeopardy and the effectiveness of any machinery set up to preserve neutralization.

The proposal to neutralize Southeast Asia assumes a homogeneity of interests among the countries of the region. Is there, in fact, such homogeneity? Do each of the states of Southeast Asia regard its independence and national welfare to be in jeopardy? Does each of the Southeast Asian states perceive itself as a bone of contention between or among outside powers for control? Do each of the states in the region regard neutralization as a more effective means of ensuring its independence and national welfare than other alternatives?

At the present, it is my impression that only a small minority of the states of the region regard their independence to be in jeopardy. I think that only three countries of the region, viz. the Republic of Vietnam, the Kingdom of Laos and Cambodia, would see themselves in that light and regard themselves as the bones of contention between outside powers for control. For the rest of the region, the idea of neutralization is unlikely to have much immediate appeal simply because only a state which finds its independence and national welfare to be in jeopardy is likely to be attracted to the idea of neutralization. But attitudes will change if the conflict in Indochina were to spread to Thailand, if the communist guerrillas were to resume armed hostilities in Malaysia and if the big power rivalry in the Indian Ocean were to heighten.

But whatever contingencies the future may bring, it is unlikely for all the countries of the region to accept neutralization. It is, for example, inconceivable to me that Indonesia would agree to be neutralized. No country with aspirations to big or middle power status could accept neutralization. The geo-political realities strongly suggest that Indonesia would seek the status of a medium power.

The proposal to neutralize Southeast Asia also assumes that the states of the region would be able to identify the outside powers which are competing or likely to be competing for control over it and that there exists a convergence of interests among these outside powers to make neutralization possible and to ensure its stability. The Malaysian government has identified China, the US and the USSR as the three potential guarantor states. Shouldn't Japan, the UK and France be added to the list? Perhaps Indonesia should be regarded more as a guarantor state than as a candidate for neutralization.

Is there a convergence of interests among the potential guarantor states to make the proposal feasible? It is difficult to demonstrate such a convergence at the present. China would not appear to have adopted a definitive policy towards Southeast Asia. Would China follow the US and the USSR by carving out an area of her special interests? If China were to adopt her version of the Monroe Doctrine, Southeast Asia would clearly constitute her sphere of special interests. In that event she could not possibly be expected to favour the idea of neutralizing Southeast Asia. As for the United States, Lau Teik Soon[3] has suggested that the neutralization proposal is incompatible with President Nixon's Guam Doctrine. Quite apart from that, it would seem unlikely for any government of the United States to be willing to become a guarantor state because American public opinion would be hostile to any commitment which could implicate her in war in

Southeast Asia. The attitude of the Soviet Union is difficult to discern at the moment. It will presumably be dependent, in part, on Chinese intentions towards Southeast Asia. Another factor is the new alignment of forces in South Asia which gives the Soviet Union an advantage over her rivals in the Indian Ocean area and new opportunities in Southeast Asia. The Japanese have remained inscrutable. Japan's attitude to the neutralization proposal cannot be clarified until her future relations with the United States and China become more defined. Only then would Japan be able to define what her role is to be towards Southeast Asia.

In conclusion, the proposal to neutralize Southeast Asia is, for the present, unlikely to achieve any mileage for several reasons. First, only a small minority of the states of the region view their independence and national welfare to be in jeopardy. Second, in so far as some of the other states perceive threats to their security, they may feel that this can be countered more effectively by unilateral or collective military forces, alliance arrangements, quasi-parliamentary diplomacy at the regional or global levels. Third, there is no demonstrable convergence of interests among the outside powers which are competing or likely to compete for influence in or control of Southeast Asia. It should, however, be said that all this could change dramatically if the conflagration in Indochina were to spread to Thailand and Malaysia, or if the big power rivalry in the Indian Ocean were to heighten. In that eventuality, neutralization could be an extremely attractive diplomatic option, especially for the small states of Southeast Asia.

Editor's Note: This paper was written at a time (1989) when the idea of neutralization was being actively debated in Southeast Asia as a possible approach to regional stability. It explains the difference between "neutralization" and "neutrality". The latter formed part of ASEAN's 1972 ZOPFAN Declaration. The paper will be of interest to those studying the history of regional co-operation in Southeast Asia, and is a good example of the intellectual role which Professor Koh has played in explaining and clarifying key ideas and concepts in regional and international affairs.

NOTES

1. See Lau Teik Soon, "Malaysia and the Neutralization of Southeast Asia" in *Trends in Southeast Asia*, No. 2, Proceedings and Background Paper for the Seminar on "Trends in Malaysia", July 1971, Institute of Southeast Asian Studies, Singapore.
2. Ghazali bin Shafie, "The Neutralization of Southeast Asia", *Pacific Community* Vol. 3, No. 1, October 1971, p. 110.
3. Lau Teik Soon, op. cit.

ASEAN AND REGIONAL ORDER: PAST AND FUTURE

ASEAN: The Force of Intra-Regional Relations

The region, Southeast Asia, stretches from Burma in the west to the Philippines in the east, from Vietnam in the north to Indonesia in the south. Within these perimeters are to be found ten states which are heterogeneous in respect of their ethnicity, culture, language and religion. One of these ten states, Burma, has for the last decade, withdrawn into its own shell and has little significant contacts with the rest of Southeast Asia. The Kingdom of Laos has been preoccupied with its internal turmoil. The Vietnamese continue to be locked in battle although the Republic of Vietnam has been much more active than the North in its contacts with the rest of Southeast Asia.

The focus of my paper will, therefore, be on the dynamics of the interstate relations between and among the five member states of ASEAN. I will highlight some problems and issues along three dimensions:

(a) The political-security dimension,
(b) The economic dimension,
(c) The psycho-historical dimension.

The Political-Security Dimension

To be meaningful, any discussion of the political-security dimension of intra-regional relations must be undertaken within the context of the international order which obtains. The international order which evolved at the end of the Second World War has suddenly shattered as a result of the split between the USSR and the People's Republic of China, the *rapprochement* between the USA and China, the emergence of Japan as a great economic and potential military power and the uncertainties which have been created by these momentous events.

The states of Southeast Asia have responded differently to the changing international order. Their responses can be broadly divided into three. There is, first of all, the proposal advocated by Malaysia to neutralize the states of Southeast Asia in order to keep out the great power rivalry from the region. The second response is typified by Singapore's preference for a "Western-orientated military-security presence in the region" and for accepting the inevitability of great power involvement in the region. The third response is typified by that of Indonesia. The Indonesian attitude can be characterized as a preference for "regional self-reliance", which is to say, that regional problems should be solved exclusively by the countries of the region.

It could be argued that each of the three responses is shaped primarily by the national interests of the proponent. The Indonesian preference for "regional self-reliance" would be perfectly explicable since, if the countries of Southeast Asia were left alone to sort out their own problems, Indonesia, as the most populous and potentially the richest and most powerful state of the region, would have the most decisive say and the greatest influence on regional affairs. In the case of the Malaysian proposal to neutralize Southeast Asia, it is difficult to decide whether the Malaysians believe that it is the best of the possible options available to Southeast Asia and that it is an achievable option, or whether the idea was manufactured in order to signal to the world a radical shift in Malaysian foreign policy from the old pro-Western anti-communist posture to a more independent and neutralist one.

In the present circumstances, it is difficult to envisage that the great powers would be willing to guarantee the neutrality of Southeast Asia and it is equally difficult to envisage that some of the Southeast Asian states, especially Indonesia and North Vietnam, would be agreeable to be neutralized. It is also probable that Indonesia would object to giving China the status of a guarantor state and it is more than likely that as a country with ambitions of becoming a middle power, Indonesia would see herself more in the image of a guarantor state than that of a state to be neutralized.

Singapore's preference for a "Western-orientated military-security presence" in the region is, of course, also a response to her perceptions of how best her security interest can be ensured. This option has the merit of continuity with the past but it is an option that is becoming decreasingly tenable. The Five Power Defence Arrangement is not really a military pact whereunder each signatory state agrees to come to the assistance of the others if attacked. It is only an agreement to consult with one another in the event that any of the five signatory powers is threatened by external aggression. The Five Power Defence Arrangement has, however, brought some psychological benefits to both Malaysia and Singapore in that it has enabled the governments and peoples of those two countries and their foreign investors to feel more secure than they otherwise would. With the election of Labour Governments in the United Kingdom, Australia and New Zealand, the continued viability of the Five Power Defence Arrangement is left very much in doubt. But even if it were to fade away, I would argue that it served a useful role while it lasted.

The states of Southeast Asia would therefore appear to have three alternatives before them. First is the Malaysian alternative of neutralizing all the states of Southeast Asia, guaranteed by the great powers. Second, the Indonesian position of excluding all foreign influence from the region and allowing the countries of the region to sort out their own affairs. Third, the position preferred by Singapore, which is not to exclude the great powers from involvement in the affairs of Southeast Asia but to balance their influence and to give each of them a stake in the stability and prosperity of Southeast Asia.

The Malaysian proposal would be ideal for the smaller countries of Southeast Asia if it were attainable. My own view is that in the short run, it is not an attainable ideal. The Indonesian alternative of regional self-reliance would be an acceptable alternative if the two potentially dominant countries of the region, Indonesia and North Vietnam, were able to convince their smaller neighbours that they have no intention to impose their hegemony over the region. The third alternative may appear to be the least ideal but it is the one which most approximates existing realities.

The Economic Dimension

In recent years, there has been an extremely interesting debate among ASEAN intellectuals on the prospects of ASEAN economic integration. On the one side of the debate are the Realists and on the other side are the Idealists. The Realists[1] argue that at the present time, the conditions for successful economic integration of the region are absent. A noted Japanese economist, H. Kitamura, has written that for successful economic integration to be possible, the member countries must be "highly inter-independent, keenly conscious of this inter-dependence and relatively well-prepared for such co-ordinated action by geographical proximity, a common historical and cultural background and a relatively homogeneous stage of economic development".[2]

The Realists argue that the economies of the ASEAN countries are mainly competitive rather than complementary and that the degree of inter-dependence is extremely low. They also argue that ASEAN countries have reached different degrees of development in the industrial sectors. An analysis of the structure of manufacturing industries in ASEAN countries reveals a low degree of complementarity in the manufactured products made by them. The lack of complementarity in both the agricultural and manufacturing sectors of the ASEAN countries is reflected in the low level of intra-ASEAN trade which accounts for something like 15 per cent of the total trade of all ASEAN countries.

Apart from the rather low level of complementarity in the economies of the ASEAN countries, it is also argued that there exists wide disparities in the overall level of economic development among the countries. The Realists argue that if economic integration were to take place, it would create very serious problems. One of these would be that the fast growing countries would grow even faster after integration as compared to their slow growing counterparts. This would, therefore, require some form of compensation scheme in order to ensure that the fruits of economic integration are equitably distributed among the member states. A second difficulty would be to work out a regional investment policy. Given the fact that each of the member governments would be concerned to maximize its own national interest, the harmonization of their national interests in the form of a regional investment policy is viewed as a Herculean task.

The Idealists[3] acknowledge the present constraints to successful economic integration of the ASEAN countries. They are, however, of the view that given a sufficient degree of political will, the economic problems are not insuperable. They argue that progress could gradually be made towards the ideal of an ASEAN Common Market by reducing and demolishing the tariff walls separating these countries not at one go, but on a product by product basis. The Idealists argue that in the case of industries of scale, which are beyond the capacity of any single ASEAN country to undertake, it would be logical and could be feasible for the ASEAN countries to collaborate in joint enterprises.

The Idealists also argue for the formation of ASEAN multinationals in order to collaborate with the transnational giant corporations in such fields as petroleum, chemicals, iron and steel, shipping, civil aviation, automobile and other kindred areas.

Not being an economist, I hesitate to take a position in this debate. My own inclination is to take a middle course between the positions held by the Realists and the Idealists. A recent study of the prospects of economic co-operation in ASEAN has suggested areas in which such co-operation is feasible and modalities by which this could be achieved. I believe that the idea of an ASEAN Free Trade Area is a feasible one and that the ASEAN countries could work gradually towards this goal by liberalizing trade among them. This could be done on a selective basis and over a period of years. I believe also that with the requisite political will, and commitment by the technocrats, progress towards a regional investment policy is possible. I also believe that in the case of industries of scale, to borrow an idea from the Malaysian economist, Dr Victor Kanapathy, ASEAN multinational corporations could be formed to undertake such industries either by themselves or in conjunction with Western-based multinational corporations.

The Psycho-Historical Dimension

To put it briefly, my thesis is that one of the major obstacles to greater regional co-operation consists of certain psychological barriers existing between the peoples and leaders of Southeast Asia. By psychological barriers I mean, *inter alia*, the stereotype images which the peoples of one country hold of the peoples of their neighbouring countries and the collective fears and suspicions harboured by the peoples of certain countries in Southeast Asia towards others. Some of these fears and suspicions are born of ancient, historical conflicts which had taken place in the era preceding the Western colonization of Southeast Asia.

During a visit to Cambodia in 1965, I was privileged to have met and held extended conversations with high officials in both the Prime Minister's Office and in the Foreign Office. It may be recalled that it was at a time when Prince Sihanouk was in power and the official line was condemnation of American incursions against Cambodian territory. In these private conversations, however, the Cambodian officials repeatedly expressed greater fears of Vietnamese and Thai territorial ambitions than of American incursions. It seemed amazing to me, then, that the Cambodian officials were so preoccupied with the events of the historical past, stretching from the 15th to the 18th century when the Vietnamese conquered the Khmers.

At the same time, the Vietnamese officials also expressed great fears of Thai territorial ambitions. The Cambodian officials could not forget the fact that in the past, the Thai state of Ayuthia had destroyed the Cambodian capital of Angkor.

The dead hand of the past appears to rule the present. The collective memory of a people stretches back for centuries and these collective memories filter through time and form stereotype images of peoples and events. Whether or not the Vietnamese and the Thais have any territorial ambitions against Cambodia is one thing. The fears which the Cambodians have is quite another matter, and the fears may not be founded upon any objective basis.

The psychological barriers which I speak of are not, however, all of ancient origin. The Singapore Ambassador to Indonesia, H.E. K.C. Lee, recently discussed a contemporary example of such an obstacle to understanding. He singled out the instance of relations between Singapore and Indonesia. "Indonesia thought of us as a 'Third China', a smuggling centre, unsympathetic towards their economic independence. On the other hand, Singaporeans have the misconception that Indonesia was an Islamic State dominated by an ethnic group supporting the Maphilindo Concept[4] – a racial concept prejudicial to Singapore's survival, although these proved to be merely misconceptions due to lack of understanding".

ASEAN: Yesterday, Today and Tomorrow

The dream of a united Europe has been shared by Europeans for more than 300 years. That dream is still not completely realized. Viewed in this light, the progress that has been achieved by ASEAN in the last seven years has been quite remarkable. Although ASEAN was formed primarily for the purpose of promoting economic and cultural co-operation among the member nations, the two outstanding achievements of ASEAN to date have been in the forging of a sense of community among the five member nations and in what I will call confidence-building. I am not denying that after seven years, the regional organization has very little to boast of in the way of concrete achievements in economic co-operation. My thesis is that the coming together of the five nations and the sense of community which has evolved and which bind them, and the increase in mutual trust and confidence are remarkable achievements and are the prerequisites for any serious attempt at economic co-operation. Based on the experience of the past seven years, my prognosis for ASEAN's future is an optimistic one. I believe that the confidence-building will continue and that this will lead to greater co-operation in all fields of endeavour among the member nations. If my prognosis is correct, then it must follow that the security of the ASEAN countries will increase with the corresponding decrease in the likelihood of conflict between and among them.

Paper presented at the International Conference on Southeast Asian Security, Singapore, 31 May–3 June 1974.

NOTES

1. In the paragraphs that follow, I am summarizing Gerald Tan's views as expressed in "Economic Problems of Regional Integration within ASEAN: A Comment", in *Economic and Political Trends in Southeast Asia* (Singapore: Institute of Southeast Asian Studies, 1973), pp. 25–38.
2. H. Kitamura, "Economic Development and Regional Co-operation in Southeast Asia", in *Economic Bulletin for Asia and the Far East*, Vol. 20, No. 2, September 1969.
3. See Dr Victor Kanapathy's paper, "Economic Trends in Southeast Asia", in *Economic and Political Trends in Southeast Asia*, op. cit., pp. 3–15.
4. The Maphilindo Concept was launched in 1963 by Malaya, the Philippines and Indonesia, and was intended as a framework for a regional association of the countries of "Malay stock". The term "Maphilindo" is an acronym taken from the first portions of the names of the countries concerned. Although its main aim was to stabilize the relationship among the three (in view of Indonesia's opposition to the formation of the Federation of Malaysia and the Philippine claim to Sabah), the scheme alienated their non-Muslim nationals and remained a stillborn concept.

ASEAN AND REGIONAL ORDER: PAST AND FUTURE

The Cambodian Conflict: The Question of Peace, Stability and Co-operation in Southeast Asia

Mr President, for the second successive year, Vietnam has proposed for the consideration of the General Assembly an item entitled "The Question of Peace, Stability and Co-operation in Southeast Asia". This year, we also have, before us, a memorandum from Laos entitled "Principles Governing Relations of Peaceful Co-existence between the Countries of Indochina and the ASEAN Countries for Peace, Stability, Friendship and Co-operation in Southeast Asia".

There are nine states in Southeast Asia. They are: Burma, Thailand, Laos, Cambodia, Vietnam, Malaysia, Singapore, Indonesia and the Philippines. Of these nine countries, the one which has the mightiest armed forces is Vietnam. It is natural for Vietnam's militarily weaker neighbours to be vigilant. They must judge Vietnam, not by what she says, but by what she does.

In 1975, the second Vietnam war came to an end. During the period 1975 to 1978, Southeast Asia enjoyed a period of relative peace. During this period, efforts were made by the leaders of the countries of Southeast Asia, through the exchange of visits and through other confidence-building measures, to reduce mutual suspicion and misunderstanding and to increase mutual trust and confidence. This process reached its zenith with the visits by the Prime Minister of Vietnam, Pham Van Dong, to the five ASEAN countries. During his meetings with our leaders, the Prime Minister of Vietnam assured them that Vietnam would scrupulously respect the sovereignty, territorial integrity and independence of all the countries of Southeast Asia. He also assured our leaders that Vietnam would not interfere in the internal affairs of other countries in the region.

Less than three months after the Prime Minister of Vietnam had made these assurances to the leaders of the ASEAN countries, Vietnam launched a large-scale military invasion of Cambodia. Vietnam continues to occupy Cambodia with more than 200,000 Vietnamese troops.

By invading and occupying Cambodia, Vietnam has completely destroyed its credibility with its regional neighbours. How can Vietnam expect us to believe her when she tells us that she would like to live in peace and friendship with her neighbours? How can we believe Vietnam when she tells us that she will respect the sovereignty, territorial integrity and independence of her neighbours? How can we be sure that after Vietnam has digested its conquest of Cambodia, she will not, under one pretext or another, seek to use her superior military force to overawe and dominate her other neighbours?

Cambodia is, therefore, important for two reasons. First, it is important because it is the victim of an aggression by its bigger and militarily more powerful neighbour. Second, it is important because it is a test case of Vietnam's sincerity and of her intention towards her regional neighbours. If Vietnam is sincere in wanting to live in peace and friendship with her neighbours, then she can best demonstrate her sincerity by agreeing to withdraw her troops from Cambodia and to allow the Cambodians to recover and exercise their right to self-determination. If, on the other hand, Vietnam persists in maintaining that her armed intervention in, and continued occupation of, Cambodia are justified and that we must accept the realities resulting from the use of force, then we are forced to conclude that Vietnam's protestations of peace and friendship are nothing more than a cynical exercise in propaganda, designed to deceive international public opinion.

Mr President, I will now comment briefly on the Laotian Memorandum contained in document A/36/561. In that Memorandum, as well as in the statements of Ambassador Sourinho of Laos and Ambassador Ha Van Lau of Vietnam, it is said that there are two groups of countries in Southeast Asia. The first group is ASEAN which consists of Indonesia, Malaysia, Philippines, Thailand and Singapore. The second group is described as Indochina, consisting of Cambodia, Laos and Vietnam. There is an important point here which I would like to identify. It is that the three countries of the former French Indochina – Cambodia, Laos and Vietnam – do not belong to a freely formed association or group. Indeed, the Government of Democratic Kampuchea has alleged that the primary reason why Vietnam invaded her in December 1978 was because of her refusal to join in an Indochinese Federation which the Vietnamese were seeking to establish under its suzerainty. It is, therefore, extremely revealing for the representative of Vietnam to assert that Cambodia, Laos and Vietnam belong to a group. It seems to confirm the accusation that Vietnam had all along dreamt of imposing its hegemony over Cambodia and Laos.

The second point in the Laotian Memorandum on which I wish to comment concerns the root cause of the present state of tension in Southeast Asia. The Memorandum states, "There still exists between the two groups of countries a number of divergences regarding the underlying cause of the potentially explosive tension in Southeast Asia". Reading the Laotian Memorandum, one gets the impression that the Vietnamese invasion of Cambodia in December 1978 never happened. In the view of the ASEAN countries, the root cause of the present state of tension and instability in Southeast Asia is Vietnam's continued occupation of Cambodia. Until Vietnam is prepared to face up to this fact, all her talk about the desirability of dialogue is hollow. Until Vietnam is prepared to admit that there is a Cambodian problem, Vietnam's proposal for a regional conference or regional consultation is nothing but a diplomatic ploy. Its aim is to remove the question of Cambodia from the agenda of the United Nations General Assembly. The regional conference or consultation will be a dialogue of the deaf because Vietnam will insist that there is no such thing as a Cambodian problem.

The Laotian Memorandum proposes that the ASEAN countries, on the one hand, and Laos and Vietnam, on the other hand, should reach agreement on a number of principles. These principles include respect for the independence, sovereignty and territorial integrity of each country, non-aggression, respect for the rights of the people of each country to choose and develop freely their political, social, economic and cultural system, and that disputes should be settled by peaceful means through negotiations and without the use or threat of use of force. These principles, which are enshrined in the Charter of the United Nations, are of unexceptional merit. The question is whether Vietnam will adhere to them in practice. Judging by Vietnam's invasion and continued occupation of Cambodia, we are forced to conclude that any agreement on paper by Vietnam to uphold these principles is worthless. Until such time as Vietnam agrees to join in the efforts, within the framework of UN General Assembly Resolution 36/5, to find a comprehensive political settlement to the conflict in Cambodia, Vietnam's protestations of peace and of friendship will be heard with deserving scepticism.

Statement delivered at the 36th United Nations General Assembly, 3 November 1981.

ASEAN AND REGIONAL ORDER: PAST AND FUTURE

ASEAN Diplomacy and the Cambodian Crisis

Mr Chairman, let me begin by stating explicitly that the ASEAN countries want a diplomatic solution to the Cambodian crisis. We do not advocate a policy of fighting Vietnam to the last Cambodian. We do not want to use Cambodia to bleed Vietnam and to bring her to her knees. Indeed, we, in ASEAN believe that an independent and prosperous Vietnam could be an asset to Southeast Asia provided, of course, that such a Vietnam would live at peace with her neighbours.

ASEAN's Cambodia policy is erected on three pillars. First, in order to interest Vietnam in seeking a political solution to the Cambodian crisis we must prevent Vietnam from imposing a *fait accompli*. This is why the ASEAN countries have supported the nationalist forces which are fighting against the Vietnamese occupation of their country, especially the two non-communist forces led, respectively, by Prince Norodom Sihanouk and Prime Minister Son Sann.

During the past year, the nationalist forces have grown in number and in the effectiveness of their attacks on the occupying army. Vietnam is unable to secure western Cambodia and to protect many of the major supply routes and communication lines. As a result of rising Cambodian nationalism against Vietnamese occupation, the number of Cambodians who are flocking to join the nationalist forces has been increasing. The two non-communist forces are unable to accept all those who come forward to join them because of the lack of supplies of arms, ammunitions, medicine and cash. The time for Vietnam to impose a *fait accompli* has passed and Vietnam can only hold on to Cambodia at a very considerable cost. We must continue to increase the military pressure on Vietnam in order to give her an incentive to come to the negotiating table.

The second pillar of ASEAN's policy is to isolate Vietnam and thereby exert political, diplomatic and economic pressure on her to come to the negotiating table. During the past five years, the ASEAN countries have succeeded in mobilizing world public opinion, including the overwhelming majority of the non-aligned countries, against Vietnam. In 1982 and 1983, 105 countries voted for the ASEAN resolution at the UN which, *inter alia*, called upon Vietnam to approach the negotiating table, and urged a political solution which would include the total withdrawal of Vietnamese forces from Cambodia and the holding of free elections under international supervision. The ASEAN countries have also been largely successful in persuading the West and Japan to withhold their bilateral economic assistance to Vietnam until the problem of Cambodia is resolved. Vietnam has been seriously embarrassed. From 1975 to 1978, Vietnam was seen by the Third World as a heroic country, having defeated first the French and then, the United States. Today Vietnam is viewed by most of the countries of the Third World as an aggressive and expansionist state.

The third pillar of ASEAN's policy is to offer Vietnam an honourable political solution which will restore Cambodia as a sovereign and independent country and, at the same time, safeguard the legitimate security interests of Cambodia's neighbours, including Vietnam. ASEAN is willing to negotiate with Vietnam within as well as outside the United Nations so long as the two basic principles of the withdrawal of Vietnamese forces from Cambodia and self-determination for the Cambodians are the bases of the negotiation. The ASEAN countries have recently expressed their support for Prince Sihanouk's proposal for a government of national reconciliation, which would imply a role for the Heng Samrin regime. At their meeting, held in Jakarta in July, the ASEAN Foreign Ministers appointed Indonesia as our interlocutor with Vietnam. If Vietnam is seriously interested in discussing Cambodia, Indonesia stands ready to engage in such a dialogue with her, on behalf of her ASEAN partners. To date, Vietnam has yet to take up ASEAN's offer.

The ASEAN countries do not call for the precipitate withdrawal of Vietnamese forces from Cambodia because this would create a vacuum which might make it possible for the Khmer Rogue to attempt to seize power. We, in ASEAN, acknowledge that Vietnam has a role to play in negotiating and arranging for an orderly, mutually agreed upon, phased withdrawal of Vietnamese troops which will ensure security and political order. We also acknowledge that arrangements should be made for the exit of certain controversial personalities such as Pol Pot.

Mr Chairman, there is a need for the active involvement of the big powers to pressure Vietnam and to offer her incentives for a diplomatic settlement of the Cambodian crisis. The solution of the Cambodian problem offers an opportunity for the big powers and for the regional states to co-operate in building an equilibrium for regional stability and co-operation. I address my final remarks to the members of the United States Congress, to the leaders of the American mass media and to the American public. In Cambodia, we are faced with three choices. First, we are faced with the choice of a Vietnamese Cambodia. Second, we are faced with the choice of a Cambodia with the hated Khmer Rogue back in power. The Cambodian people reject both these options. We, the ASEAN countries and you, the United States, have a responsibility to help the Cambodian people to find a third option. The third option is an independent, neutral, non-communist Cambodia, a Cambodia which is neither a vassal state of Vietnam nor an ally of China; a Cambodia ruled by a government freely chosen by its people and posing no threats to any of her neighbours. We, the ASEAN countries, believe that the third option is a realistic one. However, in order to achieve it we need your active involvement and support.

Speech delivered at a conference on the Cambodian crisis organized by Save Cambodia Incorporated, Washington, D.C., 11 September 1984.

ASEAN AND REGIONAL ORDER: PAST AND FUTURE

ASEAN after Cambodia: Towards Greater Dynamism

The Backdrop

When the leaders of the six ASEAN countries held their Summit in Singapore on 27 and 28 January 1992, they were very conscious of the historic significance of their meeting. In particular, they knew they had to respond to the following three challenges and opportunities. First, they had to respond to the emergence of large regional economies, such as the Single European Market (SEM) and the North American Free Trade Area (NAFTA) and the uncertain future of the world's fragile but relatively open trading system. Second, with the signature of the Paris Agreements last October putting an end to the conflict in Cambodia, ASEAN has an opportunity to normalize its relations with the three countries in Indochina and to help them in their reconstruction. Third, with the end of the Cold War, it is no longer taboo for ASEAN to talk about security co-operation among themselves or to discuss security issues with countries outside Southeast Asia. ASEAN has, however, to shed its traditional inhibition if it wants to contribute towards the evolution of a new post-Cold War security equilibrium in the Asia Pacific region.

Responding to the Economic Challenge

ASEAN has responded splendidly to the economic challenge. It has decided to establish a free trade area in 15 years. The ASEAN Free Trade Area (AFTA) will cover manufactured products, including capital goods, and processed agricultural products. The AFTA will be based upon a sectoral approach. The main mechanism for achieving AFTA is the Common Effective Preferential Tariff (CEPT). Tariff levels will be reduced to an eventual range of zero to five per cent within the 15-year time-frame. ASEAN has identified the following 15 groups of products for inclusion in the CEPT scheme for accelerated tariff reductions: vegetable oils, cement, chemicals, pharmaceuticals, fertilizer, plastics, rubber products, leather products, pulp, textiles, ceramics and glass products, gems and jewellery, copper cathodes, electronics, and wooden and rattan furniture. In order to allow for more products to qualify for the CEPT scheme, the ASEAN content requirement will be reduced to 40 per cent for the first five years. All quantitative restrictions in respect of products under the scheme shall be eliminated. Other non-tariff barriers shall be eliminated gradually within a period of five years. A Ministerial-level Council will be established to supervise, and co-ordinate the review and the implementation of AFTA.

Will AFTA Succeed?

Am I optimistic about AFTA? I am optimistic for the following reasons. The ASEAN economies have, in recent decades, made tremendous progress. From exporters of raw materials and commodities, they have become exporters of manufactured products. They have begun to acquire different comparative advantages, thereby increasing their complementarity. They have, in recent years, embarked upon the path of liberalization and deregulation. There is therefore a consensus in ASEAN that while the reduction of trade barriers among them may bring some short-term dislocation, it is in their long-term interests. There is also a realization that unless ASEAN moves rapidly from the *status quo* of six different markets to a single market, it will become less attractive to foreign investors than the European Community and NAFTA. Therefore, the combination of internal and external factors which persuaded the leaders of ASEAN to adopt the AFTA agreement will ensure its successful implementation.

ASEAN and Indochina

ASEAN has reaffirmed its commitment to the Paris Agreements on Cambodia signed in October 1991. ASEAN supports the Cambodian Supreme Council in calling on the UN Secretary-General to despatch the UN Transitional Authority in Cambodia (UNTAC) to Cambodia as early as possible. There is a danger that further delay in despatching UNTAC could result in the unravelling of the Paris Agreements.

With respect to Vietnam, the process of normalization, which was interrupted by Vietnam's invasion of Cambodia in December 1978, will be resumed. ASEAN has welcomed the requests by Vietnam and Laos to accede to the Treaty of Amity and Co-operation in Southeast Asia. ASEAN has pledged to forge a closer relationship, based on friendship and co-operation, with Cambodia, Laos and Vietnam and to play an active part in international programmes for their reconstruction.

With the end of the Cold War and the settlement of the conflict in Cambodia, there is, at long last, an opportunity for the ten states of Southeast Asia to live together in good neighbourliness. ASEAN stands ready to extend her hand of friendship to Cambodia, Laos and Vietnam, and to lead them into the mainstream of Southeast Asia.

Security Co-operation

During the Cold War, ASEAN wisely refrained from discussing security. This was so as ASEAN did not want to be seen as a defence organization allied to one side in the East-West conflict. Now that the Cold War is over, ASEAN has decided to use the Senior Officials Meeting and the Foreign Ministers Meeting to promote dialogues on enhancing ASEAN security co-operation. The Summit noted that ASEAN security co-operation could include more dialogues, consultations, exchanges of information and personnel, and other measures such as the two regional security seminars held in Manila and Bangkok in 1991, and the two workshops on the South China Sea held in Bali in 1990 and Bandung in 1991.

The Summit has made explicit ASEAN's willingness to use the annual ASEAN Post Ministerial Conference as a forum to discuss political and security matters. Apart from ASEAN, the forum includes the United States, the European Community, Japan, Australia, New Zealand, Canada and South Korea.

Conclusion

The success of the Fourth ASEAN Summit has debunked two commonly held beliefs: that ASEAN will become unstuck without the glue of the Cambodian conflict and that intra-ASEAN economic co-operation is just a lot of empty rhetoric.

As the Prime Minister of Thailand, Anand Panyarachun, said in his closing statement to the Summit:

> *The Singapore Declaration and the Framework Agreement on Enhancing ASEAN Economic Co-operation that we have signed clearly spell out ASEAN's agenda for the future. What it shows is that we are prepared and ready to move with the new trends that are shaping the emerging new world and regional order. It is a new chapter for ASEAN and a new era for Southeast Asia.*

Article contributed to the **Asian Wall Street Journal***, 3 February 1992.*

ASEAN AND REGIONAL ORDER: PAST AND FUTURE

ASEAN Charts a New Regional Order

With superpower confrontation swept from the world scene, regional diplomacy is taking on a more prominent role in shaping the Asian security agenda. A natural vehicle for this shift is the Association of Southeast Asian Nations (ASEAN), which has begun playing a more powerful part in regional relations this year.

Starting with the summit meeting in Singapore this past January, ASEAN ministers decided that, for the first time since the organization was founded 25 years ago, ASEAN's six member nations – Brunei Indonesia, Malaysia, the Philippines, Singapore and Thailand – could discuss security issues among themselves, as well as with their seven dialogue partners. These partners are Australia, Canada, the European Community, Japan, New Zealand, South Korea and the United States. The approach taken in this dialogue has been typically ASEAN. It is pragmatic, not theoretical. It is eclectic, not doctrinaire. It seeks to build upon existing structures rather than invent new ones.

ASEAN hopes that its efforts to intensify regional security discussions within ASEAN, with its dialogue partners and with China and Russia will eventually evolve into a regional process for promoting political and security co-operation.

Since the January summit, this process has been moving ahead. ASEAN held its 25th annual Ministerial Meeting and Post Ministerial Conference in Manila this July. At these meetings, ASEAN and its dialogue partners held discussions dealing with a broad spectrum of regional issues, and made headway on a number of the most difficult, such as the disputes over territory in the South China Sea claimed by several nations.

Among the other achievements in Manila last month was the accession of Vietnam and Laos to the ASEAN Treaty of Amity and Co-operation. That treaty, adopted in Bali in 1975, lays down a number of principles governing relations between states. The treaty emphasizes the duty of states to settle their disputes peacefully and prescribes procedures for doing so. By acceding to the treaty, Vietnam and Laos have signalled their wish to put an end to the confrontation of the Cold War era and to become more closely associated with ASEAN. ASEAN has reciprocated their goodwill by granting them observer status. This is a first step that will lead eventually to their full membership.

Also, though no representation of Cambodia was in Manila, the country was very much on the minds of the leaders of ASEAN and other countries. The situation in Cambodia is very precarious. There is a grave danger that the Paris Agreements will unravel. In Manila, ASEAN and its dialogue partners urged all parties to comply with the spirit and the letter of the Paris Agreements. Whether Cambodia moves down the path of peace, or toward civil war, is in the hands of the Cambodians.

If the UN Transitional Authority in Cambodia succeeds in implementing the Paris Agreements and a new government is elected, we can expect that the new Cambodian government will also want to be closely associated with ASEAN. As a first step, Cambodia may wish to consider acceding to the Treaty of Amity and Co-operation.

Another country unrepresented at the meeting but also on the ASEAN agenda is Burma. In Manila, the ASEAN countries decided that they would continue their positive engagement with Burma in order to encourage positive change in that country. They rejected the policy of isolating Burma because such a policy would be counterproductive. This does not mean that the ASEAN countries condone the behaviour of the regime in Rangoon. Singapore, for one, would like to see a peaceful transition to a constitutional government. Political instability in Burma could adversely affect the rest of the region. Internal repression could have regional consequences. For example, there is already the outflow of Rohingya refugees into neighbouring Bangladesh.

Looking also at the broader picture. ASEAN has responded dynamically to the end of the Cold War. Another achievement in Manila was the initiative exercised by ASEAN to invite the Foreign Ministers of China and Russia to attend their meeting as guests. The two ministers made several positive and useful points in their discussions with their ASEAN counterparts. The Chinese Foreign Minister put forward a number of specific proposals to strengthen ASEAN-China economic and political co-operation. These proposals will be carefully considered by ASEAN. The consulative dialogue between ASEAN and these two major regional powers is intended to strengthen a process that builds confidence, enhances co-operation and minimizes conflict.

That ASEAN discussed regional security with its dialogue partners for the first time in Manila is a sign of the organization's maturity. It also shows that ASEAN recognizes that economics and security are linked. The security of Southeast Asia cannot be isolated from the security of the larger Asia Pacific region. Countries outside Southeast Asia have legitimate interests in the region, and with the demise of the Cold War, the regional security order is likely to evolve.

Among the substantive areas of progress in the regional security discussion was the adoption by ASEAN ministers of an ASEAN declaration on the South China Sea. The declaration was intended to refer, *inter alia*, to the conflicting claims by Brunei, China, Malaysia, the Philippines, Taiwan and Vietnam to the Spratly Islands and to defuse the recent escalation of tensions among the claimants.

The declaration emphasizes the necessity to resolve the disputes by peaceful means and urges all parties to use restraint. It also resolves to explore the possibility of co-operation in a number of areas, such as safety of navigation, protection against pollution, search and rescue operations, combating piracy and campaigning against drug trafficking. The declaration also commends all parties concerned to apply the principles contained in the Treaty of Amity and Co-operation, and invites all parties concerned to subscribe to the terms it sets forth.

According to the Foreign Minister of Vietnam, Nguyen Manh Cam, the ASEAN declaration "would serve as a basis for solving the problem in the interest of peace, stability, security and prosperity of the region". The Chinese delegation issued a statement expressing appreciation for some of the basic principles contained in the ASEAN declaration. In the statement, China went on record opposing the use of force, and reiterated its proposal to "shelve the disputes and start joint development".

As ASEAN further develops its role in regional security, it is promising to note that in taking this new direction it has already achieved two things. First, it has inscribed the South China Sea declaration on the political consciousness of all the countries in the region. Second, it has made it politically costly for any country to act against the principles contained in the South China Sea declaration.

*Article published in the **Asian Wall Street Journal**, 21–22 August 1992.*

THE PACIFIC ERA: CO-OPERATING FOR PEACE AND PROSPERITY

The Idea of a Pacific Basin Community

The Pacific Ocean is the world's largest ocean. It contains 33 littoral states. The group is, however, extremely diverse. It includes the world's most populous nation, the People's Republic of China, as well as some of the world's smallest countries such as Tonga, Nauru and Vanuatu. It includes Japan, the second largest economic power in the world, Brunei, which has a per capita income of US$22,000, as well as countries such as Burma with a per capita income of less than US$200. The group includes countries which are allies, such as the United States, Japan, South Korea, the Philippines, Australia and New Zealand as well as countries which regard each other as enemies, such as China and Vietnam, North and South Korea, China and Taiwan, Vietnam and Cambodia. The Pacific Ocean is so vast that many of the countries on the eastern rim of the ocean, in Latin America, have little or no contacts with the countries on the western rim of the ocean. The group contains countries with market economies as well as those with centrally planned economies. Given the diversities which I have described, does it make any sense to talk of a Pacific Basin community?

A Network of Ties

Although the 33 littoral states cannot be said to share a sense of community, one can discern a growing network of relationships, ties and institutions. Let me briefly try to identify some of the more important components of this growing network. The United States, Australia and New Zealand are parties to the ANZUS treaty. (I shall refrain from making any comments on the current dispute between the United States and New Zealand over the latter's refusal to allow nuclear-powered and nuclear-armed US ships to visit New Zealand ports.) The United States has a treaty commitment to defend Japan, South Korea, the Philippines and Thailand against external aggression.

Six of the non-communist countries of Southeast Asia, Brunei, Indonesia, Malaysia, the Philippines, Singapore and Thailand belong to a regional association, ASEAN, which is probably the most successful regional organization in the Third World. ASEAN has established economic dialogues with the United States, Canada, Japan, Australia and New Zealand. In the South Pacific, Australia, New Zealand, Papua New Guinea, Fiji, Samoa, Solomon Islands, Tonga, Nauru, Vanuatu and Kiribati belong to a regional organization called the South Pacific Forum. ASEAN and the South Pacific Forum have expressed a mutual interest in establishing links between the two organizations. In recent years, the People's Republic of China has broken out of its self-isolation and has established good relations with most of the countries in the Pacific Basin. South Korea is seeking to expand its ties with the countries of Southeast Asia and South Pacific.

The Evolution of the Pacific Basin Community Concept

In an article entitled "Pacific Overtures" in the Winter 1984–1985 issue of *Foreign Policy*, Sean Randolph wrote that the earliest proposal for Pacific economic co-operation came from Japan in 1965. A Japanese scholar, Kojima, and a UN official, Kurimoto, proposed the creation of a Pacific Free Trade Area similar to the European Economic Community. The proposal fell on sterile ground because it was far ahead of its time. The second initiative was taken by the late Japanese Prime Minister, Masayoshi Ohira, who was very enthusiastic about the Pacific Basin community concept. Ohira appointed a brilliant Japanese economist, Saburo Okita, to head a group to produce a detailed agenda for regional economic co-operation in 1979.

In the same year, an American scholar, Hugh Patrick, and an Australian scholar, Peter Drysdale, co-authored a report for the United States Senate Foreign Relations Committee in which they proposed the creation of an organization for Pacific Trade and Development patterned after the OECD.

In September 1980, with the strong backing of Japan's Prime Minister Ohira and the then Australian Prime Minister, Malcolm Fraser, a Pacific community seminar was held in Canberra and was attended by representatives of 13 Pacific countries. The Canberra meeting created an organization called the Pacific Economic Cooperation Council (PECC).

Under the auspices of the PECC, two subsequent conferences were held, in Bangkok in June 1982 and in Bali in November, 1983. The PECC has a Standing Committee and five functional task forces. The five task forces deal respectively with trade in manufactures, investment and technology transfer, agriculture and renewable resources, minerals and energy, and capital flows and finance.

From 12 to 14 April 1984, senior trade officials from several Pacific countries met in Seoul, South Korea, at a regional trade conference sponsored by the Trade Policy Research Centre of London and the Korea Development Institute. Later that same month, the trade representatives of the Western Pacific met in Bali to discuss the possibility of a common Pacific position in the next round of multilateral trade negotiations under GATT.

Alongside the meetings which have been taking place among the representative of the governments of the region, the businessmen and scholars of the region have also been meeting and creating their own institutions. The most successful of the business organizations is the Pacific Basin Economic Council (PBEC). The scholars of the region meet regularly through a wide variety of regional conferences.

The Dynamism of the Pacific Basin

The countries of the Pacific Basin, especially those in East and Southeast Asia, have the most dynamic economies in the world. During the decades of the 1960s and 1970s, these countries grew at the annual average rate of 7.5 per cent. During the 1970s Japan, South Korea, Taiwan, Hong Kong and Singapore grew at an annual average rate of 8.2 per cent. Many of the countries of the region, such as the ASEAN countries, are blessed with abundant natural resources. The literacy rate in the region is high, and the work force is imbued with the non-Christian puritan work ethic. Most of the countries of the region have market economies and welcome foreign investment. The total United States investment in the region is estimated at US$30 billion and is increasing more rapidly than in any other region of the world. The region has become the largest market for United States agricultural exports. Since 1980, US trade with the Pacific has exceeded US trade with Western Europe. In 1983, the total United States-Pacific trade was US$135.9 billion, $26 billion more than the US trade with Western Europe.

ASEAN's Attitude towards the Pacific Basin Community

Initially, the ASEAN countries reacted with caution to the Pacific Basin community concept. They did so for several reasons. First, there were some in ASEAN who were afraid that the creation of another and larger institution could jeopardize the survival and integrity of ASEAN. Second, there were others in ASEAN who felt that a Pacific Basin community would be an organization dominated by the United States and Japan and they would be relegated to a subordinate role. Third, there were some in ASEAN who were afraid that a Pacific Basin community might take on a political complexion which would not be consistent with their professed policy of non-alignment. The attitude of ASEAN, however, underwent a dramatic change in July 1984.

The Watershed Year of 1984

At the ASEAN Post Ministerial Conference in July 1984 in Jakarta, the six ASEAN foreign ministers proposed the holding of a special meeting between the six ASEAN countries and its five Pacific Basin dialogue partners, the United States, Canada, Japan, Australia and New Zealand. This group has come to be known as the Group of 6 + 5. The meeting decided to set up a mechanism in order to explore, as a first project, co-operation in the field of human resources development. Officials of the 11 countries have been meeting, and their report will be considered at the next ASEAN Post Ministerial Conference, which will be held in 1985 in Kuala Lumpur.

Although this may seem like a very modest beginning, it is, nevertheless, an important landmark in the long quest to concretize the idea of a Pacific Basin community. The intention of the Group of 6 + 5 is to allow other countries in the Pacific Basin to participate in the project on human resources development. If this project takes off and succeeds, it will, I am sure, lead to other projects. In time, the difficult questions of the membership of the group, its objectives and institutional arrangements will be resolved in the ASEAN spirit of pragmatism and consensus.

The United States and the Pacific Basin Community

Both President Reagan and the Secretary of State, George Shultz, attach great importance to the relationship between the United States and the countries of the Pacific Basin. In the last two years, there has been an increase in the resources and in the attention devoted by the Reagan Administration to the Pacific. In January 1984, Ambassador Richard Fairbanks was given the responsibility at the State Department to deal with the Pacific in a comprehensive manner and to develop long-term US policy options toward the region. Aware of the sensitivities of some of the smaller countries in the Pacific Basin, the United States and Japan have wisely decided to let the ASEAN countries take the lead.

Conclusion

My prognosis for the future is that the economies of the countries of East and Southeast Asia will remain buoyant and dynamic. I foresee the expansion and strengthening of the existing network of institutions and relationships between countries and groups of countries in the Pacific Basin. I foresee the continued expansion of trade and investment, the increase of scholarly exchanges and the expansion of business relationships between the countries of the Pacific Basin. I foresee a growing sense of affinity and community among many of the countries of the Pacific Basin which may, one day, make the Pacific Basin community not just a concept but a reality.

Speech given to the Commonwealth Club of San Francisco, 14 February 1985.

THE PACIFIC ERA: CO-OPERATING FOR PEACE AND PROSPERITY

The Dynamic Pacific Rim in the 1990s

President Bush's second visit abroad was to East Asia. After attending the funeral of Emperor Hirohito in Tokyo, he visited the People's Republic of China (PRC) and the Republic of Korea. The visit gave him, an old Asia hand, an opportunity to tell America's allies and friends that the United States is a Pacific power and intends to remain one. The visit also gave him an opportunity to see for himself the dynamism of a region which has never been so prosperous and peaceful. What are the economic and political prospects of the region in the 1990s? What changes are we likely to see? What are the challenges and opportunities for the United States?

Who Comprises the Pacific Rim?

For the purpose of this discussion, I intend to define the Pacific Rim to include the United States and Canada, on the eastern rim and, on the western rim, Japan, China, the Soviet Union, North and South Korea, Taiwan, Hong Kong, Vietnam, Laos, Cambodia, Thailand, Malaysia, Singapore, Indonesia, Brunei, the Philippines, Australia, New Zealand and the other member countries of the South Pacific Forum. I have excluded the Latin American countries with a Pacific coast even though Chile is a member of the Pacific Basin Economic Council (PBEC) and Mexico will be admitted as a member at its next meeting. I have done so because there is very little interaction between their economies and the others and because, apart from Chile, the Latin American countries have not given the impression that they intend to participate actively in the emergent Pacific Community. I am not, however, closing the door on them.

Should the Soviet Union Be Included?

Why have I included the Soviet Union? First, because the Soviet Union is geographically a Pacific nation. It is difficult to deny them a seat at the table if the criterion is location. Second, because the Soviet Union is militarily a Pacific power. Soviet air and naval power, based in the Soviet Far East and in Vietnam, makes the Soviet Union the second most powerful nation in the Pacific. Third, in his speeches in Vladivostock in July 1986 and Krasnoyarsk in September 1986, General Secretary Gorbachev has said he wants to lower the level of military activity in the Pacific, to help resolve regional conflicts, to improve the Soviet Union's bilateral ties with all countries in the region, and to advance multilateral co-operation, particularly in the economic field. We should ask Gorbachev to translate his words into deeds. However, we can only do so if we allow the Soviet Union to engage in the constructive activities of the region, not by keeping her out. Fourth, the Soviet Union has influence with North Korea and Vietnam. The Soviet Union can, if it wishes to, help to reduce tension and the danger of conflict on the Korean peninsula. The Soviet Union can also play a constructive role in bringing the Cambodian conflict to a satisfactory conclusion.

The Sino-Soviet Summit

We are living in an unusual period of history. It is a period marked by the simultaneous reduction of tension among the four major powers of the region – the United States, the Soviet Union, China and Japan. A momentous event will occur in May when General Secretary Gorbachev travels to Beijing to hold the first Sino-Soviet Summit in 30 years. The Summit will lead to the normalization of relations between them, including the restoration of party-to-party relations.

Is the *rapprochement* between China and the Soviet Union good or bad for the region? It is good for the region. It will reduce tension between these two major powers. It is likely to lead to a reduction of tension between North and South Korea. It is also likely to have a beneficial effect on the negotiations to end the Cambodian conflict.

Is there any danger that the Soviet Union, China and Vietnam will form a communist bloc which will seek to destabilize the non-communist countries of the region? This was the nightmare which haunted some American and Asian officials in an earlier era. I don't think the nightmare is likely to become a reality for two reasons. First, China and the Soviet Union are unlikely to become allies again. Although I expect relations between China and Vietnam to improve, especially after Vietnamese troops leave Cambodia, I also do not expect China and Vietnam to become allies. Therefore, I regard the idea of a tripartite alliance between the Soviet Union, China and Vietnam as extremely remote. Second, none of the three communist countries is in an expansionist mode. The Soviet Union has just withdrawn its troops from Afghanistan and, like China, is giving priority to economic reform at home. Vietnam has pledged to withdraw its troops from Cambodia by the end of 1990 and has taken some tentative steps to rectify its economic stagnation.

Ending the Cambodian Conflict

Vietnam has occupied Cambodia since December 1978. I recall vividly the positions which Vietnam has taken on the Cambodian question at various times. Vietnam's first stand was that it had no troops in Cambodia. Vietnam's second position was that its troops were in Cambodia at the request of the puppet government it established after its invasion. Vietnam's third position was that there was no such thing as the Cambodian question and the situation in Cambodia was irreversible. Well, the irreversible is about to be reversed.

Vietnam has stated that it is prepared to withdraw its troops by September 1989 if a political solution can be arrived at. In any event, Vietnam has said that its troops will be out of Cambodia by the end of 1990. It is very important for us to agree on a comprehensive political settlement before Vietnam withdraws from Cambodia. It is crucial that such a settlement should address both the external and the internal aspects of the conflict. We do not want to create a situation like that in Afghanistan, in which the fighting continues after the foreign forces have gone. The Cambodian people have suffered enough and deserve better. We must ensure that the Vietnamese withdrawal will be monitored by an international peacekeeping force which will maintain law and order; that the PRK regime will be replaced by a coalition government, comprising all the four Cambodian factions, led by Prince Norodom Sihanouk; that free elections will be held, under UN supervision in an environment free of coercion and intimidation, to enable the Cambodian people to choose its own government; and an international conference will be held to guarantee the independence, territorial integrity, neutrality and non-aligned status of Cambodia.

The United States should increase its aid, including lethal aid, to the non-communist Cambodian resistance. The United States should play a more active role in the diplomatic efforts to find a Cambodian solution. It would not be in the interests of the Cambodian people, the US or ASEAN, for the solution to be dictated by China and the Soviet Union. The United States should also be prepared, if necessary, to break some crockery with the PRC over the need to prevent the Khmer Rouge from seizing power or achieving a position of dominance.

The US Security Role

What role do America's allies and friends expect her to play in the security field? First, to balance the military power of the Soviet Union. Second, to maintain the credibility of the US-Japan Mutual Security Treaty so that Japan will not seek to become an independent military power.

There can be no objections to efforts by the United States and the Soviet Union to agree on the mutual reduction of their military confrontation and forces in the Pacific. The United States should, however, avoid making unilateral withdrawals and reductions. For example, the US should refrain from unilaterally withdrawing its troops from South Korea. In his address to the Korean National Assembly, President Bush reassured the Koreans that he would not do so. He said that the US troops in Korea would only be withdrawn at the request of the South Korean government. The United States should do its best to seek the renewal of its air and naval bases in the Philippines, which are due to expire in 1991. The loss of those bases will have very serious implications for regional security.

The US must do nothing to undermine the credibility of the US-Japan Mutual Security Treaty. If Japanese confidence in the treaty is lost, Japan may seek to become an independent military power. This will set off alarms all over East and Southeast Asia. Japan's current defence mission of defending her home islands out to 1,000 miles from shore is wholly appropriate. The United States could also ask Japan to pay for the entire cost of the US forces in Japan. At present, Japan pays 40 per cent of the cost of US$6 billion. Although Japan is only devoting slightly over 1 per cent of her GNP to defence, her defence budget is the third largest in the world. Some members of the US Congress have called upon Japan to increase her defence expenditures to 3.5 per cent of her GNP. They have never explained how the additional money will be spent. What new defence mission do they expect the Japanese Self-Defence Forces to fulfil? Burden-sharing between the United States and Japan is a real issue. It should, however, be applied in a creative and sensitive manner.

The East Asian Economic Miracle

Ten years ago, the US had more trade with Europe than with Asia Pacific. In 1987, the US trade with Asia was US$241 billion, while that with Europe was US$170 billion. It has been estimated that by the year 2000, the value of US trade across the Pacific will be at least double that of trade across the Atlantic. The Pacific Basin contains some of the world's fastest growing economies. My prognosis is that they will continue to surge forward into the 1990s.

The first issue I would like to discuss is how to overcome the frictions which have been generated in the economic relations between the United States and her Pacific partners. I have two suggestions. I think that Japan, Korea, Taiwan and other Pacific countries should address, in a serious way, American complaints regarding the lack of reciprocity and fairness in their trade relations. Japan should continue to internationalize her economy, undertake a land reform programme which would simultaneously liberate farm land for housing and open up the Japanese market to agricultural imports and modernize her distribution system. Countries which enjoy access to the US market must reciprocate by opening their markets to US goods and services. There should be adequate protection for US intellectual property rights.

At the same time, I think the US should set its own house in order instead of blaming all its economic problems on foreign scapegoats. The US should make resolute efforts to reduce its federal budget deficit and increase its savings rate. US corporations should continue to improve the quality of its products and show more commitment to exports.

The second issue I wish to discuss is the need for the Asia Pacific countries to trade more among themselves. At present, most of the exports of these countries go to the United States and Western Europe. There is relatively little trade among the countries of the region. The United States and Europe may be reaching the saturation point as far as imports are concerned. Therefore, if the countries of the region are to continue to expand, the future demand for their exports may have to come from within the region. This means that they will have to dismantle the existing barriers – both tariff and non-tariff – which inhibit trade among them. Japan should lead the way. Japan has an opportunity to use her market, capital and technology to make the region boom into the next century.

Conclusion

There is a growing sense of community in the Pacific. There are many existing networks in the region. The Foreign Ministers of the six ASEAN countries meet annually with their counterparts from the United States, Canada, Japan, Australia and New Zealand. The business leaders of the region belong to the Pacific Basin Economic Council (PBEC). Another organization, the Pacific Economic Cooperation Conference (PECC), provides a forum for government officials, scholars and private sector leaders to discuss questions and issues of common concern. Senator Bill Bradley has proposed an organization consisting of eight Pacific nations, which he has labelled "PAC–8", to discuss problems of debt and development. Australian Prime Minister Bob Hawke has suggested the formation of an organization like the OECD. George Shultz, the former Secretary of State, spoke in Jakarta in July 1988 of the need for a Pacific forum to bring together the governments of the region. More recently, the Ministry of International Trade and Industry (MITI) has invited 12 countries – the six ASEAN countries, plus the US, Japan, Canada, Australia, New Zealand, and South Korea – to meet in Tokyo this fall to discuss how to advance economic co-operation in the Pacific.

What do these various proposals signify? First, they signify the growing importance, both economically and politically, of the Asia Pacific region. Second, they signify a growing sense – however inchoate – of community among at least some of the nations of the region. Third, they signify an ongoing quest for an appropriate forum or structure to bring together the nations of the Pacific to further their co-operation and to reduce misunderstanding, suspicion and conflict. I do not know what lies at the end of the road. I am, however, comforted by President Bush's assurance that the United States intends to remain a Pacific power. Together, we can forge a bright future for the Pacific.

Remarks delivered at the LTV Corporation Seminar, Washington, D.C., 6 March 1989.

THE PACIFIC ERA: CO-OPERATING FOR PEACE AND PROSPERITY

A Pacific Century?

Introduction

This is an opportune time for us to review some of the major trends in the Asia Pacific region. On 6 and 7 November, a historic meeting of Ministers from 12 Pacific countries took place in Canberra, Australia. As an expression of the importance which the United States attaches to its relations with the countries in that region, as well as to the Canberra Meeting, the US delegation was led by three members of the Cabinet – Secretary of State James Baker, the Secretary of Commerce, Robert Mosbacher and the US Trade Representative, Carla Hills. The other 11 countries which attended the Canberra Meeting were Japan, Australia, New Zealand, Canada, South Korea and the six ASEAN countries – Brunei, Indonesia, Malaysia, Philippines, Singapore and Thailand. I will identify four major trends in the Asia Pacific region and conclude with an exhortation to the United States of America.

A Region of Economic Dynamism

The economies of the Asia Pacific region are the fastest growing and the most dynamic in the world. On the average, they are growing at twice the rate of the OECD countries. Indeed, some of the countries in the region, such as Taiwan, South Korea, Hong Kong and Singapore, have regularly registered growth rates of over 10 per cent. This trend is likely to continue into the next decade. I also expect that countries such as Thailand and Malaysia will join the ranks of the newly industrializing economies (NIEs). The 12 countries which attend the Canberra Meeting account for more than half of the world's GNP. The fact that trade between the United States and its Pacific trading partners has exceeded US trade with its Atlantic partners is well known. In 1988, US trade with the Pacific amounted to US$280 billion whilst US trade with the Atlantic was US$190 billion. By the year 2000, experts predict that US trade with the Pacific will be twice as much as its trade with Europe. Intra-Asian trade is also increasing rapidly. In 1988 it was over US$200 billion.

Towards a Pacific Community

For the last two decades, there has been a growing sense of community among the non-Communist, market-oriented countries of the Asia Pacific region. In 1969, the business leaders of the region established an organization called the Pacific Basin Economic Council (PBEC). The Council has been meeting annually during the past 20 years and has offered the business leaders of the region a valuable forum to get together to exchange view on the opportunities and problems of enhancing Pacific economic co-operation. More recently, another organization called the Pacific Economic Cooperation Council (PECC) was established. Unlike PBEC, the national committees of PECC consist of government officials, business leaders and scholars. The Canberra Meeting is the latest and most important manifestation of this growing sense of a Pacific community and a reflection of the reality of economic inter-dependence. It is too early to say where the Canberra initiative will lead us. What I can say, with confidence, is that the 12 countries which attended the meeting have no intention to establish an Asia Pacific trading bloc. Indeed, they reiterated their commitment to the policy of free trade and to the multilateral trading system under GATT. The Canberra Meeting will not, however, be a one-shot affair. It has begun a process which is likely to endure. The 12 countries have agreed to hold their second Ministerial Meeting next year in Singapore and their third Ministerial Meeting in South Korea in 1991. Japan has offered to host a meeting of officials to prepare for the second Ministerial Meeting.

What can a Pacific forum contribute? First, it could enable the countries of the region to address the question of how to enhance co-operation and to reduce conflict in their trade relations. Countries which enjoy large surpluses and have internal barriers could be persuaded by their partners to reduce those barriers. The goal is to reduce, as much as possible, the barriers which impede trade in goods and services among the countries of the region. Second, the forum could also address the question of how to enhance co-operation in science and technology. Third, the forum could address the challenge of how to improve the communication infrastructures of the region, for example, to promote liberal civil aviation regimes and to improve the telecommunication network. Fourth, to enhance co-operation by the countries of the region in such transnational areas as the protection of the environment. Fifth, to enable the developed and the developing countries of the region to undertake practical projects of co-operation which would benefit both groups of countries.

The Emergence of Japan as an Economic Superpower

One of the most important trends of the Asia Pacific region is the emergence of Japan as an economic superpower. Those who remember the poverty and devastation which afflicted Japan at the end of the Second World War cannot help but admire what the hardworking people of this island nation have achieved in the past 44 years. Japan has the second largest economy in the world. Its per capita income has surpassed that of the United States. It has also become the world's largest creditor nation and has replaced the United States as the largest donor of aid to the Third World. Japan's neighbours in East and Southeast Asia applaud Japan's success. They derive considerable inspiration from the Japanese economic miracle. There are many lessons which countries in East and Southeast Asia can learn from Japan.

There is an increasing degree of tension and animosity in the economic relations between the United States and Japan. Japan's neighbours in Asia view this with considerable concern. Their fear is that if left unchecked, the conflict between the two countries in the economic sphere may ultimately erode the integrity of the US-Japan security relationship. If Japan should ever come to the conclusion that it can no longer depend upon the US nuclear umbrella, it may feel compelled to become an independent military power. Japan's neighbours in Asia contemplate the possibility of a re-armed Japan, independent of the United States, with the same anxiety as the Europeans contemplate the prospect of a unified Germany outside NATO.

Both the United States and Japan need to take action to arrest the continuing deterioration in their bilateral economic relations. Japan should be more aware of the fact that much of the resentment towards her in America is due to the perception that it does not reciprocate the openness of the US economy. Therefore, Japan should open its markets to US and other foreign imports more widely, more rapidly and on its own initiative. Japan should also find creative ways to facilitate foreign investment in Japan. Japanese companies in the United States should find ways to buy more from local US suppliers and must strive to bring the most advanced elements of their R & D and their productive processes to the US. On its part, the United States should avoid making Japan the scapegoat of all its problems. As long as the savings rate in this country remains low, its cost of capital high and its federal budget deficits massive, its trade and current-account deficits are inevitable. The US must therefore work harder at cutting its deficits, increasing its savings rate, lowering its capital costs and restoring competitiveness.

Reduced Perceptions of Chinese and Soviet Threats

Since the emergence of Deng Xiaoping as the paramount ruler of China in 1979, there has been a gradual reduction in the perception of a Chinese threat by the countries in the region. China has gradually reduced its support for the communist insurgencies in Southeast Asia. The 4 June tragedy of Tian'anmen Square has not significantly altered this perception. It has, however, reinforced uncertainty in the region about who will succeed Deng and whether his policy of opening the Chinese economy to the world will survive after his death.

The emergence of Gorbachev as the new leader of the Soviet Union and the two important policy statements he made in Vladivostock and Krasnoyarsk, have made a favourable impression on the countries of the region. The perception of the Soviet threat has been reduced to some extent but it has not been eliminated.

There is no Asian equivalent to the European phenomenon of "Gorbymania". Why not? First, because there has been no significant reduction of Soviet forces in the Far East. Second, relations between Japan and the Soviet Union will not be normalized until the Soviet Union returns the four Northern Islands to Japan. Third, South Korea continues to be concerned about the possibility of aggression from North Korea. The Soviet Union has recently supplied North Korea with advanced jet fighters. Fourth, the ASEAN countries are disappointed that the Soviet Union has not exercised more influence on Vietnam to seek a comprehensive political settlement of the conflict in Cambodia.

Because the Asians continue to perceive a Soviet threat to the region and because they do not want to see the emergence of Japan as an independent military power, the Asian countries would like the United

States to continue to maintain a military presence in the region. This is why countries such as Singapore have spoken publicly in support of the desirability of maintaining US bases in the Philippines. In order to make it easier for President Aquino to renew the bases agreement, my Government has recently offered the enhanced use of our military facilities to the United States. The offer has been accepted by the US Administration. In the period since the end of the Second World War, the US has been instrumental in maintaining a balance of power in East and Southeast Asia. This has created an environment of stability which has enabled Japan and the other countries of the region to prosper. The present structure of US forces in the region is, of course, not sacrosanct. The US should, however, avoid making abrupt and unilateral reductions of its forces in the region for budgetary reasons rather than in response to the reduction of threats.

Conclusion

I shall conclude with an exhortation to America. Looking to the future, I can confidently predict a bright economic future for the Asia Pacific region. It is in America's national interests to remain intimately involved with the region. Asians regard America as a benign superpower. As the former US Ambassador to the Philippines, Stephen Bosworth, has written recently, in an article in the *Asian Wall Street Journal*, "... there remains a strong conviction in Asia that the US should be actively engaged in the region in a leadership role. There is simply no other country, or combination of countries, that can assume responsibility for regional leadership, for organizing a regional consensus on key issues such as trade and security".

Remarks delivered to a meeting of the World Affairs Council of Greater Hampton Roads, 8 November 1989.

THE PACIFIC ERA: CO-OPERATING FOR PEACE AND PROSPERITY

APEC: A New Economic Architecture for the Asia Pacific

It is a truism that perception is sometimes more important than reality. I have been increasingly disturbed by the negative reporting by the world's media on the historic meeting which took place in Seattle from 14 to 20 November 1993 among the senior officials, ministers and leaders of the 15 APEC economies. Some reporters have described the informal summit as nothing more than a photo opportunity for President Clinton. Some European reporters were dismissive of the significance of the event on the grounds that the economies represented were too diverse and lacked political unity. I hold a different view. Let me attempt to summarize what I regard as the significance of the meeting.

First, the 15 economies represented in Seattle – Australia, Brunei, Canada, China, Hong Kong, Indonesia, Japan, South Korea, Malaysia, New Zealand, Philippines, Singapore, Taiwan, Thailand and the US represent 40 per cent of the world's GNP, and 50 per cent of world trade. They also include the most dynamic economies in the world.

Second, trade between the Eastern and Western rims of the Pacific Ocean has been increasing exponentially. Today, US trade with East Asia is US$345 billion whereas US trade with Europe is only US$227 billion. East Asia is America's largest export market and vice versa. At the rate at which East Asia is growing, US trade with East Asia will be double that of its trade with Europe by the end of the decade.

Third, the meeting is the message. In spite of their diversity, the leaders of the 15 economies were able to meet in Seattle and find common ground. They agreed to work for a united Asia Pacific, based upon free trade and against protectionism.

Fourth, the leaders of APEC issued a joint statement reaffirming their strong commitment to conclude the Uruguay Round by the 15 December

1993. I am sure that this has had a salutary impact on the European Union. The warning to Europe is clear. If Europe gives in to protectionist lobbies and scuttles the Uruguay Round, the Asia Pacific economies have an alternative to fall back on. It is Europe which will suffer most.

Fifth, the meeting agreed to admit Papua New Guinea and Mexico this year and Chile next year. This will bring APEC's membership to 18. The admission of Papua New Guinea, Mexico and Chile is significant in two ways. It shows that the APEC is not a rich men's club. It is also an indication that a Pacific country with a market economy, substantial economic linkages with other APEC members and which shares the collective vision, can aspire to join APEC. As President Soeharto of Indonesia has said, APEC represents a new form of co-operation between North and South, a co-operation based on trade not aid, mutual benefit and not charity and grounded on the economic logic of complementarity.

Sixth, APEC is not like the European Union. APEC has no common external tariffs. It is not a customs union. Its aspiration is to work towards the reduction of barriers impeding the flows of goods, services and technology and to enhance co-operation. It is the first example of open regionalism. There is no intention to build a Fortress Pacific to counter the threat of a Fortress Europe.

Seventh, the 14 leaders of APEC met by themselves, without aides on Blake Island, on 19 November from 9.00 am to 3.00 pm. The atmosphere at the meeting was good. All the leaders were positive about the future of APEC. They agreed that there is a growing sense of community which binds them.

Eighth, at the suggestion of President Kim of South Korea, the leaders agreed to meet again next year in Indonesia. Obviously, they would not have agreed to do so if they did not find their first encounter a useful one.

Ninth, the fact that Indonesia will be the host of next year's meeting of APEC's leaders is very important. Indonesia is ASEAN's largest member. It is also the current Chairman of the Non-Aligned Movement. The fact that President Soeharto has agreed to host the next meeting should put to rest speculations about ASEAN's ambivalence towards APEC.

Tenth, President Clinton's initiative in convening the informal summit and his commitment to APEC have succeeded in dispelling the fears, often heard after his election, that America may turn isolationist and retreat from its active engagement with East Asia. APEC is also the only forum in which the three giants of the Asia Pacific – the US, China and Japan – are members. The resumption of high-level dialogue between China and the US is to be welcomed. The fact that President Clinton and Prime Minister Hosokawa have developed a good rapport with each other is also an asset. It is no exaggeration to say that the future peace and prosperity of the Asia Pacific will depend, to a very large extent, on good relations among the US, China and Japan.

Some of the officials present in Seattle were seized with a sense of history in the making. They felt in their hearts that they were present at the founding of a new economic architecture for the Asia Pacific. Perhaps the dream of two departed Japanese leaders, Prime Minister Ohira and Dr Saburo Okita, to build a Pacific Economic Community is not an illusion after all. Such an ambitious goal must, of course, be pursued on a step-by-step basis and at a pace comfortable to all of APEC's members.

*Article published in **The Straits Times**, 27 December 1993.*

THE PACIFIC ERA: CO-OPERATING FOR PEACE AND PROSPERITY

APEC and Open Regionalism

The world should take notice of the APEC leaders' summit in Bogor, Indonesia, on Tuesday. The economies represented there already make up about 50 per cent of global production, and many of them are growing fast.

At their first meeting a year ago on Blake Island near Seattle, the APEC leaders outlined a collective vision of the Asia Pacific region in the 21st century. The big question is whether at Bogor they will agree to take concrete steps to transform their vision into reality.

Among other inputs, APEC leaders and ministers will have before them the second report of an Eminent Persons Group chaired by C. Fred Bergsten, and a report of the Pacific Business Forum (PBF), a group of 33 business leaders established by the last APEC summit.

Indonesia's President Soeharto, who will chair the Bogor meeting, has said that the reports are two important points of reference. Both envisage the eventual removal of all barriers to trade and investment between APEC economies. The Business Forum's report says that the aim should be to build a community of thriving and prosperous economies. It emphasizes the need to develop the region's human resources, bridge the existing diversity in levels of economic development, strengthen small and medium enterprises, and to protect and improve the environment.

Both reports urge APEC leaders to adopt the objective of free trade by a definite date, and to make such a decision at Bogor. The report by the Eminent Persons Group recommends the year 2000 as the starting date, with a three-tier end date of 2010 for developed economies, 2015 for the newly industrialized economies and 2020 for the developing economies. Reflecting the impatience of the business community for results, the PBF report recommends an end date of 2002 for developed economies and 2010 for developing economies.

How will APEC achieve the goal of free trade? By fully implementing the commitments of the Uruguay Round; by further liberalization unilaterally and within existing subregional free trade areas in the APEC region; and by an APEC-wide negotiation covering all goods and services.

The PBF report asks APEC leaders to adopt an immediate standstill on all new trade barriers in the region. Both reports recommend that China and Taiwan should become contracting parties of the new World Trade Organization as soon as possible.

APEC leaders are urged to adopt the goal of investment liberalization. This should create an environment conducive to foreign investment and in which business can feel confident that its investment will be secure, profitable and not beset by unnecessary and excessively restrictive or discriminatory rules and regulations.

Among specific measures suggested are adoption of a non-binding Asia Pacific Investment Code; incorporation of elements of this code into national laws where appropriate; and developing a legally enforceable and binding code as soon as possible.

The economic dynamism of the Asia Pacific region and the trade, investment, tourism and other linkages between the economies are due primarily to the multitude of business enterprises throughout the region. The main role of governments has been to facilitate such linkages.

They should go further by introducing greater transparency in administrative systems, rules and regulations; establishing common and simplified customs codes and procedures; relaxing visa restrictions; harmonizing standards; easing controls on the transfer of technology; protecting intellectual property rights; and adopting sound macroeconomic policies to keep exchange rates stable and inflation and the costs of capital low. They should also promote good business ethics and practices to eliminate corruption and anti-competitive practices.

Both reports suggest ways of developing a better partnership between government and the private sector, including the establishment of a joint public and business task force to improve infrastructure throughout the region. One important recommendation is that APEC leaders appoint a Business Advisory Forum that would report back to them.

The business forum also proposed a meeting of ministers responsible for telecommunications to help create regional and global communication networks with harmonized standards.

The world has no reason to fear the Bogor meeting. APEC leaders have no plan to create an Asia Pacific customs union or common market similar to that in Europe. Any liberalization of trade and investment will be consistent with GATT, and will be guided by the principle of green regionalism.

The fact that the current APEC chairman, Indonesia, is a developing economy should also reassure smaller members of the group that the 1994 Bogor summit will not be dominated by the strong, but will instead be conducted in the spirit of consensus.

*Comment contributed to the **International Herald Tribune**, 10 November 1994.*

ASEAN and the Asia-Europe Meeting (ASEM)

Introduction

I would like to thank the organizers of the Second ASEAN Congress for inviting me to speak to the Congress. I am pleased that I have been paired with an old friend from Indonesia, Ambassador Atmono Suryo. Pak Atmono had proposed a division of labour between us, namely, that he would focus on the economic aspect of the ASEAN-ASEM relationship and I would focus on the political and cultural aspects of the relationship. I have accepted his proposal. I am also pleased that our good friend from Thailand, Dr Suthiphand Chirathivat, is our discussant.

In my remarks, I will discuss three points. First, I will describe the role which ASEAN played in launching the Asia-Europe Meeting (ASEM) process. Second, I will discuss the question as to whether the success of ASEM has had a negative impact on the ASEAN-EU relationship. Third, I will make some suggestions on how to ensure that the ASEAN-EU process and the ASEM process remain as two intersecting circles, mutually reinforcing, but each with its own *raison d'être*.

ASEAN's Role in Launching ASEM

Why did ASEAN launch the ASEM process? My surmise is that the leaders of ASEAN decided in 1994/1995 to convene the first Asia-Europe Summit in Bangkok for the following reasons.

First, looking at the contemporary world, ASEAN's leaders must have been struck by how much the world had changed. For example, in 1995, North America, EU and the Asia ten accounted for 29.5 per cent, 29.5 per cent and 24.9 per cent of the world's GNP respectively. However, assuming that Asia grows at an average of 5 per cent per annum, and Europe and North America at 2.5 per cent, the combined GNP of North America, EU and the Asia ten in the year 2020, at 1994 prices, would be US$14,587 billion, US$14,399 billion and US$20,733 billion, respectively. In other words, by the year 2020, East Asia's economy is likely to be significantly larger than those of North America and Western Europe. Because the world economy has three co-drivers, its future therefore requires that we establish cordial and co-operative relations between those three regional economic centres.

Second, when ASEAN's leaders looked at the institutional ties existing between and among the three power centres, they were struck by the contrast. They observed that between North America and Western Europe, there existed a thick web of institutional and human ties, for example, NATO, OSCE, the Spoleto Festival of Two Worlds, etc. They also observed that, in recent years, the leaders of East Asia and North America have been building bridges across the Pacific, for example, APEC and the ARF. However, in the case of the EU and East Asia, there was a paucity of institutional and human links. The decision of the leaders of East Asia and Western Europe to convene their first summit in Bangkok in March 1996 was therefore an important first step to fill this void. The success of ASEM I has brought credit to ASEAN. ASEAN has a track record of coming up with wise and timely initiatives, especially in the post-Cold War world.

The Impact of ASEM on ASEAN-EU

What is the impact of ASEM on the ASEAN-EU relationship? Is there a danger that the attractiveness of ASEAN to the EU will be eclipsed by the three larger economies of Northeast Asia, China, Japan and Korea? Is there a danger that the ASEAN-EU relationship will eventually be subsumed by ASEM?

In February 1997, Singapore hosted two back-to-back meetings, the 12th ASEAN-EU Foreign Ministers' Meeting and the first ASEM Foreign Ministers' Meeting. Was the ASEAN-EU meeting eclipsed by the ASEM meeting? Were the European Ministers more interested in China, Japan and Korea than in ASEAN?

The 12th ASEAN-EU Ministerial Meeting

The 12th ASEAN-EU Ministerial Meeting was a success in many ways. First, it was attended by 22 Foreign Ministers, all 15 from the EU and seven from ASEAN. The meeting was also attended by Vice-President Manuel Marin of the European Commission (Sir Leon Brittan was unable to attend because of a conflicting meeting at the WTO) and the ASEAN Secretary-General, Ajit Singh. The 15 European Foreign Ministers would not have attended the meeting if they did not think it was important. If some of them had skipped the ASEAN meeting but attended the ASEM meeting, this would have been an important signal.

Second, the two "land mines", East Timor and Myanmar, which could have blown up the meeting, were successfully defused. With the help of the two concerned delegations, Indonesia and Portugal, the two Co-Chairmen, Netherlands and Singapore, managed to find an acceptable way of dealing with the East Timor question. The Dutch Foreign Minister referred to it in the context of the UN in his speech to a closed plenary session. The Singapore Foreign Minister responded by making a brief reference to ASEAN's practice of not raising bilateral issues in the regional context. The Ministers spent two hours in a frank and substantive discussion of the situation in Myanmar and of the contrasting approaches of ASEAN and the EU towards Myanmar's application to join ASEAN. The discussion was conducted in a cordial and non-confrontational manner. The discussion helped to narrow the gap between the two sides. It also helped each side to appreciate better the concerns and perspective of the other side.

Third, the meeting adopted a Joint Declaration (JD) which was substantive but fell short of the strategic vision contained in the report of the ASEAN-EU Group of Eminent Persons entitled "A Strategy for a New Partnership" and the European Commission's report entitled "Creating a New Dynamic in the ASEAN-EU Relations". The JD called for increases in the trade and investment flows between the two regions. It advocated AFTA-EU co-operation, focusing on measures for trade promotion and facilitation, such as, customs co-operation, sharing of information, and standards and conformance. The JD also encouraged greater ASEAN-EU private sector co-operation through business networking and joint ventures.

Fourth, the 12th ASEAN-EU Ministerial Meeting was not eclipsed by the ASEM Ministerial Meeting. On the contrary, since the former had gone so well, the challenge in Singapore was to consider how the latter could add value to the former.

It is, however, too early to say that the ASEAN-EU relationship will not be adversely affected by ASEM. It would be a mistake for ASEAN to become complacent. The admission of Myanmar will almost certainly affect the tone and content of the ASEAN-EU dialogue. The economic opportunities offered by Northeast Asia, especially by China, will certainly compete with those offered by Southeast Asia. Hence, it is incumbent upon ASEAN and EU to nurture this relationship. Otherwise, it will atrophy and will eventually be over-shadowed by ASEM. It is a pity that because of East Timor, Portugal continues to block the conclusion of a new generation agreement between ASEAN and the EU. The distinguishing characteristic of the ASEM Foreign Ministers Meeting was its informal format, which enabled a free flowing dialogue on a wide range of issues.

How to Revitalize the ASEAN-EU Relationship?

ASEM is in the honeymoon phase. It is new and exciting. The ASEAN-EU relationship was started in 1978. It is a marriage which is almost 20 years old. Like some 20-year-old marriages, there is a danger that the spouses will begin to take each other for granted and that they will begin to look elsewhere! Our challenge is two-fold:

(a) To keep the marriage fresh;
(b) To make the ASEAN-EU relationship and ASEM mutually reinforcing.

The following are some suggestions on how to respond to the two challenges.

Broaden and Deepen the Political Dialogue

First, I support the recommendation of the ASEAN-EU Group of Eminent Persons to broaden and deepen the ASEAN-EU political dialogue. The dialogue should be broadened to include the private sector, universities, think-tanks, other non-governmental organizations and representatives of young Asians and Europeans. The dialogue could be deepened to include such issues as:

(a) The reform of the UN;
(b) Peacekeeping;
(c) Preventive diplomacy;
(d) Human rights;

(e) Nuclear non-proliferation;
(f) International crime;
(g) Terrorism;
(h) Piracy;
(i) Health;
(j) Environment and sustainable development.

The two sides should aim to transcend dialogue and enter the world of co-operation. The ASEAN-EU dialogue is the best example of a North-South dialogue. The two sides should aspire to achieve a common action agenda which they could then pursue in the appropriate forum, such as the United Nations.

A Dialogue of Civilizations

Second, the ASEAN-EU cultural dialogue is a dialogue between several civilizations. Culturally, Western Europe is relatively homogeneous. West European values have their roots in the Judeo-Christian religions, the Renaissance and Reformation, and the Industrial Revolution. Unlike Western Europe, Southeast Asia is a region of great diversity. Buddhism, Islam, Christianity, Hinduism and Confucianism have significant followers. A successful cultural dialogue between ASEAN and EU would therefore constitute an important contribution to the dialogue of civilizations and reduce the danger that we are inexorably marching towards a clash of civilizations. The agenda could include:

(a) The role of the individual in society;
(b) The rule of law and good government;
(c) The role of the state;
(d) Human rights.

Exchange of Students and Young People

Third, ASEAN and EU should expand the exchange of students and young people between the two regions. The new ASEAN-EU programme, Junior Executive Managers (JEMS), which brings young managers from ASEAN to work with companies in Western Europe has got off to a good start. The programme should be expanded to include the bringing of young European managers to work in the ASEAN countries. One feasible way of achieving this result would be to twin an ASEAN company with an European company. I would also like to explore with the officials in charge of the intra-European exchange of university students called Socrates, the possibility of expanding the network to include the best universities in ASEAN. The EU should help ASEAN to strengthen and expand the teaching of European studies in ASEAN universities. ASEAN should help the EU to strengthen the teaching of Southeast Asian languages and studies in the EU universities. Journalists, artists, and film makers can make important contributions to better mutual understanding between Western Europe and Southeast Asia.

Conclusion

The ASEAN-EU relationship is a relationship between the world's largest and most integrated economy and the most successful regional organization in the developing world. The Southeast Asian regional economy has a combined population of almost 500 million people and is the fastest growing economy in the world. The ASEAN-EU relationship is therefore intrinsically important. It can also serve as a bridge between Western Europe and Southeast Asia and other groupings, such as ASEM and the UN. The question is: Can ASEAN-EU proceed at a faster pace and with a broader and deeper agenda than ASEM? If the answer is yes, then the ASEAN-EU relationship will have a bright future. If the answer is no, the prognosis must be that the ASEAN-EU relationship will be overshadowed and eventually subsumed by ASEM.

Speech given at the Second ASEAN Congress, Kuala Lumpur, Malaysia, 22 July 1997.

De Tocqueville Revisited: American Politics Viewed from a Foreign Perspective

Introduction

Two years ago, I was re-assigned from my post at the United Nations to the Embassy in Washington. At the UN, I had to deal with the representatives of 158 countries as well as with many key officials in the UN Secretariat – a total cast of perhaps 500 characters. When I left New York for Washington, I thought I was leaving a multilateral post for a bilateral one. However, although I am now dealing with only one government instead of 158, the US Government is, in a very real sense, a multilateral system. I do not think there is another government in the family of democratic societies in which power is so decentralized and dispersed, and in which so many institutions and individuals are involved or have inputs into the making of policy and the implementation of decisions and programmes. The following are some of my impressions of American politics as seen from the point of view of a Singaporean whose political institutions are based on the British parliamentary model.

The Influence of Hollywood, Madison Avenue and Television

Let me begin on a relatively light note. I observe that American politics has been afflicted by three unwholesome influences. These are Hollywood, Madison Avenue and television. Hollywood exerts a powerful and pervasive influence on every aspect of American life and culture. For example, I have watched with both amusement and sadness, the annual list of the ten most admired men and women in America. Apart from the President and the First Lady, those on the list consist mostly of movie stars and other entertainers. The President of Harvard University has never made the list! The winners of Nobel and Pulitzer Prizes do not seem to enjoy the same public adulation as movie stars. Hollywood has two pernicious influences on American politics. First, it has injected "a show biz" quality into American politics. Second, as Professor Garry Orren of Harvard University has pointed out, in judging the presidential debates, "the public responds overwhelmingly to the sweat on the brow, style, manner and personality" rather than to the substance of the debate.

Madison Avenue has also had a pernicious influence on American politics. The language of advertising has infected the style and content of American political discourse. Speeches by American politicians are often characterized by bombast, hyperbole and exaggerations. The influence of television on American politics has been overwhelming. As Professor Ralph Whitehead of the University of Massachusetts has said, "Television is the language of the American people, and, in politics, if you can't use television you lack the faculty of speech".

Because television is such an expensive medium, it forces politicians to over-simplify complicated issues. As the Governor of New York, Mario Cuomo, has pointed out, "having to get your message across in 28 seconds forces you to labels, shibboleths, stereotypes and simplistics". Recently, the Democratic Party requested Senator Sam Nunn to give a two-minute response, on television, to the Administration's policy on arms control. Much to his credit, Senator Nunn declined the request on the grounds that it was impossible for him to do justice to such a complex subject in two minutes. There are, unfortunately, very few Sam Nunns in American politics.

The Separation of Powers

In Singapore, as in Britain, there is a very close nexus between the Executive and the Legislative branches of government. A government is formed by the party or by a coalition of parties which commands a majority in parliament. The moment the government loses its majority in parliament, it is obliged to resign from office. Because of the close nexus between the Executive and Legislature and because of the high degree of party discipline which exists in most parliamentary democracies, the government is normally able to get its legislative programme enacted by parliament.

The situation in the United States is entirely different. There is a clear separation of powers between the Executive, the Legislative and the Judicial branches of government. Even when the same party controls the White House, the Senate and the House of Representatives, which is not a very frequent occurrence, the Administration cannot count on the automatic support of the Congress for its legislative programme. More often, the same party does not control both the White House and the two chambers of Congress. In this case, the Administration will have to negotiate its legislative proposals with the two Houses of Congress and arrive at compromises.

Let me tell you a true story which illustrates the point I am making. The new ambassador of a major country in Asia, which will remain unnamed, arrived in Washington. He called upon a senior official in the State Department. At their meeting, the ambassador complained bitterly that the Congress had just passed a law which is contrary to the spirit of a communique which had been signed by their two governments. The State Department official explained to the ambassador that the Administration could not control the Congress and advised the ambassador to lobby its members. The ambassador was taken aback by the advice. He asked, "Wouldn't it be an interference in your domestic affairs for me to lobby members of the Congress?" The State Department official replied that unless he did so, he would not be very effective in Washington.

The Administration and the Role of the Cabinet

In Singapore, every member of the Cabinet has to be an elected Member of Parliament. In the American Cabinet, the only two elected officials are the President and the Vice-President. The Cabinet Secretaries are appointed by the President and serve at his pleasure. Under the doctrine of the separation of powers, it is not possible for a member of the Cabinet to remain a member of Congress. In the current Reagan Cabinet, only the Vice-President and the Labour Secretary, Bill Brock, has previously served in Congress.

In Singapore, the Cabinet meets every week. All important questions of policies, programmes and legislation are discussed and decided in Cabinet. Decisions are usually made by consensus but, on rare occasions, by vote. I am informed that the American Cabinet does not function in the same manner. This may partially account for the fact that the different departments and agencies of the government do not seem to work harmoniously at times. As a result, it is necessary for an ambassador in Washington to work closely not only with the State Department but also with the White House, the National Security Council, the Department of Defence, the Department of Commerce, the Office of the US Trade Representative, the Treasury Department, the Department of Transportation and others. On this Administration's policy towards Southeast Asia, we have been fortunate that the Departments of State and Defence and the National Security Council have been able to work harmoniously. Credit for this happy state of affairs must go to Assistant Secretary Gaston Sigur of the State Department, Assistant Secretary Richard Armitage of the Defence Department and James Kelly of the National Security Council.

The US Congress

The US Congress has a lower chamber called the House of Representatives and an upper chamber called the Senate. The House has 435 members and the Senate has 100 members. There are more than 300 committees and subcommittees in the two houses. In addition, there are several thousand congressional staffers.

For an ambassador to be effective in Washington, he must cultivate the leadership of the two parties in the Senate and in the House of Representatives. In addition, he must cultivate the leadership and key members of the various committees and subcommittees whose work impinges upon the interests of his country. If he is wise, he would also cultivate the key congressional staffers because they possess great influence and expertise.

There was a time in the past, when Congress was ruled by a rigid seniority system. During that era the junior members of Congress would normally comply with the requests and wishes of their seniors. A revolutionary change took place in the 1970s. By 1981, 54 per cent of the members of the Senate were serving in their first term. In the 97th Congress (1981–1982) the majority of its members had served only since 1977. This has made Congress a more democratic institution. It has led to a greater degree of decentralization of power. These changes have both a positive and a negative aspect. On the positive side, Congress today is more open and more responsive to the various social and political forces in the country than it has ever been. On the negative side, it has been criticized for being too responsive, particularly to single, narrow interests. Another negative consequence of the democratization of Congress is that any of the 535 legislators can, through a variety of procedural manoeuvres, alter a bill, delay action, or tie the institution in knots.

The Role of Political Parties

In the United States, there are no national political parties. There are 50 state Democratic Parties and 50 state Republican Parties, each with its own views, rules and procedures. The two parties have no national leaders. They do not have strong national party committees. Although a lot of time and energy is spent in drafting the party platform, it is forgotten as soon as it is adopted. Congressmen and congresswomen are free to ignore their party's platform without fear of any sanction. Even in Congress, it is not always easy to enforce party discipline. In one recent case, the Democratic Party's leadership in the House of Representatives attempted to discipline a congressman from Texas, Phil Gramm, who had voted against his party. Phil Gramm promptly resigned his seat in the House, joined the Republican party and won re-election to the House. Subsequently, he succeeded in winning election to the Senate.

The Influence of Money

Members of the House of Representatives have to face an election every two years. Members of the Senate enjoy a longer tenure of six years. This means that as soon as a congressman or a congresswoman is elected, he or she must immediately set about organizing for his or her re-election campaign. Running for an election in this country is an extremely expensive business. In Singapore, a candidate may spend up to a maximum of S$6,000 or approximately US$3,000 for his or her campaign. This translates into approximately S$0.50 or US$0.25 per voter. In Singapore, the candidate does not have to raise his or her campaign funds as these come from the party's coffers.

The situation in the United States is different. First, there is no legal limit on how much money a candidate can spend for his campaign for election to a seat in the House or in the Senate. In 1984, Congressman Bill Green of New York spent US$1.1 million to retain his seat in the House and his unsuccessful challenger spent US$1.8 million. Campaigns for the Senate are, of course, even more costly. In the US, a candidate has to raise most of his campaign funds. He or she can expect little help from his political party. The advent of television has also increased the cost of running for elections. In 1984, the candidates spent a total of US$300 million on 30-second or 60-second TV and radio advertisements, mostly attacking their opponents.

Under current Federal Election Laws, a person or organization may contribute the maximum of US$1,000 per election for a candidate for federal office, US$20,000 per year to national political committees and US$5,000 to another political committee. No individual or organization may contribute more than US$25,000 directly to candidates for federal election in any one year. The federal laws, however, contain a loophole. The loophole is that there is no limit to the total amount which a political action committee (PAC) can spend on behalf of a candidate as long as the committee does not co-ordinate its activities in any way with the candidate, his or her representatives, or the campaign committee. There are approximately 4,000 political action committees in existence. In the period January 1985 to June 1986, the political action committees contributed a total of US$67 million to House and Senate candidates. Democratic candidates have reported receiving US$37 million. Republican candidates have reported receiving US$30 million. Professor Garry Orren of Harvard University has described the political action committees as phony mechanisms created to get around the finance laws. Senators David Boren and Barry Goldwater have co-sponsored a bill to deal with PACs. Senator Boren has said that, "we cannot expect members of Congress to act in the national interest when their election campaigns are being financed more and more by special interests". Senator Goldwater has stated that, "... PAC money is destroying the election process ... As far as the general public is concerned, it is no longer 'we the people', but PACs and the special interests they represent, who set the country's political agenda and control nearly every candidate's position on the important issues of the day".

The Influence of Interest Groups

Alexis de Tocqueville observed that certain American cultural values such as individuality and the need for personal achievement underlie the propensity of citizens to join groups. In a democracy, it is perfectly appropriate for a group of citizens who share a common interest or objective to form themselves into an interest group. There is nothing wrong for such groups to attempt to communicate their interests, aspirations and goals to members of the Congress or to seek to influence the course of legislation in that body. The theory is that there would be competition between various interest groups and the members of the Congress would, after taking due account of the merits of the various supplicants, decide on a policy or an issue on the basis of what is good for the nation. Unfortunately, the theory does not always accord with reality. Let me illustrate my point with the following example.

One of the thousands of interest groups which exist in this country is the tuna lobby, based in California. Due to the influence of this lobby, Congress enacted the Magnuson Act which does not recognize the rights of coastal states over tuna in their exclusive economic zones. This has caused a crisis in the relations between the United States and the island countries of the South Pacific. Many of these countries have little or no land-based resources. Their only resource is marine resource and the most valuable marine resource is tuna. Because of the refusal of the United States to recognize the rights of these countries over tuna in their exclusive economic zones, one of the countries, Kiribati, has concluded a fishing agreement with the Soviet Union and the Prime Minister of another country, Fiji, has publicly announced his intention to do the same. The South Pacific is an area of great strategic importance to the United States. It is an area in which the Soviet Union has been unable to gain a toehold for the past 40 years. It seems absurd that the policy of the United States towards the South Pacific is being controlled by the tuna lobby.

The Impact of the American Political Process on Foreign Countries

Since the United States is the leader of the free world, the choice of the US President is not only of vital importance to the United States but also to its allies and friends. The process by which the candidates of the two parties is chosen is so unpredictable and hazardous that I have once suggested, half in jest, that your allies and friends ought to have a say in the choice of your two presidential candidates.

The US system of government, characterized by the separation of powers among the three branches of government and by many checks and balances, is designed to protect the liberty of the individual. It is based upon an inarticulate mistrust of the government. The system is designed to prevent the concentration and abuse of power. It is not designed to produce a strong government, a government which has a free hand in conducting its relations with other countries.

Given the fact that power is shared between the Administration and the Congress, American foreign policy is at its best when the two institutions work in tandem and at its worse when they pull in different directions. Let me conclude my remarks by giving you two examples, one of success and the other of potential disaster. The United States played a very constructive role in assisting the peaceful transition of power which took place recently in the Philippines from President Marcos to President Aquino. One important reason for the success of US policy was that the Democrats and the Republicans, the Congress and the Administration, as well as the powerful American media were acting in unison.

My second example is in the area of trade policy. Last year, the United States suffered a trade deficit of US$150 billion. Some have estimated that the trade deficit this year could reach US$170 billion. The Administration's trade policy is based upon the following three pillars. First, to bring down the value of the US$ *vis-à-vis* the currencies of its major trading partners. Second, to knock down foreign barriers blocking the exports of US goods and services and to seek the removal of other unfair trade practices such as dumping and subsidies. Third, to launch a new round of multilateral trade negotiations and to include in its agenda such new items as agriculture, services, high technology, investments and the protection of intellectual property rights.

Instead of supporting the Administration's policy, Congress, especially the Democrats, has embarked upon the disastrous course of protectionism. On 6 August 1986, the House of Representatives came within eight votes of overriding the President's veto of the Jenkins Bill, which would have drastically curtailed the imports of textiles, especially from Asia, in violation of the United States' bilateral and multilateral treaty obligations. The House of Representatives has adopted by more than two-thirds majority an omnibus trade bill (HR 4800) which is blatantly protectionist and GATT-illegal. Since the Democratic Party has decided to exploit trade as an electoral issue in the November elections this year, the Republicans in the Senate, fearful of losing their slim majority, are feeling the heat and may therefore feel compelled to pass a protectionist trade bill of its own. The future of the world's trading system literally hangs in the balance. The outcome will not be decided by any rational consideration of the merits or demerits of the Administration's trade policy, but by the expediencies of party politics in an election year.

Remarks prepared for a Symposium at the John F. Kennedy School of Government, Harvard University, held as part of Harvard's 350th Anniversary Celebration, 5 September 1986.

ASIA AND THE UNITED STATES: PERCEPTIONS AND PRESCRIPTIONS

The United States and the Newly Industrializing Countries: The Search for a New Policy

Who Are the NICs?

One of the wisdoms we have learnt from linguistic philosophy is that it is sometimes difficult to define a term, but not difficult at all to recognize the objects to which the term is applicable. This wisdom will help us to overcome the problem of defining the term, "newly industrialising country" (NIC). One searches the economic literature in vain for a satisfactory definition. None the less, we all seem to agree that Taiwan, South Korea, Hong Kong and Singapore in Asia, and Brazil, Mexico and Argentina in Latin-America, are paradigms of NICs. It is a little less clear though whether the People's Republic of China, India, Thailand and Malaysia also qualify. Because the group is so heterogeneous, I will confine my discussion largely to the relationships between the United States and the four Asian NICs.

The US Attitude towards the NICs

The attitude of the US towards the NICs has undergone a decided change. From the 1960s to the early 1980s, the US had a very positive attitude towards them. The US was proud of the economic progress which these countries were making because their success was a vindication of the policies which the United States had been advocating in the Third World. In the last few years, however, I have noticed a change in the attitude of the United States. The pendulum has swung from the positive to the negative. The words of praise which used to be heaped on them by American leaders have been replaced by increasingly sharp attacks. An excellent example is the speech made by the Assistant Secretary of the Treasury, David Mulford, to the Asia/Pacific Capital Markets Conference in

San Francisco on 17 November 1987. In his speech, Mulford accused the four Asian NICs of contributing to global imbalances, of not behaving as responsible trading partners and of using exchange rate policy to secure and maintain their current competitive advantage. He demanded that they stop their predatory behaviour.

Reply to Mulford

Mulford's speech was greeted with disbelief in Singapore because none of the allegations are applicable to Singapore. First, how can Singapore be accused of contributing to global imbalances when it has always run a trade deficit with the world? In 1986, the deficit was 17.5 per cent of Singapore's GDP. Even on the current account, with the solitary exception of 1986, Singapore has always been in deficit. Second, how can Singapore be accused of not being a responsible trading partner when its market is more open than the US market? Ninety-six per cent of US exports to Singapore enter duty-free compared to 76 per cent of Singapore's exports to the US. It would have been more just if Singapore had complained that its trade relationship with the US is not based upon reciprocity. Third, how could Singapore be accused of using exchange rate policy to maintain its trade competitiveness when, between 1973 and 1986, the effective exchange rate of the S$ strengthened 33 per cent? When viewed against the US$ alone, the value of the S$, as of mid-November 1987, was about 11 per cent higher than in 1978. The fact that these allegations were made serves to substantiate my point that the US attitude towards the NICs has turned from friendly to hostile.

Reasons for Changed Attitude

What has brought about this change in the US attitude? The change has been brought about by three factors. First, by the growing trade and current account deficits of the United States. The trade deficit has grown from US$39.7 billion in 1981 to US$171 billion in 1987. The current account has gone from a surplus of $6.9 billion in 1981 to a deficit of $156 billion in 1986. Because of these mounting deficits, the attitude of the United States towards its trading partners has become less benign and more critical. Second, by the perception of the NICs as America's new competitors. As Professor Richard N. Cooper has written, "we tend to see the NICs ... as problems ... What exactly is the problem? It is that these countries produce goods that compete with US products. They sell goods both in the United States and in competition with US goods elsewhere in the world, and that is seen as a threat to US profits and employment.[1] The fact that in 1987, the US suffered a trade deficit of about US$48 billion[2] with the NICs, has tended to reinforce this perception. Third, by the fact that most of the NICs – South Korea, Taiwan, Brazil, Mexico and Argentina – have various forms and levels of tariff and non-tariff barriers against US goods and services. Their markets are less open than the US market. Americans therefore feel that their trade relationships with the NICS are not based upon reciprocity. This has given rise to the demand to level the playing field. I have great sympathy for the American position *vis-à-vis* the NICs. My complaint is that many Americans do not seem to know that Hong Kong and Singapore are different from the other NICs. They are free ports and have no significant tariff or non-tariff barriers against US goods and services. In fact, both Hong Kong and Singapore have more open markets than the United States. This point is often overlooked and Hong Kong and Singapore tend to get tarred by the same brush as Taiwan and South Korea. For example, the media is fond of referring to Taiwan, South Korea, Hong Kong and Singapore as the "Four Tigers". Given the significant differences which exist between Hong Kong and Singapore, on the one hand, and Taiwan and South Korea, on the other, it would have been more accurate to call them the "Four Felines". I will not argue against referring to Taiwan and South Korea as tigers, but I think it would be more accurate to refer to Hong Kong and Singapore as pussy cats!

What Is the US Policy towards NICs?

Does the US have a policy towards the NICs? If so, what is the policy? So far, no member of the Administration or Congress has outlined, in a clear and coherent manner, a policy towards the NICs. The decision of the Administration, announced on 29 January 1988, to graduate Taiwan, South Korea, Hong Kong and Singapore from the US Generalized System of Preferences (GSP), with effect from January 1989, reinforced that impression. Why do I say that? I do so for the following reasons.

First, the decision of 29 January represents the reversal of the Administration's long-standing policy of opposing the selective or accelerated graduation of countries. In 1984, the Administration defeated a bill sponsored by Congressman Richard Gephardt to graduate Taiwan, South Korea and Hong Kong, the top three beneficiaries of the US GSP. In

1986, the Administration successfully persuaded Senator Bob Dole not to press his bill to graduate a number of beneficiary countries, naming South Korea, Taiwan and Hong Kong as examples. In January 1987, the Administration affirmed the GSP status of the four Asian NICs and awarded Singapore and Hong Kong with favourable packages of GSP benefits. The Administration has yet to explain why only 12 months later, it suddenly decided to abandon its seven-year-old policy and to self-initiate the graduation of these four beneficiaries before they reach the mandatory criterion for graduation.

Second, the decision to graduate Hong Kong and Singapore would seem to be inconsistent with one of the pillars of US trade policy, i.e. to level the playing field. What does GSP mean? It means duty-free access to the market of the country giving GSP. By having no tariffs against imports, Hong Kong and Singapore are, in effect, giving GSP to the whole world, including the United States. Thus, 96 per cent of US exports enter the Singapore market duty-free. Even with the benefit of GSP, only 76 per cent of Singapore's exports enter the US market duty-free. When GSP is taken away, only 45 per cent of Singapore's exports will enter the US market duty-free. Therefore, instead of levelling the playing field, the graduation of Hong Kong and Singapore would make the current imbalance of market access between them and the US even worse.

How Should the US Respond to the NICs?

The fundamental policy question for the United States, wrote Robert D. Hormats, "is whether we will respond to these successful economies defensively (by erecting barriers around our country) or competitively (by strengthening our productivity and our export performance)".[3] Should the US welcome or lament the success of the NICs? Has their success brought benefit or harm to US industries and workers?

Professor Richard Cooper has stated that the United States "should be celebrating the economic success of these countries".[4] How does their success benefit the United States? Professor Cooper answered, "... the process of their economic transformation also leaves the average American ... better off because it provides cheaper goods than Americans can produce and it creates demand for the high-quality goods that Americans are good at producing. That process makes US consumers and producers better off and leads to a higher standard of living for the United States as well as higher standards of living in the NICs".[5]

I agree with Cooper that the United States should welcome, not lament, the success of the NICs. I agree with Hormats that the US should respond to the NICs competitively not defensively. I also agree with Hormats that, "A willingness to compete with the NICs does not imply that such competition should take place without any rules to promote fairness and reciprocity".[6] There was a time when the United States was economically pre-eminent and the NICs were backward developing countries. During that era, the US could afford a one-sided competition with them. Now that the gap between them is closing, it is not unreasonable for the United States to demand that the competition should take place on the basis of certain agreed upon rules.

The Rules of Competition

I believe that the NICs should agree to accept four rules to regulate their competition with the United States and other developed countries. First, the NICs should agree to dismantle their barriers against the import of goods from the US and other industrialized countries. The perception that the trading relationships between the US and the NICs are not based upon reciprocity is the greatest source of fuel for the engine of protectionism in American politics. The NICs should also open their markets to the exports of other developing countries. Second, the NICs should agree to negotiate new rules to govern trade in services and to bring them under the framework of GATT. On this question I would note that the NICs are divided. Hong Kong and Singapore have supported the position of the United States in the Uruguay Round whereas Brazil and India have led the opposition to it. Third, the NICs should agree to bring their domestic laws into conformity with internationally recognized principles for the protection of intellectual property. US industries have estimated that the violations of US trademarks, patents and copyrights cost them about US$20 billion annually. Of all the unfair trade practices, the "theft" of US intellectual property rights has raised the greatest moral indignation in this country. Fourth, the NICS should agree not to manipulate the values of their currencies in order to gain trade competitiveness. Instead, they should allow the relationships between their currencies and those of their trading partners to be governed by the underlying economic fundamentals. At the same time, the United States should refrain from putting pressure on any NIC, in the absence of solid economic evidence, to raise the value of its currency simply because that country enjoys a trade surplus with the United States.

Conclusion

Twenty-five years ago, no one could have foreseen that South Korea, Taiwan, Hong Kong and Singapore would have such vibrant economies today. We should all be thankful that we are gathered here to discuss the problems of success, and not how the West should rescue four basket cases. In the cycles of history, it is inevitable that some nations will rise while others decline. In the present phase of history, the countries of East and Southeast Asia, Japan, the NICs, China and the ASEAN countries, are in a dynamic mode. The question for the United States, and for the rest of the world, is how they should respond to them. I would hope that the United States would not respond to them by erecting barriers to thwart their progress. Instead, I hope the US would respond to them competitively by strengthening its productivity and export performance. The US is justified in demanding that the competition be based upon certain rules to promote fairness and reciprocity. To put it in another way, the world has a right to expect that they behave as good citizens of the world.

Paper prepared for presentation at the Overseas Development Council's Conference on "Growth, Exports and Jobs in the 1990s: The United States and the Third World", 29 February 1988.

NOTES

1. Richard N. Cooper, "The Challenge of the NICs", in Thornton F. Bradshaw, Daniel F. Burton Jr, Richard N. Cooper and Robert D. Hormats (eds.), *America's New Competitors* (Cambridge, Massachusetts: Ballinger Publishing, 1988), p. 12.
2. The US trade deficits (in US$) with the NICs were:

Brazil	$4.4 billion
Hong Kong	$6.5 billion
Mexico	$5.9 billion
Singapore	$2.3 billion
South Korea	$9.9 billion
Taiwan	$19.0 billion
Total	$48.0 billion

3. Robert D. Hormats, "New Players In The International Economy", in *America's New Competitors, supra,* Note 1, p. 7.
4. *Supra,* Note 1, p. 11.
5. Ibid, p. 13.
6. *Supra,* Note 3.

ASIA AND THE UNITED STATES: PERCEPTIONS AND PRESCRIPTIONS

ASEAN's Standing in the United States

Introduction

What is ASEAN's standing in the United States? Among the American public, I am afraid that ASEAN is a nonentity. Most Americans will probably think that the acronym is a typographical error for the word "Asian". I am sure that none of the contestants in the popular TV game show, "Jeopardy", will know what our acronym stands for. We have not yet succeeded in registering ASEAN in the consciousness of the American people. Is it unrealistic and futile to aspire to make our regional organization as well known to the American public as is, for example, the European Community?

Where is ASEAN on the US Totem Pole?

What is the standing of ASEAN and its six constituent states with the US Government? ASEAN enjoys the bipartisan support of Republicans and Democrats, the Administration and the Congress. Former Secretaries of State, Cyrus Vance, Edmund Muskie and George Shultz attended, without fail, the annual ASEAN Post-Ministerial Conference. In addition, there is an annual meeting at the UN between the US Secretary of State and the ASEAN Foreign Ministers. Former United States Trade Representatives, Bill Brock and Clayton Yeutter, have also met frequently with the ASEAN Economic Ministers. ASEAN and the US are dialogue partners. In Washington, the Economic Coordinating Committee (ECC) has served as a useful forum for the discussion of matters of mutual interest. These are not inconsiderable achievements. No other regional grouping in the Third World has achieved the stature, acceptance and support which ASEAN has. We should not, however, be complacent. Notwithstanding the nice things which are often said about ASEAN by US officials, especially in the Executive Branch, I have always suspected that on the US totem pole,

ASEAN is outranked by Japan, China, South Korea, Taiwan and Australia. In other words, in the hierarchy of the countries of East Asia and the Pacific, ranked according to US security and economic interests, ASEAN ranks near the bottom.

Examples of ASEAN's Low Standing

What evidence can I adduce to support my suspicion? Let me cite a few random examples. First, in March 1988, the US State Department published a booklet entitled "Fundamentals of US Foreign Policy". The chapter on "East and South Asia and the Pacific" contains sections on Japan, South Korea, the Philippines, China, India, Pakistan and the South Pacific. There is not a single reference to ASEAN. Second, in February 1989, President Bush visited Japan, China and South Korea. He sent his Vice-President to visit Indonesia, Singapore and Thailand. Third, the Ambassadors of Japan, China and Australia enjoyed regular access to Secretary Shultz. No ASEAN Ambassador enjoyed such access. Indeed, it has been difficult even to fix one annual meeting between the six ASEAN Ambassadors and the Secretary of State. Fourth, ASEAN enjoys even less clout with the Congress than with the Administration. Not a single senator or congressman was interested in meeting our delegates to the recent meeting to accept the report of the researchers on the ASEAN-US Initiative. I shall never forget that when the ASEAN Ambassadors co-hosted a reception for the freshmen senators and representatives of the 100th Congress, in the Capitol Building, not a single senator and only one congressman showed up.

The US Business Community

What is the standing of ASEAN with the US business community? Our standing is surprisingly low. The US business community is much more interested in each of us individually than in ASEAN. In a way, we cannot blame them because their attitude is caused by the fact that unlike the EC, ASEAN has six markets, not one. It is distressing to learn that the corporate membership of the ASEAN-US Business Council has dropped from over 60 to about 35.

How Can ASEAN's Standing Be Raised?

First, we should strengthen our relationships with this country's four leading centres of Southeast Asian studies. These are located at Cornell University,

Ohio University, Michigan University and the University of California at Berkeley. We should encourage our think-tanks and Southeast Asian specialists to establish ties with these four centres. We should exchange publications, scholars and students with them. We should encourage them to hold annual or biannual conferences, symposia and seminars on ASEAN or its constituent states. The ASEAN Missions, especially the Ambassadors, should be prepared to participate in such functions.

Second, the ASEAN Ambassadors should convene a joint meeting, in Washington, with the heads of their tourist promotion offices in the United States. The purpose of the meeting is to explore the feasibility of encouraging our tourist organizations to pool their resources and stage "ASEAN Festivals" in various cities of this country. We should also consider inviting the heads of our airlines to attend the meeting.

Third, we should investigate with the producers of the morning news programmes of ABC, NBC and CBS whether they would be interested to broadcast their shows from our capitals when the US Secretary of State or other dignitary is there. We should be alert to the value of newsworthy events which will take place in our respective countries, for example, ASEAN's 25th anniversary, and be more clever in marketing them to the US media organizations.

Fourth, we should negotiate an agreement with the State Department that the ASEAN Ambassadors should have, at least, one meeting a year with the Secretary of State. This meeting should ideally take place just before the Post-Ministerial Conference. It would be unreasonable and unnecessary for us to request regular access to the Secretary of State, but we should have more access to him than we have had in the past.

Fifth, the ASEAN Working Committee (AWC) should raise its profile and expand its network in the US Congress. Towards this end, the ASEAN Ambassadors should call on at least one senator or representative each month. The Thai Embassy has already compiled a list of senators and representatives who are important to ASEAN. We should encourage our colleagues to cultivate the staff of these senators and representatives. The staffers can open the doors for us to their bosses.

Sixth, we should continue to explore with California, Texas, Washington and Oregon the possibility of establishing in each of those states an organization similar to the Indiana-ASEAN Council.

Seventh, the US-ASEAN Business Council and the US-ASEAN Center for Technology Exchange are about to merge into a single organization to be called the US-ASEAN Council. The AWC should hold a joint meeting with the leaders of the US-ASEAN Council to discuss how we can increase corporate support for the Council and how the new organization can be made more dynamic and effective than its two predecessors.

Eighth, some years ago, the US Congress enacted legislation to create the US-Japan Friendship Commission. Half the endowment of the Commission came from the US Government, the other half came from the Japanese Government. The Commission makes grants to support studies, exchanges and meetings with a view to promoting better understanding between the US and Japan. The AWC should explore with our friends in the Congress, such as Senator Richard Lugar or Congressman Stephen Solarz, whether it would be feasible to establish a US-ASEAN Friendship Commission, along the lines of the US-Japan Friendship Commission.

Remarks prepared 26 May 1989.

ASIA AND THE UNITED STATES: PERCEPTIONS AND PRESCRIPTIONS

The US-Japan Relationship and Its Implications for ASEAN

The US-Japan relationship is a paradoxical one. It is half good and half bad. On the political and security plane, the US-Japan relationship is strong and stable. The two governments share, to a large extent, a common world view and common threat perception. The US-Japan Mutual Security Treaty is securely anchored in both countries. Japan's support for US forces in Japan has grown to over US$1.5 billion annually. At the urging of the US, Japan has been assuming more of the burden for its self-defence. Its defence budget has exceeded the ten-year-old cap of 1 per cent of GNP. Japan's decision to participate in research for the Strategic Defence Initiative (SDI) has been warmly welcomed in Washington.

The excellent political and security relationship between the US and Japan stands in stark contrast to their economic relationship. Many in Washington would characterize the present state of US-Japan economic relations as nothing less than a crisis. Some have observed that anti-Japanese sentiment in Washington has, in recent months, reached a level unprecedented since the Second World War.

Causes of the Current Crisis

What are the causes of the current crisis in US-Japan economic relations? The first cause is the size of the US trade deficit with Japan. In 1986, the US suffered a trade deficit of US$169 billion. The deficit with Japan was US$58 billion, almost one-third of the total deficit. The 1987 trade deficit with Japan is estimated at US$60 billion. The second cause is the perception in the US, especially in Congress, that Japan is an unfair trading partner who has not reciprocated the openness of the US market. US companies, seeking to break into the Japanese market, are said to confront a formidable array of tariff and non-tariff barriers. The resentment against Japan is felt by many sectors of US business and industry, such as, beef, citrus, rice, telecommunications, semiconductors, supercomputers and the construction industry.

The third cause is the prevailing view in America that Japan is not carrying its share of the burden of supporting the world economy. American leaders have often pointed out that the US is absorbing 63 per cent of the manufactured exports of the developing countries whilst Japan is absorbing only 7 per cent.

What Japan Should Do

In order to defuse the current crisis, Japan should do the following things. First, Japan should open her market to the imports of goods and services. Nothing is more corrosive to the relationship between the US and Japan than the perception on this side of the Pacific that the relationship is not based upon reciprocity.

Second, the Japanese Government should implement the main recommendations of the Maekawa Commission. The Commission of 17 wise men, chaired by the former governor of the Bank of Japan, Haruo Maekawa, was appointed by former Prime Minister Nakasone in October 1985. In its first report, the Commission observed that "The time has come for Japan to make a historic transformation in its traditional policies of economic management and in the nation's lifestyle. There can be no further developments for Japan without this transformation".

In its second report, the Maekawa Commission proposed a number of specific steps which would achieve the goals stated in its first report within the next three to five years. Among the proposed steps are these:

(a) Stimulate greater domestic consumption by providing more and better housing and improving urban facilities;
(b) Reduce domestic production of coal so as to increase imports;
(c) Accelerate transfer of production overseas;
(d) Facilitate the import of agricultural products and manufactures;
(e) Liberalize the financial and capital markets to promote the internationalization of the yen;
(f) Pursue a more active role for Japan in economic development overseas.

Some of the recommendations will be opposed by domestic interests such as mining and agriculture. Other recommendations will be implemented very slowly. Indeed, some sceptics wonder whether the purpose of the report is to appease sentiments abroad. The Japanese Finance Minister, Kiichi Miyazawa, has written that "Japan must transform its export-led economy into a grow-from-within economy". He referred to the Maekawa report as a step in the right direction and said that Japan should follow up more vigorously on its recommendations by boosting domestic demand, re-adjusting Japan's industrial structure and encouraging more imports of manufactured goods.

What the US Should Do

To be fair, one has to acknowledge that not all the faults lie with Japan. The United States is certainly not blameless. The primary reason for the trade deficit with Japan is not market barriers in Japan but the large federal budget deficits in the US. Martin Feldstein, the former Chairman of President Reagan's Council of Economic Advisers, has stated that "the primary reason for the deteriorating trade imbalance is the 70 per cent rise of the dollar which occurred between 1980 and the spring of 1985. This unprecedented increase in the exchange value of the dollar dramatically increased the price of American products relative to foreign products, causing the volume of US exports to decline while merchandise imports increased by nearly 50 per cent".

There are a number of things which the US should do to defuse the crisit with Japan. First, it should continue to reduce its federal budget deficit. Second, Americans should save more and spend less. In 1986, Americans saved only 3.8 per cent of their disposable income. Third, American industries should improve the quality of their products. Fourth, American companies should work harder to market their products in foreign markets. Fifth, the US should improve its competitiveness. This means, amongst other things, raising productivity, improving quality control, raising the standard of education in American schools, devoting a larger percentage of the GNP to civilian R & D and improving labour-management relations. Sixth, the US should resist the domestic pressure for protectionism.

The Importance of the US-Japan Relationship to ASEAN

The economic relationship between the US and Japan is important to ASEAN for several reasons. They are the two largest economies in the world. Together they account for 38 per cent of the world's GNP. They are ASEAN's two largest trading partners. The prospects of the world economy and the future of the world's trading system are very much dependent upon the interactions between these two economic superpowers.

The US should continue to exert pressure on Japan to open her market to the imports of goods and services, not only from the US but from all countries. The US should not, however, close its market to Japanese imports. The US is not the only country which has trouble exporting to Japan. The ASEAN countries confront the same obstacles in their attempts to break into the Japanese market. But, unlike the US, they do not have the leverage to pry open the Japanese market.

Japan's imports from ASEAN consist mainly of raw materials. ASEAN has been largely unsuccessful in persuading Japan to open her market to the imports of manufactured goods and agricultural products from ASEAN. Less than 10 per cent of Japan's imports from ASEAN consists of manufactures.

The US should not close its market to Japanese imports for two reasons. First, because the measures aimed at Japan are likely to hurt other countries such as ASEAN even more than Japan. Although the barriers to trade may be targeted at Japan, they will also keep out the exports of the rest of the Pacific. Second, the countries in East and Southeast Asia export between 10 per cent to 30 per cent of their total exports to Japan. If Japan is forced to reduce its exports to the US, Japan will, in turn, reduce its imports from the countries of East and Southeast Asia.

There is also a geo-strategic reason for not closing the American market to Japanese imports. In his address to a joint meeting of the US Congress, on 9 October 1985, Prime Minister Lee Kuan Yew said:

> *A Japan squeezed in such a protectionist trap has few attractive options. After thrashing around looking for market extensions in Latin America, Africa and West Asia, Japan will turn back to her two major options: closer economic links with the Soviet Union, or*

closer ties with China. She could try to do both and reconcile or postpone the conflicts inherent in the two options. In the end, she has to choose one of these two options. Either choice conjures up disquieting consequences for the rest of Asia and the world.

Japan's Role in the World

Japan's current role in the world is unique. Never before has a country with so much economic power eschewed the option of developing a military might commensurate with its economic strength. The world should reward, not punish Japan for its abstinence. This is one of the reasons which has led me to support Japan's ambition to become a semi-permanent member of the UN Security Council. If we deny Japan's ambition, we will, in effect, be saying to Japan that we cannot accept her as a great power unless she were also to become a great military power.

Right and responsibility must, however, go together. Japan must accept her international obligations. First, Japan has an obligation to abide by the rules of international trade which have made her prosperous. Japan must open her market to the world.

Second, Japan has an obligation to help the less fortunate people of the world. We should welcome the decision of the Japanese Government to increase the total amount of her economic aid during the period 1980 to 1992 by 100 per cent to more than US$40 billion. We should also welcome the fact that in consultation with the US, Japan is stepping up its aid to countries of strategic importance such as the Philippines. Japan is the largest donor of aid to the Philippines. Four members of the US Congress – Senator Alan Cranston, Senator Richard Lugar, Congressman Jack Kemp and Congressman Stephen Solarz – have proposed a new Marshall Plan for the Philippines. I hope the Government of Japan will agree to make a generous contribution to the Plan. Prime Minister Noburo Takeshita met the six ASEAN leaders in Manila in December 1987, following the conclusion of the Third ASEAN Summit. At that meeting, Japan offered the ASEAN countries a new development fund of US$2 billion, consisting of soft-term loans.

Third, Japan should play a bigger role in the multilateral development agencies. Japan is already the second largest shareholder in the World Bank and the largest shareholder in the Asian Development Bank. Japan is also playing an increasingly important role in the International Development Agency (IDA). Japan has replaced the US as the world's leading creditor country. Japan must therefore pick up the slack caused by the transformation of the US from a creditor to a debtor nation.

Fourth, Japan should be more active in transferring technology to the developing countries. This process is already ongoing and has accelerated during the last two years due to the appreciation of the value of the yen. Japanese companies in ASEAN should export some of their production back to Japan, increase the level of technology transferred and employ more local personnel in middle and top management.

Fifth, Japan should play a more active and creative role in world diplomacy and in international negotiations on scientific, social, cultural and humanitarian questions.

Conclusion

ASEAN has a great deal at stake in the US-Japan relationship. The current imbalances between the two economies are unsustainable and dangerous, and must be corrected. The correction should, however, be done in such a manner as not to plunge the world economy into a recession or to undermine the world's trading system. The world economy needs leadership. That leadership can only be provided by the US and Japan acting in tandem.

Paper prepared for presentation at the Kenneth Holland Lecture Series 1987–1988, Institute of International Education, New York, 12 January 1988.

ASIA AND THE UNITED STATES: PERCEPTIONS AND PRESCRIPTIONS

The Future of US-Japan Relations

Mr President, fellow Harvardians, Ladies and Gentlemen, I feel very humble in having been chosen by the Harvard Club of Singapore as its Guest of Honour at its annual dinner this evening. There are many other Singaporeans who deserve this honour more than I do. But, when the President of the Club, who is also my boss at The Institute of Policy Studies, asked me, I could not refuse. The story of my life is that I am the undeserving recipient of many honours which have been bestowed upon me.

An Act of Serendipity

I want to make a confession about my going to Harvard Law School in 1963. I did not apply for admission to the Law School. I do not know whether I would have been accepted if I had done so! Instead, one day, I received a letter from Dean Griswold inviting me to go to Harvard together with the offer of a handsome fellowship. It was an act of serendipity which led me to Harvard Law School. Because of our British connections, I had set my sight on going to Oxbridge. During my final year, I was examined by several external examiners including one from England, Professor Sir Jim Gower of London University. By chance, Professor Gower had spent the previous academic year teaching at Harvard Law School as a Visiting Professor. He persuaded me that because of the similarities between our Law School and those in England, it would be more interesting for me to be exposed to the American legal system and legal education.

Chasing the Shuttlecock at Radcliffe

I had a wonderful year at Harvard, intellectually, culturally and socially. I studied with some of the great professors of the Law School. In addition,

I audited a course on economic development with John Kenneth Galbraith, a course on sociology with David Riesman and a course on philosophy with Professor Twining. I was an avid badminton player in my youth. As soon as I arrived, I asked to join the badminton club. I was told that Harvard men played squash and if I wanted to play badminton, I had to go over to Radcliffe College and join the women. After some hesitation, I joined the badminton club at Radcliffe College. I want to assure you, and especially my wife, that my intentions were strictly athletic and honourable.

The Impact of US-Japan Relations on Singapore

Let me now turn to the topic of my remarks this evening. I have chosen to speak, *in my personal capacity*, about the future of US-Japan relations not only because this month marks the 50th anniversary of the outbreak of war between the US and Japan but also because I have been worrying about their bilateral relationship for the last seven years. Why should a Singaporean be concerned about the state of US-Japan relations? He should be concerned for two reasons. First, the US and Japan account for 40 per cent of the world's GNP. If the two economies turn from competition to conflict, it would have a disastrous effect on the world economy and on the Asia Pacific economies. Second, the US-Japan Security Treaty of 1960 has been an important pillar of peace and stability. If Japan stops relying upon the US nuclear umbrella and becomes an independent military power, such a development will destabilize the region. For these and other reasons, Singapore has a stake in the continued good relations between Japan and the US.

The Current State of US-Japan Relations

What are some of the salient facts concerning the current state of US-Japan relations?

Economic Interdependence

Economically, the two economies have become very interdependent. The US is Japan's largest export market. Japan is the largest export market for the US. The two-way trade in 1990 was US$140 billion. Japan enjoyed a trade surplus of US$41 billion. Japan has invested heavily in the US. Between 1985 and 1990, Japanese direct investment in the US totalled

US$110 billion. In the same period, US direct investment in Japan was US$5.3 billion. Japanese investment has, however, dropped sharply. So far this year, Japan has invested only about US$2 billion in the US. Until recently, Japanese investors bought about 40 per cent of US Treasury Bills. This figure has dropped to about 10 per cent. In recent years, an increasing number of Japanese and American companies have entered into strategic alliances.

Political Allies

Politically, the US-Japan Security Treaty of 1960 has stood the test of time. Opinion polls in the US have repeatedly revealed that the American people want America to honour its treaty commitment to defend Japan against external aggression. On all major international issues, Japan has followed America's lead. During the recent Gulf War, Japan contributed a total of US$13 billion towards the costs of the allies. The homeport of the US Seventh Fleet is in Yokusuka, Japan. Japan contributes about US$3 billion or half the non-salary cost of the US military presence in Japan. Japan's share will be increased to 80 per cent by 1995.

Problems in the US-Japan Relationship

The US-Japan relationship is in trouble. It is in trouble partly because their common enemy, the Soviet threat, has largely disappeared. The strain between them is also due to the economic imbalances between the two countries and the perception in the US that Japan is not carrying her fair share of the burden of collective security, as well as to the aspiration of Japan to transform her status from a junior partner to an equal partner.

Economic Imbalance

I referred earlier to the fact that in 1990, Japan enjoyed a trade surplus of US$41 billion. It is not just the size or the persistence of the trade deficit which causes resentment in the US. It is the widespread feeling in the US that Japan is not a fair trading partner and has taken undue advantage of the openness of the US market and economy. In an opinion poll conducted in 1990, 71 per cent of Americans believed that Japan was guilty of unfair trade practices. Sixty per cent viewed Japan's economic power as constituting a critical threat to the vital interests of the US. The Japanese view of the trade imbalance is quite different. Shintaro Ishihara, the author of *The Japan That Can Say No*, believes that the US has lost its economic vitality and has made Japan its scapegoat.

Acrimonious Dialogue

The dialogue between the US and Japan over their economic relations has grown increasingly acrimonious. As President Bush said to the Asia Society in New York on 12 November 1991, "Japan-bashing has become a minor sport in the US, and some in Japan have become equally disdainful of the US. Both our nations must reject those who would rather seek scapegoats than tackle their problems". In his speech on 7 December at Pearl Harbour, President Bush called upon Americans to stop hating Japan and to turn a new page in US-Japan relations. What then is the solution? The solution is for Japan, on the one hand, to continue to open her market and reduce her non-tariff barriers and, on the other hand, for the US to reduce her federal budget deficit and to increase her industrial and educational competitiveness. Japan should discard her old protectionist habits. Mentally, Japan does not appear to have made the transition from being a poor country to being an economic superpower. The US, on the other hand, has grown complacent with wealth and power. She does not seem to appreciate the seriousness of her economic situation. Unless she can stop living beyond her means, raise her savings and investment rates and improve the quality of her primary and secondary education, her economic decline may be irreversible.

Burden-Sharing

The problem of burden-sharing is even more difficult to resolve. After the Second World War, the US imposed a "peace constitution" on Japan. In fact, Article IX of the Japanese Constitution forbids Japan from maintaining "land, sea and air forces". Using the nomenclature of "Self-Defence Forces", Japan has built up a significant capacity to defend itself and has the world's fourth largest defence budget. Viewed from the vantage point of the US Congress, however, the *status quo* is unfair because the US is spending 6 per cent of its GNP on defence and Japan, only slightly over 1 per cent. Many Americans believe that this is why Japan is able to invest two and a half times more than the US in new plant, equipment, and research and development.

Japan's Security Role

In recent years, Washington has been pressuring Tokyo to spend more on defence and to carry a greater share of the burden of maintaining stability in East Asia. The policy of the US is unpopular within Japan and with Japan's neighbours. The people of Japan do not want Japan to become a great military power. Some of Japan's neighbours, such as China, Korea and the Philippines, who were the victims of Japan's aggression and occupation, would oppose any American plan to make Japan the policeman of East and Southeast Asia. Finally, those in Washington who want Japan to spend more on defence have not explained what they want Japan to spend the extra dollars on.

Conclusion

Singapore's capacity to influence the future course of US-Japan relations is marginal. Along with our ASEAN partners, we should, however, do everything we can to ensure good relations between these two giants. We should make ourselves useful to each of them. We should help to develop co-operative arrangements, both in the economic and security realms, which would include both. In the economic field, we have APEC which has the potential to fulfil this role.

In the security field, there is no similar institution. My hope is that one day, in the not too distant future, there will be an Asian-Pacific equivalent of the Conference on Security and Cooperation in Europe (CSCE). Such a security forum, comprising ASEAN, US, Japan, China, Russia, India and other Asia Pacific countries could lend political stability to East and Southeast Asia. The US is not convinced that the region needs such a forum. There is, however, a noticeable absence of new thinking in Washington concerning the need to evolve a new security equilibrium in the Asia Pacific region. Others feel that such a forum should only be established after various regional problems, such as peace on the Korean peninsula and differences between the US and China, have been resolved. The CSCE was, however, established before and not after the end of the Cold War in Europe. Perhaps we should proceed on a step-by-step basis and use one of the existing forums, such as the ASEAN Post-Ministerial Conference or APEC, to begin a regional dialogue about security.

Ultimately, the health of the Japan-US relationship depends upon the successful management of their economic competition and the transformation of their unequal political relationship into a global partnership. The principles of such a partnership are likely to be spelt out in a "Tokyo Declaration" which will be adopted by President Bush and Prime Minister Miyazawa, at the end of the US President's visit to Tokyo in January. We must hope that President Bush and Prime Minister Miyazawa will succeed. The alternative will be a disaster for Japan, the US and the world.

Speech delivered to the Harvard Club of Singapore, 12 December 1991.

ASIA AND THE UNITED STATES: PERCEPTIONS AND PRESCRIPTIONS

The United States and Southeast Asia: A Rationale for Partnership in the Post-Cold War Era

US Perceptions of Southeast Asia

Americans are generally not well informed abut Asia. This has been documented by William Watts in his book, *The United States and Asia: Changing Attitudes and Policies*.[1] He wrote, "... substantial misinformation about Asia and its nations does abound. Negative stereotypes about the area as a whole dominate ... These stereotypes are applied indiscriminately to specific lands and peoples, suggesting that many of the remarkable and explosive changes taking place in that part of the world have not yet been fully understood or even heard of ..."

In a survey conducted by Gallup Poll, Watts found that a majority of Americans thought mistakenly that Indonesia was not a major supplier of oil and petroleum products to the United States, that the United States still provided major economic assistance to South Korea, and that US trade with Europe was considerably larger than US trade with Asia. More recently, a Republican candidate running for the Presidency said that workers in Singapore were paid 70 US cents!

If Americans are not well informed about Asia generally, they are even less informed about Southeast Asia. If asked to name the countries of Southeast Asia, Americans would probably be able to name only two, Vietnam and the Philippines. Southeast Asia is an unfamiliar geographical entity to most Americans. It also suffers from the fact that it is eclipsed by the larger countries of China, Japan and India. Economically, Americans tend to think of East Asia as Japan writ large. Hence, East Asia is the subject of both admiration and concern to Americans.

ASEAN is the Core of Southeast Asia

No one would disagree with the proposition that the Association of Southeast Asian Nations (ASEAN) is the core of Southeast Asia. Its seven member countries are Brunei, Indonesia, Malaysia, Philippines, Singapore, Thailand and Vietnam. Of the remaining three countries of Southeast Asia, Cambodia and Laos enjoy observer status with ASEAN. Myanmar is regularly invited to attend the annual meetings of the Foreign Ministers of ASEAN. The next annual meeting of ASEAN Foreign Ministers and the Post-Ministerial Conference will be held in July 1996 in Jakarta. There will also be an informal summit of the ASEAN Leaders in Bogor, Indonesia, in December 1996. ASEAN has a three-point agenda for 1996: (a) the expansion of ASEAN, (b) the deepening of ASEAN's economic co-operation, and (c) the strengthening of ASEAN's external relations.

Founded in 1967, ASEAN is one of the most successful regional organizations in the world. It has helped to maintain peace and stability in Southeast Asia. It has shown it is capable of acting as one and pursuing successfully a diplomatic objective over many years, for example, in bringing peace to Cambodia. ASEAN stands for free trade and is a staunch proponent of the World Trade Organization (WTO) and the Asia Pacific Economic Cooperation (APEC). ASEAN has a proven track record of launching new initiatives, such as the ASEAN Regional Forum (ARF) and the first Summit of Asian and European Leaders, which was held in Bangkok on 1 and 2 March of this year. ASEAN is simultaneously engaged in the processes of broadening and deepening the organization. In July 1995, ASEAN admitted Vietnam as a full member. ASEAN has decided to accelerate the implementation of the ASEAN Free Trade Agreement from 15 to ten years. At their summit in Bangkok in December 1995, ASEAN Leaders agreed to enlarge the scope of economic liberalization beyond manufacturing products to include agriculture and services.

The Importance of Southeast Asia to the US

What is the importance of Southeast Asia to US national interests?

First, Southeast Asia is a region of strategic importance to the United States. It connects the Pacific and Indian Oceans. Several of the world's vital sea-lanes, such as the Straits of Malacca and Singapore, the Lombok Strait and the Sunda Strait, pass through Southeast Asia. In the event of war in the Middle East, US forces based in Japan will have to transit Southeast Asia on their way to the Gulf. After losing the naval and air bases in the Philippines, the United States has obtained access to facilities in Surabaya, Indonesia and Lumut, Malaysia. The end of the Cold War does not affect the objective reality that the United States, as a global power, must have reliable allies and friends in strategic regions, as well as unimpeded access to and through the strategic sea-lanes of the world.

Second, Southeast Asia is a region of growing economic importance to the United States. The region has a combined population of over 450 million. The seven ASEAN economies have consistently registered some of the highest growth rates in the world. The economic model pursued by the economies of Southeast Asia is different from the Northeast Asia model. The Southeast Asian economic model welcomes foreign direct investments, practises free trade and eschews the mercantilist policies favoured by some countries in Northeast Asia. As a result, US trade and investment in Southeast Asia has been growing rapidly.

In 1980, US trade with ASEAN was US$22.5 billion, comprising 4.7 percent of US total trade. IN 1990, the two-way trade between the US and ASEAN had grown to US$47.5 billion, comprising 5.2 per cent of US total trade. In 1994, it had increased to US$86.1 billion or 7.2 per cent of US total trade. US exports to ASEAN had grown from $9.2 billion in 1980 to US$18.9 billion in 1990 to US$32 billion in 1994.[2] Although ASEAN enjoys a trade surplus with the US in merchandise trade, the US enjoys a surplus with ASEAN in trade in services.[3] It should also be remembered that a substantial part of ASEAN's exports to the US is by US multinational corporations.

In 1980, 42 per cent of ASEAN's exports to the US consisted of petroleum and petroleum-related products. Today, more than half of ASEAN's exports to the US consists of industrial machinery and equipment, including electronics, telecommunications components, computers and computer parts. Similarly, manufactured products account for 90 per cent of US exports to ASEAN. Machinery and transport equipment make up a large part of US exports.

US cumulative investment in ASEAN had also grown from US$4 billion in 1980 to US$ 11.2 billion in 1990, to US 24.5 billion in 1994. Although US investment in ASEAN in 1994 constituted only 4 per cent of its total in the world, its income from ASEAN was 7.2 per cent of its income from the world. In other words, US investment in ASEAN was almost twice as profitable as its investment in the rest of the world.

Third, ASEAN has been a useful and effective political partner of the United States. Between 1979 and 1991, ASEAN and the United States worked closely to bring an end to the conflict in Cambodia. ASEAN helped the United States to launch the Uruguay Round of multilateral trade negotiations and to bring it to a successful conclusion. ASEAN and the United States have worked closely in the various international and regional organizations, such as the UN, APEC and the ARF. Apart from Cambodia, ASEAN and the United States worked closely to achieve the indefinite extension of the Non-Proliferation Treaty, in bringing the 1992 Earth Summit to a successful conclusion, and in various UN peacekeeping and humanitarian activities.

Fourth, the cultural relationship between the United States and ASEAN is of global significance. Southeast Asia is a region of great diversity. It has many races, religions, languages and cultural traditions. Indonesia, Malaysia and Brunei represent modern Islam. They do not see the West as the enemy of Islam. They are not opposed to development and modernity. The success of Indonesia, Malaysia and Brunei could serve as an exemplar to the Islamic world. It is a much more attractive model than that of Iran. Muslims from other parts of the world, such as Africa, are beginning to visit Southeast Asia rather than the Middle East for inspiration.

Singapore is a fusion of Asian and Western values. For these reasons, the United States has a better prospect of reaching a cultural understanding with heterogeneous Southeast Asia than with the more homogeneous societies of Japan, China or Korea. Such an understanding is of global significance because of the fear, espoused recently by Professor Samuel Hungtington of Harvard University, that future conflicts between nations may be based upon their civilizations or cultures.

Elements of a Sound US Policy towards Southeast Asia

In the context of a post-Cold War world, anyone arguing for US engagement with another country or region must show that such engagement is in the national interest of the United States. I believe that I have given four reasons why it is in America's national interest to remain actively engaged with Southeast Asia. What do Southeast Asians want from America?

First, they want the United States to continue to maintain a credible military presence in East Asia. They were heartened by the recent decision of the Clinton Administration to maintain its forward deployed military presence in the Asia Pacific and to maintain the force level at 100,000. Southeast Asians want the United States to act as a balancer and stabilizer in the Asia Pacific because they view the United States as a benign superpower.

Second, Southeast Asians would like the United States to remain strongly committed to free trade. They welcome the active role which the United States has played in the WTO and in APEC. They would like the United States to examine the possibility of linking the North American Free Trade Area and the ASEAN Free Trade Area.

Third, they would like the United States to maintain good relations with both Japan and China. Southeast Asians believe that a stable triangular relationship between the United States, Japan and China is a necessary requirement for the maintenance of peace and stability in the Asia Pacific. The US-Japan security alliance is a pillar of peace in the Asia Pacific. The United States and Japan must not allow their trade and economic differences to break the fire wall and poison their good political and security relations. Washington must be sensitive to the rising nationalism in Japan and allow her to play a less unequal role in the partnership.

In the case of China, Southeast Asia would like the United States to engage China, not to contain her. The United States, Japan and Southeast Asia should pursue a common policy of bringing China into the mainstream of the international community, including the WTO but, at the same time, insist that China must behave as a responsible global citizen. The United States should continue to abide by the three joint communiqués it has signed with China, and not encourage the development of two Chinas or of one China and an independent Taiwan. At the same time, we should all persuade China to give Taiwan more international space.

Fourth, Southeast Asia nations would like the United States to work co-operatively with them to nurture the ASEAN Regional Forum so that it could, in time, become the security equivalent of APEC. The ARF was established in Bangkok in July 1994. Its members are the seven ASEAN countries, its seven Dialogue Partners, namely, the United States, Canada, Japan, South Korea, Australia, New Zealand and the European Union, as well as China, Russia, Laos, Cambodia and Papua New Guinea.

Paper published in **The Ambassadors REVIEW**, *Spring 1996.*

NOTES

1. William Watts, *The United States and Asia: Changing Attitudes and Policies* (Lexington, Massachusetts: Lexington Books, 1982).
2. See Annexes 1 and 2.
3. See Annex 3.

ANNEX 1

US TRADE WITH ASEAN

Year	US Exports to ASEAN US$ (m)	Per cent Change	US Imports from ASEAN US$ (m)	Per cent CHANGE	Trade with ASEAN US$ (m)	Per cent Change	Trade Balance US$ (m)
1980	9,248	-	13,304	-	22,552	-	-4,056
1981	8,854	-4.3%	14,391	8.2%	23,245	3.1%	-5,537
1982	9,855	11.3%	11,873	-17.5%	21,728	-6.5%	-2,018
1983	9,858	-0.0%	14,046	18.3%	23,904	10.0%	-4,188
1984	9,683	-1.8%	16,872	20.1%	26,555	11.1%	-7,189
1985	8,109	-16.3%	15,623	-7.4%	23,732	-10.6%	-7,514
1986	8,587	5.9%	15,180	-2.8%	23,767	0.1%	-6,593
1987	9,976	16.2%	18,052	18.9%	28,028	17.9%	-8,076
1988	12,788	28.2%	21,901	21.3%	34,689	23.8%	-9,113
1989	16,056	25.6%	26,002	18.7%	42,058	21.2%	-9,946
1990	18,951	18.0%	28,577	9.9%	47,528	13.0%	-9,626
1991	20,795	9.7%	30,318	6.1%	51,113	7.5%	-9,523
1992	23,987	15.3%	37,384	23.3%	61,371	20.1%	-13,397
1993	28,294	18.0%	44,050	17.8%	72,344	17.9%	-15,756
1994	32,095	13.4%	54,022	22.6%	86,117	19.0%	-21,927

Note: ASEAN includes: Brunei, Indonesia, Malaysia, Philippines, Singapore, Thailand and Vietnam.
Source: ***IMF Direction of Trade Statistics Yearbook 1987 & 1995*** (*US perspective*).

ANNEX 2

US TRADE WITH ASEAN
(Value in US$ Million)

Country	US Exports to ASEAN 1992	1993	1994	US Imports from ASEAN 1992	1993	1994	Trade with ASEAN 1992	1993	1994	Balance of Trade 1992	1993	1994
ASEAN	23,987	28,446	32,095	37,384	44,050	54,022	61,371	72,496	86,117	-13,397	-15,604	-21,927
Brunei	453	478	376	30	32	47	483	510	423	423	446	329
Indonesia	2,778	2,922	2,811	4,704	5,887	7,020	7,482	8,809	9,831	-1,926	-2,965	-4,209
Malaysia	4,396	6,065	6,965	8,540	10,923	14,419	12,936	16,988	21,384	-4,144	-4,858	-7,454
Philippines	2,753	3,529	3,888	4,623	5,176	6,025	7,376	8,705	9,913	-1,870	-1,647	-2,137
Singapore	9,620	11,676	13,022	11,560	13,050	15,657	21,180	24,726	28,679	-1,940	-1,374	-2,635
Thailand	3,982	3,769	4,861	7,927	8,982	10,799	11,909	12,751	15,660	-3,945	-5,213	-5,938
Vietnam	5	7	172	0	0	55	5	7	227	5	7	117

Source: *IMF Direction of Trade Statistics Yearbook. 1995* (US perspective)

ANNEX 3

US SALES AND PURCHASES OF SERVICES IN ASIA

	1994			1993		
	Receipts	Payments	Surplus	Receipts	Payments	Surplus
US$ (Millions)							
Japan	29,710	13,754	15,956	26,942	12,994	13,948
Australia	3,792	1,952	1,840	3,643	2,253	1,390
China	2,181	1,444	737	1,941	1,378	563
New Zealand	843	566	277	794	544	250
Taiwan	4,242	2,695	1,547	3,563	2,413	1,150
Singapore*	2,363	1,189	1,174	2,382	1,135	1,247
Thailand*	1,455	462	993	891	399	492
Malaysia*	387	235	152	757	327	430
Indonesia*	918	465	453	883	444	439
India	1,255	769	486	1,137	724	413
Hong Kong	2,570	2,086	484	2,350	1,545	805
Philippines*	1,184	1,065	119	1,302	864	438
South Korea	4,507	2,609	1,898	3,709	1,954	1,755
Other	2,135	2,927	-792	2,238	2,490	-252

Note: * Denotes members of ASEAN.
Source: US Department of Commerce.

ASIA AND THE UNITED STATES: PERCEPTIONS AND PRESCRIPTIONS

Reflections of a Departing Ambassador: American Values and Economic Problems

By the time I leave Washington, D.C., to return to Singapore in June this year, I will have spent about 20 years in the United States, a year as a graduate student at Harvard Law School, one semester as a visiting Lecturer at the Law School of the State University of New York in Buffalo, 13 years as Singapore's Ambassador to the UN in New York and six years as Ambassador to the United States. I have lived through your good times and your bad times. I have witnessed your triumphs as well as your defeats. I agonized as America went through a nervous breakdown as a result of the divisive war in Vietnam. I watched in sorrow at the sight of Americans turning their backs on American ideals and institutions. In the 1980s, I was relieved to see the recovery of faith and self-confidence. What I would like to do today is to share with you some of my reflections on America and on its future.

Let me begin by identifying some of the things which I admire about America.

First, no other country has welcomed as many refugees and immigrants and none has assimilated them so easily as America. Since the end of the Vietnam War in 1975, the US has welcomed over 850,000 Indochinese refugees to her shores. Many of the children of these refugees, often of humble origin, have topped their classes in schools and have been awarded scholarships to study at America's elite colleges and universities. The Asian-American community is the fastest growing community in America. Because of their devotion to hard work, the high value they attach to education and the availability of opportunities, Asian-Americans will provide America with a new infusion of brainpower, especially in the areas in which the United States is in danger of losing its lead – mathematics, science and engineering. Not all the countries in the world accept immigrants. Of those which do, none is able to match the manner in which the United States assimilates them. In some countries, the immigrant, his son and even his grandson will always be treated as outsiders. In the United States, the moment a person becomes a US citizen, he or she is treated just like any other American. The absence of an aristocratic past frees America of social barriers against upward mobility. As a result, it is possible for an American child, no matter what his ethnic origin and how adverse his family circumstances, to aspire to fulfil the American Dream.

Second, American is a nation of warm-hearted and generous people who have shared their wealth, technology and markets with others. Between 1945 and 1986, the United States gave a total of $344 billion in economic assistance to other countries. No other country has been as generous in sharing its technology with other countries. Senator Jay Rockfeller (Democrat – West Virginia) has estimated that Japan has been able to purchase all the technology she wanted from the United States for between $10 billion and $17 billion. This has enabled Japan to catch up with the US and, in some areas, even to surpass the US in the technological race. American capital, technology and markets have enabled the economies of East and Southeast Asia to grow and prosper.

Third, America is a nation of volunteers. More than 80 million Americans volunteer some of their time to a cause. The average time spent is five hours a week. Half of all private high schools in the United States, including the two my sons attended, require a specified number of hours spent in community service as a graduation requirement.

Fourth, there is a strong tradition in America of giving to charity. The term "charity" includes churches, hospitals, schools, colleges, universities, public libraries, museums, symphonies, operas, ballets, etc. In 1987, American corporations, foundations and individuals gave a total of $93 billion to charity. In 1988, the figure exceeded $100 billion. As a proportion of their incomes, the poor gave more to charity than the rich.

Fifth, there is a strong spirit of entrepreneurship in America. Since 1980, 19 million new jobs have been created in America. About 75 per cent of these jobs have been created by small businesses. Americans are willing to take risks. The society encourages the spirit of entrepreneurship by rewarding those who succeed and, just as importantly, by not penalizing those who fail. There is no social stigma attached to failure. The society gives the entrepreneur as many chances as he or she has the courage and the resources to try until he or she succeeds.

Let me now turn to discuss the second aspect of my topic, the future of the United States. The persistence of the triple deficits, the merchandise trade deficit, the current account deficit and the federal budget deficit, has affected the mood in America. This mood helped to make Paul Kennedy's book, *The Rise and Fall of the Great Powers*, into a best seller even though it is highly questionable whether the author's concept of imperial overreach can be applied to the United States. In a recent opinion poll, 48 per cent of Americans regarded Japan as the strongest economic power in the world. Only 39 per cent thought that the United States was still number one. More and more thoughtful Americans are aware that the American Government and the American people must stop living beyond their means. They realize that unless America succeeds in overcoming the drug menace, which has become an epidemic, in raising the standard of education, and in increasing the rates of savings and productivity, the future of America is clouded.

What are the facts? Do you support the thesis that the American century is over and that American economic decline is irreversible?

In 1989, the US economy grew by 2.9 per cent. However, productivity increased only by 1 percent. In 1989, the United States was the world's largest exporter. However, the US suffered a merchandise trade deficit of $110 billion and a current account deficit of $123 billion. The nation continued to spend more than it saved. The net domestic savings was 2.5 per cent of GNP. Savings as a percentage of disposable income was 4.4 per cent (12.6 per cent in the West Germany and 15.2 per cent in Japan). In 1989, the US had to import between $115 billion to $120 billion of capital to bridge the gap between its low level of savings and its need for capital. The nation is also spending too little on new plant and equipment and in the building of infrastructure. Net private fixed investment as a percentage of net national product was 4.5 per cent. During the 1980s, the percentage of GNP which the federal, state and local governments had been spending in the building of infrastructure dropped to 2.2 per cent.

I would like to make three general comments on the facts and figures I cited above. First, the competitiveness of an economy depends upon its productivity. A productivity increase of only 1 percent is very unsatisfactory. Second, the low level of investment in new plant and equipment is probably one of the reasons for the low increase in productivity of the US economy compared to other economies. Third, the fact that in 1989, the US had to import about $120 billion of capital from abroad leads to a number of deleterious consequences. Peter Drucker, the guru of American management, recently pointed out that business in America is handicapped by the fact that it has to pay two to three times as much for capital as businesses in other countries.

There are other problems. According to an OECD study, cited by the John Young Report on Competitiveness, the US has one of the worst records in labour-management relations among the industrialized countries. This is one area in which the United States can learn from Japan. Another problem is the failure of government and business to work together. In the past, the US Government did not believe that it was its business to promote American business abroad. At the same time, American business tended to regard the federal government as its enemy rather than its partner. Under the Bush Administration, things have started to change for the better. Let me give you an example. AT&T is competing against a Japanese company for a major telecommunications contract in Indonesia. Suspecting that the Japanese government was pressuring the Indonesian government to award the contract to the Japanese company, President Bush wrote to Prime Minister Kaifu to tell him that the contract should be awarded on the basis of merit and not pressure. At the same time, the same message was conveyed by President Bush, Secretary Baker and Secretary Mosbacher to Ambassador Ramly of Indonesia.

In the past, most US companies contended themselves with catering for the domestic market. Given the size of the domestic market, there was little incentive to export. Things have changed. American companies must now compete in the global market place in order to survive. However, apart from the large multinational companies, most medium and small enterprises have not adjusted to this change. Even some of the large companies, such as those in the auto industry, have not totally shed their attitude of complacency. As a result, it is not unfair for me to say that American luxury cars are not competitive in the world market. In the booming economies of Japan and the other countries in the Asia Pacific, the luxury car of choice is either a Mercedes Benz, a BMW or a Jaguar. Isn't it time for Detroit to wake up when the best selling car in the United States in 1989 was the Honda Accord?

Another cause for concern is the declining level of investment in non-military Research and Development (R & D). The United States used to lead the world in the percentage of its GNP which was invested in both military and civilian R & D. This is no longer true today. Japan and West Germany are out-investing the United States in civilian R & D. If this trend is not reversed, in the long run, it is bound to affect America's technological lead.

Six years ago, the National Commission on Excellence in Education issued a report entitled "A Nation At Risk". The report deplored the rising tide of mediocrity in the schools and called for tougher high school graduation requirements, more core academic courses, higher teachers' salaries and other corrective measures. Americans are becoming increasingly aware that the economic future of their country is very much dependent on raising the quality of education in its schools, colleges and universities. On 27 and 28 September 1989, President Bush summoned the 50 governors of the nation to an Education Summit at the University of Virginia. The meeting, the first of its kind, agreed to adopt national goals to guarantee an internationally competitive standard in a number of areas.

The poor quality of American high schools was reflected in a recent study issued by the International Association for the Evaluation of Educational Achievement. Thirteen countries took part in the evaluation. In biology, the most popular science course in the US, the US ranked last. Singapore scored first. In physics, Hong Kong was first and the US was ninth. In chemistry, Hong Kong was again first, the US was eleventh and Singapore was third. The proportion of college students who major in engineering is six times as high in Japan (4 per cent) as in the US (0.7 per cent). According to *Newsweek* Magazine (9 April 1990), the US-born engineering doctorate is almost a thing of the past. Foreign nationals now receive a quarter of the natural science Ph.D.s and more than half the engineering Ph.D.s awarded in this country.

What about the federal budget deficit?

Under the Gramm-Rudman-Hollings budget deficit reduction law, the projected deficit for FY 1990 (October 1980 to September 1990) had to meet the target of $100 billion. The Office of Management and Budget project a deficit of $116.2 billion for FY 1990. Using this projection, Congress and the Administration had to agree to reduce spending by $16.2 billion in order to meet the target. The OMB projection could, however, be misleading. The Congressional Budget Office, a non-partisan office created by Congress, projected the deficit for FY 1990 at $141.3 billion.

Senator Ernest Hollings, one of the authors of the budget deficit reduction law, has denounced the whole process as a fraud upon the public. He has charged that the real deficit for FY 1990 was not $116.2 billion, not even $141.3 billion, but closer to $300 billion. Hollings explained that in order to disguise the real extent of the deficit, the Administration and Congress have resorted to a number of fiscal gimmicks such as including the surpluses of social security as revenues, placing the cost of rescuing the savings and loan industry off the budget, moving the deficit of the US Postal Service off the budget and changing the Pentagon pay day from 1 October to 29 September in order to "save" $2.9 billion.

In November 1989, an agreement was reached between the Administration and Congress to reduce spending for FY 1990 by $17.8 billion. The President was able to tell the nation that he had fulfilled his pledge of reducing the budget deficit without raising taxes. The Administration and Congress could pretend that they had met the Gramm-Rudman-Hollings target when they had not in fact done so. The sad truth is that neither the Executive nor the Legislative branches of the federal government has displayed the political will to tackle the federal budget deficit in a serious manner.

I leave America filled with admiration for its many virtues and good qualities. At the same time, I leave America worried about its future. I wonder if this fractious nation can forge the cohesion and summon the courage to put its house in order. I do not, however, believe that the United States is suffering from a case of a terminal illness. The federal budget deficit, serious as it is, is certainly not the symptom of such a disease. It can be wiped out by nothing more painful than a gasoline tax increase of 20 cents per gallon. America is, however, at a crossroads in its destiny. It could either bounce back or continue down the path of decline. There is no country or combination of countries which can replace the leadership role of the United States in the world. For this, if for no other reason, I must believe that America will regain its economic pre-eminence in the world.

Speech delivered to the Economic Club of Indianapolis, Indiana, 9 April 1990. Published in **Vital Speeches of the Day***, Vol. LVII, No. 17, 15 June 1990.*

ASIA AND THE UNITED STATES: PERCEPTIONS AND PRESCRIPTIONS

An Asian Agenda for President Clinton

A Memo to Bill Clinton

Congratulations on your election to what is probably the most powerful and important job in the world. As an Asian who has spent 20 years in your country, I naturally regard myself as a friend of America. I wish you success in your challenging task of making the US economy the pre-eminent economy in the world once more. You were right when you said that America cannot be strong abroad if it is weak at home. I hope you will not think it too presumptuous of me to share a few thoughts with you regarding the relations between the United States and East and Southeast Asia.

First, during the campaign, you never referred to the Association of Southeast Asian Nations (ASEAN) or its six member states – Brunei, Indonesia, Malaysia, the Philippines, Singapore and Thailand. ASEAN, which is celebrating its 25th anniversary this year, is probably the most successful regional organization in the Third World. It has helped to keep the peace in Southeast Asia. It played a critical role in reversing the Vietnamese *fait accompli* in Cambodia and in securing an internationally acceptable negotiated settlement of that conflict. It has conferred observer status on Vietnam and Laos and is actively helping them to move from central planning toward market economics. ASEAN is rich in natural resources and has a combined population of more than 300 million. The ASEAN economies are among the fastest growing economies in the world. President Fidel Ramos is determined to make the Philippines another Asian tiger. ASEAN is committed to free trade. It is the hospitable host of many US multinational companies and a growing market for US exports. I hope you will re-affirm the bipartisan policy of the last three administrations to support ASEAN and to work closely with ASEAN in both the political and economic arenas.

Second, it is time for the US and Vietnam to normalize their relations. Seventeen years have passed since the Vietnam war ended. Vietnam has withdrawn its troops from Cambodia and is co-operating with the UN Transitional Authority in Cambodia (UNTAC). The Vietnamese authorities have, in recent months, satisfied General John Vessey and President Bush that they are giving their full co-operation to the resolution of the difficult and emotional POW/MIA issue. The lifting of the US economic embargo against Vietnam will allow American business access to economic opportunities in Vietnam and permit the Vietnamese economy to grow at a faster pace.

Third, you have said that the US-Japan relationship is vitally important. You have described the US-Japan alliance as fundamentally strong. Referring to the trade tensions between the two countries, you have said that you aim to "gain greater access to Japan's market for American goods, while we work to improve the American economy by increasing investment and improving the education and training of our work force".

Asia's leaders are reassured by the importance you attach to the US-Japan security alliance. Any rupture of that relationship will force Japan to re-arm, which will be destabilizing to the region. On US-Japan trade relations, you have adopted a balanced approach. The US should increase its competitiveness whilst Japan must open up its market more rapidly to all imports and not just those from the US. The US should, however, avoid making Japan a scapegoat for its own failures or an excuse for protectionism.

Fourth, you have re-affirmed the US commitment to defend South Korea against any external aggression and to station US troops there for as long as there is a threat. This is good because US policy toward the Korean peninsula should be bipartisan in character. No one should be left in any doubt of the US resolve to retain a deterrent presence in South Korea for as long as its government desires it and the threat from North Korea continues.

Fifth, you have said that the US-China relationship is one of great importance and that you do not seek to isolate China. China is important to the US not just as a balancer to the former Soviet Union. Because of its size and capabilities, China is important to the peace and prosperity of the Asia Pacific region. Until the Tian'anmen Square incident of June 1989, the US had a bipartisan policy towards China. Since then, that bipartisanship has been replaced by increasing polarization between President Bush and his Democratic opponents in Congress. One of the challenges of your administration is to evolve a new consensus on China.

One of the troublesome issues is the most-favoured-nation (MFN) status for China. To non-trade experts, the term "most favoured nation" may imply some kind of privileged or preferential status. In fact, MFN is the normal basis on which trade is conducted among states and economies. For example, Singapore extends MFN status to all its trading partners. So do all the other contracting parties of GATT. Only in the US is the question of China's MFN status linked to extraneous matters and subjected to an annual review. The respected Chairman of the subcommittee on international trade of the Senate Finance Committee, Max Baucus, has proposed that granting of the MFN status to China should not be linked to non-trade considerations. I agree.

Another issue is China's record on democracy and human rights. Based on the recent experience of South Korea and Taiwan, I would argue that the best way to promote democracy in China is to support China's economic reform and its integration into the world economy. When the basic human needs of people have been satisfied, they will demand greater political openness. The best way to impede the cause of democracy in China is to subvert economic reform and impose barriers to its ability to trade. Any attempt to isolate China will only strengthen the hands of the hardliners and reduce the influence of the reformers. Such a policy will also hurt the economic interests of Hong Kong and Taiwan.

An isolated China will be an angry China and an angry China is not good for China's neighbours. The US should also remember that, unlike small developing countries, China has the capacity to retaliate. It can buy its wheat from Argentina, Australia and Canada. It can buy from Airbus instead of from Boeing or McDonnell Douglas. It can buy its plants and equipment from Japan and Germany. It can refuse to co-operate with the US in the UN Security Council and in arms control.

Sixth, the end of the Cold War has presented new opportunities as well as uncertainties. The Asia Pacific is a region of booming economies. It is a region at peace with itself. It is a region that welcomes the continued engagement of the US. There is an opportunity for your administration to contribute new ideas to design the architecture of co-operative arrangements to promote security and co-operation in the region. In the field of regional economic co-operation, the Asia Pacific Economic Cooperation (APEC) forum has the potential to make the dream of a Pacific community a reality.

Do you share our vision? Will you be our partner in the making of the Pacific century?

*Article contributed to the **Asian Wall Street Journal**, 5 November 1992.*

ASIA AND THE UNITED STATES: PERCEPTIONS AND PRESCRIPTIONS

Without a Chaperon, Asia Will Dance in the Dark

The uncertainties that mark Asia's security scene have brought senior officials from throughout the Pacific to Singapore today for the two-day Association of Southeast Asian Nation's Post-Ministerial Conference. After more than a year of hemming and hawing – Japan first proposed the idea for the gathering in July 1991 – the region looks set to make the first significant attempt to hammer out a framework for an Asian multilateral security forum.

The timing couldn't be more propitious. Gone from the region are the perverse assurances of superpower rivalry. Today, Asia confronts the possibility of a nuclear Korean peninsula, enduring tensions on the Indian subcontinent and contending claims to the Kuril, Paracel, Senkaku and Spratly Islands. The region's continental giant, China, is growing in military and economic strength. Southeast Asia has been buying and producing arms at an astonishing pace. And Japan, for the first time since the Second World War, is testing the international waters: It has dispatched 600 peacekeeping troops to monitor the 23–28 May Cambodian elections and will send 53 to Mozambique to monitor elections next month. Against this backdrop, add the spectre of an American withdrawal from the region and the result looks quite disconcerting.

Major Players

For the most part, the meeting brings together the right participants to address Asia's security challenges. Gathered are all the region's major players (except Russia and China, which should be invited to future gatherings): the six ASEAN members – Brunei, Indonesia, Malaysia, the Philippines, Singapore and Thailand – and their "dialogue" partners: Australia, Canada, the European Community, Japan, New Zealand, South Korea and America.

Indeed, the Singapore meeting's greatest success may be its convocation; never before have such senior officials from these nations come together to take up the issues of Asian security.

Although the region's hot topics – from Korea to Cambodia – will be discussed, the meeting should concentrate on accomplishing two connected goals. First, the participants should explicitly recognize the continuing importance of established bilateral security ties. The end of the Cold War does not mean Asia has to throw the proverbial baby – in this case the networks of bilateral links that helped defeat the Soviet threat – out with the bathwater. And the most important bilateral links concern the second goal. Asia must sustain and re-affirm its close working relations with Washington.

While the region's multilateral impulse has been growing for some time, the Singapore meeting is not intended as a step toward the establishment of a Conference on Security and Cooperation in Europe (CSCE)-type organization for Asia. Conditions across the Pacific are different from those across the Atlantic. Where European security organizations like CSCE are legalistic and formal, the Singapore meeting will be characterized by its informality. The region's preference for institution-building is based solely on pragmatic considerations; these leaders are gathering to discuss security concerns at an informal forum.

The most important talk at this forum concerns America's future role in the region. Most countries in the Asia Pacific region regard the United States as a benign superpower. The US fought three wars in East Asia over the last 50 years, and Asians know that America did not fight those wars in pursuit of territory or natural resources or to impose its hegemony upon other countries. In Asia, the US is viewed as the most idealistic of the great powers.

Accordingly, Asians want the US to retain a credible military presence in the region. Like a trustworthy chaperone to a dance, Washington offers an elbow on which the region comfortably feels it can rely. This is because Asians have long memories. We remember Japanese colonialism before and during the Second World War. We also remember imperial China and fear its possible revival. Only a US presence can balance the anxieties from the past with the security realities of today.

Asians accept the need for America to reduce the size of its forces in the region, commensurate with its perception of changing threats. We also understand the shift in Washington's military doctrine to emphasize air and sea power and rapid deployment. But the bottom line remains the same: the US military presence in the region constitutes the only credible deterrence against aggression. In no small way, America's presence in the region keeps Asians from provoking fights with Asians.

But addressing the fear that Washington might withdraw from the region is not only the greatest challenge facing Asian participants at the Singapore meeting. It is also the main challenge confronting the chief US delegate, Assistant Secretary of State Winston Lord.

Clearly, US self-interest is not well served by the perception that Washington may diminish its ties to the region. America's economic future is more closely linked to the economies of Asia than it is to Europe. In 1992, two-way merchandise trade between the US and Asia grew by 9.1 per cent, reaching US$345 billion, compared to about US$227 billion with Europe.

America should use the Singapore meeting to re-assert the importance of its various bilateral treaty alliances with Japan, South Korea, Australia, Thailand and the Philippines. These treaties constitute the web of bilateral relationships that have contributed to the peace and security of the region; there is no reason to do away with them or amend them.

Washington should also use the meeting in Singapore to seek enhanced access to the military facilities of friendly countries in the region. The existing arrangement between the US and Singapore – which allows America enhanced access to Singapore's military facilities – is a model that can be replicated elsewhere in the region. This is one of the ways in which countries in the region can demonstrate by deed, their support for a continued US military presence in Asia. The Singapore-US military arrangement is a 21st century example of burden-sharing.

Burden-Sharing

Indeed, burden-sharing should be the clearest message delivered when the Singapore meeting closes its doors. America must know that it no longer has to carry Asia's security burden alone; that Asians need Washington to remain active in the region and are willing to work, bilaterally, to see that it can stay under mutually agreeable terms. Short of such agreements, there is simply no way to assure any one that the region's power games will not turn into war games.

Article contributed to the **Asian Wall Street Journal**, *20 May 1993.*

AVOIDING A CLASH OF CULTURES: ASIA'S ROLE IN THE NEW WORLD ORDER

Does East Asia Stand for Any Positive Values?

In an interesting article, "Greater China Should Think Again about Being So Different" (*International Herald Tribune*, 23 November1993), George Hicks complained that most of the values proposed by Asian critics of the West were negative. He concluded by posing a challenge: Can the East offer an alternative vision of the values needed for a better world? Here are ten such values that East Asia represents.

1. East Asians do not believe in the extreme form of individualism practised in the West. We agree that every individual is important. However, he or she is not an isolated being, but a member of a nuclear and extended family, clan, neighborhood, community, nation and state. East Asians believe that whatever they do or say, they must keep in mind the interests of others. Unlike Western society, where an individual puts his interests above all others, in Asian society the individual tries to balance his interests with those of family and society.
2. East Asians believe in strong families. Divorce rates are much lower than those in the West, and Asians do not, as a rule, abandon their aged parents. They believe that the family is the building block of society.
3. East Asians revere education. Unlike the West, this is a value held not only by the elite but by all strata of society. Asian mothers would make any sacrifice to help their children excel in school. In Singapore, many parents take leave to help their children prepare for year-end examinations. As a result, Asian students consistently outperform their Western counterparts in mathematics and science. This will give Asia a competitive edge in the 21st century.
4. East Asians believe in the virtues of saving and frugality. It is no accident that Singapore's saving rate of 46 per cent of GNP is the highest in the world or that Taiwan has larger foreign exchange

reserves than any other country. East Asians believe, as individuals, families and governments, that they should lead frugal lives and live within their means. This is better than the Western addiction to consumption, paying "on time" and living under a mountain of debt.

5. East Asians consider hard work a virtue – the chief reason this region is outcompeting Europe.

6. East Asians practise national teamwork. Unions and employers view each other as partners, not class enemies. Together, government, business and employees work co-operatively for the good of the nation. This philosophy, combined with the ability to forge national consensus, is one of the secrets of the so-called East Asian development miracle.

7. There is an Asian version of a social contract between the people and the state. The government will maintain law and order, provide citizens with their basic needs for jobs, housing, education and health care. Governments also have an obligation to treat their people with fairness and humanity. In return, citizens are expected to be law-abiding, respect those in authority, work hard, save and motivate their children to learn and be self-reliant. Most Asian governments do not pay unemployment benefits, partly because there is little unemployment and partly to avoid the Western disease of welfarism. Asian governments do not make welfare payments to unmarried women with dependent children because teenage pregnancy and illegitimate birth are, fortunately, rare in Asia.

8. In some Asian countries, governments have sought to make every citizen a stakeholder in the country. More than 90 per cent of Singaporeans own their own homes. Singapore also has the world's highest percentage of citizens who own shares (50.3 per cent, compared to 16.2 per cent in Britain and 11.7 per cent in the United States). Each year, employees in the private and public sectors receive a performance-based bonus. This year, for example, every public-sector employee in Singapore will receive three and a half months' salary as bonus. Some employees in the private sector will receive even more. In these ways, we try to build communitarian societies.

9. East Asians want their governments to maintain a morally wholesome environment in which to bring up their children. A recent survey found that most Singaporeans do not want magazines such as *Playboy* to circulate in the country. Recently, the democratically elected government in Seoul refused to allow Michael Jackson to perform in South Korea. There is no reason why Asians must adopt the Western view that pornography, obscenity, lewd language and behaviour, and attacks on religion are protected by the right of free speech.

10. Good governments in East Asia want a free pass but, unlike the West, they do not believe that such freedom is an absolute right. We do not want our press to be mere mouthpieces of government. Yet, we believe that the press must act responsibly. For example, it has no right to instigate trouble between racial, religious or linguistic groups, or between countries. We also insist that the press should give those whom it has attacked the right to reply.

Taken together, these ten values form a framework that has enabled societies in East Asia to achieve economic prosperity, progress, harmonious relations between citizens, and law and order (Singapore and Tokyo are the two safest cities in the world).

For generations, Asians have learned from the West, and we continue to do so. I hope the time has come when the West should also be willing to learn from the East.

*Personal comment contributed to the **International Herald Tribune**, 11–12 December 1993.*

AVOIDING A CLASH OF CULTURES: ASIA'S ROLE IN THE NEW WORLD ORDER

The East and the West: Towards a Convergence of Values

For the past century, the values of the West have dominated the world. This assumption that West stood for the best and that the best must be Western is changing as East Asians are gaining respect for their traditional values.

This more positive self-image is largely the result of the spectacular rise of East Asia in the world economy. Led by Japan, and followed by Korea, Taiwan, Hong Kong, ASEAN, China and Vietnam, the economies of East Asia have the world's highest growth rates. Because of their increasing interdependence created through trade and investment, they have maintained their buoyancy despite the recession and comparatively sluggish growth in the OECD economies. Economic success has given East Asians the self-confidence to deal with the West as equals.

East Asians are also benefiting from the rising tide of social problems in the West – the breakdown of the family, rising crime rates and the decline of civil society. In East Asia, by contrast, the family remains strong; social welfare exists but does not erode the work ethic or the sense of personal responsibility, and cities are safe for law-abiding citizens. East Asians therefore believe that their point of view, whether on economics, moral values, social governance, or the concept of good government, is legitimate and worth sharing with others.

On the whole, East Asians prefer consensus over contention. Thus, they believe that the rights of the individual must be balanced by the rights of the family and society; that the family is the building block of society; that education is important; and that frugality is virtuous. They have faith in the work ethic, in national teamwork, and in communitarianism.

What are the consequences of the rise of East Asia? There are at least three possible scenarios – Samuel P. Hungtington's scenario of "civilizational conflict"; a world order based on universal values; and a community of nations based on partial convergence of universal values. The first two are least likely. The world does not appear to be heading toward conflict based on clashes of civilizations, but a complete convergence of values throughout the world would be an unrealistic expectation. Since there is, however, a growing core of universal values, the third scenario is the most logical. Outside this core, we must respect each other's point of view. Better still, we should learn from them.

The avoidance of future conflict requires mutual understanding. Success should not make the East smug and arrogant; it should continue to learn from the West. At the same time, the West should drop its stance of moral superiority, acknowledge that some of its moral, economic and social prescriptions have proven to be flawed, and admit that it can learn some valuable lessons from East Asia.

Article published in **Overcoming Indifference: Ten Key Challenges in Today's Changing World**, *Klaus Schwab (ed.) (New York and London: New York University Press, 1995).*

AVOIDING A CLASH OF CULTURES: ASIA'S ROLE IN THE NEW WORLD ORDER

What Holds Societies Together

I would like to examine the question, "What Holds Societies Together?", from the *yin* and *yang* perspectives. First, I would like to enumerate the six factors which hold societies together. Second, I would like briefly to discuss the four factors which could drive societies apart.

Holding Societies Together

Societies are held together by a shared memory of the past and shared aspirations for the future. Societies are also held together by a sense of common identity and a set of common values. In the case of East Asia, there are strong and positive values which hold societies together. Examples of such values are strong families, the work ethic, thrift, the importance of education and the strong emphasis on the need to maintain social harmony.

It is also very important to make every citizen a stakeholder in Singapore, we have tried to do this by giving every citizen a job, an affordable home, affordable health care, quality education and a share in the growing prosperity of the society through various schemes of profit-sharing, bonuses and asset enhancement.

In a plural society, it is very important that all citizens, irrespective of race, religion, language, sex, tribe or caste, should enjoy equal opportunity, in law and in fact.

Finally, it is important to preserve social harmony and public order. Citizens should be educated from young on both their rights and their correlative obligations to society. Children should be taught, by their families, their schools and by their elders, of the need to be virtuous and to be socially responsible.

Driving Societies Apart

There are at least four factors which could drive societies apart. First, societies fall apart when unscrupulous politicians or religious leaders exploit the explosive issues of tribe, race, religion and language. Second, societies need to strike a golden mean between too much and too little social equality. Too much social equality will dampen the drive of the achievers to create wealth. Too little social equality will threaten the social cohesion and harmony of a society.

Third, it is very important to avoid the evolution of an underclass. In most parts of Asia, there is no underclass because the poor have middle class values. They believe in strong families, the work ethic and the importance of education. They know that education is their children's passport to upward mobility.

Finally, we should avoid the danger of a breakdown of law and order and of the civil society. In many parts of the West, the law and order situation has come perilously close to a crisis. Law-abiding citizens no longer feel safe in their homes or to walk along the streets of their cities. The erosion of the belief in values and virtues, the absence of a sense of responsibility and shame, the strange phenomenon of victimhood, have all contributed towards the danger of the breakdown of civil society in some parts of the contemporary West.

Speech delivered to the World Economic Forum, Davos, 28 January 1995.

AVOIDING A CLASH OF CULTURES: ASIA'S ROLE IN THE NEW WORLD ORDER

Revisiting the "Asian Values" Debate

I want to share with you tonight some of my evolving thinking on the debate concerning our moral values. A discussion of our moral values is relevant to the theme of the Conference because the values which we have imbibed from our families, friends and society constitute part of our cultural heritage. I want also to use this opportunity to clarify my own thinking on the subject and to respond to some of my foreign critics.

First, is there such a thing as East Asian values? In a recent editorial, the highly respected British weekly, *The Economist*, described my attempt to identify ten core East Asian values (*International Herald Tribune*, 11–12 Dec 93) as vapid and empty of content. Philip Bowring, the former Editor of the *Far Eastern Economic Review*, concluded in a recent article in the *International Herald Tribune* that claims about Asian values do not stand up to scrutiny.

My response to *The Economist* and to Mr Bowring is that I have inherited from my antecedents a set of moral values which constitute my moral compass. These values include the importance of the family, the reverence for education, the virtues of saving, frugality and hard work, the concern for others and the importance of team work.

I am not saying that these values are uniquely Asian. I concede that some of these values are probably of a universal character. I also recognize that until the recent past, many of these values were the dominant values of Western societies. This is however no longer the case. This is why there is a growing movement in the West to return to their traditional values. I therefore do not understand why some Western critics have dismissed our Asian values as being "vapid".

Second, will our traditional values endure or will they be swept away by the tide of development, affluence and democratization? Some scholars contend that as a society progresses, as its citizens become better educated and more affluent, as women become liberated from their inferior status in society, the traditional values will inevitably lose their sway. They argue that as Asia becomes more developed and affluent, Asian societies will suffer the same loss of moral values as the West.

I do not agree that this is an inevitable trend. Let us take Japan as an example. Japan is as developed and as affluent as the West. Yet, Japan has managed to maintain many of the core East Asian values. The Japanese have not lost the Asian virtues of saving, frugality and hard work. They continue to revere education. The Japanese family has not suffered the same erosion as in the West. To use only one indicator, whereas only 2 per cent of children are born out of wedlock in Japan, the percentage in the UK and the US is about 33 per cent. The model of Japan therefore gives me hope that it may be possible for the rest of East Asia to become as developed, modern and affluent as Japan, and yet succeed in retaining many of our traditional moral values.

Third, some of our Western friends seem to feel both offended and threatened by East Asians talking about their Asian values. Let me give you an example. One of my good friends, who is a professor at very good university in California, recently sent me a paper he had written for a conference. He is an expert on East Asia and has spent much of his life trying to promote understanding between the United States and East Asia. I was therefore very surprised to read in his paper that he regarded the movement for "Asian values" as "an Asian cultural declaration of independence from the alleged dominion of American political morality". He also wrote that, "The case for Asian values … is inextricably linked to a critique of United States' policies at home and abroad".

I wish to use this occasion to reassure my good friend in California and all my other friends in the West that when East Asians express pride in their cultural heritage, they are not explicitly or implicitly saying that Asian values are good and Western values are bad. I readily admit that there are good Asian values and bad Asian values just as there are good Western values and bad Western values.

At the risk of offending many of my Asian friends, let me cite a few examples of bad Asian values. I regard the caste system in Hindu culture; the subjugation of women; the practice of nepotism; the attitude of subservience to those in authority; the tradition of authoritarian rulers; and the shame which parents feel towards their children with physical or mental disabilities as bad.

I would also like to point out that many of the characteristics of modern Singapore which make us successful are derived from the West. I refer, for example, to our independent judiciary; our transparent legal process; our excellent civil service based upon merit and free of corruption; science and technology; a management culture based upon merit, team work and the delegation of power; the uplifting of the status of women; the belief in affording all citizens equal opportunity; and a political system which makes the government accountable to the people through regular elections.

Fourth, where should Singapore position itself in the debate between East and West? I believe that Singapore should avoid becoming a strident spokesman for the East. Singapore is a happy blend of the East and the West. We are the most occidental of the oriental societies. We are in the fortunate position of being able to pick the best from the East and from the West, and to weave them into a beautiful tapestry. Our natural role is therefore to seek common ground between East and West, to interpret one side to the other and to avoid a civilizational clash between East Asia and the West.

Speech delivered at "Our Place in Time – A Conference on Heritage in Singapore", Guinness Theatre, The Substation, Singapore, 16 September 1994.

AVOIDING A CLASH OF CULTURES: ASIA'S ROLE IN THE NEW WORLD ORDER

Tolerance, Asian Style

The end of the Cold War was supposed to lead to a new era of peace in the world. Instead, the world has witnessed a new round of fighting and blood-letting, especially in Europe and in Africa. The main characteristic of these post-Cold War conflicts is that they are intra-state in nature. Some of these conflicts, for example, between the Hutus and the Tutsis in Rwanda, are tribal in character. Others, such as that between the Serbs and the Muslims in Bosnia-Herzegovina, are religious in character. Still other conflicts, for example those between the Armenians and the Azeris and the civil war in Sudan, combine a potent mix of race and religion. In western Europe, we have also seen the rise of growing intolerance; in Germany towards its large Turkish minority, and in France, towards the Arab minority.

From this brief survey, one can conclude that one of the challenges facing leaders around the world is the management of diversity. How should societies which are racially, ethnically, religiously or linguistically diverse govern themselves so that harmony will be maintained and conflict avoided?

Region of Great Diversity

I believe that Europe and Africa can learn some valuable lessons from the experiences of Southeast Asia, a region of great diversity. The small city state of Singapore, with a population of only three million people, has three major races, speaks four languages, and worships four different religions. Indonesia, with a population of about 190 million, is made up of 17,000 islands, many different ethnic groups and languages, religions and regional loyalties. Each of these plural societies, whether small or big, had to find its own devices to manage its diversity and maintain harmony.

The Indonesian government regards questions of ethnicity, religion, race and class as sensitive issues. The approach is to downplay these divisive issues. Indonesia chooses to emphasize instead the shared experiences which bind Indonesians together while celebrating the diversity which gives contemporary Indonesian culture a distinctive character. The national motto is "Unity In Diversity". In addition, the Indonesian Armed Forces or Abri regard themselves as guardians of the nation-state. Abri is very conscious of the need to maintain political stability and social cohesion. It has taken a firm stand against religious extremists and communist revolutionaries.

The choice of the national language is a good example of the Indonesian genius for conciliation at work. Although Indonesia's population is made up of many ethnic groups, the dominant Javanese comprise more than 50 per cent of the total population, 100 out of 190 million. It would have been natural to choose Javanese as the national language of Indonesia but this would have reinforced the fear of Javanese domination by minority ethnic groups. In order to avoid this, the founding leaders of Indonesia chose Bahasa Indonesia, a language native to only 4 per cent of the population, as the national language. The choice of Bahasa is egalitarian and politically sensitive. It is a language which is easy to learn and is widely used for interethnic communication.

Indonesia is also fortunate because contemporary Indonesian politics have been heavily influenced by Javanese cultural values which emphasize the avoidance of conflict and stress the virtues of consultation, *musyawarah*, and consensus, *mufakat*. The political culture of seeking consensus and avoiding conflict is one of the assets which has enabled Indonesia to cope successfully with its challenges of diversity. The other secret is a tolerant majority – the Javanese – which has refrained from imposing its language and culture on the minorities.

Singapore is tiny compared to Indonesia but it too is extremely diverse. Its population of three million is made up of Chinese, Malays, Indians, Ceylonese, Eurasians, Arabs, Jews and so on. Singaporeans speak English, Chinese, Malay, Tamil and several other languages and dialects. Buddhism, Islam, Christianity and Hinduism have significant number of followers.

What are some of the special features of the Singapore experiment in managing its diversity? First, although the Chinese constitute 75 per cent of the population, the group has refrained from imposing its language,

Mandarin, as the island's national language. Instead, Singapore has four official languages – English, Chinese, Malay and Tamil. English is the language of administration and is in very common use. Every child has to learn two languages in school, English and his or her mother tongue, so it is more widely spoken today than it was during the time when Singapore was a British colony.

Laws to Maintain Harmony

Second, although Buddhism is the religion of the majority, it is not the religion of the state. Singapore is a secular state. In order to maintain religious harmony, it has recently enacted the Maintenance of Religious Harmony Act. This law empowers the minister to take action, *inter alia*, against any religious leader who causes enmity, hatred, ill-will or hostility between different religious groups. The minister may prohibit such a leader from addressing his followers, publishing his views or holding office on an editorial board or committee for a period of two years. The minister's order shall cease to have effect unless it is confirmed by the President within 30 days. A Presidential Council for Religious Harmony has been established to advise the President on cases. It consists of nine persons and is chaired by a former Chief Justice. Of the nine, six are appointed to represent Sikhism, Protestantism, Hinduism, Buddhism, Islam and Catholicism.

Third, race relations are extremely important in Singapore. On at least two occasions in the recent past, racial rioting took place which resulted in death, injury and the destruction of property. The republic's Constitution created a Presidential Council for Minority Rights. The Council is chaired by the Chief Justice. It has four permanent members and 12 non-permanent members. Of the 16 members, three are Malays, three are Indians and two are Eurasians. The purpose of the Presidential Council is to advise Parliament and the government on bills passed by Parliament which are discriminatory on the grounds of race or religion.

Another interesting experiment is to ensure the representation of racial minorities in the Singapore Parliament. Of the 81 elected Members of Parliament, 21 are elected in single person constituencies and 60 are elected in 15 group representation constituencies (GRC). In such constituencies, candidates must stand for election as a group of four. Of these four, at least one must be from a racial minority. In this way, no matter which party wins the election, the racial minorities are assured of a certain minimum representation in Parliament. At present, of the 81 elected members, 62 are Chinese, 10 are Malays and 7 are Indians.

Another important point is that the government must be prepared to act firmly against anyone who tries to incite racial or religious hatred or intolerance. The Singapore Government has thus acted against communalists under the Internal Security Act. This sensitivity and respect for racial and religious differences also extends to the media, which is not available to communalists to preach their hatreds. The media instead actively encourages tolerance and discourages racial chauvinism.

Lastly, the Singapore government tries to ensure that no community is educationally or economically backward through various programmes of affirmative action and through community self-help groups such as the Singapore Indian Development Association (SINDA), the Council for the Development of the Singapore Muslim Community (MENDAKI) and the Chinese Development Assistance Council (CDAC). The government assists such self-help programmes through matching grants and ministerial encouragement. The governing principle is to encourage self-reliance and minimal subsidies.

There are at least four lessons to be learned from the relatively successful experiences of Indonesia and Singapore in managing their highly diverse societies. First, in both Indonesia and Singapore, we have a tolerant majority community which has refrained from imposing its language as the national one and its religion as the state religion. A tolerant majority is therefore a necessary requirement for the successful management of diversity.

Second, in diverse societies, the political culture should promote consultation and consensus and try hard to avoid confrontation. In addition, the government should be firmly and actively supportive of multiethnic tolerance, and equally active in stamping out racism and religious intolerance. Community leaders should equally provide leadership and guidance in favour of tolerance and harmony.

Third, legal devices can be found to ensure representation of minorities in Parliament, to prevent the passage of laws which discriminate against persons on the ground of race or religion and to prevent religious leaders from causing hatred or hostility between their different groups of followers.

Fourth, we learn that in the interest of racial and religious harmony, it may sometimes be necessary to curtail the individual's right to free speech.

As one example, Singapore did not hesitate to ban British writer Salman Rushdie's book, *The Satanic Verses*, published in 1988, because of the very strong objections expressed on it by the Muslim community, or the film, *The Last Temptation of Christ*, because of strong objections by the Christian community.

Article published in **World Link**, *the magazine of the World Economic Forum, January/February 1995.*

AVOIDING A CLASH OF CULTURES: ASIA'S ROLE IN THE NEW WORLD ORDER

This Way or That, Get on with Good Government

There is a real danger that with the end of the Cold War, a new ideological battle may occur between the West and Asia over democracy and human rights. The West asserts that economic development and democracy are inseparable. An opposed thesis, heard often in Asia, maintains that a benign but authoritarian government is superior to a democratic government in achieving economic progress.

The Western assertion is grounded on the experience of industrial nations where democracy and capitalism flourished at the same time and were mutually reinforcing. The failure of Communist dictatorships in Eastern Europe to deliver the economic goods suggests that the failure is systemic. One of the prerequisites of economic growth is political stability, and this is more likely to occur with a government elected by the people.

In the Western view, a dictatorship is more likely to grant monopolies and other forms of economic inefficiency. It is also more likely to be corrupt, and corruption retards development. Only a democratically elected government, it is argued, can motivate people to support the development imperative by working hard, saving, accepting social discipline and being willing to accept short-term sacrifices in the interest of longer-term gain.

Some Asian leaders, however, have argued that democracy does not necessarily lead to economic progress. On the contrary, democracy often retards growth. An authoritarian but benign government could be a better vehicle to achieve development.

Advocates of this view can point to the fact that South Korea's most rapid economic growth took place under two non-elected regimes, while Taiwan's occurred under unelected President Chiang Ching-kuo. Hong Kong has developed under the benign but authoritarian rule of British colonialism. Eastern Europe failed to deliver the goods not because it was totalitarian, but because it followed the wrong economic model, that of central planning.

Democracy, a number of Asian leaders assert, often leads to contention and political instability. And it is very difficult in a democracy to persuade the electorate to accept wise policies that may be painful in the short term. There is often no industrial peace because management and unions are locked in a class conflict. As the current political crisis in Italy shows, corruption is a disease of democratic as well as authoritarian systems. Western democracy is a fragile flower that cannot be easily transplanted to the soil of some Asian countries, such as China, which have no democratic tradition.

I agree with neither the Western nor the opposed thesis. There are democratic governments that have succeeded in promoting economic development and others that have failed. There are authoritarian regimes that have succeeded and those that have failed. It is not possible, on the basis of the empirical evidence, to assert a causal link between democracy and economic development, or between authoritarianism and economic development.

Instead, what the world needs is not one system or the other, but good government. Agreement on the need to promote it could act as a bridge between Asia and the West. Such a regime could be democratic or authoritarian, presidential or parliamentary, a constitutional monarchy or a republic.

There are indicators of good government: wise and honest political leaders; a competent and clean bureaucracy; economic policies that promote growth and reward enterprise and achievement; social policies in such fields as housing, education and health care that make every citizen feel a stakeholder; national teamwork and partnership between government, business and labour; acceptance of the rule of law and an independent judiciary.

A good government accepts the obligation to face the electorate, at fixed intervals, in a free election to win the people's mandate. It fosters the growth of a civil society, pursues a policy of good neighbourliness toward other countries, and abides by the rules of international law and the norms of international behavior. It strikes an equitable balance between economic development and protection of the environment, and between order and liberty.

Of these indicators, the most important is the quality of political leaders. For example, Anand Panyarachun served on two occasions in recent years as Prime Minister of Thailand. He was not elected to office, yet most Thais and most Asians would agree that his caretaker administrations had many of the characteristics of good government.

It is possible, on the basis of evidence, to assert that economic development will lead to demands by the people for more political openness, greater participation and accountability. Those in the West who wish to promote democracy in Asia should promote, not subvert, economic development in the non-democratic countries of Asia.

Comment contributed to the **International Herald Tribune**, *6 May 1993.*

AVOIDING A CLASH OF CULTURES: ASIA'S ROLE IN THE NEW WORLD ORDER

Asians Too, Want Good Environment

There is a link between development, on the one hand, and environment, population and poverty on the other. Some Asian states, such as Indonesia, have shown remarkable progress in economic development and the reduction of population growth. Others, such as Malaysia, have made impressive strides in reducing poverty. Yet, major environmental challenges remain.

As China and India industrialize and grow, they will exert tremendous pressure on the earth's carrying capacity unless they avoid the path of progress at any cost, and follow a course of sustainable development.

In the past, due to institutional and policy weakness, the needed infrastructure in many Asian countries and cities, such as sewerage and industrial waste disposal systems, failed to keep pace with economic expansion. As a result, many Asian cities suffer from serious pollution.

Tokyo and Singapore are exceptions to the rule – models that other Asian cities can emulate. According to studies by the World Health Organization, five of the seven cities with the worst air pollution – Beijing, Calcutta, Jakarta, New Delhi and Shenyang – are in Asia. Two of the cities with the best air quality, Tokyo and Singapore, are also in Asia.

When Singapore began to industrialize in the 1960s, the government legislated and enforced high environmental standards to protect the land, air and water. Contrary to a belief then prevalent in the Third World, the increased costs to industry did not deter investment.

The government also built common treatment facilities to help industries, including facilities to process and dispose of toxic and hazardous wastes. As a result of these policies, three decades of rapid industrialization in Singapore have not despoiled the land, air or water.

Singapore has adopted a radical approach to protecting the quality of its air and preventing the city from strangulation by motor vehicles. The government has invested heavily in public transport. There is an underground Mass Rapid Transit service, an island-wide bus system and many taxis.

Growth of the motor vehicle population is controlled by setting a quota for each month, auctioning that quota by tender, and imposing a tax of about 200 per cent on the price of a vehicle plus a heavy road impost based on engine size. The government keeps the central business district free of congestion by making drivers of vehicles buy a licence to enter the area. It encourages the scrapping of old vehicles and provides a tax incentive to use lead-free petrol and to discourage the use of leaded petrol.

In another two years, Singapore will introduce an electronic road pricing system. Each vehicle will be fitted with an electronic tag. Drivers will be billed monthly based on their usage of the roads. If Singapore succeeds in its experiment, it will have set an example for the world, not just for Asia.

I am confident that in the years ahead, Asia will meet the environmental challenge, not because of external pressures, but because Asians are demanding the right to live in a clean and healthy environment, as well as the right to development.

Comment contributed to the ***International Herald Tribune***, *1 February 1994.*

AVOIDING A CLASH OF CULTURES: ASIA'S ROLE IN THE NEW WORLD ORDER

Asia and Europe: From Prejudice to Partnership?

There is a stark contrast between the economic landscape of western Europe and East Asia. In western Europe, the economies are either in recession or mired in slow growth, millions of people are out of work, and the future looks uncertain. In East Asia, the economies are booming, the people are busy saving, investing, learning, producing and trading; and they look to the future with optimism. The question is: Does the rise of the East Asian economies pose an economic threat to Europe?

There are two schools of thought in Europe. One school, comprising the leaders of France, Belgium, Italy, Spain and Portugal, views East Asia as an economic threat to Europe. Let me cite four examples. In February 1993, the President of France, Francois Mitterrand, said in a television interview that, "competition from Southeast Asia, which because of low prices and absence of social protection, sells everything and anything ... has caused a dramatic crisis in the western industrial world". The Prime Minister of France, Edouard Balladur, has criticized foreigners with different values in Asia and elsewhere for undermining the prosperity and social system of France through unfair trade. During his visit to the US in July 1993, the President of the French Senate, Rene Monory, stated that "Europe and the United States should take on the one formidable commercial adversary: Southeast Asia".

Similar sentiments were echoed by the current President of the European Council of Ministers, Willy Claes, the Deputy Prime Minister and Foreign Minister of Belgium. In his address to the European Parliament on 14 July 1993, President Claes said, "The EC should not become a victim of a naive and unilateral free trade liberalism" and that "the newly industrializing countries in Southeast Asia and elsewhere must be requested to respect minimal social and environmental norms".

The second school of thought, comprising Germany, UK, Netherlands and Denmark, views the rising economic competitiveness of East Asia as a challenge, but also as an opportunity. In presenting a special study on Asia to the German cabinet, the Foreign Minister, Klaus Kinkel, said on 22 September 1993:

> *The economic dynamism of Asia is breathtaking ... We must not make the mistake of seeing Asia as an economic threat. We must see Asia as a challenge and an opportunity for our economic policies and the ability of our companies to innovate.*

Speaking in Bonn, on 25 September 1993, the German Chancellor, Helmut Kohl, said Germany will expand its presence in Asia with an eye to boosting economic ties, mutual investment and co-operation in high technology industries. Writing in the weekly magazine, *Welt am Sonntag*, Chancellor Kohl wrote, "Asia could become the most important continent of the 21st century. An active German Asian policy aimed at enhancing relations with this region ... serves our basic political and economic interests. As an export-dependent nation, we must be involved in Asia's dynamic markets through trade and investments".

In several of the member states of the European Community, bashing Asia is an increasingly popular sport among politicians and labour leaders. Why is this so? Writing in the *International Herald Tribune* (14 September 1993), Robert Elegant attributed it to "a condescending, racist attitude toward East Asia that is common among Europeans. It is a compound of ignorance, prejudice, fear and envy ... Too many Europeans still look on Asians as strange little yellow and brown people who may be cunning, even competent, but are not to be taken seriously. In their minds, Europe remains the only true civilization, the hub around which all else revolves". There is another explanation. At a time of growing unemployment and economic recession, some European leaders find it convenient to look for a scapegoat instead of having the courage to tell their electorates the truth. Fortunately, they constitute a minority in Europe, albeit a vocal minority.

Some European leaders may be guilty of the sin of ignorance. They do not seem to be aware of the fact that for the last two years, East Asia has overtaken North America as the largest market for the EC's exports. They think of East Asia as "low-wage" economies, forgetting that Japanese wages are as high as those in the West. Even in Singapore, wages for professionals are sufficiently high to attract Westerners to work in Singapore on local, not expatriate, terms. Wages in Indonesia are substantially lower than in France but so is the output per worker. The differential wages and productivity among nations are the economic facts which make the international division of labour an economic reality. This reality is good for world trade, and free trade benefits all nations.

Some European leaders think that the success of East Asia is due to the fact that they have "different values". In a major study of the so-called "East Asian Miracle", the World Bank (September 1993) concluded that it is not a miracle after all. The East Asians have "achieved high growth by getting the basics right. Private domestic investment and rapidly growing human capital were the principal engines of growth. High levels of domestic financial savings sustained the ... high investment levels. Agriculture, while declining in relative importance, experienced rapid growth and productivity improvement. Population growth rates declined more rapidly ... than in other parts of the developing world". I hope my European friends will not regard the Asian's habit of saving and his thirst for education as evils which are incompatible with the European value system. Perhaps, Europe can learn something from the Asian ethos of high saving, not living beyond one's means, reverence for learning, working hard and striking the right balance between the rights of the individual and his obligations to society?

I am well aware of the danger of making straight line projections. There is certainly more than one plausible scenario regarding the future of East Asia. Everything could go wrong and the East Asian Miracle could become a mirage. The greater likelihood is, however, for the East Asian economies to continue on the path of high growth. They are likely to be joined by Vietnam and India. As the Asian economies expand, they will afford a myriad of opportunities for European business and industry. The Asian economies are not only expanding rapidly, but they are also deregulating and opening up to the world. Although intra-regional trade and investment are growing at an explosive rate, the Asians do not seek to emulate the Europeans in creating a regional economic bloc. They prefer to live in a world governed by free trade and a world which grows increasingly borderless. They are prepared to compete on a level playing field. They will abide by internationally accepted norms regarding labour rights and the protection of the environment. They hope that Europe will eschew the self-destructive path of protectionism in whatever guise, and refrain from the politics of envy. Asia would like Europe to be its economic partner and for that partnership to be grounded on mutual benefit and reciprocity. The question is: Can Europe discard its prejudices and accept Asia as an equal?

Dinner address to the Association of Dutch Businessmen, Hollandse Club, Singapore, 11 October 1993.

PERSONAL EXPERIENCES

My First Year at the UN

Singapore's independence in 1965 was not planned for. Therefore, when independence came, there was no foreign service in place. One had to be invented. Individuals were talent-spotted and persuaded to serve abroad. They came from the civil service, teaching service, university and the business community. The HQ staff was small and equally inexperienced. We, the pioneers, therefore went abroad without the benefit of an introductory or orientation course. We had to sink or swim.

Baptism by Fire

I arrived in New York in early August 1968. My first team consisted of Tan Siak Leng (who joined the Singapore Mission from the UN Secretariat and subsequently returned to it), Mahesh Sharma (a teacher who died prematurely) and Ng Chwee Tee. Later, See Chak Mun took Siak Leng's place and T. Thirunagaran took Mahesh's place.

Asian Group Chairman

HQ either did not know or had forgotten to tell me that Singapore was the Chairman of the Asian Group for the month of August. Imagine my surprise when, a few days after I arrived, I was told to chair a meeting of the Asian Group. The other Ambassadors must have wondered who that kid from Singapore was. A few tried to take advantage of my youth and innocence by trying to pull a fast one. I saw through their schemes and politely declined.

Czechoslovakia Invaded

During the same month, the Warsaw Pact countries invaded Czechoslovakia to crush Dubcek's government. His Ambassador called on me in my capacity as Chairman of the Asian Group. I tried to help him to no avail. I quickly learned about the awesome power of the veto. I was amazed at the way the then Ambassador of the USSR, Jacob Malik, could tell a pack of lies with utter conviction.

Afro-Asian Group Chairman

In the following month of September, I found to my horror that Singapore was the Chairman of the Afro-Asian Group. In those days, the Afro-Asian Group was still a political force in the world and several visiting African and Asian Heads of State or Government requested to speak to the Group. The third blow came when the Secretariat drew the name of a delegation to occupy the first seat in the General Assembly Hall. This is done annually in order to avoid a situation in which countries whose names begin with the alphabet "A" would always sit in the first row and countries whose names start with "Z" would always sit in the last row.

The Luck of the Draw

Unfortunately for me, the country chosen to occupy the first seat was Saudi Arabia. Singapore's seat was in the first row, right in front of the rostrum. For three months I felt like a prisoner. I had to pretend to be interested even if the speakers were deadly boring. I also had to reply to the toasts by the hosts at many lunches and dinners. The reason was that the hosts would often follow the seating arrangement in the General Assembly. I was so nervous at first that I could hardly eat my meals. After a while, I learnt not to show my nervousness. If I found that I was occupying the seat of honour, I would mentally compose my response to the toast. I always followed a three-point agenda: first, start with a humorous story; second, praise the host country; and third, praise the host and hostess. I also observed the different customs regarding the time for toasting. At a Japanese party, the toast and response are made before the meal. At a Scandinavian party, the host proposes a toast before the meal but the guest of honour has to wait until after the meal to reply. At all other functions, excepting the Chinese, the toast and response are made after the dessert and before coffee. At Chinese functions, *mao tai* flows freely and there are many "*ganbeis*" throughout the meal. *Mao tai* is lethal stuff and I quickly learned to sip it rather than to empy the cup with each toast.

Rahim Ishak

The Singapore delegation to the UN General Assembly in 1968 was led by Rahim Ishak and included David Marshall, Aziz Mahmood and the long-time MP of Hougang, Ng Kah Ting. Rahim Ishak was then the Minister of State for Foreign Affairs. He was very successful at the UN. He was good looking, intelligent, knowledgeable, spoke well and had a charming manner. The first night Rahim arrived in New York, the delegation took him to a restaurant in Chinatown for dinner. Rahim brought along a bottle of pickled chillies which was supposed to last him for the entire duration of his stay. He generously offered to share his hot chillies with us. It was a mistake, because we finished the entire bottle at that dinner!

David Marshall

David Marshall was also a member of the delegation. I had worked for him, as his pupil, following my graduation from the Law Faculty, from 1961 to 1962. David must have been amused by the fact that six years later, he was working under me. I assigned him to the Third Committee which covered social, cultural and humanitarian affairs. In those days, most of the delegates to the Third Committee were women. The women delegates found him charming. So did the famous Ambassador of Saudi Arabia, Jamil Baroody. Ambassador Baroody was actually a Syrian Christian. He was close to the Saudi royal family. He had served at the UN since the beginning and was a walking encyclopaedia about the UN.

One day, Baroody submitted a draft resolution to the Third Committee. It was not well crafted. Marshall offered his help and redrafted the text for Baroody. Baroody was delighted. In introducing the revised text of his draft resolution, Baroody acknowledged the help he had received from his "young brother" from Singapore. I never found out whether it would have made any difference if Baroody had known that David Marshall is a Jew. I think it would not because Baroody was an anti-Zionist, but not an anti-Semite.

David Marshall had rented a small apartment. He was, however, hopelessly undomesticated. He rang me one morning and asked whether I knew how to percolate coffee. I said yes, drove over to his apartment and showed him how to do it. On another occasion, we had to attend a black-tie function. When I arrived to fetch him, I found that he had not dressed. The reason was that his tuxedo was crumpled. He did not know how to iron it. I ironed it for him.

Aziz and Kah Ting

In 1968, my rent ceiling was US$600. It took me three months before I located a small three-bedroom apartment on 76th Street between Lexington Avenue and 3rd Avenue. See Chak Mun's rent ceiling was even lower. He had to rent a basement apartment. My wife was then in her final year at Medical School. She did not join me until February 1969. I therefore invited Aziz Mahmood and Ng Kah Ting to stay with me. We had a lot of fun together.

Kah Ting and I did the cooking. Aziz could not cook, so we asked him to do the dishes. Kah Ting was a very good cook. His fried "beehoon" was delicious. Aziz had one peculiar food habit. He liked his meat to be well done and would complain if it was not. One day, Kah Ting was frying an egg for Aziz. He deliberately fried it until the edges were burnt. When Aziz complained, Kah Ting innocently replied, "Oh, I thought you liked all your food well done".

U Thant and Narasimhan

U Thant was the Secretary-General. He had been a teacher in Burma before U Nu drafted him to serve at the UN. U Thant was a genuinely good man. He was honest, principled, kind and humble. He was a good Secretary-General. His powerful Chef-de-Cabinet was an outstanding Indian civil servant, C.V. Narasimhan. They were very kind to me and treated me like their nephew. Through them, I got to know the very distinguished Permanent Representatives of Burma, U Soe Tin, and of India, G.P. Parthasarathi. I used to regard them as my gurus and learned a lot from them about international politics, diplomacy and the UN. Another person who taught me a lot about the UN is the current Prime Minister of Thailand, Anand Panyarachun. Anand and I have been good friends for 24 years.

Conclusion

I look back on my first year at the UN with amazement and gratitude. In 1968, I was only 30 and did not have any diplomatic experience. I had learned international law but did not realize the limits of its efficacy in international relations. I had followed international politics as the Secretary of the Singapore Institute of International Affairs but did not know how often principle could be overwhelmed by the power of force. My idealism was tempered by reality. I had to make a quick transition from the placid world of academia to the turbulent world of international politics. I am grateful to all my friends, in Singapore and at the UN, for helping me to make that transition.

Article written for the Ministry of Foreign Affairs (MFA) Club special publication to commemorate its 5th Anniversary, September 1992.

PERSONAL EXPERIENCES

My Favourite UN Stories

Madam President, Mrs Anna Tham, ladies and gentlemen, before preparing my remarks for this evening, I sought my wife's advice. As usual, she gave me good advice. She said a speech to an audience at dinner should resemble a woman's bikini – it should be brief, but it should also cover all the vital points. I have decided to tell you some of my favourite UN stories.

As some of you will recall, the United Nations has had five Secretaries-General. The third Secretary-General was an Asian. He was U Thant of Burma. U Thant was a kind, gentle and meditative man. He had a serious demeanour which misled some people into thinking that he had no sense of humour. He was actually a witty person who appreciated good humour. The following was one of the stories he told me. One day, U Thant was invited to speak to an American audience. The end of his speech was greeted with warm applause. Before U Thant left, many members of the audience went up to shake his hand and to congratulate him. One elderly lady shook U Thant's hand very warmly and said, "Mr Secretary-General, that was a wonderful speech. You must have it published posthumously". U Thant was slightly taken aback by the latter remark and before he could recover from his surprise, the lady added, "And you must do it as soon as possible".

The fourth Secretary-General, Dr Kurt Waldheim of Austria, told me the following story. Once, a certain gentleman in an unnamed country, was elected its Prime Minister. Before he took office, his predecessor called on him and gave him three envelopes. The envelopes were marked 1, 2 and 3 and were sealed. His predecessor said to him, "I hope you will have a long and successful tenure as Prime Minister. I hope you will not be confronted with any crisis. But if you should be confronted with a crisis, you may find the advice contained in the first envelope helpful to you. If, after surviving your first crisis, you should confront a second and third crisis, you could consult the contents of the second and the third envelopes". Several months later, the Prime Minister was confronted by a major political crisis. Failing to think of a solution to the crisis, he suddenly remembered the three envelopes his predecessor had given him. He opened his safe and took out the first envelope. He broke the seal and opened the envelope. Inside the envelope was a piece of paper containing the following three words: Blame your predecessor. He followed the advice and blamed his predecessor for the crisis. Soon the storm blew over and he survived his first crisis. A year passed before he was faced by a second crisis. He took the second envelope from his safe and opened it. On the paper inside the envelope were written these words: Promise the people you will institute a major reform. He followed the advice and told the people that he would institute a major reform. The people were lulled by the promise and the crisis was ended. A few uneventful years rolled by before the Prime Minister was confronted by his third crisis. He tore open the third envelope, and took out the piece of paper inside with great anticipation. The paper read: Prepare three envelopes.

In the fall of 1980, His Holiness, John Paul II went to address the United Nations. After his visit, some wit at the UN concocted the following story. His Holiness called on Secretary-General Waldheim. The two men paid each other compliments and began discussing the difficulties of their respective jobs. The Secretary-General said to the Pope, "Mine has been described as the most impossible job in the world. The peoples of the world expect me to solve all the major problems of the world but the member states are not prepared to give me the power to do my job effectively. It is very frustrating". The Pope responded thus: "My responsibilities as head of the Catholic Church are also very difficult. Many young couples refuse to follow the teachings of the church on birth control. I have to contend with the radical clergy who support the communists as well as with those on the right who align themselves with the corrupt and oppressive oligarchies of the Third World. Some of the temporal rulers have no respect for the Church. Do you remember Stalin asking 'How many battalions does the Pope have?'" After some reflection, the Pope added: "I must, however, admit that I have two advantages over you. First, I am infallible. Second, I only have to be elected once".

One of my favourite UN stories is a story about Cyprus. As some of you may remember, Cyprus is an island-state situated in the Mediterranean Sea. Its population is made up of two ethnic communities: Greek Cypriots and Turkish Cypriots. As a result of clashes between the two ethnic groups, the United Nations Security Council sent a peacekeeping force to Cyprus to assist in the maintenance of peace on the island. The story is about a young soldier from Toronto, Canada, who had just completed an assignment with the UN peacekeeping force in Cyprus. Upon his return to Toronto, a group of his good friends took him out to their favourite restaurant for dinner. After several rounds of cocktails, one of his friends asked him, "What was the weather like in Cyprus?" The soldier replied, "Cyprus has a Mediterranean climate. Most of the time, the weather was lovely". Another friend asked, "What was the place like?" The soldier answered, "The place was very interesting. There are many archaeological finds on the island dating back thousands of years". Yet another friend asked, "Was the food good?" "Yes, the food was delicious", replied the soldier. Finally, someone asked, "What were the Cypriots like?" The soldier remained silent for a few seconds, scratched his head and said, "That is funny. During the time I was there, I met many Greeks. I met many Turks. But I never met any Cypriots". This is a very insightful story because the root cause of the problem in Cyprus is the weakness of Cypriot nationalism and the dominance of Greek and Turkish communalism in the political life of Cyprus.

During the height of the Polish crisis, another UN wit concocted the following story about Poland and President Brezhnev. It seemed that one day, President Brezhnev went to his barber in the Kremlin for a haircut. After Brezhnev had settled himself into the barber's chair, the barber asked him, "Comrade President, how is the situation in Poland today?" Brezhnev glared at his barber and said, "I am tired today. I don't want to discuss politics". After a while, the barber asked, "Comrade President, are you planning to invade Poland?" Brezhnev got very cross and said, "I have already told you that I am very tired today and I don't want to talk about Poland. Just cut my hair". After the haircut was over, Brezhnev got up, thanked the barber and as he was leaving the shop, he turned to the barber and asked, "By the way, why were you asking me so many questions about Poland today?" The barber replied, "Comrade President, the reason why I asked you so many questions about Poland is because every time I mentioned the word 'Poland', your hairs stood on their ends. It made it easier to cut your hair".

I will conclude by sharing with you a story I like to tell whenever I am asked how you can have faith in the UN when it has so many glaring shortcomings and defects. One day, three priests, two elderly priests called Peter and John and a very young priest called Thomas, went fishing in a lake. After a while, Peter ran out of bait. He got up, stepped confidently over the side of the boat and walked on the water towards the shore.

Peter collected some fresh bait and walked back to the boat and resumed fishing. A little while later, John ran out of bait. John got up, stepped confidently over the side of the boat and walked on the water towards the shore. He collected his bait and returned to the boat and resumed fishing. Thomas could hardly believe what he had just seen. Sometime later, Thomas ran out of bait. He closed his eyes and said a fervent prayer. He got up, stepped confidently over the side of the boat and sank to the bottom of the lake. Thomas, you see, could not swim. Peter and John fished him out and pulled him over the side of the boat. After drying him and allowing him to recover his breath, Peter and John put their arms around Thomas' shoulders. The two older priests said to their young colleague, "My son, it is all right to have faith but you must know where the rocks are". My attitude towards the UN is similar. Yes, I have faith in the UN but I think I also know where the rocks are.

Speech delivered at the annual dinner of the Methodist Girls' School (MGS) Alumni Association, Singapore, 23 July 1982.

PERSONAL EXPERIENCES

Reflections on a Diplomatic Career

Mr Minister, colleagues and friends, I would like to share with you some highlights of the 23 years I have spent with the Singapore Foreign Service, 13 of them at the UN, six in Washington and four in the Ministry of Foreign Affairs (MFA's) HQ in Singapore.

My diplomatic career began in 1968, three years after Singapore's unexpected independence. I was asked to be Singapore's first resident Ambassador to the UN in New York. I had no prior diplomatic experience. Because the MFA was new, I was given very little guidance before I was shipped off to New York. When I arrived in New York, I found to my surprise that it was Singapore's turn to chair the Asian Group. The month of August 1968 was also memorable because Czechoslovakia was invaded by the Soviet Union and the other members of the Warsaw Pact. That episode made me understand the limits of the efficacy of international law. It also taught me about the power of the veto in the UN Security Council. In the following month, September, I found to my horror that Singapore was the Chairman of the Afro-Asian Group. I had to chair several meetings of the Group. My first five months at the UN were very challenging. I felt like a non-swimmer thrown into the deep end of a pool. But, as they say, nothing concentrates the mind so well as the absence of an alternative! I learnt to swim very quickly.

I remember two funny incidents from that period of my life. Because I was only 30, I was about one generation younger than the average Ambassador at the UN. One evening, my wife and I were the guests of the Philippine Ambassador at dinner. A young lady mistook the two of us for the children of the Philippine Ambassador. She asked my wife whether I was the son of the Philippine Ambassador. My wife said, "No, he is the Ambassador of Singapore and he is married to me". On another occasion, a visitor to our home for dinner did not recognize me. When I opened the door and greeted him, he asked me whether my father was in. He was very embarrassed when I explained that my father was not in and did not live there and that I was his host! Now that I am an old man, I am no longer mistaken for the son of the Singapore Ambassador. Let me tell you another story. At the Earth Summit, in 1992, a myopic member of the Italian delegation asked me whether one of my colleagues, Foong Chee Leong, was my son! On another occasion, I was asked whether Burhan Gafoor was my son!

As I look back on my work with the UN over the last 26 years, five things stand out.

First, my presidency of the Third UN Conference on the Law of the Sea. It took eight years of very difficult negotiations to complete the treaty. The treaty is like a constitution for the world's oceans. I am pleased that the 1982 UN Convention on the Law of the Sea will come into force on 16 November this year. Second, my chairmanship of the Preparatory Committee for and the Main Committee at the Earth Summit. It was a miracle that the more than 170 countries of the world were able to put aside their differences and arrive at a consensus in Rio de Janeiro. Third, the battle with Vietnam and her backers at the 1979 UN General Assembly over Cambodia and the subsequent 13-year diplomatic campaign, from 1979 to 1991, to secure a diplomatic solution to the conflict in Cambodia. At the 1979 UN General Assembly, the odds seemed to favour Vietnam because the world was glad to be rid of the genocidal regime of Pol Pot and the Soviet camp was at the height of its power. Although the odds were against us, the ASEAN delegations succeeded in persuading the UN to censure Vietnam for its invasion and occupation of Cambodia. Simultaneously, ASEAN launched a campaign to stop the fighting and to negotiate an internationally acceptable solution to the conflict. We finally succeeded in Paris in 1991. Fourth, the struggle with Cuba and the pro-Soviet camp of the Non-Aligned Movement in Havana in 1979 to prevent the Soviet takeover of the Movement. Fifth, my appointment last year by Secretary-General Boutros Ghali as his Special Envoy to Russia, Estonia, Latvia and Lithuania.

In 1984, I was transferred from the UN in New York to the Embassy in Washington, D.C.. Although the physical distance between the two postings was not great, the agenda and the nature of the work were very different.

At the UN, my agenda was to strengthen the UN system so that the world would be made a safer place for small states; enhance Singapore's stature and reputation in the international community; protect Singapore's national security and economic interests; make friends for Singapore; and be useful to the international community.

In Washington, my agenda was different. It was to strengthen the bilateral relations between Singapore and the United States; to encourage the United States to remain actively and constructively engaged with East Asia; to work with the Economic Development Board (EDB) in promoting US investment in Singapore; to work with the Trade Development Board (TDB) in promoting trade between our two countries; to work with the Singapore Tourist Promotion Board (STPB) in promoting tourism; to facilitate the operations of Singapore business enterprises in the US; to look after our students and visitors; and to cultivate a broad constituency for Singapore.

In pursuit of these objectives, I travelled all over America to promote Singapore, to visit our students and to encourage the American people to view East Asia as a region of opportunity and of nations friendly to America. My wife and I helped to raise money for the National Symphony Orchestra; the Asia Society, the Multiple Sclerosis Society, the National Rehabilitation Hospital and other good causes.

The high point of my six years in Washington was to secure an invitation for the Senior Minister to address a joint session of the US Congress in October 1985. It was a formidable challenge to secure that invitation, but we succeeded. The Senior Minister made a brilliant address to the US Congress on the geo-strategic and geo-economic importance of free trade. I think it helped to convince Congress that protectionism would be a disastrous course for the US and for the world.

In 1990, I had the honour of leading the Singapore delegation to negotiate with China for the establishment of diplomatic relations between our two countries. The negotiations were successfully concluded and formal relations between Singapore and China were established on 3 October 1990.

Let me address an issue which a young Foreign Service Officer once asked me. Is it necessary for a good diplomat to smoke, drink and womanize? My answer is no. I do not smoke. I do like good wine and it would be useful for a diplomat to know his wine. I have never gone to bed with another woman in the national interest. Talking about sex and diplomacy reminds me of a story. A Singapore officer at our embassy in Moscow was seduced by a Soviet agent. She was, of course, a lovely blue-eyed blonde. When they blackmailed him, he gave in and handed over state secrets to her. I asked the former Foreign Minister of Malaysia, Tan Sri Ghazali Shafie, how he dealt with such problems. He said it was easy. He would see every Malaysian officer before he or she was posted to Moscow. He would warn them that the Russians might try to seduce them. He told them that they should try to resist temptation. However, if they succumbed they should not panic. If the Russians tried to blackmail them with incriminating photos they should simply reply, "Please give me two sets of the photos. My Foreign Minister would like to have one set of them!"

I shall conclude. If your aim in life is to make money, the Foreign Service is not for you. If, however, you are looking for a career of adventure and achievement, the Singapore Foreign Service is one option you should consider. If you have a good mind and a charming personality, an interest in international affairs and an aptitude for learning languages, and if you are a good communicator with excellent social skills, a love for foreign travel and an ability to live happily in foreign countries and among foreign peoples, the Foreign Service is certainly a good option for you. I look back on the 23 years I have spent in Singapore's Foreign Service with great satisfaction. Why do I do so? I do so because it has enabled me to serve my country and to build a better world. The Singapore Foreign Service offers you a career, an adventure and a way of life.

Career talk given for the Ministry of Foreign Affairs, Singapore, 25 June 1994.

THE QUEST FOR WORLD ORDER
PERSPECTIVES OF A PRAGMATIC IDEALIST

Ambassador Tommy Koh, the new Permanent Representative of Singapore to the United Nations, is seen here presenting his credentials to the Secretary-General, U Thant, at the UN Headquarters in New York. (1968)

Ambassador Anand Panyarachun, Mrs Anand, Mrs Koh Siew Aing (pregnant with first son Wei) and Ambassador Koh. (1969)

Ambassador Koh presenting his credentials to UN Secretary-General Kurt Waldheim. (1974)

The Singapore delegation at a session of the UN General Assembly. Seated in the front row are S. Rajaratnam (left), Minister for Foreign Affairs, and Ambassador Koh, Permanent Representative to the UN, while Michael Cheok, Lee Chiong Giam and Peter Chan (left to right) are seated behind. (1974)

Ambassador Koh signing the Final Act of the Third UN Conference on the Law of the Sea, Montego Bay, Jamaica, December 1982. Standing behind the Ambassador (from left to right) are Kumar Chitty, Legal Officer; the late Bernardo Zuleta, Secretary-General of the Conference; Roy Lee, Legal Officer; and Erik Suy, Legal Adviser to the UN.

Lighter moments at Montego Bay. From left to right, Mrs Edward Seaga, wife of the Prime Minister of Jamaica; Mrs Javier Perez de Cuellar, wife of the UN Secretary-General; the UN Secretary-General, Mr Javier Perez de Cuellar; Alvarode Soto, UN Assistant Secretary-General; Ambassador Koh; and Imre Hollai of Hungary, President of the UN General Assembly. (1982)

Ambassador Koh with Pierre Trudeau, Prime Minister of Canada (right), and Ramon del Rosario (centre), the Philippine Ambassador to Canada. (1983)

Ambassador Koh and Mrs Koh with President and Mrs Reagan. (1988)

At the White House with President George Bush, Secretary of State James Baker (left), and National Security Adviser, General Brent Scowcroft (right). (1989)

Ambassador Koh practising his diplomacy with a Kikuyu woman in Masai Mara, Kenya. (1990)

Ambassador Koh, Chairman of the United Nations Conference on Environment and Development's (UNCED's) Preparatory Committee, is seen here in Nairobi, Kenya, with Ambassador Bo Kjellen of Sweden (on his right), Chairman of one of the three committees of the Preparatory Committee, and Bukar Shaib of Nigeria (on his left), Chairman of another of the committees. (1990)

Ambassador Koh shaking hands with China's former Deputy Foreign Minister, Xu Dunxin, at the successful conclusion of negotiations in Beijing to establish formal diplomatic relations between Singapore and the People's Republic of China. (1990)

President Wee Kim Wee of Singapore conferrring the Distinguished Service Order (DSO) on Ambassador Koh. The photograph bears the President's signature. (1990)

The opening meeting of the United Nations Conference on Environment and Development (UNCED). Ambassador Koh is seen addressing the meeting in his capacity as Chairman of the Preparatory Committee of UNCED. In the centre is Maurice Strong, Secretary-General of UNCED, with the Deputy Secretary-General, Nitin Desai, on the extreme left. (1992)

Ambassador Koh with President Soeharto of Indonesia at a luncheon of world leaders held during the United Nations Conference on Environment and Development in Rio de Janeiro, Brazil. (1992)

Ambassador Koh chairing a meeting of the UNCED Preparatory Committee in New York. The photograph was taken just after Secretary-General Boutros Ghali had read one of the pages of his speech twice, thus repeating a compliment which he had paid to Ambassador Koh, whereupon Ambassador Koh stopped the Secretary-General midway to tell him that he did not have to honour him with the same compliment twice over. It was only at that juncture that the Secretary-General realized that he had unwittingly repeated the same page of his address. The meeting broke up in laughter. (1992)

The Singapore delegation at the Earth Summit, Rio de Janeiro. In the front row (left to right) are Chew Tai Soo, Ahmad Mattar, Tommy Koh, Lim Chuan Poh and K. Kesavapany. In the back (also left to right) are Foo Kim Boon, Richard Grosse, Viji Menon, Foong Chee Leong, Khoo Seow Poh and Burhan Gafoor. (1992)

Ambassador Koh, as Director of The Institute of Policy Studies, presenting Dato' Seri Anwar Ibrahim with a token of appreciation. Dato' Ibrahim was in Singapore to give a public lecture at the Raffles Hotel. (1992)

Ambassador Koh being conferred the Commander of the Order of the Golden Ark by Prince Bernhard of the Netherlands. (1993)

Ambassador Koh, the UN Secretary-General's Special Envoy to Russia, Estonia, Latvia and Lithuania, in Moscow with the Russian ambassadors who were negotiating with Estonia, Latvia and Lithuania. (1993)

Ambassador Koh, after having been conferred the Grand Cross of the Order of Bernardo O'Higgins by Chile. Pictured with him (left to right) are Mrs Koh, Ambassador Tudela, Mrs Tudela, Mdm See Tsai Ying (the Ambassador's mother), Jimmy Koh (the Ambassador's brother) and Mrs Geraldine Koh (the Ambassador's sister-in-law). (1997)

Ambassador Koh receives the Elizabeth Haub Prize for Environmental Law. With him are (left to right) the Representative of the Free University of Brussels, Minister Klaus Toepfer of Germany, Mrs Helga Haub and Wolfgang Dehane of the IUCN. (1997)

Ambassador Koh with UN Secretary-General Kofi Annan. (1997)

Ambassador Koh, Mrs Koh and their two sons, Wei (left) and Aun (right). (1992)

A BIOGRAPHICAL NOTE

Professor Tommy Thong-Bee Koh is currently Ambassador-at-Large at the Ministry of Foreign Affairs and Executive Director of the Asia-Europe Foundation.

Professor Koh was Singapore's Permanent Representative to the United Nations from 1968 to 1971 (concurrently accredited as High Commissioner to Canada) and again from 1974 to 1984 (concurrently accredited as High Commissioner to Canada and Ambassador to Mexico), and served as the Ambassador to the United States of America from 1984 to 1990. He was President of the Third UN Conference on the Law of the Sea from 1981 to 1982 and Chairman both of the Preparatory Committee for and the Main Committee of the UN Conference on Environment and Development (UNCED) from 1990 to 1992. Professor Koh had the further distinction of being appointed as the Special Envoy of the United Nations Secretary-General to the Russian Federation, Estonia, Latvia and Lithuania in August/September 1993.

Professor Koh was Chairman of the National Arts Council from 1991 to 1996 and Director of The Institute of Policy Studies, Singapore, from 1990 to February 1997. He was the Second Arthur & Frank Payne Visiting Professor at the Institute for International Studies, Stanford University, for 1994/95. He was also a member of the UN's High-Level Advisory Board on Sustainable Development from 1993 to 1995, and a member of the Earth Council from 1993 to 1996. Professor Koh is on the Board of Directors of the Institute for the Study of Diplomacy at Georgetown University. He is also a member of the Toyota International Advisory Board.

Professor Koh received a First Class Honours degree in Law from the University of Singapore. He has a Masters degree in Law from Harvard University and a postgraduate Diploma in Criminology from Cambridge University. He was Dean of the Faculty of Law, University of Singapore (now known as the National University of Singapore), from 1971 to 1974, and was conferred a full professorship in 1977. In 1984, Professor Koh was awarded an Honorary Degree of Doctor of Laws from Yale University. He has also received awards from Columbia University, Stanford University, Georgetown University and the Fletcher School of Law and Diplomacy.

For his service to the nation, Professor Koh was awarded the Public Service Star in 1971, the Meritorious Service Medal in 1979 and the Distinguished Service Order Award in 1990. He was appointed Commander of the Order of the Golden Ark by HRH Prince Bernhard of the Netherlands in March 1993. He was also presented with the Arts and Culture Award by the Japanese Chamber of Commerce & Industry (JCCI) Singapore Foundation in March 1993. Professor Koh received the award of the Grand Cross of the Order of Bernardo O'Higgins from the Government of Chile on 3 April 1997. He was awarded the 1996 Elizabeth Haub Prize for environmental law and policy by the Free University of Brussels and the International Council on Environmental Law on 17 April 1997.

Professor Koh is married with two sons.

INDEX

A
Abdul Rahman, Tengku, 239
Afghanistan
　conflict, 3, 276
　Geneva Accords, 46, 50
　Soviet invasion, 2, 3
Alatas, Ali, 219
Alders, J.G.M., 163
Algeria, xix, 5
Amerasinghe, Hamilton, xxv, 127
America, Central, 13
America, Latin
　and Pacific Community, 274
　territorial sea, 133
America, North
　gross national product (GNP), 291, 292
　-Western Europe institutional ties, 292
Anand Panyarachun, 264, 366, 375
Angel, Norman, xviii
Angola
　Cuban troop withdrawal, 13, 46
ANZUS treaty, 269
Arab-Israeli War
　1948, 35
　1956, 36
　1967, 48
　1973, 37–38
Argentina
　territorial sea, 133
armed conflicts, 33, 64, 65
arms control, 66–67
arms race
　conventional, 52, 53, 67
　nuclear, 52
Asia
　cities, 167
　democracy, 364
　economic bloc, 371
　environment
　　good, 367–68
　-Europe relations
　　from prejudice to partnership, 369–71
　gross national product (GNP), 291, 292
　health problems
　　contaminated water, 167
　infrastructure, 367
　pollution, 367
　security, 345–48
　　burden-sharing, 347–48
　tolerance, 359–63
　trade
　　intra-Asia, 281
　　with US, 334, 347
　values, xxvii, xxviii, xxix, xxx, 356–58, 371
　　bad, xxviii, 357–58

Asia, East, xxvii, xxviii
　cities, 173
　　safe, 352
　economic
　　grouping, 227–28
　　growth, 370
　　miracle, 278–79
　　success, 352
　economies, 214, 352, 369
　　rise of, 203
　-EU links, 292
　-US relations, xxix
　values, 349–51
　　consensus, 352
　　education, 349
　　environment, wholesome, 350
　　family, 349, 352
　　frugality, 350
　　individualism, 349
　　press freedom, 351
　　saving, 349
　　social contract, 350
　　society, 349, 352, 354
　　stakeholder, 350
　　teamwork, 350
　　welfarism, 350
　　work ethic, 352
Asia, Northeast
　economies, 329
Asia, Southeast, 255
　arms race, 345
　development
　　sustainable, 157
　diversity, 295
　economies, 329
　environment
　　prospects for co-operation and conflict, 151–57
　　relations with extra regional states, 156
　forum, 15
　neutralization of, 239, 245–47
　　guarantor states, 246
　population, 296, 329
　regional co-operation
　　psycho-historical dimension, 252–53
　regional order
　　new, 226, 232–35
　regional security, 250
　　and US, 329–31
　　importance to US, 328–30
　　Southeast Asian desires, 330–31
　　US perceptions, 327
　　US policy, 330–31
Asia-Europe Foundation, 233
Asia-Europe Meeting (ASEM), 233, 294, 296

403

and ASEAN, 291–96
  Ministerial Meeting, 293–94
Asia Pacific
  Canberra Meeting, 280, 281
  economic
    dynamism, 280–81
    growth, 280
  newly industrializing economies (NIEs), 280
  security, 325
  trade
    intra-regional, 278
  See also Pacific Basin; Pacific Rim
Asia Pacific Centre for Environmental Law
    (APCEL), 173
Asia Pacific Economic Cooperation (APEC),
    182, 214, 234–35, 325, 331
  Asia Pacific Investment Code, 289
  Bogor Meeting, 219, 220, 288
  Business Advisory Forum, 290
  co-operation, 286
  Eminent Persons Group
    second report, 288, 289, 290
  gross national product (GNP), 285
  infrastructure, 289
  investment liberalization, 289, 290
  membership, 285, 286
  Ministerial Meeting
    Second, 226
  open regionalism, 288–90
  production, 288
  Seattle Meeting, 285–87, 288
  trade, 285
    free, 288, 289
    liberalization, 290
Association of Southeast Asian Nations
    (ASEAN), xix, 14, 15, 21, 22, 23, 24, 25, 87,
    194, 212, 219, 253–54, 270, 328, 341
  achievements, 212–13, 253
  in APEC, 226, 234
    attitude towards, 286
  and Asia-Europe Meeting (ASEM), 233,
    291–96
    role in launching, 291–92
  Burma policy, 266
  Cambodian crisis
    diplomacy, 258–60
    International Conference on Cambodia,
      82, 83, 90
    International Conference on Kampuchea,
      114, 115
    policy, 24, 213, 232
  challenges and opportunities, 261–64
  -China relations, 266
  Common Market, 251
  confidence-building, 253
  development, 68
  dialogue partners, 265, 266
    Pacific Basin, 271–72
  economic
    challenge, 261–62
    co-operation, 224, 225
    development, 251
    dialogues, 270
    integration, 250–52
  economies, 262
  environment
    ASEAN Environment Programme (ASEP),
      153–54
    ASEAN Senior Officials on the Environment
      (ASOEN), 154
    ASEAN Subregional Environmental Trust
      (ASSET), 154
    bilateral co-operation, 155
    co-operation and conflict, 153–56
    Co-ordinating Body on the Seas of
      East Asia (COBSEA), 154–55
    Indonesia-Singapore Joint Committee
      on the Environment (ISJCE), 155
    Malaysia-Singapore Joint Committee
      on the Environment (MSJCE), 155
  -EU relations
    cultural dialogue, 295
    impact of ASEM, 292
    Junior Executive Managers (JEMS)
      programme, 295
    Ministerial Meeting, Twelfth, 293–94
    political dialogue, 294–95
    revitalizing, 294–96
    student exchange, 295
  exports to Japan, 318
  Foreign Ministers Meeting, 263
  and Indochina, 262–63
  intra-regional relations, 248–54
    political-security dimension, 248–50
  investment policy, regional, 251
  -Japan relations
    development fund, 319
  membership
    admitting Myanmar, 294
    expansion, 226, 232, 234
  Ministerial Meeting
    23rd, 224–25
    25th, 265, 266, 267
    Post-Ministerial Conference, 263, 272, 345
  multinationals, 251, 252
  Pacific Basin Community
    attitude towards, 272
  population, 341
  regional order
    charting new, 265–68
  regional security, 267
  -Russia relations, 266
  security co-operation, 263
  Senior Officials Meeting, 263
  South China Sea declaration, 267
  trade
    free area, 252
    intra-ASEAN, 251
  Treaty of Amity and Co-operation, 263,
    265, 267
  US-Japan relationship
    importance to ASEAN, 318–19
  -US relations
    Business Council, 312, 314

Center for Technology Exchange, 314
Council, 314
cultural, 330
Economic Co-ordinating Committee (ECC), 311
investment, 329
political partners, 330
standing in US, 311–14
standing with US business community, 312
trade, 329, 332, 333
ASEAN Free Trade Area (AFTA), 213, 232, 261–62, 328
-ANZCERTA link, 232
Common Effective Preferential Tariff (CEPT), 261–62
content requirement, 262
tariffs, 261
ASEAN Regional Forum (ARF), 213, 233
members, 331
Australia, 211, 250, 279
APEC, 234
international civil aviation policy, 21
International Conference on Cambodia, 90
-Singapore relations
Joint Ministerial Committee (JMC), 235
new partnership, 235
UN Conference on the Law of the Sea Third, 116
UN Convention on the Law of the Sea, 147
Austria
joining EEC, 243
neutralization, 242, 244–45
Aziz Mahmood, 375

B
Balladur, Edouard, 369
Baroody, Jamil, 374
Baucus, Max, 343
Beebe, Christopher, xxv
Belgium, 37
East Asia as economic threat, 369
Bergsten, Fred, 188
Boren, David, 302
Bosnia-Herzegovina, 56
conflicts, 359
Bosworth, Stephen, 284
Bradley, Bill, 279
Bretton Woods
institutions, 120
Brezhnev, Leonid, 37, 379
Brittan, Sir Leon, 293
Brunei, 328
income per capita, 269
Burma, 248, 266
income per capita, 269
refugees, 266
See also Myanmar
Bush, George, 13, 98, 279, 338, 339, 342
on environment, 159, 160
on US-Japan relations, 324
visit to East Asia, 274, 277, 312

C
Cambodia, 15, 87–88, 213, 252, 253, 262, 263, 266, 342
conflict, 219, 224, 255–57, 275, 283, 382
choices, 260
ending, 225–26, 276–77
elections, 225, 276
famine, 25, 40
independence, 246, 277
International Conference on, 82, 83, 87–96, 219, 225
failure, reasons for, 94
participation, 89–90
procedural rules, 92–93
role of great powers, 93
structure, 90–91
timing, 94–95
International Conference on Kampuchea, 114, 115
Jakarta Informal Meeting (JIM), 219
lessons from Singapore, 204–9
neutrality, 245
Paris Agreements on, 262, 266
political settlement, 47, 50
self-determination, 23
at UN, 88
Vietnamese invasion, xix, 2, 3, 22, 23, 24, 88, 256, 258–60
withdrawal, 13, 15, 88, 259
Canada
International Conference on Cambodia, 90
UN Conference on the Law of the Sea Third, 116
capacity building, 173
Caradon, Lord, 45
Castaneda, Jorge, 141
Castlereagh, Lord, 10
Castro, Fidel, 71
Central America. *See* America, Central
Centre for Human Settlements, 167
Chan Chin Bock, 20
Chew Tai Soo, 21
Chiang Ching-kuo, 364
Chile, 274
in APEC, 286
China, 83, 249, 275, 276, 342, 343, 345
ARF, 233
on Cambodia, 277
democracy, 343, 365
development
sustainable, 367
economic reform, 276
economy
opening, 283
energy demands, 166
engaging, 331
external relations, 270
guarantor state, 249
imperial, 346
-Indonesia relations
diplomatic, 228
International Conference on Cambodia, 90

International Conference on Kampuchea, 114, 115
isolation, 343
neutralizing Southeast Asia, 246
-Singapore relations
  diplomatic, 228, 383
  economic, 228
-Soviet Union relations
  Summit, 275–76
  threat, 283
-US relations, 342–52
  MFN status, 342
-Vietnam relations, 276
Chou En-Lai, 39
Churchill, Winston, 33
civilizations
  clash of, xxix
Claes, Willy, 369
Clinton, Bill, 285, 286, 287
  Asian agenda, 341–44
Cold War
  end, 13, 228, 263, 346, 359
  conflicts, 359
collective security
  principle of, 11
Concert of Europe, 10
conciliation, xvii
Congo
  crisis, 37
  independence, 37
Congress of Vienna, 10
Coomarasamy, Punch, xxiv
Cooper, Richard, 308
Cordorvez, Diego, 46
Costa Rica, 52
Cuba
  crisis, 39, 40
Cuomo, Mario, 298
Cyprus, 46, 49, 378–79
Czechoslovakia
  invasion of, 1, 2, 373

D

de Cruz, Simon, 236
de Cuellar, Javier Perez, 41
de Gaulle, Charles, 239
de Tocqueville, Alexis, 302
decolonization, 134
democracy, 365
  and economic development, 364, 365
  parliamentary, 181
  political instability, 365
Deng Xiaoping, 283
developed countries
  Earth Summit
    finance, 162
developing countries, 59, 62–63
  Earth Summit
    finance, 162
  economic development, 67–68
development, xx

and environment, 158, 166–68, 170–71
sustainable, 152, 156, 174
  challenge of, 166–68
Dhanabalan, S., xvii, 201
dictatorship
  Western view, 364
diplomacy, xvi, xvii
  multilateral, xxii
  with US Congress, 106–9
disarmament, 66–67
Dole, Bob, 308
Drucker, Peter, 337
Dubcek, Alexander, 1

E

Earth Summit, xxvi, 151, 152, 153, 169, 382
  Agenda 21, 160, 153, 167
  assessment, 158–65
  attendance, 159
  carbon dioxide protocol, 159
  Convention on Biological Diversity, 159–60, 172
  Convention to Combat Desertification, 172
  desertification, combating, 161
  "Earth Charter", 153
  financial resources, 162–63
  fisheries, 161–62
  forests, 160–61
  Framework Convention on Climate Change, 159, 166, 171
  negotiating process, 97–105
  Preparatory Committee, 98, 101, 153
    organizational session, 99, 100
  progress, 170–74
    development and environment, 170–71
    green movement, 171
  Rio
    achievements, 158, 159–63
    Declaration, 105, 160
    negotiating process in, 104
  technology transfer, 163
East Asia. See Asia, East
East Asian Economic Caucus (EAEC), 214
East-West
  confrontation, 13, 58
  cultural differences, xxviii
  values
    convergence of, 352–53
economic growth
  prerequisites, 364
Egypt, 37, 38
Encomienda, Alberto, 236
environment, xx, 158–65, 151, 152
  and development, 158, 166–68
  movement, 171
Europe
  -Asia relations
    East Asia as economic threat, 369
    East Asia as opportunity, 370
    politics of envy, 371
    from prejudice to partnership, 369–71

protectionism, 371
Conference on Security and Cooperation in Europe (CSCE), 17, 325, 346
  imports, 279
  19th century, 10
Organization for Security and Cooperation in Europe (OSCE), 17
  united, 253
Europe, Eastern, 159
  failure of Communism, 364, 365
Europe, Western
  culture, 295
  economies, 369
  intolerance, 359
  -North America institutional ties, 292
European Community (EC), 262
  agricultural subsidies, 227
  Asia bashing, 370
  exports to East Asia, 370
  Single European Market (SEM), 261
European Economic Community (EEC), 116
European Union (EU)
  -ASEAN relations
    cultural dialogue, 295
    impact of ASEM, 292
    Junior Executive Managers (JEMS) programme, 295
    Ministerial Meeting, Twelfth, 293–94
    political dialogue, 294–95
    revitalizing, 294–96
    student exchange, 295
  -East Asia links, 292
  gross national product (GNP), 291, 292
  Uruguay Round, 286
Evensen, Jens, 141

F
Fairbanks, Richard, 273
Feldstein, Martin, 317
Fiji
  fishing agreement, 303
Fisher, Roger, 7
Five Power Defence Arrangements (FPDA), 211, 249, 250
force
  use of, 3, 4
foreign policy
  moral, 1–8
  Moralist school, 7
  national interest, 4
  Realist school, xvi, xvii, xviii, xx, 4, 6, 7, 237
France
  East Asia as economic threat, 369
  International Conference on Cambodia, 88–89, 91, 95
  intolerance, 359
  UN Conference on the Law of the Sea
    Third, 116
Franck, Thomas M., 16, 17
Fraser, Malcolm, 270

G
Gardner, John, 45
General Agreement on Tariffs and Trade (GATT), 120, 124
  Uruguay Round, 120, 289
    conclusion, 285
    Ministerial Meeting in Brussels, 227
Geneva Conference
  on Indochinese refugees, 25, 40
Gephardt, Richard, 307
Germany
  annexations, 11
  East Asia as opportunity, 370
  intolerance, 359
  UN Convention on the Law of the Sea, 147
Germany, West
  savings, 337
Ghazali Shafie, 239, 384
global economic negotiations, 60–62
  development, 61
  energy, 61–62
  finance, 61–62
  raw materials, 60–61
  trade, 61
Global Environment Facility (GEF), 162
global warming, 166
Goh Chok Tong, 220, 222, 223, 235
Goldwater, Barry, 302
Gong Ro–Myung, 236
Gorbachev, Mikhail, 3, 13, 15, 275
  policy statements, 283
  on UN, 15–16
Gottlieb, Allan, xxiv, 180
government
  good, 365–66
Gramm, Phil, 301
Great Britain. *See* United Kingdom
Greece
  civil war, 36
greenhouse gases, 166
  emission of, 171
Grotius, Hugo, xxxi, 132
Group B, 21, 116
Group of 77, 21, 30, 67, 68, 159
  UN Conference on the Law of the Sea
    Third, 116, 117, 118, 119
Guyana, 41

H
Ha Van Lau, 256
Haig, Alexander, 82
Hammarskjold, Dag, 39
  plane crash, 37
Hawke, Bob, 279
Heng Samrin, 25, 40, 259
Hollings, Ernest, 339
Hong Kong
  development, 364
  economic model, 197–99

GSP, 308
  graduation, 308
  hinterland, 197
  income per capita, 198
  market, 307
  population, 197
human settlements, 172–73
human solidarity, 59–60, 62
humanity
  crime against, 2
Hun Sen, 89, 94, 95, 225, 226
Huntington, Samuel, xxix, 330, 352

I
idealism, pragmatic, xviii, xix, xxx
idealists, xx
India
  ARF, 233
  development
    sustainable, 367
    economic growth, 370
    energy demands, 166
  International Conference on Cambodia, 90
  Kashmir, 50
Indochina, 256
Indonesia, 193, 259, 286, 330
  Abri, 360
  achievements, 218
  -China relations
    diplomatic, 228
  contributions, 219
  cultural values
    Javanese, 360
  diversity, 217
  East Timor question, 293, 294
  economic development, 218
  economy, 290
  foreign policy, 218
  guarantor state, 249
  independence, 35, 217
  International Conference on Cambodia, 89, 91
  Jakarta Informal Meeting (JIM), 89, 95, 219
  language, national, 360
  maritime boundaries, 148
  national motto, 360
  on neutralization, 246
  Non-Aligned Movement, 219
  political culture, 360
  population, 217, 359, 360
    growth, reducing, 367
    Javanese, 360
  productivity, 370
  regional
    ambitions, 218
    self-reliance, 249
  -Singapore relations, 220–21, 224
    Air Services Agreement, 220
    defence co-operation, 220–221
    Growth Triangle, 220, 224
    investment, 220

Karimum, development of, 220
Ministerial Committee on Indonesia–Singapore Tourism Co-operation, 220
  misconceptions, 253
  Tourism Co-operation Agreement, 220
  trade, 220
society, plural, 359, 360
territory, 217
tolerant majority community, 362
wages, 370
INF Treaty, 13
Institute for International Economics, 188
Integrated Programme for Commodities, 60
  Common Fund, 60
international aggression, 11
International Association for the Evaluation of Educational Achievement, 339
international co-operation, 168
International Council on Environmental Law, 170
International Maritime Organization, 150
international relations, xvii, xviii, xx, xxii, xxx, 58
  cultural identity, xxviii
  influence, xxiii
  international law, 6, 7
  Liberal–Idealist tradition, xviii
  non-interference, xix, 5
  old days, 10
International Sea-bed Authority, 139
international system, xx
  aggression, 3, 4
International Tribunal for the Law of the Sea, 148
Iran, 41
  Azerbaijan, 35
Iran-Iraq War, 41
  cease-fire, 46
Iraq, 41
  invasion of Kuwait, 229–30
Islamic world, 330
Ismail, Tun Dr, 239
Israel, 35, 36, 37, 38
  Earth Summit
    Rio Declaration, 162, 163
  Golan Heights, 49
Italy
  colonization of Ethiopia, 11
  corruption, 365
  political crisis, 365

J
Japan, 248
  -ASEAN relations
    development fund, 319
  colonialism, 346
  conquering Manchuria, 11
  constitution
    peace, 324
  creditor country, 320

defence, 277, 315, 325
  budget, 278, 315, 324
economic
  aid, 319
  links, 318, 319
  superpower, 282–83
economy
  internationalize, 278, 279
family, 357
Gulf War contribution, 323
imports from ASEAN, 318
International Conference on Cambodia, 90
international waters, testing, 345
Maekawa Commission, 316
  recommendations, 316, 317
market opening, 316, 318, 319
military power, 277, 282, 283, 322
Ministry of International Trade and Industry (MITI), 279
moral values, 357
nationalism, 331
neutralizing Southeast Asia, 247
Pacific economic co-operation, 270
protectionism, 324
savings, 337
-Soviet Union relations, 283
technology transfer, 320
-US relations, 322–25, 342
  economic, 282, 315–18, 322–23
  Friendship Commission, 314
  investment, 323
  military presence, 323
  Mutual Security Treaty, 277, 315, 322, 323
  political and security plane, 315, 323
  problems, 323–25
  technology, 336
  trade, 322, 323, 324
wages, 370
world role, 319–20
  multilateral development agencies, 319, 320
  in UN, 319
John Paul II, 378

K
Kennedy, John, 39
Khieu Samphan, 89
Khmer Rouge, 82, 83, 87, 88, 115, 225, 259, 260, 277
Khrushchev, Nikita, 39, 40
Kim Young Sam, 236
Kinkel, Klaus, 370
Kiribati
  fishing agreement, 303
Kirkpatrick, Jeane, 84
Kissinger, Henry, xviii, 37, 85
Kohl, Helmut, 370
Korea, North, 283
Korea, South, 270, 277, 283, 307
  economic growth, 364
  -Singapore relations, 236
Korean peninsula
  tension, 275
Korean War, 36
Kuwait
  Iraqi invasion, 229–30

L
Lang, Winfried, 173
Laos, 248, 263, 266
  independence, 246
  International Conference on Cambodia, 92
  memorandum, 255, 256, 257
  neutralization, 244
Latin America. *See* America, Latin
leader
  entrepreneurial, xxv
  intellectual, xxxi
  structural, xxv
League of Nations, 10–12, 17
  Covenant
    Article 11, 11
    Article 16, 11
  decisions, 12
  failure
    causes, 11–12
Lebanon, 35, 36, 49
  Beirut, 49
Lee K.C., 253
Lee Kuan Yew, 195, 211, 220, 222, 223, 318
  addressing US Congress, 383
  foibles, 177
  foreign policy legacy, 175–79
  impact on foreign leaders, 175–76
  relations with foreign media, 176
Lichenstein, Charles, 28
Lie, Trygvie, 38, 39
Lon Nol, 87
London Dumping Convention, 167
Luger, Richard, 194
Luxembourg
  neutralized state, 242

M
Machiavelli, 1, 2, 3, 4
Mahathir Mohamed, 161, 214
Malayan Communist Party, 20
Malaysia, 250, 330
  foreign policy, 239
  neutralizing Southeast Asia, 249
  poverty, reducing, 367
  –Singapore relations, 224
    agreements, 224
Malik, Jacob, 373
Mao Zedong, 237
Marin, Manuel, 293
Marshall, David, 374–75
Matsunaga, Spark, 191
Mauritania
  occupation of Western Sahara, xix, 5
media
  role
    in nation building, 72–73

in society, 72
Mediterranean Sea
  marine pollution, reducing, 154
Mexico, 274
  in APEC, 286
  territorial sea, 133
Middle East, 13
Mill, John Stuart, xviii
Mitterrand, Francois, 369
Miyazawa, Kiichi, 317
Mochtar Kusumaatmadja, 219
Moldan, Bedrich, 103
Monory, Rene, 369
Montreal Protocol, 166
Morgenthau, Hans, xviii
Morocco
  occupation of Western Sahara, xix, 5
Mulford, David, 305
Myanmar, 293
  ARF, 233
  See also Burma

N
Namibia, 50
  independence, 13, 46
Nandan, Satya, 142, 147
Nasser, Gamal Abdel, 48
national interest, xviii, 8
negotiations
  multilateral
    example of, 87–95
    practice of, 110–15
    rules of, xxi, 110–15
    timing, 103
    with US, 81–86
negotiator
  qualities, 85
neutralization, 240
  advantages and disadvantages, 243
  concept, 239–40
  and demilitarization
    difference, 242
  guarantor states, 242, 243, 245
  rights and duties, 242, 244
  and neutralism
    differences, 241
  and neutrality
    differences, 240–41
  paths to, 244–45
  preconditions for success, 245
  purposes, 242
  rights and duties of neutralized state, 242–43
New International Economic Order, xxiii, 62, 63
New Zealand, 211, 235, 250, 269
newly industrializing countries (NICs), 305–10
  competition rules, 309
  exchange rates, 309
Ng Kah Ting, 375
Nguyen Manh Cam, 267

Nicaragua, 13
Niebuhr, Reinhold, 4
Nixon, Richard
  Guam Doctrine, 246
Non-Aligned Movement (NAM), xix, xxii, xxiii, 29, 30, 34, 53, 382
  countries, 42
  International Conference on Cambodia, 90
  pro-Soviet faction, 67
  strengthening the UN, 64–69
North American Free Trade Area (NAFTA), 261, 262
North Atlantic Treaty Organization (NATO), 53
North Korea. *See* Korea, North
North–South
  confrontation, xxii, xxiii
  dialogue, 30, 62, 68
  divisions, xxvi
  beyond, 58–63
  negotiations, 68
Nunn, Sam, 298

O
Ohira, Masayoshi, 270, 287
Okita, Saburo, 270, 287
O'Neill, Tip, 182
Organization for Economic Cooperation and Development (OECD)
  homeless, 206
  Human Development Index (HDI), 205
  jobless growth, 205
  unemployment, 205

P
Pacific Basin
  dynamism, 271
  economic growth, 271
  See also Asia Pacific; Pacific Rim
Pacific Basin Community, 269–73, 281–82
  building, 234
  contributions, 281–82
  evolution of concept, 270–71
Pacific Basin Economic Council (PBEC), 271, 274, 281
Pacific Business Forum, 288
  report, 288, 289, 290
Pacific Century, 280–84
Pacific Economic Cooperation Council (PECC), 178, 214, 270, 271, 281
  task forces, 271
Pacific Ocean, 269
Pacific Rim
  definition, 274
  dynamic, 274–79
  See also Asia Pacific; Pacific Basin
Pakistan, 83
  Kashmir, 50
Palestine Liberation Organization (PLO)
  Earth Summit
    Rio Declaration, 162, 163
Papua New Guinea
  in APEC, 286

Pardo, Arvid, 134
Pham Van Dong, 255
Phan Hien, 25, 40
Philippines, 341
  Marshall Plan for, 319
  -Singapore relations, 236
  US bases, 284
Pol Pot, 22, 23, 259
Portugal
  East Timor question, 293, 294
Preston, Lewis, 162
Pronk, Jan, 162
protectionism, 21
Prussia, 10

R
Rafeeuddin Ahmed, 90
Rahim Ishak, 374
Rajaratnam, S., xvii, 68
Ramos, Fidel, 341
Reagan, Ronald, 3, 272
Recupero, Reubens, 162
regional conflicts
  solving, 46–47
  in Third World, 13–14
regional diplomacy, 265
Richardson, Elliot, xxi, 86, 117
Romulo, Carlos P., xxi
Roosevelt, Franklin, 33
Ruggiero, Renato, 121, 123
Russia, 56
  attack on Finland, 11
Rwanda
  conflicts, 359

S
Sadat, Anwar, 37
Saudi Arabia
  Earth Summit, 159
Schlesinger, Arthur, 4
Shultz, George, 57, 84, 272, 279
Sea, 169–70, 172
  Law of, 22
    evolution of traditional, 131–32
    Hague Codification Conference, 132–33
    Mare Clausum school, 132
    Mare Liberum school, 132
    territorial sea, 135
See Chak Mun, 375
self-determination, 4, 5
Serbia, 56
Sihanouk, Norodom, 87, 88, 89, 91, 94, 225, 258, 259, 276
Singapore, 250, 330
  in 1950s and 1960s, 20
  air quality, protecting, 368
  area, 175, 210
  -Australia relations
    Joint Ministerial Committee (JMC), 235
    new partnership, 235
  birth rate, 208
  Changi Airport, 20

-China relations
  diplomatic, 228, 383
  economic, 228
community self-help groups, 362
current account, 306
defence
  expenditure, 211
  military service, 211
diplomacy, 237
Earth Summit
  interests and role, 163–64
  negotiating process, 214
Economic Development Board (EDB), 20
economic model, 197–99
economy
  growth, 200, 208–9
education, 205, 349
  characteristics, 205
  tertiary, 205
election
  campaign, 301
environmental protection, 209
equal opportunities, 207
exchange rate, 306
export market, 200, 237
external relations, 222–30, 231–38
  Prime Minister, change of, 222–24
foreign policy, xxiii, 175–79
  alert, 215
  characteristics, 215
  frugal, 215
  pragmatic, 215
  relevance for Africa, 210–16
  scenario planning, 215
  seven pillars, 177–78, 223–24
foreign reserves, 209, 210
Foreign Service, 372, 384
GATT, role in, 214
gender equity
  education, 207
  employment, 207
  politics, 208
globalization, 200–1
governance, good, 208–9
  bureaucracy, 208
  democracy, participatory, 209
  political leadership, 208
government, 298, 299
  Cabinet, 299
gross domestic product (GDP), 210
  per capita, 210
gross national product (GNP)
  per capita, 204
Growth Triangle, Southern, 214
GSP, 308
  graduation, 308
harmony, maintaining, 361–63
  Maintenance of Religious Harmony Act, 361
  Presidential Council for Minority Rights, 361
  Presidential Council for Religious

Harmony, 361
health care, 206
  communicable diseases, 206
  doctors, 206
  expenditure, 206
  financing, 206
  immunization programme, 206
  tuberculosis, 206
housing, 206
human resources, xxiv
income per capita, 198
independence, 20, 178, 217, 372
-Indonesia relations, 220–21, 224
  Air Services Agreement, 220
  defence co-operation, 220
  Growth Triangle, 220, 224
  investment, 220
  Karimum, development of, 220
  Ministerial Committee on
      Indonesia–Singapore Tourism
      Co-operation, 220
  misconceptions, 253
  Tourism Co-operation Agreement, 220
  trade, 220
industrial peace, 208
industrialization
  environmental standards, 367
infant mortality rate, 204
intellectual property rights
  protection of, 196
Internal Security Act, 362
investment outflow, 214
-Korea, South, relations, 236
languages, 360
legitimacy, 210–11
life expectancy, 206
-Malaysia relations, 224
  agreements, 224
market, 306, 307
maternal mortality rate, 204
media, 362
  role, 76–77
miracle
  explanation for, 204–9
  lessons for Cambodia, 204–9
  modern characteristics, 358
moral power, 238
multinational corporations, 198
National Trades Union Congress, 207
National Wages Council, 207
Parliament, 361–62
-Philippines relations, 236
population, 175, 210, 359, 360
race relations, 361
realism, 177
regional security, 249
regionalization
  guidelines, 201–2
  objective, 201
  preparation, 203
  vision, 201–3
religions, 360, 361
saving rate, 208, 349
security, 211–12
"school", xxviii
self-reliance, 177
share owning, 208, 350
social mobility, 207
society, plural, 359, 360, 361
-Soviet Union relations, 229
stakeholder, 207, 354
state economic role, 198
strengths, 202
survival, xvii
-Taiwan relations, 228
technical co-operation programme, 237
tolerant majority community, 362
trade deficit, 306
trading nation, xxiv, 210
transport
  congestion free, 368
  electronic road pricing, 368
  motor vehicle curb, 368
  public, 368
UN agenda, 383–84
UN experience, 19–26, 214, 215
  benefits, 20–24
unemployment, 205
US-Japan relations
  impact on Singapore, 322
  on US military presence in Asia Pacific,
      211–12, 229, 283–84
-US relations, 236
  facilities for US military, 212, 229, 284,
      347
  importance to US, 194–95
  Washington embassy, 180–90
volunteers abroad, 214
wages, 370
  bonus, 207, 350
  increase, 207
weaknesses, 202
work force
  foreign workers, 205
  world ranking, 205
Singapore International Foundation, 214
Singapore National Iron and Steel Industry, 20
society
  diverse
    managing, 362
    driving apart, 355
    social inequality, 355
    underclass, 355
  holding together, 354
    stakeholder, 354
  laws, xx
    law and order, 354
    upward mobility, 354
Soeharto, 178, 218, 219, 220, 288
  on APEC, 286
Soesilo Soedarman, 218
Sohn, Louis, 142
Solarz, Stephen, 189
Somalia, 56

Son Sann, 88, 89, 258
Sourinho, 256
South China Sea
  disputes, 265
South Korea. *See* Korea, South
South Pacific Forum, 270
Southeast Asia. *See* Asia, Southeast
Southeast Asia Nuclear Weapon Free Zone
  (SEANWFZ), 225
Soviet Union, 13, 14, 34, 35, 37, 38, 39, 53
  248, 275
  allies, 67
  attitude towards developing countries, 58
  attitude towards mass media, 74
  Austrian neutralization, 243, 244
  on Cambodia, 277
  -China relations
    Summit, 275–76
  International Conference on Cambodia,
    90, 95
  invasion of Afghanistan, 2, 3
    withdrawal, 13, 276
  –Japan relations, 283
  neutralizing Southeast Asia, 246
  in Pacific Rim, 275, 277
  sea
    law, 136
    territorial, 134
  subjugating Hungary and Czechoslovakia,
    4
  threat, 283
  UN
    proposals to strengthen, 15
  UN Conference on the Law of the Sea
    Third, 112, 127
Spanish Sahara. *See* Western Sahara
Spratly Islands, 219
Stalin, Joseph, 33, 237
Strategic Arms Reduction Talks (START),
  13
Strong, Maurice, 101
Swarztrauber, Sayre A., 132, 133
Sweden
  neutral state, 240, 241
Switzerland
  neutralized state, 240–41, 242, 243
  outside UN, 243
Syria, 35, 36, 37
  Golan Heights, 49

T
Taiwan, 307, 331
  economic growth, 364
  foreign reserves, 349, 350
  -Singapore relations, 228
Tang I.F., 20
technology transfer, 61
Thailand, 252, 253, 366
Thant, U, xvi, xxi, 39–40, 375, 377
Third World, 44, 74
  communist countries

  mass media, 74
  conflicts, 229
  independence
    challenges, 74
  sea law, 135
  small countries
    threat to, 53–54
  and Western mass media, 70–80
    complaints against, 77–78
Toepfer, Klaus, 161, 169
trade
  MFN status, 343
traditional values, 356–57
Truman, Harry
  proclamations on sea, 133
Tshombe, 37

U
United Kingdom, 250
  Earth Summit, 161
  gross national product (GNP)
    per capita, 204
  press freedom, 71
  sea law, 132, 133
  share owning, 350
United Nations (UN), xxii, xxiv, 32–45, 55–57
  Advisory Committee on Administrative
    and Budgetary Questions (ACABQ), 29
  Afro–Asian Group, 373
  arms control, 43
  budget, 29
  bureaucracy, 56
  Cambodia question, 257
  Charter, 2, 12, 17, 23, 27, 32, 33, 42, 44,
    51, 55, 257
  collective security system, 12–13, 33, 34, 54
    failure, 34, 65
  Commission on Human Rights, 43
  Commission on Sustainable Development
    (CSD), 166, 167
    role, 168
  committees, 29
  Conference on Disarmament, 52
  Conference on Environment and
    Development. *See* Earth Summit
  Conference on Human Settlements
    second, 172
  Conference on the Human Environment
    in Stockholm, 135, 151–52
    Declaration of Principles, 152
  Conference on the Law of the Sea,
    First, 134
    conventions adopted, 134
  Conference on the Law of the Sea,
    Second, 134
  Conference on the Law of the Sea,
    Third, xxvi, 22, 88, 110, 111, 112, 116–
      19, 127–30, 382
    Castaneda Group, 141
    Evensen Group, 141
    fisheries, 136–37

interest groups, 141
issues negotiated, 135–40
mineral resources on sea-bed, 138
negotiating process, 140–42
procedural rules, 118
Conference on Trade and Development (UNCTAD), 21, 22
Fourth, 60
Convention on the Law of the Sea, 22, 131–43
  1994 Amendment Agreement, 146
  archipelagic waters, 145
  dispute settlement, 147
  Exclusive Economic Zone, 137, 145
  fisheries, 148, 161–62, 172
  in force, 167
  implications for Southeast Asia, 144–50
  islands disputed, 148
  marine environmental protection, 145-46
  Part XI, 129, 146
  provisions, 145–46
  ratification advantages, 149–50
  Resolution II, 138–39
  sea-bed provisions, 146
  significance, 142–43, 148–49
  territorial sea, 136, 145
  transit passage, 136, 145
deficiencies, 64
disarmament, 52–54
Disarmament Commission, 52
Economic and Social Council on Sustainable Development, 164
Environment Programme (UNEP), 158, 154, 155
  East Asian Seas Action Plan, 154
financial crisis, 55
Food and Agriculture Organization (FAO)
  Code of Conduct for Responsible Fisheries, 167
forum, 26
Forum of Small States, 215
General Assembly, 12, 17, 22, 23, 32, 41–42, 64
  common jury of the world, 41
  Convention against Torture, 42
  disarmament, 52
  human rights questions, 43
  negotiating forum, 42
  prestige and credibility, 66
  sea-bed declaration, 138
  "Uniting for Peace Resolution", 41
  Universal Declaration of Human Rights, 42
High Commissioner for Refugees (UNHCR), 25, 40
human rights, 42–43
Institute of Disarmament Studies, 52
International Court of Justice, 6
junkets, 29
Observer Missions, 50
  UN Good Offices Missions in Afghanistan and Pakistan (UNGOMAP), 50

UN Iran–Iraq Military Observer Group (UNIIMOG), 50
UN Military Observer Group in India and Pakistan (UNMOGIP), 50
UN TRUCE Supervision Organization (UNTSO), 50
peacekeeping
  characteristics of operations, 48–49
  forces, 38, 47–49
  functions of operations, 47–50
  new era, 46–51
  operations, 55, 56
  perception of, 55, 64
  personnel policy and management, 27–28
  prestige, 32, 64
  reforming, 27–31
  renewal, 55–57
  revitalization, 45
Secretariat, 27, 28, 43, 71–72
  recruitment, 44
  salaries, 29
Secretary–General, 28, 38–41, 43, 47, 48, 54
Security Council, 12, 17, 27, 33, 34, 35, 36, 37, 38, 41, 42, 48, 49, 54, 57, 90
  Berlin crisis, 38
  permanent members, 225
  Resolution 338, 37
  Resolution 435, 46
  Resolution 598, 50
  Soviet Union walk-out, 36
  veto power, 34
  and small states, 19–26
  strength, 27
strengthening, 64–69
successes, 50
survival, 44
Transitional Authority in Cambodia (UNTAC), 262, 266
West, role of, 30–31, 45
world order
  quest for, 10–18
United States, 12, 13, 34, 35, 37, 38, 39, 53 248, 303
  agricultural subsidies, 227
  -ASEAN relations
    Business Council, 312, 314
    Center for Technology Exchange, 314
    Council, 314
    cultural, 330
    Economic Coordinating Committee (ECC), 311
    investment, 329
    political partners, 330
    standing in US, 311–14
    trade, 329, 332, 333
  -Asia, East, relations, xxix
  and Asia, Southeast, 327–31
    importance to US, 328–30
    military facilities, 329
    Southeast Asian desires, 330–31

US perceptions, 327
US policy, 330–31
Asian-American community, 335
budget deficits, 317, 339–40
on Cambodia, 189, 277
  International Conference on Cambodia, 88–89
capital import, 337
charity, giving to, 336
-China relations, 342–43
  MFN status, 343
competitiveness, 317, 338
Congress, 106–9, 181–82, 300, 301
  election, 301, 302
  House of Representatives, 300
  private sector influence, 186
  Senate, 300
  staffers, 192
  working the, 183–86
current account deficits, 306, 337
debtor nation, 320
defence
  budget, 324
  treaties, 269, 347
diplomat
  cultural idiosyncracies, xxix
Earth Summit, 159, 161
  Rio Declaration, 162, 163
economic
  assistance, 336
  growth, 337
  problems, 278, 283, 337–40
education, 339
  National Commission on Excellence in Education, 339
entrepreneurship, 336
export market, 237
foreign policy, 303
future, 337
Generalized System of Preferences (GSP), 307, 308
  graduation, 307, 308
government, 299–300, 303
  branches, 181
  Cabinet, 299
  checks and balances, 181
  decentralized, 297
  Executive branch, 182
  powers, separation of, 181, 298–99
  system, 192
government-business relationship, 338
immigrants
  Indochinese refugees, 335
imports, 279
infant mortality rate, 204
infrastructure, 337
intellectual property rights, 278
  losses, 309
interest groups, 187
interests, 311, 312
invasion of Grenada, xix, 5

investment, 337
  in non-military R & D, 338
  in Pacific Basin, 271
-Japan relations, 322–25, 342
  anti-Japanese sentiment, 315
  economic, 282, 315–18, 322–23
  Friendship Commission, 314
  investment, 323
  Mutual Security Treaty, 277, 315, 322, 323
  political and security plane, 315, 323
  problems, 323–25
  trade, 322, 323, 324
  trade deficit, 315
labour-management relationship, 338
League of Nations, 10
liberty of individual, 181, 303
lobbies, 187, 194
market, 318
maternal mortality rate, 204
media, 72, 84, 186
  journalists, 72
negotiating with, 81–86
negotiators, 81, 82
  weaknesses and idiosyncracies, 83–85
neutralizing Southeast Asia, 245, 246
and newly industrializing countries, 305–10
  attitude towards, 305–7
  competition rules, 309
  policy towards, 307–8
  response to, 308–9
  trade deficits with, 310
and Pacific Basin Community, 272–73
politics
  foreign perspective, 297–304
  impact on foreign countries, 303–4
  influence of interest groups, 302–3
  political action committee, 302
  political parties, 301
  unwholesome influences, 297–98
press freedom, 70, 192
productivity, 337
protectionism, 304, 309, 317
savings, 317, 337
sea
  law, 133, 136
  territorial, 134
security role in Pacific, 277–78, 283, 284, 331, 346, 347
  bases in Philippines, 277
  military facilities, 347
  troops in South Korea, 277, 342
share owning, 350
-Singapore relations, 236
social mobility, 336
technology sharing, 336
think-tanks, 188
trade
  with Asia, East, 285
  with Asia Pacific, 271, 278, 280, 281,

334, 347
 deficit, 304, 306, 307, 337
 with Europe, 271, 279, 280, 281, 285, 347
 free, 331
 policy, 304, 308
 in UN
  arrears, 55
  contributions, 31
 UN Conference on the Law of the Sea
  Third, 82, 111
 UN Convention on the Law of the Sea, 131, 147
 values, 335–36
 –Vietnam relations, 342
Vietnam War
 anti-war sentiments, 71
 volunteers, 336
 wars in East Asia, 346
Washington
 diplomatic environment, xxiv
 in WTO
  agenda, 121
urbanization, 167
Urquhart, Brian, xxi
Uruguay Round. *See* General Agreement on Tariffs and Trade (GATT)
USSR. *See* Soviet Union

V
Vance, Cyrus, xviii
Venezuela, 41
Vienna Convention for the Protection of the Ozone Layer, 166
Vietnam, 23, 24, 82, 88, 213, 219, 224, 225, 226, 248, 249, 252, 253, 255, 262, 263, 265, 266, 275, 276, 283, 342
 ASEAN membership, 232
 -China relations, 276
 economic growth, 371
 hegemony, 256, 257
 image
  aggressive, 24, 259
  heroic, 24, 259
 independence, 246
 intention towards neighbours, 256
 International Conference on Cambodia, 90, 92, 94, 95
 invasion of Cambodia, 2, 3, 4, 22, 23, 24, 88, 256, 257, 258–60, 382
  withdrawal, 13, 14, 88, 259, 276
 refugees, 24, 25, 40
 -US relations, 342
Vietnam War, 87
 end, 255

W
Waldheim, Kurt, 25, 40, 377
wars
 conventional, 54, 67
Warsaw Pact countries, 53
Washington Conference on the Protection of the Marine Environment from Land-based Activities, 172
Washington Global Programme of Action for the Protection of the Maritime Environment from Land-based Activities, 167
Watts, William, 327
West
 democracy, 364
 law and order
  breakdown of, 355
 moral superiority stance, 353
 social problems, 352
 traditional values, 356
 UN role, 30–31, 45
Western mass media, 70
 and the Third World, 70–80
  complaints against governments, 77–78
Western Sahara, 4, 5, 47, 50
 occupation of, xix
 Polisario, 5
Wheeler, Joe, 162
Wilson, Woodrow, xviii, 10
Winsemius, Albert, 20
World Bank, 218
 "East Asian Miracle", 371
 International Development Agency (IDA), 150
World Conference on Human Settlements
 Second, 162
World Conservation Union (IUCN), 172
 Commission on Environmental Law, 170
world order
 quest for, 10–17
World Trade Organization (WTO), xxvi, 173, 289
 Article IV, 120
 Green Room, 124
 members, 120
 Ministerial Conference, First, 234, 235
  Information Technology Agreement, 234, 235
 negotiating process, 120–26
Worldwide Fund for Nature (WWF), 154, 172

Y
Yeo Cheow Tong, 123
Young, Oran, xxv
Yugoslavia, 36

Z
Zimbabwe
 International Conference on Cambodia, 90
Zone of Peace, Freedom and Neutrality (ZOPFAN), 225
Zuleta, Bernardo, 129